REFORMERS, CRITICS, AND THE PATHS OF GERMAN MODERNITY

Reformers, Critics, and the Paths of German Modernity

*Anti-Politics and the Search for
Alternatives, 1890–1914*

• • •

KEVIN REPP

HARVARD UNIVERSITY PRESS

Cambridge, Massachusetts

London, England • 2000

Library of Congress Cataloging-in-Publication Data
Repp, Kevin.
 Reformers, critics, and the paths of German modernity : anti-politics and the search for alternatives, 1890–1914 / Kevin Repp.
  p. cm.
 Includes bibliographical references and index.
 ISBN 0-674-00057-9 (alk. paper)
  1. Political culture—Germany—History—19th century.
 2. Social reformers—Germany—History—19th century.
 3. Germany—Politics and government—19th century.
 4. Germany—Social policy—19th century.
 5. Germany—Intellectual life—19th century.
 I. Title

DD228.5.R38 2000
943.08'4—dc21   00-020603

For my folks,
Bob and Millie Repp,
in Colfax

Contents

• • •

Acknowledgments

Though often seemingly a lonely enterprise, historical scholarship is always a collective work in progress, and I would like to thank the many individuals—friends, colleagues, critics, and mentors—who have pushed, pulled, nurtured, inspired, and guided this project through its manifold guises far beyond my own limited horizons. While its shortcomings are entirely mine, the present study owes whatever strengths it possesses largely to the sustaining efforts of these individuals, and in this sense, the credit belongs to them. From this study's beginnings as a Stanford dissertation prospectus, James J. Sheehan has taken an active interest in seeing the project through to its completion, guiding the process with subtle hints and suggestions at every stage, planting with a few carefully chosen words the seeds of ideas I often failed to recognize until they had already grown to become major aspects of the work in progress. Despite his claim to have "stood by and cheered from the sidelines," Professor Sheehan deserves my immense gratitude and all the credit due the best coach a young scholar could ask for. I am also indebted to the other members of my dissertation committee, Professors Paul Robinson and Timothy Lenoir, who read several early drafts, providing diligent and constructive criticism along the way, as well as to the Stanford-Berkeley reading group in German history. Reinhard Rürup and Nicolaus Sombart also offered useful advice for the dissertation during a year spent in the archives and libraries of the Federal Republic in 1991–1992. On the long, harrowing road from dissertation to publishable manuscript, I have enjoyed continued support from many old friends and a number of new colleagues at Yale University who have carefully read through entire drafts and given thoughtful suggestions and priceless encouragement over the past three years: Professors Henry Ashby Turner,

Jr., Frank M. Turner, Glenda Gilmore, Robert Johnston, and Peter Gay. Beyond my immediate environs—and far beyond the call of duty—David Blackbourn has devoted painstaking attention to the manuscript, as well as a detailed, thorough, immensely helpful response, for which I am especially grateful. Finally, I would like to thank Jonathan Sperber, who offered concrete suggestions for improving the manuscript, along with another, anonymous reader for Harvard University Press, whose challenging critique provoked some serious rethinking in the final revisions and helped produce a substantially strengthened final draft.

But scholarship does not live on intellect alone. In addition to its enrichment from scholarly minds, this study owes much to the material, logistical, and personal support of many other parties. A four-year fellowship and numerous other grants from the Stanford History Department allowed me to devote myself exclusively to the project; in addition, the German Academic Exchange Program (DAAD) funded a year of research in the Federal Republic that turned out to be as productive as it did thanks to the help of staffs at several research institutions: the Technical University of Berlin; the Federal Archives in Potsdam, Merseburg, and Koblenz; the State Archive and Library in Berlin; and the International Institute for Social History in Amsterdam. There is, finally, the support of friends and family who both inspired and sustained this effort with sparkling insights, steadfast encouragement, confidence, advice, and a fortifying sense of humor. I especially wish to thank Steve Irish; Brad Abrams; Robert Grathwol, who first inspired my interest in history; and my wife, Susan Imhoff, who saw me through the struggle to finish with intelligence, wit, patience, and compassion. But above all, the completion of this work stands as a testimonial to the steady support of my parents, who taught me lessons about honesty, courage, and the rewards of hard work that sustained me even in the most difficult times. It is to them I dedicate the following pages as a token of my deepest gratitude and heartfelt respect.

Coming to Terms with the Future

There must be an abandonment of the old conception that the only business of organized society is to protect the individual from domestic and foreign aggression. There must be a wide extension of public ownership, a greater control of the aggressions of privilege and property, a big programme of social legislation, a change in our system of education, and the exclusion of privileged and business interests from the long ascendancy which they have enjoyed in our political life.

FREDERIC C. HOWE, 1915

Returning from a tour of Germany in 1914, the progressive reformer Frederic Howe found it difficult to describe the country in terms an American audience could understand. "[C]rushed under the heel of the autocratic caste" in "feudal" Prussia, the country lacked the democratic institutions that seemed indispensable to modern capitalism in the West, yet Germany was also rapidly asserting its leadership as a dynamic force in the world economy. "Administrative and industrial efficiency are a scientific study in which hundreds of thousands of the best minds of the state are engaged," Howe wrote. "There is efficiency in transportation, scientific thought to every process and every social and industrial problem; there is the greatest concern for human life, for health and well-being, for education and training of workers, artists, commercial men, and scientists, and the coordination of the individual into a machine of national rather than purely personal dimensions." Far from being a handicap, the failure of laissez-faire liberalism was the key to Germany's success. "The individual German receives more from society . . . His dignity and his personal liberty are on a different, and from our point of view lower plane than in America and

1

Great Britain, but his daily and his hourly needs, and those of his wife and family are better cared for," the reformer insisted. "And the individual man is more efficient. He is better prepared for his work. He enjoys a wholesome leisure life. He is assured protection from *la misère* in old age." Combining anachronistic political structures with an advanced industrial economy, "dual Germany" had thus discovered an alternative route to modernity that "evades Anglo-Saxon analysis" but was crucial for the West to comprehend. Socialized Germany was already a quarter century ahead "in social consciousness, in an understanding of the new statecraft," Howe warned, and unless Americans abandoned the outdated belief "that the only business of organized society is to protect the individual from domestic and foreign aggression," they would fall still further behind in years to come.[1]

After 1945 things looked different. Bizarre and ghastly, the images of torchlit spectacles and gas chambers that conveyed the inconceivable barbarism of National Socialism again brought home the magnitude of Germany's divergence from the path of liberal democracy, which could now be grasped only in terms of "a peculiar view of man and society which seems alien and even demonic to the Western intellect."[2] Seeking to come to terms with the past, scholars looked to the same factors Howe had stressed in looking ahead before the First World War—rapid industrialization in the absence of liberal, democratic traditions—but rather than situating Germany at the forefront of modern development, this "special path" appeared to lead to a wholesale "attack on modernity, on the complex of ideas and institutions that characterize our liberal, secular, and industrial civilization."[3] In his now classic study *Society and Democracy in Germany*, sociologist Ralf Dahrendorf traced the moment of aberration to a failure to complete "those two revolutions that Marx combined in a brilliant turn of thought," the bourgeois and industrial revolutions, upon which the "reality of the liberal principle depends." Having botched the first in 1848, "the faulted nation" was banished from the sunlit trail of Western modernization into a freakish netherworld of paradox and dis-

---

1. Frederic C. Howe, *Socialized Germany* (New York: Charles Scribner's Sons, 1915), pp. vi–vii, 1–8.
2. George Mosse, *The Crisis of German Ideology: Intellectual Origins of the Third Reich* (New York: Schocken, 1964), p. 1.
3. Fritz Stern, *The Politics of Cultural Despair: A Study of the Rise of the Germanic Ideology* (Berkeley: University of California Press, 1974), p. xvi.

tortion: "the history of industrialization in Germany could be written as a history of non-industrialization." Particularly troubling from this view was the "social consciousness" that had impressed Howe so much in the Wilhelmine era. The "peculiarly German blend of social tradition and modern industrialism" had prompted reliance on public ownership, non-partisan notions of the "common good," and a "preference for things national over things rational" that prevented "a self-confident bourgeoisie with its own political aspirations" from taking matters into its own hands. "[P]ublic agencies in Germany consistently felt responsible for the welfare of workers," Dahrendorf darkly observed; "the official attitude toward the social question strikingly documents the preindustrial combination of a severe and benevolent paternal authority." "What is remarkable about Imperial Germany," he wrote, was that "it managed to miss the road to modernity and instead consolidated itself as an industrial feudal society with an authoritarian welfare state."[4]

During the 1960s and 1970s, the bundling of "liberal, secular, and industrial" institutions into the cohesive picture of a benign postwar modernity held together something of a consensus among Western historians that Germany's special path had reached crisis rather than coordination by 1914. Sketching out the predominance of "pre-industrial elites" in government, bureaucracy, and army, Hans-Ulrich Wehler's influential survey *The German Empire* emphasized the bourgeoisie's exclusion from positions of power under the "Bonapartist dictatorship" of Otto von Bismarck, who masterfully combined repressive tactics of "negative integration" with paternalistic social policy to manipulate the masses and orchestrate the "gathering" of illiberal forces that led industrialists to seek protection in the "alliance of iron and rye." With normal routes to modernization effectively blocked, pressures of rapid social and economic growth continued to build behind Germany's ossified political structures, and with the fall of Bismarck in 1890, the fragile balance of opposing parties exploded into a "permanent crisis of state," until the groundswell of Social Democratic agitation eventually forced the ruling elite into a portentous "flight forward" through war and revolutions that came to a halt only in 1945.[5] At the same time,

4. Ralf Dahrendorf, *Society and Democracy in Germany* (New York: Doubleday, 1967), pp. 31–37, 46–49, 60, 120–23.

5. Hans-Ulrich Wehler, *The German Empire, 1871–1918* (Dover: Berg, 1985). For similar accounts, see Wolfgang Mommsen, *Der autoritäre Nationalstaat: Ver-*

intellectual historians showed how the "crisis of modernity" drove broad segments of the populace to flee from the rational, scientific, and emancipatory impulses of Western Enlightenment, or *Zivilisation,* into the cozy, unpolitical world of a specifically German *Kultur.*[6] While a small group of "modernists" endorsed the new, pragmatic, and empirical fields that undermined the privileged position of the humanities toward the end of the nineteenth century, most of the professors in Fritz Ringer's foundational work *The Decline of the German Mandarins* stubbornly clung to the cultivation of traditional, aristocratic sensibilities and airy notions of subjective freedom, tightening their pact with the ruling classes, who protected their status in return for ideological services rendered to the state.[7] As enrollment at German universities skyrocketed, the elitism, nationalism, and "disdain for politics" encouraged by this neo-humanist idealism spread through Wilhelmine political culture, where it "coalesced into a widespread academic illiberalism, which molded students for scholarship, professional careers, and citizenship into conformist patterns, thus deflecting pressures for change away from the state and society toward *Wissenschaft* and personal development," Konrad Jarausch argued in a later study.[8] By far the gravest "consequences of the Unpolitical German" were to be found in the "vulgar idealism" Fritz Stern documented in *The Politics of Cultural Despair.* Julius Langbehn's anguished attack on liberalism, science,

    fassung, Gesellschaft und Kultur im deutschen Kaiserreich (Frankfurt: Fischer Taschenbuch Verlag, 1990); Volker Berghahn, *Imperial Germany, 1871–1914: Economy, Society, Culture, and Politics* (Providence: Berghahn, 1994).

6. On the antithesis between *Zivilisation* and *Kultur,* see Norbert Elias, *The Civilizing Process,* vol. 1, *The History of Manners* (New York: Pantheon, 1978), pp. 1–34; Fritz Ringer, *The Decline of the German Mandarins: The German Academic Community, 1890–1933* (Cambridge, Mass.: Harvard University Press, 1969), pp. 88–123; Stern, *Despair,* pp. 196–97; Mosse, *Crisis,* pp. 68–69. On the conformist withdrawal into impotent aestheticism, see Wolfgang Mommsen, *Bürgerliche Kultur und künstlerische Avantgarde: Kultur und Politik im deutschen Kaiserreich 1870 bis 1918* (Frankfurt: Propyläen, 1994).

7. Ringer, esp. pp. 7–13, 201–24; Leonard Krieger, *The German Idea of Freedom: History of a Political Tradition* (Boston: Beacon, 1957).

8. Konrad Jarausch, *Students, Society, and Politics in Imperial Germany: The Rise of Academic Illiberalism* (Princeton: Princeton University Press, 1982), p. 404.

cities, and Jews has long become emblematic of the "crisis of the 1890s" that pushed ever widening circles to "leap from despair to utopia across all existing reality," plunging the German people into the irrational currents of religious fervor, nationalism, anti-Semitism, and self-delusion that ultimately swept the nation into the waiting arms of Hitler.[9]

While the consensus on Wilhelmine Germany as a culture in crisis continues to hold sway, a more critical perspective on Western rationality and Enlightenment has called into question the view of National Socialism as a culminating paroxysm of anti-modern despair along with the notion of a German special path. This challenge was issued early on by David Blackbourn and Geoff Eley, whose provocative critique of modernization theory in *The Peculiarities of German History* sparked intense debate on which the dust has only recently—and fitfully—begun to settle. Seeking to uncouple the bourgeois and industrial revolutions Dahrendorf had joined in a single model, the British social historians shattered the composite of liberal, secular, and democratic elements that formed the normative standard of postwar modernity against which German deviance had been measured. While Blackbourn argued for a strong bourgeois influence over cultural and legal affairs, Eley emphasized that the authoritarian features of Wilhelmine political culture were by no means inimical to the interests of German industrialists, who had good reasons for wishing to suppress organized labor and to resolve social conflicts outside parliament. Like Howe, in fact, Eley insisted that the combination of non-political coordination, paternalistic social policy, and authoritarian control fostered a breakthrough in rationalization that put the country at the forefront of a modernity quite at odds with the liberal models of his contemporaries: "by comparison with Britain it was precisely the most 'modern' and 'progressive' aspects of Imperial Germany's capitalist development—namely, the higher levels of concentration, the rapid investment in new plant and technology, the experimen-

---

9. Stern, *Despair*, p. xi; Stern, "The Political Consequences of the Unpolitical German," in Stern, *The Failure of Illiberalism: Essays in the Political Culture of Germany* (New York: Knopf, 1972); see also Mosse, *Crisis*; Shulamit Volkov, *The Rise of Popular Anti-Modernism: The Urban Master Artisans, 1873–1896* (Princeton: Princeton University Press, 1978); Peter Paret, *The Berlin Secession: Modernism and Its Enemies in Imperial Germany* (Cambridge, Mass.: Harvard University Press, 1980).

tation with more sophisticated divisions of labour—that first permitted the repressive labour relations . . . to develop." In addition, Blackbourn and Eley also rejected the view of nationalism as a tool of Bonapartist manipulation, describing it instead as a powerful destabilizing force emerging spontaneously from below in a thoroughly modern process of grassroots mobilization that pushed government and bourgeoisie into increasingly radical corners. Far from an aberration, Blackbourn concluded, the peculiarities of German history were in fact "a heightened version of the norm."[10]

The ensuing debates over modernization and the special path nourished a rich scholarly literature on Imperial Germany that has yielded a copious new portrait of the complex dynamics at work in Wilhelmine political culture. Centered in Bielefeld and Frankfurt am Main, collective research projects have mapped the composition, status, and proclivities of the German "bourgeoisie," which has ceased to be an easily definable class "with its own political aspirations," dissolving under competing social and cultural definitions to assume diffuse, but significant roles comparable to those played by the middle classes throughout Western Europe before 1914. At the same time, studies of political mobilization have revealed a far-reaching process of democratization in an expanding "German-National public realm" that challenged the conservative status quo from many directions.[11] "Wilhelmine Germany appeared not as a static social and po-

---

10. David Blackbourn and Geoff Eley, *The Peculiarities of German History: Bourgeois Society and Politics in Nineteenth-Century Germany* (New York: Oxford University Press, 1984), pp. 109, 263.

11. For a recent overview of the Bielefeld and Frankfurt projects, see Jonathan Sperber, *"Bürger, Bürgertum, Bürgerlichkeit, Bürgerliche Gesellschaft:* Studies of the German (Upper) Middle Class and Its Sociocultural World," *Journal of Modern History* 26, no. 2 (June 1977): 271–97; Jürgen Kocka, "The European Pattern and the German Case," in Kocka and Allan Mitchell, eds., *Bourgeois Society in Nineteenth-Century Europe* (Oxford: Berg, 1993), pp. 3–39. While challenging Eley's views on the role of notables in grassroots mobilization, Roger Chickering also depicts a considerable radicalization of the "German-National public realm," particularly after 1908, in his study of the Pan-German League, *We Men Who Feel Most German: A Cultural Study of the Pan-German League, 1886–1914* (Boston: Allen and Unwin, 1984); Geoff Eley, *Reshaping the German Right: Radical Nationalism and Political Change after Bismarck* (New Haven: Yale University Press, 1980). For more on political mobilization, see David Blackbourn, "The Politics of Demagogy in Imperial Germany," *Past*

litical system locked into a pre-programmed authoritarian rigidity, but as a rapidly changing, turbulent society in which new developments of all kinds were possible," Richard Evans concludes in one of the many reassessments published in recent decades.[12] In contrast to the earlier focus on anti-modernism and cultural despair, a burgeoning scholarship has begun to explore the highly modern and prolific explosion of fin-de-siècle cultural production, not only in literature and art, but above all in the natural sciences, where close cooperation among state officials, local communities, and the private sector pioneered advances in public health and productive efficiency that made German *Wissenschaft* a model for Howe and many others besides.[13]

and Present 113 (November 1986): 152–84; Marilyn Coetzee, *The German Army League: Popular Nationalism in Wilhelmine Germany* (New York: Oxford University Press, 1990); Beverly Heckart, *From Bassermann to Bebel: The Grand Bloc's Quest for Reform in the Kaiserreich, 1900–1914* (New Haven: Yale University Press, 1974); Richard Evans, *Rethinking German History: Nineteenth-Century Germany and the Origins of the Third Reich* (Boston: Allen and Unwin, 1987); Helmut Smith, *German Nationalism and Religious Conflict: Culture, Ideology, Politics, 1870–1914* (Princeton: Princeton University Press, 1995); Gangolf Hübinger, *Kulturprotestantismus und Politik: Zum Verhältnis von Liberalismus und Protestantismus im wilhelminischen Deutschland* (Tübingen: Mohr, 1994). While preserving its broad outlines, Wehler has substantially revised his initial thesis regarding Imperial German political culture in light of this new evidence; Hans-Ulrich Wehler, *Deutsche Gesellschaftsgeschichte,* vol. 3: *Von der "Deutschen Doppelrevolution" bis zum Beginn des Ersten Weltkriegs* (Munich: Beck, 1995), esp. pp. 700–72, 1038–1120; Hans-Ulrich Wehler, "A Guide to Future Research on the Kaiserreich? *Society, Culture, and the State in Germany, 1870–1930,* edited by Geoff Eley," *Central European History* 29, no. 4 (1996): 566–67.

12. Evans, *Rethinking,* p. 2. See also Jack R. Dukes and Joachim Remak, eds., *Another Germany: A Reconsideration of the Imperial Era* (Boulder: Westview, 1988); Thomas Nipperdey, *Nachdenken über die deutsche Geschichte: Essays* (Munich: Beck, 1986).

13. On literature and art, see Carl Schorske, *Fin-de-Siècle Vienna: Politics and Culture* (New York: Vintage, 1981); Peter Jelavich, *Munich and Theatrical Modernism: Politics, Playwriting, and Performance, 1890–1914* (Cambridge, Mass.: Harvard University Press, 1985); Jelavich, *Berlin Cabaret* (Cambridge, Mass.: Harvard University Press, 1993); Peter Fritzsche, *Reading Berlin 1900* (Cambridge, Mass.: Harvard University Press, 1996); Mommsen, *Kultur,*

Imperial Germany is thus once again beginning to look increasingly modern, if hardly benign. Far from illuminating the hopeful prospects Howe glimpsed there in 1914, in much of the recent scholarship Wilhelmine political culture serves as a "fascinating foreground against which to track the dark shadows of modernity," to borrow Peter Fritzsche's evocative description of the Weimar Republic, especially in the area of progressive social policy and the welfare state.[14] While acknowledging "alternatives in thinking and acting" that might have emerged from the "network of social-scientific theories and methods on the one hand and social institutions and practices on the other that had been set up to solve the 'social question'" at the turn of the century, Detlev Peukert's oft-cited essay "The Genesis of the 'Final Solution' from the Spirit of Science" combined the Frankfurt School's critique of instrumental rationality with a Foucauldian sensitivity to the disciplining power of "bio-politics" to mark out a path leading from the "progressive optimism" of Wilhelmine reformers to the "philanthropic pathos" of Himmler's secret exhortations to the SS in what

pp. 43–57; Gangolf Hübinger and Wolfgang Mommsen, eds., *Intellektuelle im Deutschen Kaiserreich* (Frankfurt am Main: Fischer Taschenbuch, 1993). On science, see Timothy Lenoir, *Instituting Science: The Cultural Production of Scientific Disciplines* (Stanford: Stanford University Press, 1997); Alan Beyerchen, "On the Stimulation of Excellence in Wilhelminian Science," in Jack R. Dukes and Joachim Remak, eds., *Another Germany*, pp. 139–68; Paul Weindling, *Health, Race and German Politics between National Unification and Nazism, 1870–1945* (New York: Cambridge University Press, 1989); Jeffrey Allan Johnson, *The Kaiser's Chemists: Science and Modernization in Imperial Germany* (Chapel Hill: University of North Carolina Press, 1990); David Cahan, *An Institute for an Empire: The Physikalisch-Technische Reichsanstalt, 1871–1918* (New York: Cambridge University Press, 1989); Gangolf Hübinger, Rüdiger vom Bruch, and Friedrich Wilhelm Graf, eds., *Kultur und Kulturwissenschaften II: Idealismus und Positivismus* (Stuttgart: Franz Steiner, 1997); Rüdiger vom Bruch, *Wissenschaft, Politik und öffentliche Meinung: Gelehrtenpolitik im Wilhelminischen Deutschland, 1890–1914* (Husum, Germany: Mathiesen, 1980); Bruch, "Bürgerliche Sozialreform im deutschen Kaiserreich," in Bruch, ed., *"Weder Kommunismus noch Kapitalismus": Bürgerliche Sozialreform in Deutschland vom Vormärz bis zur Ära Adenauer* (Munich: Beck, 1985), pp. 61–179.
14. Peter Fritzsche, "Did Weimar Fail?" *Journal of Modern History* 68, no. 3 (September 1996): 632.

has since become a classic depiction of the "pathologies of modernity."[15] The influx of scientific social workers and eugenicists into welfare administration, particularly at the municipal level, has been the focus of intensive examination with an eye to later developments. Major works like Paul Weindling's massive study *Health, Race and German Politics between National Unification and Nazism* and George Steinmetz's *Regulating the Social* often emphasize the discontinuities in this trajectory, but the Nazis' gruesomely efficient destruction of "life unworthy of life" inevitably casts a very dark shadow over the "disciplined rationality" pervading the new, integrative systems of social and health services devised by Wilhelmine progressives from the early 1890s.[16] Confirming the influence of German

---

15. Detlev Peukert, *Max Webers Diagnose der Moderne* (Göttingen: Vandenhoeck & Ruprecht, 1989), pp. 106, 111–12.
16. Weindling, *Health;* see also Weindling, "Eugenics and the Welfare State During the Weimar Republic," in W. R. Lee and Eve Rosenhaft, eds., *The State and Social Change in Germany, 1880–1980* (New York: Berg, 1990), pp. 134–63; George Steinmetz, *Regulating the Social: The Welfare State and Local Politics in Imperial Germany* (Princeton: Princeton University Press, 1993); Christoph Sachße, *Mütterlichkeit als Beruf: Sozialarbeit, Sozialreform und Frauenbewegung 1871–1929* (Frankfurt: Suhrkamp, 1986), quotation p. 86. See also Ute Frevert, "The Civilizing Tendency of Hygiene: Working Class Women under Medical Control in Imperial Germany," in John Fout, ed., *German Women in the Nineteenth Century: A Social History* (New York: Holmes and Meier, 1984), pp. 320–44; Dietrich Milles, "Industrial Hygiene: A State Obligation? Industrial Pathology as a Problem in German Social Policy," in Lee and Rosenhaft, eds., *State,* pp. 164–202; Nancy Reagin, *A German Women's Movement: Class and Gender in Hanover, 1880–1933* (Chapel Hill: Univeristy of North Carolina Press, 1995), pp. 71–98; Peter Becker, *Zur Geschichte der Rassenhygiene: Wege ins Dritte Reich* (New York: Thieme, 1988); Carsten Klingemann, ed., *Rassenmythos und Sozialwissenschaft in Deutschland: Ein verdrängtes Kapitel sozialwissenschaftlicher Wirkungsgeschichte* (Opladen, Germany: Westdeutscher Verlag, 1987); Jürgen Kroll, *Zur Entstehung und Institutionalisierung einer naturwissenschaftlichen und sozialpolitischen Bewegung: Die Entwicklung der Eugenik/Rassenhygiene bis zum Jahre 1933* (Tübingen: dissertation, 1983); Peter Weingart et al., *Rasse, Blut und Gene: Geschichte der Eugenik und Rassenhygiene in Deutschland* (Frankfurt: Suhrkamp, 1988); Robert Proctor, *Racial Hygiene: Medicine under the Nazis* (Cambridge, Mass.: Harvard University Press, 1988); Renate Bridenthal, Atina Grossmann, and Mar-

industrialists over the formation of municipal social policy, Steinmetz notes both the "individualizing, disciplinary dimension" of the Elberfeld System, which served to inculcate self-imposed norms of bourgeois subjectivity in workers under laissez-faire principles before 1890, and the "ideological and practical seeds of Nazi eugenics" that "were sown during the latter years of the empire" by scientific social workers and neocorporatists. Eley has recently suggested that "the logic of the Final Solution was inscribed" into German social policy already before 1914.[17] Returning to questions of "The Bourgeoisie, the State, and the Mastery of Reform," Eley has particularly stressed the influence of Peukert and Foucault in setting a research agenda to explore "modernity's dark side" in five regions of Imperial German political culture: (1) the "radical nationalism" of populist movements on the right, which agitated for efficiency and order in "extraparliamentary" actions and were "profoundly antisocialist and antidemocratic in the core of their political being"; (2) the "industrial paternalism" and "authoritarianism" uniting factory owners across the political spectrum; (3) "social imperialism" arising from the aggressive colonialist aims of liberals, progressives, and Social Democrats in foreign policy, which "were powerfully reinserted within the metropolitan society"; (4) the gendering of public discourse, especially in the professionalized regulation of welfare; and (5) the "eugenicist consensus" that "convened biomedical knowledge, public health, and racial thought on the ground of social policy" to become a "restlessly aggrandizing ideological field" between 1870 and 1945.[18]

In coming to terms with the past, historians have thus moved from benevolent to malign conceptions of a modernity that in either case continues to provide a steady compass for charting the extremes that impelled German political culture on a course (whether divergent or true) toward the worst-possible-case scenario we now know it reached in 1945. But if "the fantasies of omnipotence heaping up at the turn of the century in the

ion Kaplan, eds., *When Biology Became Destiny: Women in Weimar and Nazi Germany* (New York: Monthly Review Press, 1984).

17. Steinmetz, *Regulating*, pp. 120–22, 198–203; George Steinmetz, "The Myth of the Autonomous State: Industrialists, Junkers, and Social Policy in Imperial Germany," in Eley, *Society*, pp. 289–91; Geoff Eley, "Introduction 1: Is There a History of the Kaiserreich?" in Eley, *Society*, p. 28.

18. Geoff Eley, "German History and the Contradictions of Modernity: The Bourgeoisie, the State, and the Mastery of Reform," in Eley, *Society*, pp. 97–102.

human sciences and social professions cannot be overlooked" from the vantage point of "historical hindsight skeptically sharpened by the knowledge of subsequent events," as Peukert rightly argued, those fantasies should also not obstruct our view of the moderate, critical aspirations for a livable future that were far more visible to those who built these institutions as they looked ahead from the past, since without it our own horizons begin to look quite narrow.[19] Without losing sight of the "ideology of radical nationalism" that ultimately won out in 1933, historians need also to chart the other competing visions Eley postulated in his initial challenge to the monolithic "pre-industrial" variety featured in earlier accounts by applying Gramsci's model of hegemony. If nationalist ideology was "continually renegotiated in accordance with the shifting strength (economically, culturally, politically) of the subordinate classes" in processes that were "open to contest and hence unpredictable" while "areas of bureaucratic and repressive control" remained "steadily constrained," then the less radical strains of that ideology were equally significant in sustaining a dynamic that pushed in many directions at once, as indeed did Wilhelmine modernity.[20] Although Wehler's defense of modernization theory does little to bring out these alternative trajectories, his complaint that the "power-monism" of much post-Foucauldian analysis is equally restrictive hits the mark, and it also serves as a useful reminder of just how unsteady this compass heading has proven to be: "The opposite pole would be a more skeptical interpretation of modernity."[21]

Meanwhile, the ongoing exploration of the rich, complex, protean landscape of Wilhelmine modernity seems well on the way to supplying such an interpretation. In her pathbreaking study *Languages of Labor and Gender,* Kathleen Canning has given us a finely nuanced portrait of the "coalescing of discourses and subcultures" in the fin-de-siècle debates over female factory work, where feminists "reinforced the dominant consensus regarding eugenicist solutions to the increasingly complex tangle of social questions" while simultaneously seeking "to disrupt and contest the rationalization of reproduction and the disciplining of the body."[22] Possibil-

---

19. Peukert, *Diagnose,* p. 111.
20. Eley, *Reshaping,* pp. 163–64.
21. Wehler, "Guide," pp. 546–48, 552.
22. Kathleen Canning, *Languages of Labor and Gender: Female Factory Work in Germany, 1850–1914* (Ithaca: Cornell University Press, 1996), pp. 213–14.

ities for creative resistance from within the "authoritarian" structures of Imperial Germany have also been critically evaluated in the flourishing scholarship on the maternalist "service ideology" often linked to the rise of fascism. Thus, by 1914, "the discourse on motherhood was so powerful in the feminist movement that it encompassed the widest possible spectrum of positions, from strident nationalism to pacifism," Ann Taylor Allen concludes in her recent study *Feminism and Motherhood in Germany.*[23] While stressing the less malleable boundaries dividing Wilhelmine political culture, Helmut Smith's *German Nationalism and Religious Conflict* argues that, "far from possessing an archaic worldview," those who were fighting to claim nationalist identity for competing confessional groups "often perceived themselves as forward-looking, and that the central drama—national unity in a polity with a divided memory—posed, and poses, a peculiarly modern problem."[24] Celia Applegate's *Nation of Provincials* also brings out the diverse potentialities of nationalist identity, depicting the *Heimat* movement as a parallel, but distinctly alternative response to the social and cultural transformations resisted by anti-Semites and anti-modernists, a conclusion recently seconded by William Rollins's study *A Greener Vision of Home,* which documents the innovative use of technology and scientific impulses behind environmental reform initiatives.[25] Anne Harrington has uncovered the progressive and subversive side of German organicism and holistic discourse in *Reenchanted Science,* while the diverse potentialities hidden beneath the guise of the "Unpolitical German" have emerged from painstaking studies by Peter Jelavich, Rüdiger vom Bruch, Gangolf Hübinger, and many others.[26] Sketching out the "shadow lines"

---

23. Ann Taylor Allen, *Feminism and Motherhood in Germany, 1800–1914* (New Brunswick, N.J.: Rutgers University Press, 1991), p. 233.
24. Smith, *Politics,* p. 235.
25. Celia Applegate, *A Nation of Provincials: The German Idea of Heimat* (Berkeley: University of California Press, 1990), pp. 59–107; William Rollins, *A Greener Vision of Home: Cultural Politics and Environmental Reform in the German* Hei-matschutz *Movement, 1904–1918* (Ann Arbor: University of Michigan Press, 1997).
26. Anne Harrington, *Reenchanted Science: Holism in German Culture from Wilhelm II to Hitler* (Princeton: Princeton University Press, 1996); see also above, note 13.

National Socialism casts over Wilhelmine cultural traditions (which he persisted in describing as special path), Thomas Nipperdey also emphasized "the great potential of the unpolitical man and woman in German culture," which had been "actualized in a one-sided manner and beyond [an] original ambivalence by political events—1914, 1918–19, 1929–30— and so helped determine the way things went."[27]

The following chapters contribute to this emerging portrait by exploring both the potential and the ambivalence and limitations of the Wilhelmine search for alternatives within a broad milieu of intellectuals and activists who stood firmly on modern ground at the fin de siècle but who were determined to reform that modernity in order to free it from the darkening shadows already plainly visible on the horizon before the First World War. Like the "hundreds of thousands of the best minds" Howe discovered in 1914, the reformers of this milieu strove to apply "scientific thought to every process and every social and industrial problem" while showing "the greatest concern for health and well-being, for education and training of workers, artists, commercial men," and in this sense, they certainly belonged among the rationalizing professionals and efficiency experts whose "progressive optimism" Peukert found so ominous in retrospect. Promoting "the co-ordination of the individual into a machine of national rather than purely personal dimensions," Wilhelmine social and cultural reformers were also quite at home in the discourse of "integral nationalism" Geoff Eley and Roger Chickering have mapped on the radical right in the expanding public sphere, where indeed many of them joined Pan-Germans, Navy League imperialists, and anti-Semites to push for extreme solutions. But many also did not. In fact, one of the most resilient bonds uniting these socially conscious men and women—who often agreed on little else—was a firm rejection of the new politics in a "sharper key" as a grave threat to the unity, prosperity, and strength of the German nation.[28] Nor was paternalistic social policy or the "*Herr-im-Haus* outlook" of National Liberal factory owners the culmination of Wilhelmine reformist visions. The Bülow Bloc, the "Cartel of Productive Estates," Delbrück's gloating proclamation of a "realistic social policy" were anathemas in the reform milieu, (momentary)

---

27. Thomas Nipperdey, *Deutsche Geschichte 1866–1918* (Munich: Beck, 1992), vol. 1, p. 824.

28. Schorske, *Vienna,* pp. 116–20.

triumphs for the despised creed of "Manchesterism" that evoked powerful resistance and, in one important case, bitter outbursts of despair from progressive reformers in the last decade of peace.[29] It was indeed this renunciation of nineteenth-century liberal models of progress along with the weapons of political struggle that brings the search for alternatives so close to the ground of anti-modernism that was plowed over by historians in the 1960s and 1970s. Decrying the rationalizing, alienating, depersonalizing forces of modern industrial capitalism as the evisceration of living *Kultur* by mechanistic *Zivilisation* at the same time that they sang the praises of modern science and technology, Wilhelmine reformers felt just as at home with the discourse of cultural despair as they did with the discourse of progressive optimism.

The Wilhelmine reform milieu inhabited a familiar landscape common to the antimodernists and hypermodern technocrats and populists who have given us such starkly contrasting pictures of late Imperial Germany, and while its territory overlaps with each of them, it is co-extensive with none. In competing for discursive ground with extremists on all sides, moderate social and cultural reformers used the same terms to mark off a contiguous region in Wilhelmine political culture that fell short of radical positions in debates over science and humanism, nationalism and cosmopolitanism, liberalism and socialism, and other issues dividing Germans into the opposing camps they wished to avoid, and from which this middle ground itself was scarcely visible. Both more and less than a composite of those extremes, the search for alternatives has been obscured not only by discourse that later became the exclusive property of radicals but also by the resolve to sidestep the spectacular clashes between right and left in the political arena for the quiet labyrinth of indirect avenues that led into the subterranean world of Wilhelmine anti-politics: scientific studies, detailed proposals, legalistic reports, privately run seminars for public officials, professional careers, personal connections, model institutions, popular education, alternative lifestyles, and many other strategies designed to make an immediate, palpable difference in the quality of people's lives. Facing the realities of Germany's sham constitution, which reduced stormy sessions in the Reichstag to episodes of tragi-comic opera, reformers defended this choice as a hardheaded, practical attempt to dispense with the illusions

---

29. Eley, "Contradictions," p. 98; Eley, *Reshaping,* pp. 257–77, 317–30.

of official culture and to get down to the business of laying concrete foundations for a more humane and prosperous national community in the gray area, neither private nor public, that was their undisputed terrain. Far from a path into complacency and complicity, the "line of least resistance" seemed to offer a most "resourceful way of struggling" for East European dissidents like George Konrád, who defined *Antipolitics* as a "network of conversations uncontrollable from above" little more than a decade ago, while Václav Havel discovered "The power of the powerless" in the "prepolitical" sphere of "self-education," artistic creativity, civic attitudes, and "self-organization" that fortified the "independent life of society" against the "enslaving" lies of a "post-totalitarian" regime.[30] This struggle was, of course, remote from the *Anti-Politik* of Wilhelmine reformers, but it was among the latter that the term was coined in 1907, when disenfranchised critics of the conservative regime used it to describe a similar "ineradicable suspicion toward the mass of political judgments that surround us"; and the parallel seems suggestive in other ways as well.[31] Without smashing the barriers between hostile camps in the repressive and fragmented political culture of Imperial Germany, the men and women of the milieu slipped past those barriers to explore possibilities for constructive resistance, achieving modest successes that informed the contours of public life in subtle, but significant ways before the First World War, and in some cases well beyond.

Superimposed on existing maps, the moderate, faint image of Wilhelmine anti-politics hardly effaces the bold outlines etched by radicals, but it seems worth fitting into the complex historical portrait of the period that is emerging. Along Germany's troubled path into the twentieth century, the search for alternative modernities was another of the forces jostling toward an unthinkable future, our unforgettable past, in a struggle that ended in disaster. This search too belongs to the storyline leading to

---

30. George Konrád, *Antipolitics: An Essay,* trans. Richard Allen (New York: Harcourt Brace Jovanovich, 1984), pp. 198–202; Václav Havel, "The Power of the Powerless," trans. Paul Wilson, in Havel et al., *The Power of the Powerless: Citizens against the State in Central-Eastern Europe* (London: Hutchinson, 1985), pp. 47–48, 52–54, 65.

31. Konrád, p. 232. See also the concluding section of Chapter 4, "Sombart, Naumann, and the Fight for *Anti-Politik.*"

1933. Yet it also pushed in other directions. Like the "loyal critics" of H. Stuart Hughes's study of European social thought, *Consciousness and Society*, and alongside the intellectuals and activists of James Kloppenberg's *Uncertain Victory*, the reformers of the milieu strove to correct the abuses and injustice of the modern world without relinquishing the promise of scientific and technological advance. Refusing flight into utopias or resignation, they took a stand on contemporary ground, fully aware of the potential dangers, and in seeking to avert disaster they helped bring it on. Like the broad tapestry of Western modernity to which it unquestionably belongs, their story contains both shadows and bright prospects, a perilous texture from which our future too must one day be woven.

•   •   •

The following chapters portray the thick web of crisscrossing paths that brought young men and women from a variety of backgrounds to join the search for alternatives in the diverse array of reformist circles, movements, and institutions that comprised the milieu of anti-politics. Behind all their varied commitments stood the "social question," the central issue around which hopes, fears, and expectations regarding modernity revolved at the turn of the century. Chapter 1 begins by looking at the way this question was posed in what became a defining moment for the "younger generation," the proclamation of Kaiser Wilhelm II's social reform decrees in 1890. After briefly recounting the crisis leading up to the February Decrees—and the fall of Bismarck—our initial survey turns to the formative experiences that made this moment so memorable, focusing in particular on debates over the social question since the founding of the Empire, debates that were strongly informed by the discourses of national economics and biology, prestigious sciences that also played a decisive role in shaping responses of young Germans who later went on to become leaders of the reform milieu after 1890. The chapter concludes by considering two prominent members of this generation, Friedrich Naumann and Max Weber, whose careers offer an illuminating contrast to the less famous intellectuals and activists at the core of this study. The following three chapters explore the milieu at ground level, from the perspective of individual reformers, in order to examine in some detail the processes by which these men and women learned the social question through interaction with a wide network of circles, movements, and journals that gave access to contemporary social discourse. The same network also provided each reformer with a distinct

set of personal and institutional ties, both of which enabled them to mobilize support for precise answers that were posed and refined in conflicts
with others competing for the same discursive terrain. While largely forgotten today, all three individuals achieved prominence in the reform
milieu at the fin de siècle using the languages of scientific progress, nationalism, and cultural despair to promote moderate solutions that explicitly rejected the extremes demanded by anti-Semites, Pan-Germans,
Navy Leaguers, and technocrats.

Chapter 2 follows the early career of Adolf Damaschke from the back
of one of Berlin's notorious "rental barracks," where he grew up as the
son of a struggling artisan family, through a bewildering variety of circles
and causes that reappear in subsequent chapters and that receive intro-
ductions here—pedagogical reform, workers' education, Egidy's "United
Christendom," Ethical Culture, natural medicine, utopian settlements,
the Friedrichshagen colony of playwrights and poets, the National Social
Association—to Damaschke's position as leader of the League of German
Land Reformers (*Bund Deutscher Bodenreformer,* or BDB), focusing on
Damaschke's deployment of popular nationalist rhetoric in his clashes with
anti-Semites, Conservatives, and Naumann's enthusiasm for colonies and
fleets.

Chapter 3 covers much of the same ground through the eyes of Gertrud
Bäumer, the daughter of a middling civil servant, while also introducing
new terrain, above all the conflicts between radicals and moderates in the
bourgeois women's movement that culminated in her election as chairwoman of the League of German Women's Associations (*Bund Deutscher
Frauenvereine,* or BDF) in 1910. Bäumer's integration of eugenicist discourse and anti-modern tropes of cultural despair into a progressive, organicist synthesis defending the social impulse of 1890 alongside the subjective individualism of humanistic *Kultur* forms the core of this case study.
The chapter concludes by exploring her visions of a non-partisan cultural
politics of womanhood as the means to achieve a "bright renaissance" of
industry in 1914.

Chapter 4 retraces Werner Sombart's journey from the affluent household
of an *haut bourgeois* landowner and National Liberal politician through a
cultural and environmental critique of capitalism that brought him close
to the revisionist wing of German Social Democracy as a leading voice
among the young national economists in the early 1890s. We then move
on to his technocratic visions of productive efficiency at mid-decade, his

harassment by Conservatives, and his central role in the reform milieu as author of the founding statutes for the Society of Social Reform in 1900, and further still to his profound cynicism and cultural despair—again linked to eugenicist discourse—after the turn of the century, his flight into aestheticism, apocalyptic visions of a "Twilight of the Gods," and ultimate commitment to the transcendental values of neo-humanist idealism that evoked his final, public repudiation of the Nazis' "scientific" social policy after 1933.

After having provided a concrete image of the diverse trajectories that carried socially conscious young Germans through the terrain of Wilhelmine anti-politics at the fin de siècle, as well as of the bold shifts in direction often concealed beneath subtle nuances in the fluctuating meanings of national economic and biological discourse, the study returns to the by now familiar common ground on which these paths met—in some cases, collided—in order to map the broader contours of the milieu in sharper relief. Canvassing the universities and social circles in which the generation of 1890 learned the social question, Chapter 5 offers a group portrait of Wilhelmine social and cultural reformers that is based on a prosopographical study of some four hundred individuals who rubbed shoulders with Damaschke, Bäumer, and Sombart, providing thumbnail sketches of other lives to illustrate diverging paths and resonances while laying out the intertwining sets of personal ties that wove together the complex, tangled fabric of feuds, alliances, and divided loyalties sustaining the search for alternatives. The chapter then moves on to survey some of the institutions, practices, and professions constructed on the basis of these relationships and, after examining what might be considered anti-political successes, closes with a look at the debates surrounding two attempts to consolidate a "scientific" paradigm legitimating the milieu's vision of the future, the institution of racial hygiene and sociology as academic disciplines in the first decade of the twentieth century. A brief epilogue traces the continuing struggle over the milieu and its discourse in a process of negotiation and compromise that continued through war and revolutions, suggesting other end points for the story to accentuate its ambivalence, but concludes in 1914, when its scattered trajectories still trembled at the cutting edge of Howe's modernity and had yet to burst apart.

CHAPTER 1

The Generation of 1890

"There are days that remain unforgettable for a lifetime," wrote Friedrich Naumann, the rebellious "workers' pastor" and self-proclaimed socialist, who was just beginning his rise to fame as spokesman for the "younger generation" in Wilhelmine Germany: "It was such a day for us when the social reform decrees of the Kaiser came in February 1890."[1] With extraordinary precision, Naumann thus pinpointed to the day, almost to the hour, the impulse that would propel his career through its many stages: from leader of what Damaschke later called "the *first* national social movement," through his attempt to forge a progressive alliance "from Bassermann to Bebel," into the "civic peace" of the Great War, and beyond, to his final roles as founder of the German Democratic Party and one of the architects of the Weimar constitution. Through it all, Naumann never lost sight of the promise contained in Wilhelm II's early pledge to maintain "peace between employers and employees" by guaranteeing workers "free and peaceful expression of their wishes and complaints" and "equal rights before the law."[2] However fleeting this vision of "social peace" proved to be for the Kaiser, it left a permanent imprint on the life of Naumann, who in turn personified the hopes—as well as the fears and disappointments— of many young, socially conscious Germans in the Wilhelmine era. Seen

---

1. Friedrich Naumann, "Wochenschau," *Die Hilfe* 1, no. 7 (February 17, 1895): 1.

2. Wilhelm II, "Decree to the Prussian Minister of Commerce and to the Minister of Public Works" of February 2, 1890, in Hans-Jörg von Berlepsch, *"Neuer Kurs" im Kaiserreich? Die Arbeiterpolitik des Freiherrn von Berlepsch 1890 bis 1896* (Bonn: Verlag Neue Gesellschaft, 1987), pp. 28–29.

in this light, the February Decrees of 1890 seem to be not a chimera, or even the blueprint for a single, albeit significant, career in politics, but instead might justly be called the birth certificate of an entire generation.

Whatever else it might be, a generation is in one sense a group of people who pose the same questions to themselves and their society, who see the same problems as central and the same issues as urgently demanding attention.[3] It is, after all, not so much the answers they come up with that identify members of a single generation as the questions they ask, and for Naumann's generation the "social question," posed so dramatically by the young Kaiser himself, occupied "hundreds of thousands of the best minds." What precisely was the nature of this question, how did it come to be framed in this particular way, and why did it remain so unforgettable? Before exploring the specific "answers" of Damaschke, Bäumer, and Sombart, let us first investigate the broader contours of the question they were asking and the role it played in the hopes and fears of their generation, the generation of 1890.

At the Dawn of an Uncertain Future

> The times were charged with electricity. Everywhere the old earth seemed shaken by underground thunder, and here and there a dark, yawning abyss opened up where green meadows had been laughing only moments before.
>
> LILY BRAUN

As the first to come of age in the new German Empire, the generation of 1890 grew up in an atmosphere of tense uncertainty, where every aspect of life seemed open to flux and change. Germany's rise to the unfamiliar status of major world power, its accelerated transition from an agrarian to an industrial, capitalist economy, the sudden appearance of new cities and the refashioning of ancient capitals in wave after wave of urban construc-

---

3. Karl Mannheim noted this in his classic essay on social generations by pointing out different patterns of response to key historical developments that together defined the "entelechy" of a given generation; see Robert Wohl, *The Generation of 1914* (Cambridge, Mass.: Harvard University Press, 1979), pp. 73–78. On the role of generational factors in the ability to "see" problems in the first place, see Thomas Kuhn, *The Structure of Scientific Revolutions* (Chicago: University of Chicago Press, 1970), pp. 77–110, 151–59.

tion made "modernity"—as this bewildering jumble of transformations came to be perceived—an inescapable fact of life for the children of "Bismarck's Empire." Both electrifying and ominous, images of altered landscapes punctuate their memoirs, vividly conveying the impression of youth standing on the threshold of a new age. "Triumphantly the factory chimney climbed toward the heavens, where the castle's tower was slowly crumbling," Lily Braun wrote of an aristocratic outing that was rudely interrupted by the Ruhr miners' strike of May 1889. "I fled its sight and would so dearly have loved to escape from myself on the opalescent, spanned wings of fantasy into the sun-drenched realm of legend, but reality snared me again and again in its thick, gray webs."[4] Writing of his childhood at the opposite end of the social scale as a "renter-nomad" on the outskirts of "small town Berlin," Franz Oppenheimer remembered the untamed wilderness that vanished to make room for elegant nightlife and opulent villas in the city's new West End. "With some of technology's achievements, it seems somewhat doubtful to me whether or not they should be viewed unconditionally as progress," he sighed, reflecting on what had been lost in the process; "but I won't let anything stand in the way of my electric light. . . . Berlin without gas, electric light, without telephone, indeed, even without pneumatic post, without radio, without express trains; what young Berliner can imagine that?!"[5]

Germany was changing, but where that change would lead was open to doubts, especially in the unsettled political climate of the 1870s and 1880s. Alongside new mansions for its prosperous entrepreneurs, the giddy boom of the "founders' years" brought lurid scenes of poverty and homelessness that evoked acrid critiques of "Mammonism" even before the speculative bubble burst in 1873. Massive layoffs, lower wages, and heightened demands on labor followed, as economic growth fluctuated erratically for the rest of the decade in what proved to be the worst depression to hit the country before 1929. The fortunes of the German state thus seemed inextricably bound up with the "social question" from the start, and passionate debates over the nation's vulnerability to the vicissitudes of the new economic order and the excesses of economic individualism undoubtedly

---

4. Lily Braun, *Memoiren einer Sozialistin*, vol. 1, *Lehrjahre* (Berlin: Hermann Klemm, n.d.), p. 325.

5. Franz Oppenheimer, *Erlebtes, Erstrebtes, Erreichtes: Lebenserinnerungen* (Düsseldorf: Melzer, 1964), p. 25.

did much to prepare the ground for Bismarck's "refounding of the Empire" in 1879 by eroding popular support for the Liberal Era on all sides. The impressive social legislation of the 1880s, which introduced mandatory workers' insurance against accidents, illness, and disability (though not unemployment) as well as a national pension program, merely underscored the ambivalence surrounding the country's transition to industrial capitalism, winning Germany a "forerunner's role in modern societies" while at the same time serving alongside other policies of negative integration and charismatic rule as a cornerstone of Bismarck's "authoritarian interventionist state."[6]

Increasingly, however, the Chancellor's solutions began to seem inadequate. Social policy experts who were demanding collective bargaining rights and factory safety regulations as part of a more expansive approach called "workers' protection" condemned Bismarck's refusal to move beyond insurance measures as proof that his vision was too narrow to address the problems of a modern industrial nation,[7] while radical anti-Semites and xenophobic nationalists rode the crest of a potentially revolutionary wave of social protest that swept the countryside in the late 1880s. Far from heralding successful "Bonapartist" manipulation from above, these renegade populists tapped volatile currents of social unrest erupting from below to challenge the hegemony of traditional elites, as the revisionist historiography of recent decades has persuasively demonstrated.[8] The mounting tensions surrounding Germany's social and economic transformations seemed to demand a radical shift in course, though what direction it would take was difficult to say. As rumors of an imminent coup d'état began circulating in government circles, a major strike "broke out with elementary force" and "spread like a prairie fire" through the Ruhr coal mines on May 1, 1889, sparking violent confrontations between workers

---

6. Wehler, *Gesellschaftsgeschichte*, vol. 3, pp. 552–58, 907–15, 934–38; Nipperdey, *Geschichte*, vol. 1, pp. 335–59.

7. Martin Wenck, *Geschichte und Ziele der deutschen Sozialpolitik* (Leipzig: Wiegand, 1908), pp. 111–17; Leopold von Wiese, *Posadowsky als Sozialpolitiker* (Cologne: Christlicher Gewerkschaftsverlag, 1909), pp. 16–19; Nipperdey, *Geschichte*, vol. 1, p. 359.

8. Blackbourn and Eley, *Peculiarities*, pp. 144–49, 265–85; Blackbourn, "Demagogy," pp. 152–84; Eley, *Reshaping*, pp. 21–40; Evans, *Rethinking*, pp. 6–14, 47–50.

and soldiers that had many in the younger generation convinced Bismarck's Empire was about to collapse in bloody civil war.[9] "I believe we are standing on the brink of a great upheaval," Lily Braun wrote from her aristocratic refuge amid the violence; "the power of capital must be destroyed. A hundred years ago a revolution toppled absolutism and feudalism—they deserved it!—a future revolution will destroy capitalism, and we will live through this wonderful drama, in which nobles and workers march together."[10]

A Workers' Kaiser?

Capturing the imagination of young Germans like Braun, the social question once again seemed to hold the key to the nation's future at a crucial moment in its history, an impression etched all the more keenly in the minds of this generation when the Ruhr miners' strike helped to provoke a quarrel between Bismarck and the new Kaiser, Wilhelm II, that precipitated the Chancellor's fall and so opened the door to exciting new possibilities, just as these young men and women were entering adult life and preparing for future careers. While Bismarck hoped to use the spectre of social revolution hovering over the strike to frighten the Reichstag into extending his repressive legislation against the Social Democrats indefinitely, Wilhelm loudly refused to send "his troops" to defend "the villas and rose gardens of industrialists," from whom he instead demanded concessions on behalf of the striking workers.[11] This sudden and unexpected intervention in matters of Bismarck's social policy hardly ended well for the miners (whose leaders were jailed after refusing to accept the settlement), but in the aftermath of the strike, the Kaiser conferred with reform-minded officials and industrialists of the Ruhr, whose suggestions quickly found their way into the famous February Decrees, in which he promised to embark on a "New Course" the following spring. Impressed by the proposals of Count Hans von Berlepsch, a Ruhr administrator who had prevented an escalation of the strike in Düsseldorf, Wilhelm named him

---

9. Helga Grebing, *Arbeiterbewegung: Sozialer Protest und kollektive Interessen-vertretung bis 1914* (Munich: Deutscher Taschenbuchverlag, 1985), p. 9; Berlepsch, *Kurs*, pp. 15–19; Wenck, *Sozialpolitik*, pp. 121–22.

10. Braun, *Memoiren*, vol. 1, p. 336.

11. Grebing, *Arbeiterbewegung*, pp. 24–39.

Prussian Minister of Commerce and Industry on January 31, 1890 and asked him to outline his plans for mediating future social conflicts in a statement on the new Imperial social policy. Bismarck had meanwhile dissolved the Reichstag, which had rejected his Anti-Socialist Bill by a wide margin six days earlier, and new elections were called. With anticipation that the rules of German politics were about to change significantly hanging palpably in the air, the Kaiser published his reform decrees on February 4th.[12]

The first was addressed to Berlepsch and echoed the frustration of social policy experts over Bismarck's opposition to workers' protection. Insurance schemes would take a back seat to an overhaul of the industrial code guided by the assumption "that it is one of the tasks of executive power to regulate time, duration, and types of work in a manner that provides for the preservation of health, the dictates of morality, the economic needs of the workers, and their legitimate claim to equal rights before the law." Legislation was also needed to ensure that "workers, through representatives possessing their confidence, will be involved in the regulation of matters of common interest and empowered with the organs of My Government." Linking these demands to the recent upheaval in the Ruhr, the Kaiser promised that Prussia's state-owned mines would become "model institutions" for the "care of workers," while private ones were to be subjected to factory inspections. Finally, he proposed a conference of European states to discuss international workers' protection—necessary if German industry was to maintain its competitive edge—and in a second decree he instructed Bismarck to begin making immediate arrangements.[13]

At a moment of intense apprehension, political parties on almost every side responded to the Kaiser's message with jubilation, especially on the left. "In light of the Imperial Decrees, the campaign slogan for German workers must read: elect labor representatives, elect Social Democrats, as many as you can!" the *Berlin People's Newspaper* cheered on February 7. Voters seemed to agree. In the Reichstag elections held on February 20th, the SPD claimed the single largest block with 19.7 percent, while the Progressive delegation more than doubled in size and Bismarck's political allies

12. Berlepsch, *Kurs,* pp. 16, 31–48; Karl Erich Born, *Staat und Sozialpolitik seit Bismarcks Sturz* (Wiesbaden: Franz Steiner, 1957), pp. 7–29. See also Canning, *Languages,* pp. 137–38.

13. See above, note 2.

lost 85 seats. As Wilhelm Liebknecht put it, the Social Democrats had won 1.5 million votes in support of the Kaiser's struggle against capitalism, and a week later Berlin's proletariat rallied in the streets to greet an Imperial procession with "Cheers for the Workers' Kaiser!"[14] After decades at an impasse, German political culture seemed to be breaking free of past constraints and opening up to the possibility of significant change, particularly with regard to the social question. On March 15 Wilhelm II hosted an International Conference on Workers' Protection in Berlin, as promised. Two days later Bismarck resigned, and in October the Chancellor's twelve-year ban on Social Democracy finally lapsed, ending the SPD's days as an "outlawed party." Addressing the Prussian House of Deputies a month later, his successor Leo von Caprivi left no doubt about the direction of the New Course: "In an age when the social question is assuming such outstanding prominence, when we are standing before such difficult tasks regarding social questions, all steps taken by the government and the legislature must be examined in light of the question: how will they affect social reforms?"[15] By this time the Reichstag had already begun reviewing plans for the promised overhaul of the industrial code, which eventually included maximum shifts for certain types of work, restrictions on night and Sunday labor, child labor laws, factory safety regulations, expanded competency for factory inspectors, the mandatory posting of legally binding factor ordinances stipulating shift hours, breaks, and payment procedures, and provisions for labor arbitration courts in cities with more than 20,000 inhabitants. A cornerstone of Wilhelmine social policy for decades to come, the new code was passed on June 6, 1891.[16]

"Through a Turning Point in the Times"

The sudden thaw in domestic relations "when the social reform decrees of the Kaiser came in February 1890" was not confined to government offices but spread vitality into the deepest layers of Wilhelmine political culture, where it stirred a "new, rich interest in social policy" that quickly took root in a sudden proliferation of organizations and movements. "It blossomed in bourgeois circles, seized the non-Social-Democratic workforce, which

14. Berlepsch, *Kurs,* pp. 31–32; Born, *Staat,* pp. 9–10.
15. Born, *Staat,* p. 93.
16. Ibid., pp. 98–105.

had previously had little interest in social policy," Martin Wenck later remembered; it "created a union life that unfolded with increasing fertility,
and drove doubt into the Social Democratic movement—however strong
its upturn since 1890—whether the standpoint of pure negation against
state and society is the right thing for a workforce that is striving socially
upward."[17] Major reform institutions like the Protestant Social Congress
and the German Women's League were founded in 1890, and many of the
others we will later encounter—the Ethical Culture Society, the "university extension" movement, and Naumann's National Social Association—
also traced their origins back to this "crucial year." Artists and writers
too played active roles. While prominent Naturalists experimented with
socialistic alternatives on the outskirts of Berlin, more radical poets like
Bruno Wille and Julius Türk joined the SPD itself, founding the Free People's Stage with Franz Mehring as a venue for workers to act out "social
dramas" for the benefit of their comrades.[18]

Of course, not everyone shared the youthful enthusiasm behind this
sudden flowering of artistry and activism. The New Course also unleashed
forces of a very different kind, provoking anger among members of the
traditional elite, who accused Caprivi of "class betrayal."[19] Within four
years a vicious campaign from within the Kaiser's own entourage forced
the new Chancellor from office, and in 1896, Berlepsch fell at the hands
of Baron von Stumm, the famous Saar industrialist who insisted on remaining "master in his own house" and "more or less embodied the social
political reaction."[20] Faced with the "Revolution Bill" of 1894 and the
"Prison Bill" of 1899, the Reichstag spent the "Stumm era" considering
ways to rescue the ruling class from strikes and from Social Democrats
rather than new measures of workers' protection. The fears that nipped
the spring thaw in the bud, like the hopes the thaw released, also seeped
far down into Wilhelmine political culture, producing a similar rash of

---

17. Wenck, *Sozialpolitik*, p. 171.
18. Katharina Günther, *Literarische Gruppenbildung im Berliner Naturalismus*
    (Bonn: Bouvier Verlag Herbert Grundmann, 1972), pp. 61–101, 124–26; Eu-
    gene Lunn, *Prophet of Community: The Romantic Socialism of Gustav Lan-
    dauer* (Berkeley: University of California Press, 1973), pp. 52–54.
19. Kenneth Barkin, *The Controversy over German Industrialization* (Chicago:
    University of Chicago Press, 1970), p. 102.
20. Wiese, *Posadowsky*, p. 40.

new organizations and movements—the League of German Agrarians, the German National Commercial Clerks' Union, the Pan German League, among others—in what proved to be an ominous radicalization of the "German-National public realm."[21] "Agrarian romanticism and hostility to the metropolis" were strong motifs in the response to the "controversy over German industrialization" provoked by the New Course, and many undoubtedly answered this "crisis of modernization" with cultural despair.[22] After all, 1890 was also the year of Julius Langbehn's confused and anguished *Rembrandt as Educator.*[23]

As it was posed in the February Decrees, the social question thus seemed to demand a fundamental stance with regard to modernity as a whole from the young men and women of the Wilhelmine era. Capitalism, industry, urbanization, socialism all spelled uncertainty, and while some greeted the prospects of an uncharted future, others drew back in fear. The "underground thunder" in the coal mines of the Ruhr had certainly issued a strong warning about the "elemental forces" at work in Germany's social and economic transformations. The Hamburg cholera epidemic of 1891 soon provided another as it crept out of squalid "rental barracks" in proletarian districts to invade the homes of the city's elite, killing hundreds each day.[24] The question was how to confront such dangers. One could deploy troops against striking workers, hide sources of contagion, and wield art as a weapon in the revolt against modernity. Or one could study the economic factors behind labor unrest, discover the biological causes of and medical remedies for disease, and use the awesome productive capacity of German industry to bring art to the masses on a previously unimaginable scale. Either way, "modernity" remained the central question for the generation of 1890.

---

21. Chickering, *Men,* pp. 47–57, 152–77; Hans-Jürgen Puhle, *Agrarische Interessenpolitik und preußischer Konservatismus im wilhelminischen Reich* (Hanover: Verlag für Literatur und Zeitgeschehen, 1966), pp. 33–36.

22. Chickering, *Men,* p. 47; Barkin, *Controversy,* passim; Klaus Bergmann, *Agrarromantik und Großstadtfeindschaft,* (Meisenheim: Hain, 1970), p. 87; Thomas Nipperdey, "Probleme der Modernisierung in Deutschland," in Nipperdey, *Nachdenken,* pp. 44–59.

23. Stern, *Despair,* pp. 97–180.

24. Richard Evans, *Death in Hamburg: Society and Politics in the Cholera Years, 1830–1910* (New York: Oxford University Press, 1987), pp. 346–402.

Looking back a hundred years later, it might seem clear where these choices were bound to lead in the end. Whether fixed on anti-modern manias or on distinctly modern pathologies, the historian's gaze easily obscures the view of an uncertain future—and the alternative modernities discernible within it—that confronted these young men and women as an inescapable reality in 1890. Heartened by the moment's promise, but equally mindful of its disastrous potential, reformers like Damaschke, Bäumer, and Sombart believed they were living through "a turning point in the times," that it was up to them to determine the shape modernity would take "in days to come."[25] At the same time, the only viable path out of the present also led through a career, with its mundane demands for hard work, technical skills, and compromise—constraints that tempered this strong sense of mission and, for most, ruled out the extremes on either side from the start. Determined to find realistic answers to the burning questions of the day, many agreed with the noted economist Lujo Brentano, who in 1890 told a gathering of students that "the true danger of social crisis . . . is not to be found in the appearance of economic change and the advancement of new social classes" but in rash attempts to divert these developments suddenly and violently through "revolutions and reaction."[26] Between the utopian reefs on left and right there was plenty of room to chart new courses; all that was needed was careful study and commitment to gradual change.

Among Brentano's students was Naumann, who conveyed the exhilaration and sense of responsibility this challenge still evoked when he presented his own plans for a new German economic policy sixteen years later. "While earlier, quieter times were able to sun themselves in the splendor of how magnificently far they had come and believed themselves to be at the end of a long line of development, the opposite feeling is common among us," he wrote, "that we are living just at the beginning of new forms of life, on the eve of an age whose essence is just beginning to reveal itself to us. After us, only after us, we feel, will the truly new age come, the age

---

25. Adolf Damaschke, *Aus meinem Leben,* vol. 2, *Zeitenwende* (Leipzig: Grethlein, 1925); Gertrud Bäumer, *Lebensweg durch eine Zeitenwende* (Tübingen: Wunderlich, 1933); Walther Rathenau, *In Days to Come* (London: Allen & Unwin, 1921).

26. Quoted in Rüdiger vom Bruch, "Bürgerliche Sozialreform im deutschen Kaiserreich," in Bruch, *Kommunismus,* p. 62.

of the machine in all of its power, magnificence, and rapine, the age of the world market and the spanning of the globe, the period of perfected capitalism and thus, perhaps, the rosy dawn of socialism, yet at the same time thus also the ultimate sinking and drowning of 'Hermann and Dorothea.' "[27]

Socialists of the Lectern

If the February Decrees made so memorable an impression, Brentano and his colleagues could certainly claim at least as much credit as the "Workers' Kaiser," who soon turned his back on the hopeful vision of 1890. The historical school of national economics had set the terms of debate when the social question emerged as a cipher for the Empire's future two decades earlier, and it was here that many turned for help in interpreting the potential of the New Course during the spring thaw. "The writings of bourgeois social policy experts grew out of the ground like mushrooms," Wenck tells us. "The old works of the first Christian Social movement were pulled out again and checked for accuracy. Social theoreticians were studied." Seeking "whatever experience and knowledge had been recorded by social scientific associations," young reformers learned to value the work of the economists in "the Association for Social Policy, founded already in 1873,"[28] which continued to inform their search for answers long after the fall of Berlepsch and Caprivi. National economics thus left an indelible imprint on the memory of 1890, and in order to decipher its meaning for the younger generation we will need to retrace these early steps for a closer look at the "socialists of the lectern" who advanced the prestigious discipline and shaped the evolving discourse of the social question at an earlier turning point in the times.

National Economics

Often translated as 'political economy,' *Nationalökonomie* (or *Volkswirtschaft*) has no precise equivalent in the English language. Stressing integrative functions of commerce and industry that seemed to be producing coherent systems of economic activity at the national and international

---

27. Friedrich Naumann, *Neudeutsche Wirtschaftspolitik*, 3rd revised ed. (Berlin: Fortschritt, 1911), p. 14.
28. Wenck, *Sozialpolitik*, pp. 140–41.

level, the field first emerged as a distinctive response to the theories of Adam Smith and other "classical economists" in the 1820s and 1830s.[29] This focus on community at the expense of individual interests may have formed the basis for a conservative paternalism in the writings of Adam Müller,[30] but Friedrich List soon presented a markedly different version of the new science in his *National System of Political Economy,* the first volume of which appeared in 1841.[31] An ardent advocate of railways and democracy, List strongly promoted the Prussian customs union of 1832, which he saw as a springboard for Germany's transformation into a modern, industrialized nation-state. Once it reached this level of development, his country would be able to join England and others to realize Smith's dream of a world economy governed by the principles of free trade, List fervently believed, but first the material foundations of a prosperous *national* economy had to be in place.

Rebelling against Müller's hazy romanticism, the empiricist List felt the same impatience with the tranquil world represented in *Hermann and Dorothea* as the Young German poets and playwrights, whose aesthetic of radical immanence helped inspire Marx's "materialistic view of history" a generation later.[32] The authors of *The Communist Manifesto* were by no means alone, however, in using economics to critique "the German ideology." The founders of the historical school of economics who followed after List shared many of Marx's basic assumptions, as Albert Müssiggang has shown. Wilhelm Roscher, Bruno Hildebrand, and Karl Knies were virulently materialistic and, like Marx, tended to insert economics in place

---

29. Albert Müssiggang, *Die soziale Frage in der historischen Schule der deutschen Nationalökonomie* (Tübingen: Mohr, 1968), pp. 46–80.

30. Robert M. Berdahl, *The Politics of the Prussian Nobility: The Development of a Conservative Ideology, 1770–1848* (Princeton: Princeton University Press, 1988), pp. 160–79.

31. Friedrich List, *Das nationale System der politischen Oekonomie* (Berlin: Cotta'sche Buchhandlung Nachfolger, 1925); W. O. Henderson, *Friedrich List: Economist and Visionary, 1789–1846* (Totowa, N.J.: Frank Cass and Company, 1983).

32. Ernest K. Bramsted, *Aristocracy and the Middle-Classes in Germany* (Chicago: University of Chicago Press, 1964), p. 309; Nigel Reeves, "Heine and the Young Marx," *Oxford German Studies* 7(1972–73): 44–97.

of idealism as a kind of "ersatz religion" sustaining an intense "belief in progress" that was again conceived in remarkably similar terms. Both Marxist and national economic schools described social problems as the result of the current transition from an agrarian/artisan-based economy to a socialistic order of the future, in which such problems would ultimately disappear. The founders of the historical school differed strongly with Marx in their continued emphasis on national difference as a factor in the character and timing of economic development, but by combining Müller's organic metaphors with List's empirical orientation they firmly established national economics as a second strand of historical materialism that evolved alongside Marxist political economy in the 1850s and 1860s.[33]

The Association for Social Policy and the Crisis of the Founders' Years

The belief that the future socialist order would rest on national foundations seemed quite relevant in the political struggles of the decades before 1871. Ferdinand Lassalle's sensational attempts to rally a nascent workers' movement to the cause of German unity with symbols drawn from national tradition made an especially deep impression on the students of Roscher, Hildebrand, and Knies in the early 1860s. For Gustav Schmoller, Albert Schäffle, and others in the younger historical school, the Progressives' refusal to admit Lassalle's workers into the National Association in 1863 was a tragic event epitomizing a lost opportunity to integrate the working classes into the German nation that was as unforgettable for them as the February Decrees later became for Naumann and his followers.[34] Had the bourgeoisie welcomed workers, they might never have been seduced by Marx's radical hostility to the nation, the spectre of revolution would never have risen, and Bismarck could not have driven the wedge of fear between

---

33. Müssiggang, *Frage,* 82–116, 229–31. See also Smith, *Politics,* pp. 175–77.
34. Müssiggang, *Frage,* pp. 125–37; Shlomo Na'aman, *Lassalle* (Hannover, 1970); Peter Gay, *The Dilemma of Democratic Socialism* (New York: Columbia Univeristy Press, 1952), pp. 20–35; Guenther Roth, *The Social Democrats in Imperial Germany* (Totowa, N.J.: Bedminster, 1963), pp. 42–51; James J. Sheehan, *German Liberalism in the Nineteenth Century* (Chicago: University of Chicago Press, pp. 91–93.

the forces of social progress. Or so it seemed to Schmoller and Schäffle, who drove these lessons home as teachers of the younger generation. Whatever its actual significance, the tale of Lassalle's lost bid for social peace thus found its way into the historical memory of reformers like Damaschke, Bäumer, and Sombart, in whose writings it echoes loudly as a warning motif.

Brentano also studied economics in the 1860s, but preferred the methods of "classical economics" and—like Lassalle's Progressive opponents—promoted self-help rather than "state socialism" as the best answer to the "workers' question." Called to the University of Berlin at the onset of the Liberal Era, in 1871 he published the first volume of his controversial *Workers' Guilds of the Present,* which used an analysis of the British union movement to depict the possibility of negotiating a partnership between organized labor and organized industry on the principles of a free market economy. Although firmly anchored in liberal economic theory, Brentano's message nevertheless provoked angry, frightened responses from representatives of business and finance in the new Empire, who dismissed it as "pure class-hate propaganda" at a time when August Bebel was openly invoking the bloodshed of the Paris Commune as a "battle cry of the entire European proletariat."[35] Nor were Social Democrats the only ones threatening Liberals with socialistic ideas amid the glaring contrasts of the founders' years. Bebel's turn to Marxist rhetoric partly reflected unwelcome competition from "bourgeois" economists like Eugen Dühring, who published his *Critical History of Political Economy and Socialism* in 1871,[36] and the historical school of national economics began voicing increasingly radical views on capitalism in these years as well. "I criticize the principles of our entire economic law, personal freedom and private property," the young economist Adolf Wagner wrote a year after his conversion from "liberal Saul" to "state socialist Paul" in 1871. Having already acknowledged the validity of Marx's methods in a speech, "On the Social Question," Wagner now insisted that "Marx and Lassalle" were "more than a match" for liberal economists "in terms of scholarship," and privately he

---

35. Sheehan, *Liberalism,* p. 154; Sheehan, *The Career of Lujo Brentano* (Chicago: University of Chicago Press, 1966); Günter Brakelmann, Martin Greschat and Werner Jochman, *Protestantismus und Politik* (Hamburg: Hans Christians, 1982), p. 87; Roth, *Social Democrats,* pp. 171–83.

36. Roth, *Social Democrats,* pp. 173–78; Gay, *Dilemma,* pp. 94–103.

even considered joining the Social Democratic party itself.[37] Even without this step, however, his vitriolic attacks on Manchesterism and Mammonism seemed worrisome enough. Schäffle's attempt to calm Liberal anxieties by outlining the scientific side of Marx's "bitingly critical and undeniably clear-sighted work" in an 1874 treatise, *The Quintessence of Socialism,* did little to improve matters.[38]

In light of such views, the Liberals' repudiation of Brentano was not entirely surprising, and the young scholar soon felt pressured to join with his more radical colleagues in order to defend his views as the lines of battle became more clearly drawn. A decisive moment in these escalating debates came when the prominent National Liberal Heinrich Oppenheim denounced the historical school as "socialists of the lectern" after another professor of national economics, Gustav Schönberg, praised socialism in his inaugural address at the University of Freiburg in 1871. Instantly adopted and worn with pride by Schönberg and Wagner, the label stuck, becoming a permanent marker that later resurfaced with serious consequences for the generation of 1890, as we will see. The same was true of "Mammonism," the accusation with which Wagner returned fire against the Jewish Oppenheim, tainting the conflict with anti-Semitic overtones in a characteristically vile outpouring of spleen. While the press war between national economists and Liberals was over by 1876, it left deep scars behind, and the caricatures it provoked on both sides lived on in the popular imagination, where they joined Lassalle's ghost, Manchesterism, and other straw men as significant players in the Wilhelmine discourse on the social question.

A more tangible outcome of the dispute was the Association for Social Policy, which Brentano, Wagner, and Schmoller founded in October 1873 as a counterweight to the influential Congress of German Industrialists.[39]

---

37. Bruch, "Sozialreform," pp. 69, 156n42; Martin Heilmann, *Adolph Wagner— Ein deutscher Nationalökonom im Urteil der Zeit* (New York: Campus, 1980), p. 33; Barkin, *Controversy,* pp. 141–42; Müssiggang, *Frage,* pp. 142–44.

38. Albert Schäffle, *The Quintessence of Socialism* (New York: Charles Scribner's Sons, 1894), p. 6.

39. Irmela Gorges, *Sozialforschung in Deutschland 1872–1914 Gesellschaftliche Einflüsse auf Themen- und Methodenwahl des Vereins für Socialpolitik,* 2nd ed. (Frankfurt: Anton Hain Meisenheim), pp. 37–75; Sheehan, *Brentano,* pp. 67–72; Müssiggang, *Frage,* pp. 149–50; Dieter Lindenlaub, *Richtungskämpfe im Verein für Sozialpolitik* (Wiesbaden: Steiner, 1967), pp. 2–5.

Adopting the middle ground between Brentano's free market principles and Wagner's state socialism, Schmoller also invited prominent National Liberals to the Association's founding congress, at which he hoped to reconcile the warring parties of academe and industry, and went out of his way to assuage their suspicions about "socialism of the lectern." In his opening address, the moderate economist expressed grave concern about the threat of revolution arising from the "deep divide" between workers and employers, and he depicted the emergence of the historical school of national economics as a scientific means to eliminate this danger. Distancing himself from the goal of "leveling in the socialist sense," Schmoller went on to acknowledge the principles of free enterprise and wage labor. Here he stopped to express the concerns of his fellow economists, however, declaring that "we will not suffer the most glaring abuses and allow them to grow for the sake of a doctrinaire principle." Economic freedom was certainly desirable, but it required careful supervision "by the public sphere," and in cases "where a public sphere is in fact lacking," Schmoller believed, "the state [should] intervene by investigating and, without involving itself in the enterprise in question, publishing the results." Having defined scholarship as the Association's primary task and endorsed a conception of state "intervention" limited to purely informative, or at most advisory functions, Schmoller concluded his speech with a passionate appeal for the Liberals' solidarity in pursuit of the national economist's integrationist ideal: "to call an ever greater segment of our nation to participation in all higher forms of culture, in education, and in affluence. This can and must be the great mission of our development, democratic in the best sense of the word, just as it appears to be the goal of world history in general."[40]

Coming at the height of the controversy, Schmoller's middling position failed to satisfy either of the extremes represented at the Association's founding congress. Rudolf Gneist, the Liberals' spokesman, responded by flatly rejecting the idea that government should intervene in the affairs of private enterprise at all. Brentano also objected to Schmoller's visions of a "social monarchy," and disagreement over Bismarck's social policy eventually caused a break between the two economists and friends in the early 1880s.[41] At the same time, Schmoller's readiness to compromise with the

40. Gustav Schmoller, *Zur Social- und Gewerbepolitik der Gegenwart: Reden und Aufsätze* (Leipzig: Duncker & Humblot, 1890), pp. 1–13.

41. Sheehan, *Brentano,* pp. 80–84.

Liberals inevitably alienated Adolf Wagner. The state socialist's calls for nationalizing the railroad industry and extending communal property rights in turn sparked an angry exchange with Brentano, and even though Schmoller took his side on the issue, Wagner resigned from the Association for Social Policy in protest in 1878.[42] Despite this immediate failure, however, the moderate economist remained the magnetic center of discussions concerning social policy in the following decades, alternately attracting and repelling Wagner, Brentano, and their supporters, but all the while reinforcing the message of social integration he had outlined in 1873, and which continued to resonate loudly a generation later in the writings of Damaschke, Bäumer, and Sombart.

The Science of Anti-Politics

After his break with the Association, Wagner joined the "first Christian Social movement" Wenck named as the other major source of social-political discourse in the spring thaw of 1890. The Christian Social Party was founded in 1878 by Wilhelm I's court preacher, Adolf Stöcker, who asked the anti-Semitic socialist of the lectern to write its statutes, hoping to lure workers away from Social Democracy and to "lay a conquered Berlin at the feet of the Hohenzollern."[43] Wagner's program echoed the agenda of the Association for Social Policy in these years and even borrowed some of Brentano's proposals, including the recognition of organized labor and the creation of labor arbitration courts. Similar demands later appeared in the February Decrees and in the industrial code of 1891, as did other planks from Wagner's Christian Social platform, such as international regulation of workers' protection, child labor laws, maximum shifts, and health and safety regulations. Such overlap was certainly due to the social policy Association's scholarly publications, which Berlepsch consulted during his experiments with communal administrative reform in Düsseldorf, but it may also indicate Stöcker's influence on the young Wilhelm II, whom he served as tutor and almost certainly introduced to Chris-

---

42. Barkin, *Controversy,* pp. 142–43.
43. Hellmut von Gerlach, *Von Rechts nach Links* (Hildesheim: Gerstenberg, 1978), p. 105; Peter Pulzer, *The Rise of Political Anti-Semitism in Germany and Austria* (New York: Wiley, 1964), pp. 88–102.

tian Social goals.[44] What is perhaps more surprising is that a similar set of proposals was also contained in the Social Democrats' Eisenach Platform, which the specific proposals of Wagner's program mimic in both form and content.[45] And while the court preacher's bid for the hearts of German workers failed miserably, it successfully disseminated the national economists' integrationist agenda to ever wider circles of young Germans, who grew impatient with the Christian Socials' embarrassing political entanglements with the Conservatives and finally rejected Stöcker's anti-Semitism as worthless packaging.[46]

Wagner's excursion into Conservative politics after 1878 departed from the "social scientific" Association and its mainstream approach in more ways than one. Shaken by the clashes of the founders' years, Schmoller soon directed the national economists' attention away from issues of immediate political interest and back to the empirical, narrowly descriptive approach he had outlined at the founding congress. While in its first years the Association's research had generated reform proposals on joint-stock companies, arbitration courts, old age and invalid insurance, the legal status of labor contracts, and municipal tax structures, after 1878 the socialists of the lectern investigated questions concerning German agriculture—including "internal colonization" and "usury in the countryside"—and devoted more of their time to training civil servants.[47] Reflecting government interests after the conservative turn of 1878, the Association's new agenda was not necessarily a turn away from politics in a broadly defined sense, but it certainly removed the national economists' efforts from the limelight of controversy, marking a crucial tactical shift from direct political engagement to the indirect channels of anti-politics.

Both contemporaries and later historians have often condemned the Association's newfound distaste for political conflict as a serious handicap on its ability to effect meaningful change,[48] yet the advisory role Schmoller

---

44. Born, *Staat*, pp. 7, 29.
45. Brakelmann, *Protestantismus*, p. 86, 114–15.
46. Gerlach, *Rechts*, pp. 102–7.
47. Gorges, *Sozialforschung*, pp. 76–102, 161–82.
48. Lindenlaub, *Richtungskämpfe*, vol. 1, pp. 22–27. Damaschke was among the contemporary critics of the Association for Social Policy and of Schmoller in particular. The "purely historical" approach, Damaschke felt, led to "such an objective view that it cripples the will to the deed, which after all must

prescribed achieved dramatic results in cases like Berlepsch's. By excluding political questions, the new agenda allowed economists to avoid quarrels and to focus their efforts on problem-solving in areas of mutual interest, a condition Kuhn has described as the decisive advantage of scientific research communities more generally.[49] The Association's weakness may thus also have been its strength, as Rüdiger vom Bruch suggests: "untroubled by political/ideological discussions of principle, it directed all of its energy with remarkably concentrated force toward pragmatic solutions, which indeed were often well-suited to serve as levers for gradually loosening up the political system as a whole."[50] The same was true of other institutions in which national economists met privately with government ministers, bureaucrats, factory owners, financiers, and others capable of influencing German social policy during the 1880s, such as the Central Association for the Welfare of the Working Classes, the Wednesday Society, and the Political-Scientific Society Schmoller founded in 1883, where industrialists Heinrich Freese and Ernst Abbé conferred with professors and civil servants to hammer out the principles of "factory constitutionalism." Such organizations, Bruch argues, "mirrored the specific milieu that enabled communication between the middle class and the government and should be seen as a decisive segment of Imperial political culture."[51]

Here national economists perfected anti-political techniques that won them considerable influence on public policy while at the same time penetrating regions of German society far removed from official culture. Albert Schäffle, for instance, consulted with Bismarck on details of the workers' insurance program—inspiring the Chancellor's long-range plans for a neo-corporate parliament of economic affairs—but in 1879 the Social Democratic press chose to publish his *Quintessence of Socialism* from exile in Switzerland.[52] When Wilhelm II launched his initiative a decade later, it was Wagner's and Schmoller's turn to give the advice, but the pervasive

always express itself in a one-sided manner." Of Schmoller he wrote: "He 'cleverly' rejected the organized struggle for acknowledged truths"; Adolf Damaschke, *Geschichte der Nationalökonomie: Eine erste Einführung* (Jena: Fischer, 1929), vol. 2, p. 72.
49. Kuhn, *Structure*, pp. 160–73.
50. Bruch, "Sozialreform," p. 83.
51. Ibid., p. 85.
52. Born, *Staat*, p. 41; Gay, *Dilemma*, p. 43.

influence of national economics at the university ultimately proved more decisive. "Nearly all the important economic chairs in Germany were occupied by socialists of the lectern after 1890," Karl Erich Born has noted in discussing the impulses behind Wilhelmine social policy.[53] "Schmoller's and Wagner's handbooks on national economic theory were the standard works of the time. In professional journals, countless articles by the socialists of the lectern on specific issues were printed," while "the number of advisors who had gone through Schmoller's and Wagner's school steadily increased" in the ranks of the civil service. Yet the educational imperative of the 1880s reached a much wider audience at the university and in less privileged social circles beyond, as we will see in Chapter 5, and according to Born it was national economics that "made the idea of social reform popular in public opinion for the first time."[54]

What appealed to progressive minds of the younger generation in the works of the Association for Social Policy and the socialists of the lectern was precisely the promise of avoiding potentially ruinous political conflicts that was contained in their status as "science." Confronted by the upheaval in the Ruhr, national economics responded with countless empirical studies and detailed reform proposals compiled from decades of painstaking research that seemed to offer a rational explanation and "objective" answers to the social question during the spring thaw of 1890. The other science that was swiftly gaining prestige alongside national economics in the years prior to the New Course was biology, which similarly came to the rescue in the country's major crisis of modernity, the Hamburg cholera epidemic, identifying both cause—poor sanitation leading to a contaminated water supply—and remedy—increased supervision and, where a public sphere was lacking, state intervention in matters of the nation's health. In other words, the biologists and physicians who responded to this crisis agreed with the socialists of the lectern in stressing "the inadequacy of classical liberal practice in the face of urban growth and social change."[55]

The "scientific" messages of national economists, biologists, and physicians had in fact long blended together in a common message of social integration that strongly informed the younger generation's response to the February Decrees, which, as we have seen, named "the preservation of

---

53. Born, *Staat,* p. 44–45.
54. Ibid., p. 33.
55. Evans, *Death,* p. 565.

health" as the first objective of workers' protection. Already in 1873, the year of Schmoller's opening appeal to the Association for Social Policy, physicians had joined with "engineers, builders, and experts on water supply and sewers" to found the National Society for Public Health, promoting sanitation as a means to increase the nation's physiological "capacity for service."[56] Later in the decade Wagner's reform agenda came to include "protection of the working population from conditions detrimental to health at the workplace and at home," a demand that later found its way into the new industrial code of 1891 along with other planks in the Christian Socials' platform, but which again also resembled Social Democratic calls for prohibitions on labor "hazardous to health and morality" and "sanitary checks on workers' apartments" to safeguard the "life and health of workers."[57] Behind such reforms lay the works and debates of medical reformers, physiologists, Darwinian embryologists, "germ plasm" theorists, and a colorful assortment of other biological practitioners, to whom we now turn to examine this second strand in the "scientific" discourse of the social question.

The Health of the Nation

The link between national economics and biology can be traced back to the materialist impulse of the 1830s and 1840s, when students of the life sciences joined the revolt against romantic idealism that also inspired List and the founders of the historical school along with Marx and the Young Germans. In biological terms this revolt expressed itself in the mordacious repudiation of any notion of an immaterial "life force" by young students lashing out at the perceived idealism of teachers like Johannes Müller and Karl Ernst von Baer.[58] Among this generation was Carl Vogt, who reputedly enjoyed shocking audiences with the assertion that ideas and urine were analogous products of the brain and bladder, while Jacob Moleschott sug-

56. Weindling, *Health,* pp. 157–58.

57. Born, *Staat,* pp. 98–99; Brakelman, *Protestantismus,* p. 98; Allan Mitchell, "Bourgeois Liberalism and Public Health: A Franco-German Comparison," in Kocka and Mitchell, *Society,* pp. 346–64.

58. Timothy Lenoir, *The Strategy of Life* (Chicago: University of Chicago Press, 1982); Frederick Gregory, *Scientific Materialism in Nineteenth Century Germany* (Boston: Reidel, 1977).

gested that the hunger crises of the 1840s could be relieved by using corpses as fertilizer in the fields.[59] Equally determined to root out all vestiges of biological idealism, but more reserved than these "scientific materialists," Emil du Bois-Reymond and Hermann von Helmholtz sought to trace the physical sources of organic energy through respiration in experiments that led to significant breakthroughs in microscopy as well as to Helmholtz's discovery of the first law of thermodynamics in 1847.[60] Such efforts were rooted in the same social and cultural milieu as historical materialism, and Anson Rabinbach has even suggested that it may have been Helmholtz who supplied the "physiological model of labor power" underlying Marx's *Capital*, while Engels "explicitly integrated Helmholtz" into his *Dialectics of Nature*.[61]

Biologists also took active parts in the political struggles of the decades prior to unification. In 1848 some went to the barricades, including both Vogt, who led Giessen's citizens' corps before being sent to the Frankfurt parliament, and Ludwig Büchner, the author of *Force and Matter*, a "bible of the new materialism" that was later published to spite the Reaction in 1855 (his more famous brother Georg, the playwright, had also become a biologist after being exiled in an earlier wave of social protest in the 1830s).[62] The young anatomist and physician Rudolf Virchow served as a delegate in Frankfurt too, but he quickly turned to more anti-political methods in light of the disillusioning pace of events at the Paulskirche. Founding the journal *Medical Reform*, Virchow called on his fellow physicians to convene a separate congress in order to consider a medical bill of rights that included proposals for a national public health agency, an academy of medicine, a health council, municipal health boards, and stan-

---

59. Gregory, *Materialism*, p. 64. Dieter Wittich, *Vogt, Moleschott, Büchner* (Berlin: Akademie-Verlag, 1971), p. lxi.

60. Lenoir, *Strategy*, pp. 195–243.

61. Anson Rabinbach, *The Human Motor: Energy, Fatigue, and the Origins of Modernity* (Berkeley: University of California Press, 1990), pp. 52–83; Timothy Lenoir, "The Social Interests of the Organic Physics of 1847," in Lenoir, *Instituting*, pp. 77–89; Lenoir, "The Politics of Vision: Optics, Painting, and Ideology in Germany 1845–95," in Lenoir, *Instituting*, pp. 135–38.

62. Wittich, *Vogt*, pp. l–li; Ludwig Bücher, *Im Dienste der Wahrheit* (Giessen: Roth, 1900), p. xiii; Georg Büchner, *Danton's Death, Leonce and Leona, Woyzeck*, trans. Richard Price (New York: Oxford University Press, 1971), p. xi.

dardized medical training.[63] While such revolutionary commitments cost many their jobs in the conservative backlash of 1849, more cautious biologists like du Bois-Reymond, Helmholtz, and Carl Ludwig subscribed to similar "social programs" and quietly preserved the link between organic science and the progressive impulse of 1848 as they established a strong presence at German universities in the reactionary 1850s.[64] After a brief spell of official disfavor, even Virchow managed to secure a full professorship at the University of Berlin by 1856, followed by a place at the Prussian Royal Deputation for Health Care in 1860. In the following decade, Büchner (now a private physician) pushed for a Liberal alliance with workers in the Democratic People's Party before joining the Internationale in a desperate bid to win the support of Marx and Engels.[65]

It was Virchow, however, who played the most visible (and notorious) role in the political battles of the 1860s and 1870s. A founding member of the Progressive Party and one of Bismarck's fiercest adversaries during the Prussian constitutional crisis, the famous Berlin professor passionately defended the Liberals' secularizing policies in the "Kulturkampf," a term he himself coined in a polemical address to the Prussian parliament in 1873. The year before, Virchow had declared that "only dreamers and scoundrels opposed" the progressive force at work in scientific research: "It rules not only in factories and kitchens, but also in the arts of war and diplomacy, in art and trade—it rules everywhere! Why should we then preclude its entrance into the ordinary thought of the people? Let the light shine openly into people's minds! No more hypocrisy, no fabrication, no attempts at mediation!"[66] Amid the turbulence of the founders' years, Virchow's bellicose "confession of faith" merely heightened the tensions and perceptions of ruthlessness that were already undermining the foundations of the Liberal Era, and it drew a sharp response from more circumspect biologists like du Bois-Reymond, who spent the rest of the decade countering highly

63. Byron Boyd, *Rudolf Virchow* (New York: Garland, 1991).

64. Lenoir, "Interests," pp. 79, 85–86; Timothy Lenoir, "Science for the Clinic: Science Policy and the Formation of Carl Ludwig's Institute in Leipzig," in Lenoir, *Instituting*, pp. 116–24.

65. Gregory, *Materialism*, pp. 105–14; Büchner, *Dienst*, p. xviii; Dieter Fricke et al., eds., *Lexikon zur Parteiengeschichte* (Cologne: Pahl-Rugenstein, 1986), vol. 1., pp. 508–10; Weindling, *Health*, pp. 93–95.

66. Boyd, *Virchow*, p. 158.

politicized versions of science with his famous dictum *ignoramus, ignora-bimus:* "we do not know it, we will never know it."[67] Insisting that scientists had no answers to questions about the meaning of life and the existence of God, du Bois-Reymond ruled the noisy political conflicts of the 1870s out of bounds and drew the limits of the biologists' mission as narrowly as Schmoller did for economists in the Association for Social Policy. Still, the principle of "value-free scholarship" left plenty of room for "techno-cratic anti-politics" in both fields.[68]

At the University of Berlin, du Bois-Reymond, Helmholtz, and others built up major biological and medical research facilities on the basis of the same cooperation among officials, industrialists, and academics we en-countered in Schmoller's Social-Scientific Society and the other institutions of the city's anti-political milieu. Under Helmholtz's direction, the Physical Institute provided laboratory space, instruments, and other materials for biologists and physicists, who were encouraged to cooperate. Du Bois-Reymond assisted in fund-raising for Helmholtz's Institute, while Werner von Siemens helped secure government support, and the three also came together behind Anton Dohrn's efforts to found a marine biology research station in Naples.[69] The work done at such facilities often had direct ap-plications for both industry and the public sector. While "Social Helm-holtzianism" began to offer practical tips for the efficient configuration of physiological labor with the new science of work, Berlin laboratories iso-lated the bacterial agents for tuberculosis, pneumonia, and tetanus, placing significant technical possibilities for the prevention of disease in the hands of government. In return, Bismarck's national insurance legislation proved to be "the making of the medical profession."[70] This community of inter-ests continued to grow in the following years, as Prussian Minister of Cul-

---

67. Emil du Bois-Reymond, *Über die Grenzen des Naturerkennens* (Leipzig: Veit, 1891); Gregory, *Materialism*, pp. 148–51; Erwin N. Hiebert, "The Transfor-mation of Physics," in Mikulas Teich and Roy Porter, eds., *Fin de Siècle and Its Legacy* (New York: Cambridge University Press, 1990), pp. 241–44.

68. Weindling, *Health*, p. 20.

69. Cahan, *Institute*, pp. 12–72; Peter Ruff, *Emil du Bois-Reymond* (Leipzig: Teubner, 1981), pp. 42–53; Theodor Heuss, *Anton Dohrn: A Life for Science* (New York: Springer, 1991), pp. 166–67, 244–48, 288–92, 315.

70. Weindling, *Health*, p. 17.

ture Friedrich Althoff poured funding into biological and medical research facilities both at universities and in the private sector.[71]

Through hidden channels of anti-political technical expertise, German biologists directly shaped the response of government and industry to questions of health, safety, and productive efficiency, but they also quietly educated an entire generation of officials and socially conscious citizens in much the same spirit as the socialists of the lectern had done. The new methods of bacteriology and pathophysiology that were introduced to a rapidly growing number of German physicians by teachers like du Bois-Reymond and Virchow encouraged a synthetic, functionalist approach to the treatment of disease, which may help to explain the marked shift from "democratic individualism to corporate professional authority" Paul Weindling has noted among Virchow's students beginning as early as the 1880s.[72] By the 1890s, in any case, one young physician trained at the University of Berlin was ready to declare himself the "first medical socialist of the lectern."[73] Yet the social message emanating from the life sciences, like that of the national economists, reached far beyond an elite corps of social policy experts trained at the universities. Above all, the rising prestige of biology was linked to the reception of Darwin's theories, and the highly publicized debates over evolution and heredity attracted a broad popular audience, shaping the younger generation's responses to the social question in equally potent ways.

Between Weismann and Lamarck

> As Darwin has discovered the law of development in organic nature, so Marx discovered the law of development in human history.
>
> FRIEDRICH ENGELS

Published in 1859, the same year as Marx's *Critique of Political Economy,* Darwin's treatise *On the Origin of Species* hit the unsettled political atmosphere of Germany like a storm in the 1860s, threatening to drown out

---

71. Beyerchen, "Stimulation," pp. 152–54.
72. Weindling, *Health,* pp. 17–25, 218; Ruff, *du Bois-Reymond,* pp. 42–53.
73. See the section below, "The University of Berlin: Center of Centers," in Chapter 5.

the message of scientific socialism with its radical appeal. Even at Marx's graveside, Engels felt compelled to draw his friend from behind the shadow of the English biologist who "discovered the law of development in organic nature." For decades, the concept of "evolution" shaped public discussions of virtually every topic, from art history to sociology and the social question. Dominating the popular imagination in this response were two powerful images, neither of which was tied to Darwin's theory in any strict sense. First, the idea of mutation fascinated young Germans, who grasped it as an expression for the flux and dynamism surrounding them in Bismarck's Empire. Second, the "struggle for existence" seemed to evoke both the dangers and excitement of life at a turning point in the times, conjuring a world filled with worthy opponents locked in battle for vitality, growth, power—an image vividly captured in Nietzsche's "splendid blond beast prowling about avidly in search of spoil and victory."[74] Shattering the deterministic constraints of a "mechanistic" universe, visions of evolution driven by instinct and striving also revived notions of a voluntaristic "life force" the scientific materialists had rejected in the 1830s. "The essence of life," Nietzsche wrote, was "its will to power."[75]

Paradoxically, the theory most closely associated with biology in the popular imagination thus helped to undermine the materialist and positivist foundations on which the science had built its prestige a few decades earlier. While Bergson hailed the spiritual force of *élan vital* and Stravinsky celebrated "the mystery and great surge of the creative power in spring," the most famous proponent of "Darwinian" evolution in Germany, Ernst Haeckel, portrayed man as a microcosm and promoted the quasi-religious belief that all matter was endowed with the spiritual forces of life.[76] The

---

74. Friedrich Nietzsche, *The Genealogy of Morals* (New York: Vintage, 1967), pp. 40–41.

75. Ibid., p. 79.

76. Henri Bergson, *Creative Evolution,* trans. Arthur Mitchell (Boston: University Press of America, 1983), pp. 268–71; Modris Eksteins, *Rites of Spring: The Great War and the Birth of the Modern Age* (New York: Anchor Books, 1989), p. 9; Niles Holt, "Ernst Haeckel's Monist Religion," *Journal of the History of Ideas* 32 (1971): 265–80; Peter Bowler, *The Non-Darwinian Revolution: Reinterpreting a Historical Myth* (Baltimore: Johns Hopkins University Press, 1988), pp. 83–90, 193; Daniel Gasman, *The Scientific Origins of National So-*

primitivist and neo-vitalist currents sustaining this vogue for the organic also evoked more disturbing sentiments in the elitism of Stefan George's "pagan-gnostic circle" or, worse yet, the "Aryan mysticism" of Ludwig Schemann, Houston Stewart Chamberlain, and the other racial anti-Semites who founded the Gobineau Society in 1894.[77] Given such irrational and even violent responses to Darwin, how justified are we in viewing biology as the "other science" available to young Germans wishing to confront the crisis of modernization with realistic and constructive solutions?

While certainly significant, the vitalistic work *Reflections on Violence* that swept across Europe in Darwin's wake should not obscure less sensational interpretations that competed for public attention in debates over the social meaning of evolution throughout this period. The revolt against positivism was not always a revolt against science and modernity any more than the revolt against Manchesterism was always a revolt against the principles of individual liberty and free enterprise. In fact, even Bergson's immensely popular treatise *Creative Evolution* marshaled evidence from empirical studies to defend his beliefs in a rather dry exposition on the controversy over the inheritance of acquired characteristics.[78] Within the scientific community itself, inability to isolate the precise mechanism responsible for the transmutation of species inspired something of a consensus that "natural selection is not enough," and many biologists subscribed to the view of life as a creative force striving to surmount obstacles and actively adapting to its environment ascribed to the French zoologist Jean-Baptiste Lamarck.[79] Unprepared to face the nightmare of a destiny governed solely by the laws of physics, but equally unwilling to abandon an enlightened faith in science, "loyal critics" of Wilhelmine modernity

cialism: Social Darwinism in Ernst Haeckel and the Monist League (New York: Elsevier, 1971), pp. 64–69.

77. Steven Aschheim, *The Nietzsche Legacy in Germany 1890–1990* (Berkeley: University of California Press, 1992), pp. 71–84; Mosse, *Crisis,* pp. 88–107, 209–11; Herman Glaser, *The Cultural Roots of National Socialism* (Austin: University of Texas, 1978), pp. 139–59.

78. Bergson, *Evolution,* pp. 76–84.

79. Peter Bowler, *The Eclipse of Darwinism: Anti-Darwinian Evolution Theories in the Decades around 1900* (Baltimore: Johns Hopkins University Press, 1983).

could thus appeal to the authority of organic science in asserting a lasting significance for the personal struggles in life, just as young reformers were able to promote the humane improvement of working-class environments as a "scientific" means to augment the health of the nation as a whole.

Beginning in the early 1880s, however, these "neo-Lamarckian" views faced a stern challenge from German embryologist August Weismann, and for the next three decades scientific debates over "hard heredity" absorbed the attention of those who had staked so much on the biological underpinnings of their "modern" social views. At the center of these debates was Weismann's theory of the "germ plasm," a cellular substance he insisted was always completely isolated from the environment and fully capable of transmitting all characteristics necessary for survival. However much it might creatively adapt in the struggle for survival, the adult organism could never pass these benefits on to future generations through the impenetrable wall around the germ plasm.[80] Weismann's followers gradually succeeded in convincing most of their colleagues that embryology could be reduced to "developmental mechanics," or the unlocking of chemical forces contained in the fertilized egg at conception,[81] but in the 1890s, a former student, Hans Driesch, caused a major stir by announcing that germ plasm was merely a physical means employed by an immaterial life force he described in Aristotelian terms as "entelechy." Restoring creative potential to the organic world, Driesch's neo-vitalism also offered reformers a compelling biological model for social integration in his conception of life as a "harmonious equipotential system," or self-regulating dynamic equilibrium, in which the organism's health depended on the well-being of its individual cells, which in turn it ensured through a network of feedback loops and control mechanisms designed to foster each cell's uninhibited development to its fullest potential.[82] Despite such allures, how-

---

80. Paul Weindling, *Darwinism and Social Darwinism in Imperial Germany: The Contribution of the Cell Biologist Oscar Hertwig (1849–1922)* (New York: Fischer, 1991), pp. 138–52; Bowler, *Revolution,* p. 113.

81. Frederick Churchill, "From Machine-Theory to Entelechy: Two Studies in Developmental Teleology," *Journal of the History of Biology* 2 (1969): 165–85.

82. Hans Driesch, *Lebenserinnerungen: Aufzeichnungen eines Forschers und Denkers in entscheidender Zeit* (Basel: Reinhardt, 1951), pp. 74–77; Driesch, *The*

ever, Driesch's theory provoked skepticism in a generation trained to think in empirical, materialist terms, and many agreed with du Bois-Reymond, who denounced neo-vitalism as a relapse into the "mental illness of Romantic nature philosophy."[83]

Seeking new ground between the extremes of Weismann and Driesch, theories of "energetic" or "emergent vitalism" proliferated in response to the debates over heredity and evolution at the turn of the century. Explaining organic properties in terms of a "mechanistic structure anorganisms lack,"[84] adherents of these theories stressed the material basis of life but also argued that the configuration of elements in organic compounds gave rise to unique interactions among physical forces that combined to produce a fundamentally new dynamic, which could not be reduced to the simple laws of inorganic nature. Thoroughly infused with throbbing rhythms and active responses to its environment, this "emergent" life force had all the appeal of Driesch's "entelechy" but was firmly grounded in the materialist foundations that ensured Weismann's supporters the respect of the scientific community. Translating the theory into social terms for the progressive readers of Naumann's journal *Assistance* in 1913, one reformer wrote that the "peculiar combination of biological energies" in the nation created a heightened "social energy," which depended on the "physical and psychic energies of the individual people belonging to the state," but was more than a sum of its parts. "If the state is to be an organism in which the collective will of everyone is uniformly expressed, then within it the demand must be raised that all of its components can join together for the same resultant," Kurt Gebauer wrote; "in other words, all citizens of the state must be able to work together in the same way on legislation, just as we imagine it as Liberals under the influence of universal and equal elections."[85]

Science and Philosophy of the Organism (London: Black, 1908), vol. 1., pp. 55–66, 129.

83. Emil du Bois-Reymond, "Über Neo-Vitalismus," in du Bois-Reymond, *Vorträge über Philosophie und Gesellschaft* (Hamburg: Felix Meiner, 1974), p. 212; O. Bütschli, *Mechanismus und Vitalismus* (Leipzig: Engelmann, 1901), p. 57.

84. Bütschli, *Mechanismus,* p. 75.

85. Kurt Gebauer, "Ist der Staat ein Organismus?," *Hilfe* 19, no. 4 (January 23, 1913): 54–56.

Ultimately, of course, all notions of creative evolution and life force lost out in battles that reduced them to the status of mere "pseudo-science," but the final blow did not come until 1915, with Thomas Hunt Morgan's chromosome theory, and until then progressive reformers went on contesting the claims of radicals and mystics to the discourse of vitalistic biology, which also sustained such moderate visions of alternative German modernities, at once scientific and humane. Even in conceding victory to Weismannism, the revisionist Social Democrat Eduard David continued to insist that environmental reforms effectively eliminated "degenerative hereditary transmissions," allowing even the most "constitutionally weakened" to join in the upward social evolution of the nation. "As severely contested as the inheritability of acquired characteristics is," David wrote in an essay on "Darwinism and Social Development" in 1909:

> It is nevertheless undeniably certain that improvement or deterioration in the parental organism, as soon as it exercises a constitutive influence on the germ plasm, is passed on to the offspring. Healthy persons with normal chemistry, that is, with well-nourished cellular material, will have healthier children with a better organic predisposition than parents whose organism is weakened and poisoned by adverse living conditions. The hygienic configuration of labor will thus eliminate infinitely more degenerative hereditary transmissions than could be effected by the premature extinction of constitutionally weakened male and female workers.[86]

Socialist Darwinism

Stumbling through this awkward jargon, David struggled to preserve a crucial link between the *scientific* materialism of Marx and Darwin that many Germans saw as the essence of modern social movements, even in the contemporary "life reform" fads devoted to health, beauty, and youth later associated with cultural despair. "A rational bodily training for youth and development of bodily culture for adults" corresponded to the "principles of social hygiene" just as much as the "hygienic configuration of labor," and the prominent Social Democrat therefore called for the "systematic utilization of the hygienic factors water, air, and sunshine, in ad-

---

86. Eduard David, "Darwinismus und soziale Entwicklung," in Max Apel, ed., *Darwin im Ringen um Weltanschauung und Lebenswert* (Berlin: Buchverlag der *Hilfe*, 1909), p. 57.

dition to more rational nutrition."[87] While the gradual turn toward Weismannism infused the debates over heredity with darker and noticeably more conservative strains after the turn of the century, the cynical creed known today as "Social Darwinism" made slow inroads in a country where the appeal of evolutionary discourse had long been found almost exclusively on the left.[88] "German popular Darwinism was a continuation of the old eighteenth-century Enlightenment tradition," Alfred Kelly has argued, and its most prominent spokesmen "sought to crush superstition, to inform, to liberate, and, indirectly, to democratize."[89]

Like socialism of the lectern, socialist Darwinism emerged from the polemics and press wars of the 1870s as a subversive *bête noire* for Liberals and Conservatives alike. Haeckel provoked much of the fear and anger surrounding the new theory of evolution when he championed it as "incontrovertible" scientific evidence against the "ephemeral dogma" of Christianity at the height of the *Kulturkampf,* demanding that Darwinism become the centerpiece of the secular curriculum being introduced in German schools in 1877. Such radical immanence went too far even for Virchow, who denounced Haeckel's godless materialism before the Association of German Scientists and Physicians. "I hope that the theory of evolution will not bring us all the horrors which similar theories have actually wrought in a neighboring country," he warned. "After all, if pursued logically, this theory has an unusually ominous side; and I hope it hasn't escaped you that socialism is in close sympathy with it."[90] Haeckel quickly responded with sharp denials of any "natural" connection between Darwinism and Social Democracy, but the clash only deepened the taint of radicalism clinging to the idea of evolution.[91] Denounced and equated with Marxism from right to left, Darwin's theory continued to provoke public outrage, even-

---

87. Ibid., pp. 56–57.
88. See Hans-Günther Zmarzlik, "Social Darwinism in Germany, Seen as a Historical Problem," in Hajo Holborn, ed., *Republic to Reich: The Making of the Nazi Revolution* (New York: Pantheon, 1972), pp. 435–74.
89. Alfred Kelly, *The Descent of Darwin: The Popularization of Darwin in Germany, 1860–1914* (Chapel Hill: University of North Carolina Press, 1981), p. 7.
90. Ibid., p. 59.
91. Ernst Haeckel, "Deszendenztheorie und Sozialdemokratie," in Günther Alther, ed., *Der Darwinismus: Die Geschichte einer Theorie* (Darmstadt: Wissenschaftliche Buchgesellschaft, 1981).

tually reaching the floor of the Prussian parliament; in 1883 the teaching of evolution was officially banned from the largest state in the new Empire, not to be resumed until after the revolution in 1918.[92]

Meanwhile, orthodox Marxists, revisionists, and renegade socialists continued to explore the radical immanence and potentially subversive dynamism of biological materialism that had been so deeply inscribed in the social message of Darwinism in the conflicts of the Liberal Era. While Bebel read the works of Darwin, Haeckel, and Büchner in prison during the 1870s, two decades later the same authors had become favorites of the working class; and by 1898, four out of the ten most requested titles from German workers' libraries were listed as "Darwiniana."[93] In what turned out to be the opening salvo in the campaign for revisionist socialism, Georg von Vollmar's famous El Dorado speeches of 1891 turned to evolutionary discourse, advocating "slow, organic development,"[94] an image that reappeared in Bernstein's famous manifesto, *Evolutionary Socialism*. And on the non-Marxist left, the aging scientific materialist Ludwig Büchner transformed the cynical elitism of Herbert Spencer's followers into one of the most interesting and illuminating expressions of socialist Darwinism. After abandoning his overtures to Marx and Engels in the 1860s, Büchner had struck out on his own, calling for an end to "hereditary capitalism," which he complained was stifling the immense social energy contained in the German proletariat and German women. Insisting that the Marxists' future state would merely reverse the roles in this oppressive system of class rule, the organic socialist instead championed the natural evolution of a "social, productive, or labor aristocracy" through free competition among the unrestrained energies and talents of all. "[T]rue socialism ... does not wish the domination of a single social class," he proclaimed, "but instead the liberation of the entire society ... by a more equitable distribution of property and the means with which every individual must fight in the struggle for existence."[95] Drawing on precisely the same features of natural

---

92. Kelly, *Descent*, pp. 60–71.

93. Ibid., pp. 127–28.

94. Beverly Heckart, *From Bassermann to Bebel: The Grand Bloc's Quest for Reform in the Kaiserreich, 1900–1914* (New Haven: Yale University Press, 1974), p. 19.

95. Ludwig Büchner, *Darwinismus und Sozialismus oder Der Kampf um das Dasein und die moderne Gesellschaft* (Stuttgart: Alfred Kröner, 1906), p. 43; Büch-

selection as Social Darwinism, Büchner thus demanded state intervention to level the playing field so that the upward striving could not only survive but also prosper in the economic life of a strong and healthy nation.

Naumann, Weber, and the Legacy of 1890

In February 1890, Wilhelm II's reform decrees proclaimed a message of social integration young Germans had been hearing for decades. What made this message so unforgettable was not its novelty, but the hope that it had finally reached a Kaiser capable of leading the nation from the brink of civil war to the long-envisioned goal of "social peace." While that hope quickly faded, its memory survived the social-political reaction of the Stumm era to become the legacy of a generation determined to prove its mettle in another round of battles for Germany's future. "I would like to refer to Count von Stumm as a chap—in a good, not a dismissive sense," the reformer Leopold von Wiese wrote; "that is, as someone whom we must fight unconditionally as long as one of us still has the life necessary to struggle for life and death, a chap on whose grave one yet lays a laurel wreath with the inscription: Thus I wish it for all my enemies."[96] Rather than looking to politics, however, many chose to follow the example of their teachers, the national economists and organic materialists, quietly laying the foundations for what they hoped would be a more humane and productive alternative by formulating technocratic administrative proposals behind the scenes, while simultaneously bringing "scientific" enlightenment to the masses in order to calm fears on both sides of the social divide as they extended the educational impulse of the older generation beyond the walls of the university to reach the workers themselves.

Sharing the hopes, fears, and lessons contained in this legacy, Friedrich Naumann and Max Weber are today by far the most familiar representatives of the younger generation's search for answers to the social question. Like so many others, both combined the social messages of economics and biology, Marx and Darwin, to depict the conflicts of the 1890s as a struggle between "rising" and "falling" classes for mastery of an evolving economic

---

ner, "Die Frauenfrage," in Büchner, *Am Sterbelager des Jahrhunderts* (Giessen: Emil Roth, 1898), pp. 305–40.

96. Wiese, *Posadowsky*, p. 41.

order. While the productive strength of industry would inevitably sustain Germany's future prosperity, Weber and Naumann viewed agrarians and artisans as atavistic holdovers threatening to strangle the vital forces necessary for the nation's survival in the modern world. Given this sense of urgency, the progressive orientation of the two young reformers easily hardened into partisanship, and both became entangled in the political clashes between left and right many of their peers were seeking desperately to avoid in the controversy over German industrialization. The decision to engage in liberal politics alienated many socially conscious men and women of their generation, as we will see; yet it is precisely this distance from the antipolitical milieu of Wilhelmine social reform that may account for the prominence of Naumann and Weber in subsequent historical accounts, where they often appear as heroic, but isolated figures of tragic importance in an otherwise bleak landscape. Complaining that "there was never a significant reform movement designed to shift German liberalism toward the left," for instance, Kloppenberg notes: "Yet there is one thinker who merits consideration as a progressive manqué, Max Weber. Weber wanted to unbuckle liberalism from laissez-faire, broaden its focus from the middle class, and secure greater social justice than was possible within the boundaries of Bismarck's *Sammlungspolitik*. Given those interests, Weber never found a political home."[97] And discussing Naumann's short-lived National Social Association (*Nationalsozialer Verein*, or NSV), Werner Conze has drawn similarly dismal conclusions about the potentialities of Wilhelmine political culture, dismissing the Association's efforts as the "politics of illusion."[98]

But Naumann and Weber were hardly alone. On the contrary, the goals of social justice and integration had been formulated decades earlier by the socialists of the lectern and their medical colleagues to become stock phrases for the generation of 1890. If historians have searched in vain for a *political* response, it is because this message resonated most loudly among

---

97. James T. Kloppenberg, *Uncertain Victory: Social Democracy and Progressivism in European and American Thought, 1870–1920* (New York: Oxford University Press, 1986), p. 321.

98. Werner Conze, "Friedrich Naumann: Grundlagen und Ansatz seiner Politik in der nationalsozialen Zeit," in Walther Hubatsch, ed., *Schicksalswege deutscher Vergangenheit: Beiträge zur geschichtlichen Deutung der letzten hundertfünfzig Jahre* (Düsseldorf: Droste-Verlag, 1950), p. 356.

social and cultural reformers who heard it as a call to a different kind of action, in a sphere remote from parties and parliaments. The aggressive strains of nationalistic power-politics and the tendency to fall into fits of desperate resignation that later seemed to link Weber and Naumann most firmly to the context of late Imperial political culture in fact obstructed their appeal to many in these circles, with whom they otherwise shared so much in common.[99] The critiques of the iron cage and the spirit of capitalism that have since become such a ubiquitous presence in European intellectual and cultural history were likewise quite at home in this environment, where they initially emerged from discussions of the social question that reveal a surprisingly sophisticated appreciation for the contradictions of modernity and often had little to do with cultural despair. Weber and Naumann were a part of this world, but they also stood apart from it in important ways, and it is this contrast that makes them instructive examples in exploring the legacy of 1890.

From Christian to National Social

However isolated they might appear from today's perspective, in the 1890s Naumann and Weber belonged to the national economic "boys" (*Jungen*), a group of young scholars and reformers including Sombart, Ferdinand Tönnies, Gerhart von Schulze-Gävernitz, Heinrich Herkner, and Alfred Weber, who had studied under the socialists of the lectern and followed in their footsteps by demanding a fresh look at Marx's writings and seeking contacts with Social Democracy.[100] Unlike most of the boys, however, Naumann and Weber were latecomers to the study of economics, having first

---

99. Ibid.; Peter Theiner, *Sozialer Liberalismus und deutsche Weltpolitik: Friedrich Naumann im Wilhelminischen Deutschland* (Baden-Baden: Nomos, 1983); Wolfgang Mommsen, *Max Weber and German Politics, 1890–1920*, trans. Michael S. Steinberg (Chicago: University of Chicago Press, 1984).

100. Dieter Krüger, "Max Weber and the 'Younger' Generation in the Verein für Sozialpolitik," in Wolfgang Mommsen, ed., *Max Weber and His Contemporaries* (London: Allen & Unwin, 1987) pp. 71–87; Lindenlaub, *Richtungskämpfe*, pp. 273–91; Volker Kruse, "Von der historischen Nationalökonomie zur historischen Soziologie," *Zeitschrift für Soziologie* 19, no. 3 (June 1990): 149–65.

discovered an interest in the social question through their involvement in the Christian Social movement—a pattern of development that was typical of many in this generation. It was in fact Adolf Stöcker who initially inspired Naumann's career as a social worker; after hearing the court preacher speak in Leipzig, the young student organized a campaign in support of Stöcker's Anti-Semitic Petition in 1881 before leaving school to work at a halfway house for juvenile delinquents in the early 1880s. Returning to complete his degree in theology, Naumann then took a job as pastor for a proletarian congregation in Saxony, where he wrote a controversial "Worker's Catechism" in 1888, and two years later he joined the leadership of the Inner Mission, a Protestant organization for social and charity work in Frankfurt am Main.[101] Naumann's new responsibilities prevented him from attending the first Protestant Social Congress, convened by Stöcker and Wagner in the crucial year 1890, but Weber was in attendance, and it was at the Congress that the two reformers met the following year.[102]

Weber had come to the Christian Social movement through his mother's Pietist sympathies,[103] and after studying for a career in law, he had decided instead to devote his interest entirely to the social question. Joining the Association for Social Policy in 1888, Weber was commissioned to study problems of internal colonization in Germany's eastern rural provinces, an assignment that established his reputation as an expert on the "agrarian question" among younger Christian Socials and won him a professorship in national economics at the University of Freiburg in 1893.[104] In the meantime, Naumann had also developed an interest in Weber's new discipline as a result of his growing sympathy for the workers' movement. Inspired by Schulze-Gävernitz's influential treatise *On Social Peace*, Naumann fol-

101. Theodor Heuss, *Friedrich Naumann: Der Mann, das Werk, die Zeit*, 2nd rev. ed. (Stuttgart: Wunderlich, 1959), pp. 42–65.
102. Wilhelm Spael, *Friedrich Naumanns Verhältnis zu Max Weber* (Sankt Augustin: Liberal-Verlag, 1985), pp. 13–42.
103. Arthur Mitzman, *The Iron Cage: An Historical Interpretation of Max Weber* (New York: Knopf, 1970), pp. 34–35, 37–38; Spael, *Verhältnis*, p. 16.
104. Lawrence A. Scaff, *Fleeing the Iron Cage: Culture, Politics, and Modernity in the Thought of Max Weber* (Berkeley: University of California Press, 1989), pp. 34–59; Mommsen, *Politics*, pp. 22–27; Spael, *Verhältnis*, pp. 20–23.

lowed the example of the national economic boys in seeking closer ties to organized labor, both in the Christian Social movement, where he supported the Protestant Workers' Associations that had begun spreading throughout Germany during the 1880s, and among Social Democrats, whose party congress he attended in open defiance of Stöcker and the older generation in 1894.[105]

Inside the Protestant Social Congress, Weber and Naumann joined a circle of young Germans who were growing impatient with Stöcker's conservatism. "He could not be moved to take a stand against [Bismarck's] Socialist Law, even though it was the most screaming injustice for workers," Hellmut von Gerlach later remembered. "For overcoat seamstresses he found the strongest words. After all, he could whip up his listeners' instincts against the 'Jewish clothiers' at the same time. But the rural proletariat, which stood there with far fewer rights and much more pitifully— oh don't touch that, no, not that! The *Junker* would have held it against him."[106] At the annual Congress in 1894, the younger Christian Socials aggressively staked out their opposition to Stöcker's reactionary mentors, declaring their solidarity with the "rural proletariat" amid mounting political tensions that brought the New Course to an end in October. In a joint presentation with Paul Göhre, a young minister who had recently spent three months as a factory worker in order to expose the wretched conditions of German labor, Weber called for the dismemberment of the aristocracy's unprofitable agricultural estates and the distribution of their lands among rural workers.[107] An angry clash with Conservatives followed but remained unresolved at the Congress, and in the fall Naumann founded *Assistance* as an independent power base from which the younger Christian Socials continued their assault on Stöcker in the months after Caprivi's fall. It was here that the workers' pastor affirmed the lasting impact of the February Decrees in January 1895, in remarks launching a campaign against the Revolution Bill that galvanized support from far beyond his immediate circle. When Naumann won the Christian Socials' endorsement

105. Heuss, *Naumann*, pp. 69–79; Paul Göhre, *Die evangelisch-soziale Bewegung: Ihre Geschichte und ihre Ziele* (Leipzig: Grunow, 1896), pp. 105–19.
106. Gerlach, *Rechts*, p. 105.
107. Spael, *Verhältnis*, pp. 22–27; Mommsen, *Politics*, pp. 31–32; Göhre, *Bewegung*, pp. 123–26.

of a petition against the bill at the Congress later that year, Stöcker resigned, but by then it was too late.[108]

Convinced that the campaign to revive the New Course had achieved
sufficient momentum, Naumann, Weber, Schulze-Gävernitz, and others
in the Congress began laying groundwork for a political party to advance
the social views of the younger generation, and on October 4, 1896 the
committee announced a founding congress to be held in Erfurt that November.[109] Although the invitation was addressed merely to all "non-
Conservative Christian Socials," it summoned delegates from a broad
range of causes: supporters of the 1895 petition, national economic boys,
women's activists, land reformers (including a young Adolf Damaschke),
and others promoting the goal of social peace, who rejected the proposed
confessional basis of the new party as too narrow and divisive. This view
was shared by the younger Christian Socials, who had themselves become
skeptical about the religious mainsprings of the movement. Defending his
agrarian reform proposals at the 1894 Protestant Congress, Weber had
already declared that sentimental moral and religious attachments to outdated modes of production had no place in a realistic approach to the
social question. "We wish to give external relationships this form not because people will then feel so good," he insisted, "but because the best in
them, the attributes—physical and spiritual—that we wish to preserve in
the nation will be protected under duress in the unavoidable struggle for
existence."[110] Profoundly impressed by this brash Darwinian challenge to
the older Christian Socials and by the aggressively nationalistic themes of
Weber's famous inaugural address at Freiburg, Naumann had also moved
away from religious appeals to charity, and at Erfurt he stressed the hard-
boiled material interests at stake in continuing to integrate the working
classes into an efficient, powerful, reformed national community. "In 1870
we did not reach the end of German history, but the beginning of further
history," Naumann proclaimed in his opening speech. "Now that states are

---

108. Göhre, *Bewegung,* pp. 163–200; Heuss, *Naumann,* pp. 96–97; Friedrich Nau-
     mann, "Der 6. evangelisch-soziale Kongress," *Hilfe* 1, no. 24 (June 16, 1895):
     1–2.
109. Dieter Düding, *Der Nationalsoziale Verein 1896–1903: Der gescheiterte Ver-
     such einer parteipolitischen Synthese von Nationalismus, Sozialismus und Lib-
     eralismus* (Munich: Oldenbourg, 1972), pp. 42–43.
110. Spael, *Verhältnis,* p. 25.

prospering and expanding, it is a matter of dividing up space on the globe." Abandoning Christian Socialism for the more compelling, modern claims of science and nationalism, the delegates agreed to make a new start and founded the National Social Association on November 26.[111]

The Politics of Misery?

While most greeted the opening to reform-minded Catholics, Jews, and Social Democrats afforded by the Association's secular agenda, Naumann's enthusiasm for military adventures and colonial exploits subsequently sparked controversies over the meaning of national strength that weakened the movement's solidarity, and Weber's merciless calculation of the National Socials' political interests vis-à-vis the working classes met with an indignant response even at the founding congress. Unmasking sympathy for "the irksome and the burdened, those with shoes that are too tight," as the true motive behind Naumann's "supposed realism," Weber warned the delegates that such "miserabilistic principles" would transform the new party into a band of "political Raggedy Annes." This was no time to be sentimental:

> All rising strata of the nation, even rising strata of the working class, become natural opponents of the national social movement simply by rising. Only the dregs of the population remain among them. A party that counts only the weakest among its members will never attain political power. . . . You have one choice today, and one only: which of the conflicting interests do you want to support: the bourgeois or the agrarian/feudal. Politics that does not take that into account is a utopia.[112]

However keen Weber's assessment of Wilhelmine political realities may have been, a strategy acknowledging open confrontation between "conflicting interests" as the legitimate aim of public life seemed to offer little hope for social reconciliation in the already tense atmosphere of the 1890s. The unmistakably Spencerian undertones of the economist's remarks provoked a sharp rebuttal from Hellmut von Gerlach, who angrily refused to have any part in a politics of "Nietzschean master morality," while Nau-

---

111. Ibid., p. 53; Düding, *Verein*, pp. 36–39; Mommsen, *Politics*, pp. 31–32, 54–55, 69–70; Conze, "Naumann," pp. 357–58; Marianne Weber, *Max Weber: Ein Lebensbild* (Tübingen, 1926), pp. 219–52.
112. Spael, *Verhältnis*, pp. 55–56.

mann and Göhre passionately defended their attempts to achieve closer ties with the workers' movement.[113] Among the delegates, only the elderly Rudolf Sohm shared Weber's dread of such entanglements, and even he insisted on the paternalistic duty of intellectuals to care for the "dregs of the population." Unwilling to sacrifice the social "utopia" of 1890 for a "realistic" political party, the Erfurt congress decided to found a more flexible Association instead. After this repudiation, Weber withdrew to the margins of the movement, watching Naumann's illusory politics unravel over the next seven years, and when the National Socials voted to dissolve the organization after the disastrous elections of 1903, the "progressive manqué" could bitterly note the accuracy of his predictions.[114]

Yet it was possible to argue—as Damaschke did—that election results were a poor means to gauge the success of a movement that had never defined its task in political terms.[115] Immediately after the founding congress, the NSV began mobilizing support for striking dock workers in Hamburg, raising 40,000 Marks through publicity, and the following summer Berlin textile workers received a similar show of solidarity. In 1899 the Association responded to the Prison Bill with a campaign much like the one against the Revolution Bill four years earlier. Denouncing repression of "the union movement, the healthiest, best part of the workers' movement," the National Socials adopted Brentano's proposals for recognizing organized labor at the NSV congress that year and actively encouraged revisionists in the debates sparked by Bernstein's appeal for Social Democratic cooperation with bourgeois reformers in his work *Evolutionary Socialism*.[116] Such efforts preserved the memory of the February Decrees during the social-political reaction and forged associative ties that later solidified in important institutions, laying the groundwork for some of the most impressive success stories of Wilhelmine anti-politics, as we will see.

At the same time, however, Naumann's increasing attention to controversial issues of foreign policy—naval expansion, the Boer War, the Kaiser's

---

113. Ibid., p. 57; Düding, *Verein*, pp. 58–60.

114. Weber, *Max Weber*, pp. 252–54.

115. Damaschke, "Die nationalsoziale Partei und die Bodenreform," *Deutsche Volksstimme* 14, no. 18 (September 20, 1903): 530–35; Damaschke, *Zeitenwende*, p. 441.

116. Düding, *Verein*, pp. 105–17; Heuss, *Naumann*, pp. 157–58; Sheehan, *Brentano*, pp. 143–44.

"Hun Speech"—threatened to split the movement along political lines, and the NSV leader began to reconsider Weber's advice about electoral strategy. Convinced that the socialist label he had once proudly adopted had become a stumbling block, Naumann repackaged his message for a bourgeois audience to call for a "renewal of liberalism" even before the Association was dissolved in 1903.[117] Such appeals inevitably opened old wounds, conjuring up polemical phantoms from the battlegrounds of the 1870s, and many of Naumann's colleagues decried his turn from socialism to liberalism as betrayal,[118] but his goal still remained the integration of the working classes into the national community, now framed in terms of "democratizing" the social and economic order. In the *New German Economic Policy* of 1906, the erstwhile National Social drew on the ideas of Brentano, Schulze-Gävernitz, Weber, and Sombart to promote an alliance between bourgeoisie and proletariat as an objective means to protect the interests of both in a rousing manifesto of the "new liberalism."[119]

While a "technological" approach revealed only mechanistic forces at work in history, and "idealistic" methods focused solely on spiritual or psychological factors, Naumann opted for an "anthropological" analysis of German social, economic, and political development in his treatise, which revealed "the main process of the modern age" to be "the intensification of human life force, the first sign of which is a rising population." Blending the views of Marx and Darwin much as Weber had done in Erfurt ten years earlier, Naumann now delivered what might be considered his definitive rebuttal to the economist's devastating critique of "national socialism" as a sentimental utopia. "In every nation there are at the same time sinking and rising elements, but it makes a big difference which of them is in charge," he argued. "A rising nation is one in which the rising social strata attain leadership of economic life. In the struggle with sinking strata, economic policy comes into being. Rising strata, however, are only possible where increasing [population] statistics are present."[120] Since the industrial working class was undeniably the fastest-growing segment of the

117. Heuss, *Naumann*, pp. 172–84; Paul Göhre, *Vom Sozialismus zum Liberalismus: Wandlungen der Nationalsozialen*, 2nd ed. (Berlin: Verlag der sozialistischen Monatsheft, 1902), pp. 35–37.

118. Göhre, *Sozialismus.*

119. Heuss, *Naumann*, p. 190.

120. Naumann, *Wirtschaftspolitik*, pp. 15, 19.

population, it represented a vast reservoir of the "life force" Germany needed to adapt and survive in the modern world. Social and economic policies geared toward the proletariat were thus a matter of *Realpolitik,* not "miserabilistic principles," and Naumann went on to enumerate the concrete interests linking workers to the other rising element in Germany's economic struggle for existence, the bourgeoisie. "Liberals and socialists are related in their optimistic overall assessment of economic development," he wrote. They "do not let themselves be frightened off by foreign competition or new labor methods, by cartels or unions" and "want nothing other than to serve history as it marches ever onward." As a result, "all measures binding us to the commercial, technical, [and] economic present just because progress upsets customs and comforts are repulsive" to both classes. Finally, liberals and socialists had "inscribed the preservation of personal liberty onto their banners."

Here Naumann paused to consider recent developments in Germany's rapidly evolving economic life that were bringing these rising strata even closer together and demanding radical transformations in the obsolete political ideologies of both: "What is new is the fact that the individual liberal entrepreneur can no longer see himself as the ultimate norm in the national economy." Cartels and unions had now assumed this role, so that liberalism lacked "the predominant pre-requisite for its old economic order," the autonomous economic subject, while socialists were at the same time confronted with "the surprising discovery that the practical socialization of society, that is, centralized regulation of production, is not being accomplished by the proletariat, but instead by the property-owning class." The world in which the two parties had evolved no longer existed, except in the fossilized dogmas that were hindering the formation of a healthy alliance on both sides. "The German nation is growing, growing, growing. This growth will mean privation and bondage if it is not accompanied by technology and freedom," Naumann warned. "A growing nation with a backward economic policy is a nation running into the arms of fear and revolution. . . . Everyone who has the spirit of the future in his soul, who understands a new will, fresh hope, everyone who wants to rise up himself and smooth the paths of life for his children must stand untiring and energetic where the new German economic policy has been recognized, and where the attempt is being made to realize it, on the German left."[121]

---

121. Ibid., pp. 379–81, 385–86.

It was on the German left that Naumann had found a political home in 1903. Joining the Radical Coalition *(Freisinnige Vereinigung)*, he hoped to use the existing liberal parties as building blocks for a more solid platform from which to launch his campaign for an alliance with Social Democracy. First, however, he needed to quell rival factions that had splintered the movement ever further since National Liberals and Progressives first split over Bismarck's path to national unification in the 1860s. This task required patience and compromise, but by 1910 Naumann and others like him managed to fuse the three left-liberal parties into a new Progressive People's Party *(Fortschrittliche Volkspartei,* or FVP). Launching a campaign for democratic suffrage reform in Prussia, the Progressives formed tactical alliances with National Liberals to the right and Social Democrats to the left, and for a moment it seemed Naumann's oft-repeated calls for a united front "from Bassermann to Bebel" were about to be realized. For several years, state governments in Baden and Bavaria had been experimenting with liberal-socialist coalitions, and the "new liberalism" was becoming increasingly popular among National Liberals of the youngest generation throughout the country. "The Social Democrats moved closer to reformism; the Left Liberals espoused democracy and unity; the National Liberals revived their liberal ideals," Beverly Heckart has written of this intriguing juncture. "All three were searching for a new and more effective policy, and this search increased the possibilities for their cooperation."[122] Anticipation reached its height in 1912, when Progressives, Social Democrats, and many National Liberals joined to support Bebel's candidacy for Reichstag president.

As spectacular as Naumann's success appeared, the bid to transform liberal politics from within raised a "red flag" among industrialists and National Liberals, who remained as suspicious of socialism of the lectern as ever, and only a year later they revived the conservative "alliance of iron and rye" in the Cartel of Productive Estates, sealing the fate of the new liberalism in the Wilhelmine era.[123] Even before this decisive setback, the Progressives' daring political strategies proved helpless in facing Bethmann-Hollweg's bu-

---

122. Heckart, *Bassermann,* pp. 43, 154–208; Peter Theiner, "Friedrich Naumann und der soziale Liberalismus im Kaiserreich," in Karl Holl et al., *Sozialer Liberalismus* (Göttingen: Vandenhoeck & Ruprecht, 1986), pp. 195–217.

123. Heckart, *Bassermann,* pp. 274–76; Theiner, "Naumann," p. 196; Eley, *Reshaping,* pp. 317–30.

reaucratic government "above the parties," where a new "social-political reaction" set in behind the scenes in 1911. "A reasonable social policy is in my view one of the sources of strength for the German Empire," Klemens von Delbrück proclaimed, turning Naumann's arguments against him as he justified the government's intent to roll back the social legislation of recent decades in a state address on January 20, 1914. "By reasonable I mean one that gives not just the worker but also the employer that which is his, that gives him the economic and moral elbow room to fulfill the great missions our industry has fulfilled up until now and must fulfill to an ever greater degree in the future, if its proud position in the world is to be retained."[124]

Delbrück's mocking translation of Naumann's message into a final vindication of "Manchesterism" came as no surprise to many. However much the new liberalism resembled the old aims of the National Socials, it remained too closely associated with lost opportunities of earlier times—too "burdened by history," as Damaschke put it—to seem trustworthy in the eyes of most socially conscious Germans of his generation, and the decision to abandon the anti-political world of Wilhelmine reform circles led Naumann to embarrassing compromises of principle that soon appeared to confirm these suspicions. After the Liberals' sudden "mating" with Conservative agrarians in 1906, his support for the Bülow Bloc made a jarring contrast to the heroic campaign against Stumm ten years earlier. Particularly galling to many was the "professional politician's" acceptance of the notorious language paragraph, which excluded Polish nationals and other minorities from political life, as the price for reform of the Law of Association in 1908, and the step cost Naumann the friendship of many, including Brentano, who had initially encouraged his turn to liberalism in 1903.[125] And while the campaign for Prussian suffrage reform stemmed from the noblest motives, the Progressives' tactics of open confrontation on the political stage merely heightened alarm among the Liberals and the Chancellor, upon whom a true democratization of German society ultimately depended. It was in fact precisely this fear that could be heard in Delbrück's humiliating speech. From this perspective, the workers' pastor and former National Social seemed to have become just one more fickle,

---

124. Born, *Staat*, p. 246.
125. Heuss, *Naumann*, pp. 255–56; Sheehan, *Brentano*, pp. 168–70.

self-deluded politician who no longer knew what he stood for. In the guise of "party politician," Naumann thus stood as a powerful warning example for the generation of 1890, the personification of its most bitter disappointment.

Posadowsky's Lessons

For young men and women still hoping to lay foundations for an alternative modernity beyond the arena of politics, the career of Count Arthur von Posadowsky-Wehner offered a striking contrast to Naumann's depressing path in these years. Among those denouncing Delbrück's speech in 1914,[126] Posadowsky too had come a long way since the 1890s, when as Imperial Minister of the Interior he championed the first social-political reaction after the fall of Berlepsch. "Gentlemen, we will not allow ourselves to be moved by the agitations of Social Democracy or the scholarly opinions of its conscious or unconscious fellow travelers *(Mitläufer)* to regulate all branches of industry with police regiments," he had informed the Reichstag in 1897. Such measures would only lead to "a socialistic police state, in which workers are no better off than before, but in which the property-owning classes would grow to be conscious enemies of the state."[127] Instead, the new Minister's first task was to put together legislation backing the Kaiser's sensational promise that his soldiers would never have to face striking workers again, since "anyone, whoever he might be or whatever his name, anyone at all who tries to prevent a worker from performing his work or even incites a strike will be punished with a prison sentence."[128] Yet as he worked out the details of the Prison Bill, Posadowsky soon realized that even a much more cautiously worded attempt to reinstate Bismarck's Anti-Socialist Law would find no support in the Reichstag. Convinced he needed a different, less confrontational strategy for social peace, the Minister began conferring with the same progressive reformers who had inspired the February Decrees, and even before the Prison Bill

---

126. Born, *Staat,* p. 247.
127. Ibid., p. 144.
128. Ibid., pp. 146–64, quotation p. 147; Eleanor Turk, "Thwarting the Political Will: A Perspective on the Labor Regulation Bill and the Press of Wilhelmine Germany," in Dukes and Remak, *Germany,* pp. 115–38.

was defeated in November 1899—only the Conservatives and some National Liberals voted for it—he announced new measures for improving the national insurance system.[129]

The Prison Bill taught Posadowsky an important lesson about the limitations of Wilhelmine political culture, just as Delbrück and the Cartel of Productive Estates did for Naumann a decade later, but from the other side. Noisy clashes in parliament and the political press may have been exciting, but the conservative Minister gained no more from the results than the progressive politician. Still motivated by religious loyalty to the Hohenzollern dynasty and hatred of Social Democracy, Posadowsky now sought a more effective means to serve the Kaiser's interests, immersing himself in detailed economic reports on factory conditions and intricate proposals for change in mining regulations, to become a "master of social policy minutiae."[130] This change in tactics did not merely reflect despair over an inhospitable political climate, but it also revealed a growing conviction that the socialists of the lectern and their "scholarly opinions" had been right after all. In the six years following the insurance reforms of 1899, Posadowsky therefore launched a major social policy initiative, introducing industrial courts and funding for workers' housing (1901), a merchant marine code (1902), the extension of child labor laws to cottage industry (1903), commercial courts (1904), and a new Prussian Mining Law (1905), which represented "the furthest extent of accommodation to workers' demands made by state social policy before the First World War" and came in response to another strike in the Ruhr.[131] While it also included new protective tariffs (1902–1903), "Posadowsky's New Course" was hardly a victory for conservative agrarians in the controversy over industrialization, and the Minister firmly rejected any attempt to return to Bismarck's Empire as unrealistic and misguided.[132] "There are indeed factions that want a State Secretary against social policy," he recognized in 1907. "I am, however, as long as I remain in this Office, a State Secretary for social policy."[133]

---

129. Born, *Staat*, p. 178.
130. Wiese, *Posadowsky*, p. 87.
131. Born, *Staat*, pp. 183–200, quotation p. 188.
132. Barkin, *Controversy*, p. 5.
133. Born, *Staat*, p. 208.

With the formation of the Bülow Bloc, these opposing factions had suddenly entered the ruling coalition, and Posadowsky's time was running out. Since 1904 he had been working toward legal recognition of labor unions and workers' advisory councils—measures promised by the February Decrees, as the Catholic politicians pushing for them steadily reminded him—but with the Center Party banished to the opposition, Posadowsky now found himself without a strong base of support for his reforms inside the government. Facing attacks from Conservatives and National Liberals, the Minister defiantly told the Reichstag that he intended to see both measures through and announced further plans for a ten-hour day for women workers and a new Imperial Law of Association. To the surprise and dismay of progressive reformers, Posadowsky was ordered to step down two months later. As his successor, Theobald von Bethmann-Hollweg followed through on many of these initiatives before going on to become Chancellor, but the workers' councils and legal recognition of unions never came.[134] Naumann's colleagues in reform circles watched in disbelief as the Liberals sacrificed Posadowsky's New Course on the altar of political compromise.

The bizarre twist of fortunes that propelled the careers of these two men past each other to this confusing intersection speaks volumes about the potentialities of Wilhelmine political culture. Almost mirror images of one another, Naumann and Posadowsky could each inspire the admiration of socially conscious Germans in 1907. Naumann's belief in the upward-striving, his firm repudiation of the paternalistic conservatism behind Posadowsky's social reforms embodied the youthful confidence and optimism released by the spring thaw in 1890. Yet the professional politician's methods clearly left something to be desired. The master of social policy minutiae, Posadowsky, had come round to a more modern view of the social situation almost in spite of himself, and his determination to realize the promise of the February Decrees confirmed the younger generation's belief that empirical research paved the way for "objective," scientific solutions upon which even the most passionate political enemies could agree. Describing one of the last exchanges between Naumann and Posadowsky in the Reichstag, the reformer Leopold von Wiese offered a poignant indication of the lessons both men's careers seemed to hold for the generation

---

134. Ibid., pp. 209–32.

of 1890. While he was pleased that "the national social leader . . . was now finally among the people's representatives, where the German nation had missed him for so long," Wiese thought the minister's absence would be felt more keenly: "If Naumann's speech of April 11, 1907 was good, Posadowsky's was better. It was not anchored as much in the philosophy of history; but it had the advantage of demonstrating tangible work in the present and offering, instead of an inspiring but airy construction, a realistic working program that could be carried out directly."[135]

Between the Minister's bureaucratic office and the Progressive leader's seat in parliament, there was plenty of room for the two exemplary leaders to meet, on the vast terrain of anti-politics. Outside government, outside political parties, "hundreds of thousands of the best minds" came together to apply lessons of national economics and the life sciences to every imaginable concern of modern life in Wilhelmine Germany. This terrain is in some sense familiar to us, through Naumann and Weber, the crisis of liberalism, the unpolitical *Observations* of Thomas Mann, perhaps even brother Heinrich's *Man of Straw*. But the landscape connecting these well-known stations in German political and intellectual history is perhaps not quite as familiar as it might at first appear. Having traced the broad contours of the social question and its meaning for this generation, we now move on to explore this world up close through the perspectives offered by three less prominent locations in Wilhelmine political culture: Damaschke's path from the rental barracks to the National Socials and land reform; Bäumer's from the "women's segment" to the Progressive People's Party and the Garden City of Hellerau; and Sombart's from the spirit of capitalism to racial hygiene, sociology, and the "Twilight of the Gods." The careers of each of these reformers crossed the others at a surprising number of places, to which the prosopographical study in Chapter 5 will return in order to map the associative and institutional networks that sustained the Wilhelmine reform milieu. But they also moved across this common ground in different directions, facing alternatives and roads not taken that alone give concrete meaning to the choices made by the generation of 1890, and it is this dimension the following chapters seek first to restore.

---

135. Wiese, *Posadowsky*, p. 179.

Adolf Damaschke and the Language of Popular Nationalism

On the evening of November 24, 1915, enthusiastic admirers crowded into a large lecture hall in Berlin to honor a great "leader of our nation." Prominent politicians, intellectuals, religious and labor leaders praised the reformer, who had seen the promise of strength in the idea of "national community" long before war had "imposed" it as grim necessity. Celebrating his courage in standing up against "cunning interest groups," the parasitic speculators and usurers who were sapping Germany's strength, stealing the fruits of common labor in the name of Mammon and Manchester, congratulatory letters came from the Chancellor, the leaders of the war effort—Hindenburg, Ludendorff, Falkenhayn, Tirpitz—from ordinary soldiers in the trenches and all segments of society on the home front. In closing, a double quartet from Berlin's Cathedral Choir sang a hymn by the guest of honor, "The Fatherland to Its People!" Adolf Damaschke was fifty years old.[1]

Today, Damaschke is entirely forgotten. The celebrations many foresaw for his hundredth birthday never came. What emotions might his memory have evoked in those filling the hall that night, those who were still alive to think of him fifty years later? Bitterness, disappointment, cynicism, perhaps even a twinge of conscience? In 1965 Germany was torn between a capitalist "economic miracle" in the West and the iron grip of communism in the East; there was little room for festivals commemorating the author of "Neither Mammonism nor Communism." The confident predictions of fame given in 1915 have a strange ring today, a sad, disturbing quality

---

1. Heinrich Erman, *Das große Bekenntnis zur Deutschen Bodenreform* (Frankfurt/Oder: Trowitzsch & Sohn, 1928), pp. 119–52.

that inevitably stirs ghosts of the recent German past. Even if Damaschke
has been forgotten, after all, the language he used is all too familiar, and
his impassioned appeal to a "mystique of the land" finds unsettling echoes
in the mind of today's reader: "yes, the land has a mystical power! Today
this mystique is revealed to our people! Only for the land called Germany
can we demand sacrifices from our people, sacrifices unheard of in history
since Germans were destined to live upon this piece of earth. Not money,
not any goods or values that can be shoved back and forth—only the
'mystique of the land' speaks: I am the Fatherland, I am the Holy!"[2] Mystical powers and Mammonism, parasites, usurers, sacrifices to the Fatherland—Damaschke was a master at manipulating such tropes of chauvinistic nationalism, anti-Semitism, and cultural despair. One might therefore
easily include the land reformer and his followers among the conservative
revolutionaries who paved the road for Hitler, and a few spokesmen for
the radical right did turn up in 1915. Yet most of Damaschke's admirers
held political views ranging from the moderate right to the moderate left.
At his sixtieth birthday celebration in 1925, representatives of the German
Nationalist, Center, Democratic, Social Democratic, and German People's
Parties spoke on his behalf, but Communist and Nazi officials refused his
invitation to join this "parliamentary front of unity."[3] Couched in the language of popular nationalism, Damaschke's message failed to reach the extremes on either side, appealing instead to moderate Germans across the
political spectrum.

   German nationalism clearly helped define—and delimit—potential paths
to the future in the Wilhelmine era, but similar constraints can be found in
all cultures at all times. The pervasiveness of such influences easily masks
the different meanings assigned to them in various circles, as we saw in
the competing strands of historical materialism and socialist Darwinism.
The same was true of nationalist symbols, which were absorbed even into
the alternative culture of socialist labor that Vernon Lidtke has recently
described.[4] Just how restrictive was their influence, how narrowly did it
define choices for the generation of 1890? Emerging slowly from the diverse
circles of German social and cultural reform, Damaschke's nationalistic

---

2. Ibid., p. 115.

3. Ibid., pp. 17–29.

4. Vernon Lidtke, *The Alternative Culture: Socialist Labor in Imperial Germany*
   (New York: Oxford University Press, 1985).

critique of modern industrial capitalism borrowed commonplace tropes and images to achieve a broad resonance between right and left, and it offers a good place to begin exploring both the potentialities and the limits of the Wilhelmine reform milieu.

From the Rental Barracks to Land Reform

"My poor childhood showed me my path," Damaschke wrote in his memoirs,[5] a carefully crafted piece of propaganda weaving together personal memories, common stereotypes, and "objective" statistics in a narrative that leads us ineluctably through the bewildering landscape of Wilhelmine social movements to land reform as the sole practical answer to the social question. The story begins in a Berlin rental barracks—that powerful symbol of Manchesterist greed and ruthlessness—where two of Adolf's siblings had already died before he was born in November 1865, the son of a nurse who had given up her career to marry his father, a cabinet-maker soon struggling to survive the frenzied speculation of the founders' years. Squeezed between wealthy middlemen and a public wanting cheap instead of fine products, the elder Damaschke resembles the image of heroic master craftsmen disseminated by the urban artisans' movement at the time.[6] Slow sales force him first to sell a house the family owned on the outskirts of Berlin to a speculator (who makes 15,000 marks on it within six weeks) and finally to abandon his workshop. Despite such hardships Damaschke's father remains proud, honest, and dedicated to his trade, somehow escaping the vices of alcoholism and violence into which so many other artisans plunged as he led the family from one bad neighborhood to the next throughout Adolf's youth.[7] Summing up the meaning of this experience for his readers, the land reformer wrote: "And if many friends fighting honestly by my side today shake their heads over the passion that still overwhelms me when it's time to lead the cause of honest labor in city and countryside, they just don't know how vividly misery stands before me with all its humiliations and fears, in Father's restless labors, in Mother's pallid face."[8]

---

5. Adolf, Damaschke, *Aus meinem Leben* (Berlin: Hobbing, 1928), p. 225.

6. Volkov, *Rise,* pp. 29, 135–42.

7. Damaschke, *Leben,* pp. 19–27.

8. Ibid., p. 31.

As an accurate record of his path from the rental barracks to land reform—and it is the only major one available—Damaschke's autobiography
is of limited use, but for the generation of 1890 it contained important
lessons. Lost opportunities at times of crisis, dreams of escape into utopias
of revolution or reaction, futile and senseless clashes in the sphere of politics—all reappear as variations on familiar themes in the land reformer's
tale of his struggles against the ills of unbridled capitalism. Read with
caution, as a social *Bildungsroman* of sorts, Damaschke's memoirs reveal
much about the common beliefs he absorbed and the way they shaped
personal memories to inform attempts at narrative persuasion intended to
reach a broad audience, whose concerns and interests the land reformer
had come to understand quite well.

Into the Spring Thaw

From the rental barracks, Damaschke's social education led through Preparatory School and the Berlin Seminary for Municipal School Teachers
to an early career in education. Teaching provided an opportunity not
only to escape the dim prospects of his father's trade but also to guide
other poor children away from perils he had faced himself a few years
before. While still in Preparatory School, Damaschke began teaching Sunday school—not at Stöcker's City Mission, he hastens to tell us, but at
Christ's Church, under the direction of Paulus Cassel, a Jewish convert
who often clashed publicly with his anti-Semitic rival—and it was here that
Damaschke met his wife, Hedwig Bonus, as a fellow instructor in the mid-
1880s.[9] Graduating from Seminary in 1886, he had the opportunity to work
in private schools at a higher salary but chose instead to remain in the
public school system, where he felt he could do the most good. When one
of his students confided that his father would beat his mother if she gave
him money he needed for books, the young teacher launched a campaign
to provide free learning materials in Berlin schools. Speaking to Radical
Workers' Associations and Progressive rallies, Damaschke gained twenty
resolutions in favor of his demand, and by 1890 public pressure was strong
enough to prompt a compromise in the City Council that increased public
funding for education by 66 percent.[10]

---

9. Ibid., pp. 64–67.
10. Ibid., pp. 129–37.

This successful first experiment in social reform had important reper-cussions for Damaschke's career. The young teacher's zealous commitment to social activism raised suspicions in the conservative Prussian bureau-cracy, and after ignoring the thinly veiled threats of a Berlin superinten-dent, he was transferred to a notorious, poverty-stricken neighborhood in the northernmost suburbs.[11] The campaign for free learning materials also introduced him to Berlin's social and cultural reform circles just as the February Decrees were inspiring hope and determination in the younger generation. Meeting socialists and feminists, philosophers and scientists, economists, playwrights, and doctors, Damaschke thus joined in the search for knowledge and expertise Wenck described, gaining critical exposure to currents of social thought that awakened a belief in scientific solutions and eventually led him to land reform.

First, however, Damaschke's activism brought him into contact with Socialists. After writing an article on free learning materials for the Social Democratic *People's Newspaper* in 1890, the young teacher joined its edi-torial staff, where he befriended Franz Mehring. At the time, it will be remembered, Mehring was working with Wille and Türk to found the Free People's Stage, and Damaschke joined in this enterprise. When the two radical young Naturalists were expelled from the SPD in 1891, he left Mehr-ing's theater, following them into the New Free People's Stage and also as-sisting Wille in founding the Free College as another new forum for workers' education.[12] At the same time, however, Damaschke continued working alongside Social Democrats in the natural medicine and abstinence move-ments. After joining the Association for Natural Health Care in 1892, the respectable teacher was soon appointed chairman in hopes of evading police harassment due to the presence of socialists on its executive committee, and he also entered the League of Associations for Popular Health Care that year, becoming chief editor of its journal, *Nature's Doctor,* as well as its yearbook and almanac.[13] The young teacher's early interest in the social question thus quickly led him to socialism, and from there to the same "hygienic factors water, air, and sunshine" Eduard David promoted several decades later.

The position on the *People's Newspaper* brought Damaschke into contact with non-socialist circles as well by introducing him to Moritz von Egidy,

---

11. Ibid., pp. 143–45.
12. Ibid., pp. 195, 215–18.
13. Ibid., pp. 227–40.

a retired cavalry officer who suddenly began promoting "United Christendom" as a means to overcome Germany's social tensions after moving to Berlin in the fall of 1891.[14] Denouncing the authoritarian power structures of church and state, Egidy urged his followers to support the struggles of the working class and the women's movement and declared his personal sympathy with pacifists and even anarchists.[15] His emotional appeals attracted a surprisingly diverse crowd of followers, including "intellectual debaters and workers, Social Democrats and officials, anti-Semites and Jews, practitioners of natural medicine and celebrities of medical science, anarchists and privy councilors, leaders of the women's movement of all leanings," who gathered in public halls and at Egidy's home hoping to find answers to the social question.[16] Such an enthusiastic response made a strong impression on Damaschke, who kept a close eye on Egidy's movement and even endorsed his candidacy in the Reichstag elections of 1898.[17] In the end, however, United Christendom failed to produce lasting results. Criticizing Egidy's "lack of clear, objective engagement," Damaschke was careful to distance himself from the movement in his memoirs, and the maverick aristocrat serves as the first of many warnings about the seductive charms of utopian visionaries.[18]

At the opposite extreme from Egidy's sentimental appeals to brotherly love, the German Society for Ethical Culture attracted a similarly eclectic following with calls for social unity based on an enlightened, humanitarian ethic free from the strife of religious dogma, and Damaschke joined this group as well in 1892. Following the lead of Ethical Culture movements in the United States and Britain, the Society's founders Georg Gizycki and Wilhelm Förster blended Marxist and national economics with socialist Darwinism to promote the utilitarian principle of "the greatest good for

---

14. Ibid., pp. 203–5.
15. On Egidy, see Heinrich Driesmans, *Moritz von Egidy: Sein Leben und Wirken* vol. 2 (Dresden: E. Pierson, 1900), pp. 1–108; Mosse, *Crisis*, pp. 46–51; "Erklärungen gegen die Umsturzvorlage," *Hilfe* 1, no. 9 (March 3, 1895): 3–4; "Verwandte Bewegungen," *Hilfe* 3, no. 5 (January 31, 1897): 8–9; "Frauenvereine," *Frau* 6, no. 1 (October 1898): 57; "Versammlungen," *Hilfe* 3, no. 11 (March 14, 1897): 5.
16. Driesmans, *Egidy*, p. 60.
17. "Aus der Bewegung," *Deutsche Volksstimme* 9, no. 11 (May 20, 1898): 316.
18. Damaschke, *Leben*, p. 207.

the greatest number." Gizycki particularly strove to dispel bourgeois fears of socialism and encouraged revisionist tendencies in the SPD, an aim he unwittingly did much to advance by winning over one of Egidy's early supporters, the future socialist and women's activist Lily Braun.[19] With his scholarly interest in Marx, the Berlin ethics professor also enlisted the support of the national economic boys Tönnies, Herkner, Ignaz Jastrow, and (occasionally) Sombart, as well as leading representatives of the bourgeois and socialist women's movements, including Jeanette Schwerin, Hanna Bieber-Böhm, Marie Stritt, and Bäumer's mentor, Helene Lange.[20] Damaschke, who later took it upon himself to write a two-volume layman's introduction to *The History of National Economics* and integrated contemporary arguments about the impact of industrialization on the "women's question" into his appeals for land reform, clearly learned much from such contacts. But he later complained of Ethical Culture's turn to abstract philosophical interests after Gizycki's early death, which merely inspired "well-fed men and women" to dabble with the ideas of Nietzsche and Darwin "in self-satisfied comfort."[21] In fact, Förster's refusal to focus the Society's attention on land reform may provide a better explanation for Damaschke's bitter remarks—and for his resignation from the movement in 1893. By this time, the young teacher had already become convinced that land reform represented the only serious road to the goal of social unity he was encountering everywhere in Berlin's reform circles, and in his memoirs, Ethical Culture stands alongside United Christendom as a well-meaning, but insubstantial cause that betrayed the empirical impulse of the younger generation's search for concrete, scientific solutions.

Given these opinions, one would not expect to find Damaschke in the company of the Berlin Naturalists, who are hardly remembered for their practical engagement with social issues, but the refined aesthetic sensitivities of this group came closest to claiming his allegiance before the young teacher made the final commitment to land reform during his early years of activism. In fact, he had run across members of the circle from the start, working with Wille and Türk on their various experiments in popular education, and he almost certainly met others in Egidy's home, the natural health movement, and the Ethical Culture society, all of which attracted

19. Braun, *Memoiren*, vol. 1, pp. 429–536; Fricke, *Lexikon*, vol. 3, pp. 39–41.
20. For membership information, see *Ethische Kultur*, vols. 1–2 (1893–1894).
21. Damaschke, *Leben*, pp. 210–15.

the so-called Friedrichshagen circle. This group included Gerhard Hauptmann; Wilhelm Bölsche (one of the most widely read popularizers of Darwin and Haeckel); the prominent literary critics Heinrich and Julius Hart,
other well-known writers such as Otto Hartleben, Konrad Alberti, and
Richard Dehmel; and finally a smattering of women's activists, socialists,
physicians, and reformers, including—to name just one example—Franz
Oppenheimer.[22] Long before their controversial "social dramas" brought
them into the limelight in 1889, the Berlin Naturalists had founded loosely
knit organizations like the Breakthrough Association and the Ethical Club,
which brought young people together to discuss "the social consequences
of industrialization in Germany," and it would perhaps have been more
surprising if Damaschke had not attended some of these gatherings as he
explored possibilities in the early 1890s.[23]

"It fermented, foamed, and boiled in a quite peculiar way, and blew
many a wonderful bubble," Damaschke wrote of the atmosphere at the
Leipzig Street bar, where between thirty and forty members and associates
of the Friedrichshagen circle met every week. While the line between scatterbrained dreamers and practical reformers was not nearly as distinct as
he liked to suggest, the contrast thus obviously suited the rhetorical strategy
of his memoirs. Intoxicated by the euphoria of the meetings, the young
teacher comes perilously close to abandoning his career in a whimsical
urge to indulge "my creative, that is, my poetic talents," but in the nick of
time memories of his "poor childhood" rush in, pushing him back onto
the right path, and the narrative swiftly turns to the sober realities of land
reform.[24] Yet in pausing to ridicule the Taoist penchant of the Naturalists'
New Community—a group that was not founded until 1900—Damaschke
also reveals that his contacts in Friedrichshagen lasted long after he rose
to become national leader of the land reform movement. The colorful
circles and causes that blossomed in the spring thaw could not be so easily
disentangled, a fact Damaschke understood quite well after exploring the
underbrush of Wilhelmine social and cultural reform quite thoroughly
during his early years in Berlin.

22. Roy Pascal, *From Naturalism to Expressionism: German Literature and Society,
   1880–1918* (New York: Basic, 1973), pp. 19–20; Lunn, *Socialism,* pp. 52–64;
   Kelly, *Descent,* pp. 129–34.
23. Günther, *Gruppenbildung,* p. 24.
24. Damaschke, *Leben,* pp. 219–22.

The League for Land-Ownership Reform

In August 1890, while he was still fighting for free learning materials and just venturing into those circles, Damaschke attended a meeting of the German League for Land-Ownership Reform. Not particularly impressed, he nevertheless signed up on the mailing list and was soon surprised to find himself considered a dues-paying member of the League. Despite these inauspicious beginnings, the mailings he received soon convinced Damaschke that land reform did indeed represent the realistic solution to the social question he was looking for, and by 1891 he was already gathering resolutions for land reform from Berlin's shoemakers, construction workers, tailors, machinists, and metal-workers.[25] Initially just one among many of the young teacher's causes, it quickly pushed all others aside.

Like Ethical Culture, land reform took its cue from developments in America, where in 1879 San Francisco journalist Henry George launched a nationwide reform movement with his sensational critique of modern social conditions, *Progress and Poverty.* Seeking to discover the link between America's unprecedented prosperity and the social misery following in the wake of industrial capitalism, George's treatise also found obvious resonance in Germany, where similar contrasts had provoked the angry debates of the founders' years. For George, the key to this tragic contradiction lay in revenue from rising land values, which derived from the advancing industry and enterprise of society as a whole, not from that of individuals, and so had to be returned to the community for the promise of modern development to be fulfilled. While early German adherents like Michael Flürscheim and C. von Helldorf-Baumersrode agreed with this analysis, they rejected George's "single-tax" on land revenue as a solution, instead adopting the more radical goal of nationalized land-ownership championed by the outspoken socialist of the lectern Adolf Wagner. Denouncing private property as a "product of illegality and violence," Wagner had pushed hard for nationalizing Prussia's railways after his defection from the Liberal camp in the early 1870s, and he also called for the state's systematic acquisition of urban properties. During the 1880s Flürscheim and Helldorf-Baumersrode blended the ideas of George and Wagner to attract a small, but diverse following of Social Democrats, left liberals, progressive industrialists, and others. After a number of unsuccessful attempts to or-

---

25. Ibid., p. 252.

ganize the movement, the League for Land-Ownership was finally founded in 1888.[26]

The marriage of George's relatively moderate approach with Wagner's radical crusade proved unsatisfying to both sides. Flürscheim's call for nationalized land-ownership seemed extreme and unrealistic to moderates like Damaschke, who blamed it for his cool response to the League, and once he overcame his initial suspicions the young reformer encountered far more visceral reactions from progressive leaders like Max Hirsch. Alarmed by Damaschke's success in winning supportive resolutions from Berlin's Artisans' Associations, Hirsch strove to defend the liberal principle of self-help by overturning these endorsements in the Central Committee, forcing the land reformer back to the local branches for a long and bitter grassroots campaign that is clearly flagged in his memoirs as a first lesson in the senseless and harmful game of party politics.[27] Yet any attempt to overcome this obstacle by diverting attention from the movement's radical goals provoked similar outcries from Marxists. When Heinrich Freese led a campaign to protect construction workers' legal rights as the land reformers' chairman, the Social Democratic vice-chairman Leo Arons brought a vote of no confidence against him at the League's 1892 congress, charging that Freese was undermining its commitment to land nationalization. Damaschke, who actively supported Freese's campaign, could see no harm in working for "the immediate and vital interests of wide segments of the population" and insisted that such efforts would provide good publicity in any case. After a heated discussion, the Social Democrats rejected a compromise requiring the movement to pursue issues of more immediate concerns alongside the ultimate goal of land nationalization, and when Arons refused to stand for re-election as vice-chairman, Damaschke took his place.[28]

Damaschke's election proved to be a turning point. Using his rapidly growing influence to keep the League from the pitfalls of political dog-

26. Henry George, *Progress and Poverty: An Inquiry into the Cause of Industrial Depressions and of Increase of Want with Increase of Waste: The Remedy* (Garden City: Doubleday, Page & Co., 1923); Heinrich Freese, *Die Bodenreform: Ihre Vergangenheit und ihre Zukunft* (Berlin: Weichert, 1918), pp. 20–29, 51–59, 75–89.

27. Damaschke, *Leben*, pp. 252–57.

28. Freese, *Bodenreform*, pp. 212–24, 275, 288–91.

matism and unrealistic schemes he had encountered elsewhere in reform circles, the new chairman strove to establish a solid reputation for land reform as a practical solution to the immediate problems of the 1890s. When a rival group began advertising utopian settlements in Africa and Mexico, he hastily distanced the League from such ventures as editor of its journal *Free-Land* and sharply criticized Flürscheim himself when the movement's founder became involved in them. Playing down land nationalization, Damaschke promoted less ambitious financial and tax reforms but also tried to keep the League open to Social Democratic participation. While the results were encouraging—*Free-Land*'s circulation tripled within months—the land reformer was convinced that the movement needed to reach a broader audience. When offered a position as editor of two Kiel newspapers with a nationwide circulation of ten thousand, Damaschke therefore accepted, on the condition that both the *Kiel Newest News* and the *German People's Voice* would serve as official organs of land reform. By this time, however, the Berlin leadership felt unable to continue without the vice-chairman's energetic handling of day-to-day affairs, and in August 1896 they voted to dissolve the League, calling on its members to join the German People's League that was headed by Damaschke's new patron in Kiel, Johannes von Lehmann-Hohenberg. German land reformers had thus gained their first national organ, but in doing so, they had to leave behind the institutional foundations Flürscheim had built since the 1870s.[29] It was time for a new beginning.

Onto the National Stage

Damaschke's experience in Kiel proved disappointing. As a close friend and business partner of Egidy, Lehmann-Hohenberg was involved in risky settlement schemes not unlike those Damaschke opposed in *Free-Land*, and when the ventures collapsed, he was forced to sell the *Kiel Newest News* (KNN) to avoid financial ruin less than six months after the land reformer had arrived. "Every failure of this kind costs our nation valuable energies," Damaschke complained in his memoirs. "Noble people who step forward in life with the highest idealism," only to plunge into disasters of their own making, simply frightened away others "who, in recognition of their most

---

29. Damaschke, *Leben*, pp. 265, 273–78, 315–19, 329–37; Freese, *Bodenreform*, pp. 272–73.

pressing duties, might have remained capable of working successfully for the cause of social justice."[30] Despite this setback, Damaschke managed to profit from his brief stay in Kiel, where he explored a thriving network of reform movements much like the one he had left behind in Berlin. Continuing his work in popular education, the young reformer helped found a local Reading Hall Society to raise funds for a public library and formed a Free Social-Scientific Union that offered lectures on topics such as social health and hygiene. And when a KNN investigation uncovered an alarming rate of accidents involving Kiel's transit system, Damaschke launched a campaign demanding a nine-hour day for tram drivers.[31] Returning to Berlin the following spring, he thus brought back the encouraging discovery of a distant circle of like-minded reformers—as well as the *German People's Voice*, which he had managed to retain in his otherwise frustrating dealings with Lehmann-Hohenberg.

By far the most significant event during his brief stay in Kiel, however, was Damaschke's election as delegate to the National Socials' founding congress at Erfurt in November 1896. While Naumann's aggressive nationalism soon became a bone of contention between them, his calls for social integration on a secular, "scientific" basis echoed many of the lessons the land reformer had learned in his early years of activism, and Damaschke spoke out forcefully in favor of religious neutrality at the congress, sponsoring a motion to strike the paragraph containing a profession of the Christian faith from the Association's proposed platform. When this failed to satisfy a majority, he worked out a successful compromise resolution stating that confession was "not to act as a moral constraint on individual members. Everyone who wishes to cooperate in [pursuit of] our national and social goals is welcome to work with us."[32] Damaschke's skillful performance at Erfurt won him the chair of the Regulations Committee, and he quickly rose through the ranks to become one of the Association's most prominent national spokesmen.[33] Joining the staff of Naumann's short-lived daily, *The Times*, upon returning to Berlin, Damaschke also briefly took over as editor of the *World on Monday*, which he added to the biweekly *German People's Voice* as another organ promoting both land reform and

30. Damaschke, *Zeitenwende*, pp. 27, 44; Driesmans, *Egidy*, pp. 25–26.
31. Damaschke, *Zeitenwende*, pp. 17–18, 22–23.
32. Düding, *Verein*, pp. 50–51. See also Damaschke, *Zeitenwende*, p. 77.
33. Damaschke, *Zeitenwende*, pp. 84–85.

the National Socials' progressive agenda.[34] The same year, 1897, he became the NSV's first candidate for the Reichstag, running in a promising campaign that, though falling short of victory, proved to be encouraging for the young movement, and in 1898 he was elected to the Executive Committee, where he became acting chairman of meetings Naumann could not attend. When Paul Göhre left to join the SPD, Damaschke succeeded him as the NSV's new vice-chairman in 1901.[35]

Traveling through Germany on nationwide lecture tours and enjoying free access to the National Social presses,[36] Damaschke thus stepped onto a national stage after his debut at Erfurt, a move that vastly enhanced the appeal of his land reform initiatives at the same time it exposed very real constraints in the tensely charged political atmosphere in the 1890s. As a Reichstag candidate in Plön-Oldenburg, the young reformer faced bitter attacks from both right and left, as well as the grim realities of parish-pump politics in Germany's isolated rural districts: harassment from local authorities, intimidation of voters, marked ballots distributed to workers on large landed estates.[37] Angry political feuds also surfaced within the NSV itself, where Göhre's sympathy for the socialist labor movement sparked an angry exchange with Sohm (Weber's ally against the politics of misery) at the Association's first annual congress in 1897, and the controversy continued to sputter and fume until Göhre finally turned his back on the National Socials in 1900. At the same time, Naumann's attempt to receive official endorsements for his bellicose stance on foreign policy issues and fundamentally "anti-agrarian position" in the controversy over German industrialization simultaneously threatened to alienate supporters on both left and right. Damaschke did his best to smooth over these tensions, temporarily ending the dispute between Sohm and Göhre with a compromise resolution at the 1897 congress, which he followed up with conciliatory articles in the *German Peoples' Voice* and by setting up an Agrarian Committee in the NSV leadership to allay Conservative fears in

---

34. Ibid., pp. 88–92.
35. Damaschke, *Zeitenwende,* pp. 135–38; Adolf Damaschke, "Die Tage von Darmstadt," *Deutsche Volksstimme* 9, no. 19 (October 5, 1898): 565; Nachlaß (hereafter NL) Naumann 53, archival pagination, pp. 48, 110.
36. Campaign reports, *Hilfe* and *Deutsche Volksstimme,* 1896–1903.
37. Damaschke, *Zeitenwende,* pp. 109–58, 423–40; Düding, *Verein,* pp. 124–27; Gerlach, *Rechts,* pp. 156–62.

1901, but the struggle proved tiring.[38] When members of the Executive Committee began trying to thwart his influence after the National Socials added a land reform plank to the Association's platform, Damaschke threatened to resign in 1901,[39] and while he openly denounced the decision to dissolve the NSV two years later, the vice-chairman privately greeted the opportunity to devote himself entirely to the anti-political cause of German land reform.[40]

The National Socials' failure to avoid the political fray had in fact convinced Damaschke early on that land reform needed to preserve its independence. While gearing up for a second Reichstag campaign in Plön-Oldenburg in the spring of 1898, he called for a meeting to discuss proposals for reviving the League for Land-Ownership Reform on April 2.[41] Urging the League not to join the NSV, Damaschke instead called on land reformers to protect its status as "neutral ground . . . on which Conservatives and National Socials, Anti-Semites and Progressives, National Liberals and democratically-oriented men can come together." When old differences over the goal of land nationalization resurfaced, he quickly warned the group not "to create psychological obstacles through the choice of misleading formulations" and (once again) found the appropriate wording for a compromise resolution that satisfied most of those present. Marking a clean break with the movement's quarrelsome past, the assembly voted for a new institutional foundation, founding the League of German Land Reformers (*Bund Deutscher Bodenreformer,* or BDB) and defining its goals in terms calculated to encourage the participation of as many interests as possible: "The League of German Land Reformers strives to ensure that the land, the foundation of all national being, is placed under laws encouraging its

---

38. Damaschke, "Die Tage," pp. 438–43; Damaschke, *Zeitenwende,* pp. 386–87.

39. Damaschke, *Zeitenwende,* pp. 386–91; Damaschke, "Zum Kampfe um die Bodenreform," *Deutsche Volksstimme* 10, no. 17 (September 5, 1899): 514–25; Damaschke, "Die Tage von Göttingen und die Bodenreform," *Deutsche Volksstimme* 10, no. 20 (October 20, 1899): 614–15; report on BDB meeting of April 24, 1900, *Deutsche Volksstimme* 11, no. 9 (May 5, 1900): 282–83; NL Naumann, archival pagination, pp. 80, 110.

40. Damaschke, *Zeitenwende,* p. 441; Damaschke, "nationalsoziale Partei," pp. 530–35; NL Naumann, archival pagination, p. 142.

41. Report on BDB meeting of April 2, 1898, *Deutsche Volksstimme* 9, no. 7 (April 5, 1898): 194–202.

use as workplace and residence, excluding any possibility of its misuse, and making the increases in value it attains without the labor of the individual useful for the nation as a whole."[42] At the conclusion of the meeting, Heinrich Freese stepped aside to allow Damaschke to take over as chairman of the new League, a post he held continuously until his death in 1935.

However frustrating Damaschke's experiences in the NSV proved to be, they had also taught him important lessons about the potential of nationalist rhetoric as a medium for carrying the message of social unity to a broad audience of Germans with diverse political affiliations, an insight the new League's cautiously worded statutes built into the foundations of his movement. The land reformer had also learned from Naumann's mistakes, however, and he defined his "truly national" mission with exquisite care to avoid stirring up political tensions on either left or right. Drawing on his intimate knowledge of Wilhelmine reform circles, Damaschke couched his appeals in a critique of industrial capitalism with nationalistic undertones that seem deeply suspect today but managed to skirt the extremes to reach moderate, socially conscious Germans of nearly all political camps. What did this language mean to the land reformer and his contemporaries? How did it emerge from his struggle to find "neutral ground?" Let us take a closer look at the process, which may contain other lessons about alternative potentialities in the Wilhelmine era.

"In Service to the Father*land*"

> Land reform, that is, an organic rootedness of German national-
> ity in German soil, finally many German children in air and light
> and sunshine, German children healthy in body and soul—Ger-
> man future, German ascendance.
>
> ADOLF DAMASCHKE

A capital gains tax on "unearned" increment, higher excise taxes on land sales, a tax on undeveloped land, changes in assessment and mortgage procedures, the legal separation of land ownership from the ownership of buildings—land reform hardly seems adequate for the task of national redemption as Damaschke conceived it.[43] The BDB's first campaign goals

---

42. Damaschke, *Zeitenwende,* p. 178.

43. For a survey of the BDB's reform program, see Damaschke, *Bodenreform,* pp. 96–142; Damaschke, *Aufgaben der Gemeindepolitik,* 4th rev. ed. (Jena: Fi-

were so narrowly defined that they could be justified only with "purely legalistic arguments, or at best ones involving credit technicalities,"[44] and even the more ambitious drive for a "German homestead act," which the League launched after some encouraging early successes in 1912, paled in comparison with the radical aims of the early German land reformers, or even with the single-tax movement in the United States.[45] In his attempt to steer clear of utopias, Damaschke had anchored the League's efforts within the existing social and economic order to such an extent that Franz Oppenheimer later accused him of having "denigrated the humanitarian idea introduced by Henry George into a bourgeois tax affair."[46]

Yet from the beginning Damaschke claimed that Germany's fate hinged on the League's modest and uninspiring efforts. If land was the "foundation of all national being," the BDB's mission was to force it from the speculators' exploitative grasp into productive use, and by placing secure and affordable homes within reach of the underprivileged, the movement would inspire a "love of homeland" in the people.[47] But land reform was more than mere sentimental idealism: "it is the strength of the German nation that deteriorates in the housing shortage and the bondage of debt," Damaschke warned, echoing Naumann's arguments for the new liberalism, so that the League's agenda was "Realpolitik" in the truest sense of the word.[48] In fact, the land reformer, in his struggle against the greed and ruthlessness of Manchesterism, actually rendered "the same [service] to the whole of the nation as every soldier who stands in arms against an external enemy."[49]

scher, 1901), pp. 87–120; reports "Aus der Bewegung" in *Deutsche Volksstimme* (after 1908 *Die Bodenreform*).

44. Dorothea Berger-Thimme, *Boden- und Wohnungsreform in Deutschland 1873–1918* (Frankfurt: Peter Lang, 1976), p. 97.

45. "Ein deutsches Heimstättenrecht?" *Bodenreform* 23, no. 5 (March 5, 1912): 88–94; Berger-Thimme, *Wohnungsreform*, pp. 107–11.

46. Oppenheimer, *Erlebtes*, p. 154.

47. Damaschke, *Aufgaben*, p. 136.

48. Adolf Damaschke, "Vom Wesen des Staates," *Deutsche Volksstimme* 16, no. 19 (October 5, 1905): 553.

49. Report on 1900 BDB Congress, *Deutsche Volksstimme* 11, no. 24 (December 20, 1900): 722.

A Place in the Sun?

Damaschke's image of German land reformers standing shoulder to shoulder with armed soldiers in defense of "our Father*land*" perfectly captures the way the BDB leader twisted popular turns of phrase to suit his own narrow purposes, crudely, perhaps, but often with great impact.[50] This particular slogan came in his opening speech to the League's annual congress in 1900, just as public interest in fleets and colonies was reaching new intensity, and Damaschke followed it up with a report on his own strident efforts in matters of colonial policy. Since 1898 he had used the issue to put land reform in the headlines at every opportunity. While stressing the BDB's neutral stance—neither promoting nor opposing the acquisition of colonies—Damaschke argued that even the critics of imperialism could have nothing against policies benefiting native inhabitants in German colonies that already existed. The push for land reform in the colonies had sparked major debates in the Reichstag in 1899, with Admiral Tirpitz himself speaking in favor of the League's proposals, and when the Navy took over the colonial administration of Kiautschou later that year, it promptly introduced the desired measures. It was Damaschke's campaign to reveal the corrupt policies of the Colonial Office in Cameroon, however, that had yielded the most spectacular results. Exposing Director von Buchka's shady dealings with land speculators in German East Africa in the *Deutsche Volksstimme*, he had circulated petitions demanding Buchka's dismissal and even mailed his pamphlet *Cameroon or Kiautschou?* to all members of parliament when the Reichstag Bureau refused to distribute it. A scandal ensued, and Buchka was forced to resign, and at the BDB congress a month later, in June 1900, Damaschke was able to claim credit for saving another German colony from exploitation and corruption. One could only hope that similar policies would soon serve the national interest at home, he added, concluding his speech with a patriotic "Long live Wilhelm II!"[51]

---

50. Ibid.

51. Ibid., p. 723. See also Damaschke's articles: "Ein Schritt Vorwärts," *Deutsche Volksstimme* 9, no. 23 (December 5, 1898): 689–92; "Die Regierung, der Reichstag und die Bodenreform," *Deutsche Volksstimme* 10, no. 4 (February 20, 1899): 97–105; "An Seine Durchlaucht, den Herrn Reichskanzler," *Deut-*

Damaschke also translated grassroots enthusiasm for fleets and colonies into a resounding cry for land reform. "A German policy that, in the midst of the ongoing distribution of the last scraps of the Earth's surface, dutifully seeks to preserve its 'place in the sun' will in the long run be able to fulfill the new great tasks emerging in this area only . . . if that policy is sustained by the complete understanding of a throng of German people interested in politics," he warned in the petition for Buchka's dismissal.[52] "The people," it seemed, were demanding land reform, and officials might continue to enjoy the good will of Pan-Germans, Navy League pundits, and others in the "throng" clamoring for a more forceful "German policy" by giving in to this demand. Angry opposition blended together with enthusiastic patriotism in response to the Colonial Office scandal, and Damaschke skillfully orchestrated this ambivalent hubbub into a resounding call for land reform.

Internal colonization presented another chance to tap the currents of popular nationalism. It was this issue that inspired Max Weber's Darwinistic arguments about the economic foundations of national strength, as we have seen. While his demand for the subdivision of Junker estates shocked conservative Christian Socials, it was greeted by the radical nationalists, who were promoting internal colonization along the Polish frontier, and Weber himself joined the Pan-German League to support the campaign in the 1890s.[53] As the movement gained strength, Damaschke adopted its rhetoric to depict land reform as a "special national interest" that would sustain a healthy rural population, which he called a "fountain of youth for the nation," despite the fact that most of the BDB's own efforts

---

sche *Volksstimme* 10, no. 7 (April 5, 1899): 193–95; "Zur Kolonialfrage," *Deutsche Volksstimme* 10, no. 9 (May 5, 1899): 257–58; "Die nächste Aufgabe deutscher Kolonialpolitik," *Deutsche Volksstimme* 10, no. 23 (December 5, 1899): 705–8; "Wer ist der Vormund unseres Reichstags?" *Deutsche Volksstimme* 11, no. 8 (April 20, 1900): 225–27; "Vom Kampf um unsere Kolonien," *Deutsche Volksstimme* 11, no. 9 (May 5, 1900): 257–64; "Herr von Buchka geht," *Deutsche Volksstimme* 11, no. 10 (May 20, 1900): 289–95; "Der Ausgang unseres Kolonialfeldzuges," *Deutsche Volksstimme* 11, no. 12 (June 20, 1900): 357–58; and Damaschke, *Zeitenwende,* pp. 233–49.

52. Damaschke, "Durchlaucht," 194.

53. Mommsen, *Politics,* pp. 54–55.

focused on urban issues.[54] As "the greatest social deed of the German people in the middle ages," settlement of the eastern territories had demonstrated the historic importance of land reform by laying "the foundations of German greatness."[55] The Germanic custom of *Allmende,* or communal property ownership, had protected the land from exploitation under the Roman legal principle of *usus et abusus* as far away as the Carpathians, with the result that even today the land reform colonies of Transylvania remain islands of German culture in a sea of foreign peoples.[56] Damaschke was also proud to note that Otto von Gierke, the most prominent theorist of "Germanic law" and a strong voice in the drive for internal colonization, was himself an outspoken member of the League.[57]

Modern Ills

In his eagerness to establish land reform's relevance by using the most popular nationalist slogans of the day, the BDB leader thus toyed with tropes of agrarian romanticism, but after his experiences in Plön-Oldenburg, he did so with considerable misgiving, keeping the League at arm's length from the conservative populists of the Agrarian League and remaining suspicious when Pan-German leaders enlisted in his cause.[58] Yet the virulent strains of anti-urbanism feeding these movements did respond to many of the same threatening aspects of modernity that had initially led Damaschke to land reform. Far from sharing Naumann's "anti-agrarian position," he emphasized that the League understood and shared these concerns: "Only when

---

54. Adolf Damaschke, "Das Agrarproblem und die Bodenreform," *Deutsche Volksstimme* 13, no. 19 (October 5, 1901): 577.

55. Adolf Damaschke, *Geschichte der Nationalökonomie: Eine erste Einführung* (Jena: Fischer, 1929), vol. 1, pp. 75, 78.

56. Adolf Damaschke, "Die Bodenreform und der österreichische Nationalitätenkampf," *Deutsche Volksstimme* 9, no. 16 (August 20, 1898): 465–68; Damaschke, *Aufgaben,* p. 153.

57. "Heimstättenrecht?" pp. 90–92; cf. Adolf Damaschke, *Bodenreform,* p. 228.

58. "Rundschau," *Deutsche Volksstimme* 9, no. 20 (October 20, 1898): 621; Adolf Damaschke, "Der Bund der Landwirte und die deutsche Bodenreform," *Deutsche Volksstimme* 2, no. 17 (September 5, 1897): 373–80; report on the 1908 BDB congress, *Bodenreform* 19, no. 9 (May 5, 1908): 278.

our rural population is doing well enough that excessive migration to industrial areas does not result is a high standard of living for the urban
population possible, and thus a prosperous economic life for the nation as
a whole."[59] Refusing to take sides in the controversy over German industrialization, such remarks nevertheless indicate the subordinate status of
the "agrarian question" in Damaschke's eyes, and it was in his depictions
of the plight of the urban poor that he found the language of popular
nationalism and cultural despair most effective in rallying support for his
cause.

The suffering experienced by millions, especially women and children,
in the cramped, overcrowded rental barracks of German cities always remained the point of departure for Damaschke's critique of modernity. "On
December 1, 1910 in our much admired, shining Imperial Capital there
were 9,935 apartments that did not have a single heated room, that consisted only of a cubicle without a stove or a kitchen," he revealed at the
outset of *Land Reform: Fundamentals and Historical Material for the Recognition and Conquest of Social Need.* "Of the apartments with at most one
heated room, 41,963 were permanently occupied by 5 and more than 5
(up to 13) persons of differing ages and sex!"[60] While he often related
touching stories of human misery to awaken pity in his readers, Damaschke
understood that appeals to charity were not the most effective rhetorical
means at his disposal. As a site of racial degeneration, the rental barracks
linked his cause to widespread nationalist anxiety about life in the modern
metropolis. "What does the misery of the city apartment mean for the
defense force of our people?" the land reformer asked, echoing the appeals
of racial hygienists and population policy experts. It came as no surprise
to learn that thirty out of a hundred second-generation Berliners were unfit
for military duty.[61] "[I]n overfilled rear apartments without air and light
even the most highly gifted, noble race must waste away and degenerate
in less than the span of a human lifetime!"[62] Still more shocking, the Hamburg cholera epidemic sent an ominous warning of the perils lurking in
the rental barracks Damaschke addressed specifically to his middle-class
readers: "when death arose out of these conditions, it did not stop before

---

59. Damaschke, *Bodenreform*, p. 176.
60. Ibid., p. 10.
61. Ibid., p. 11.
62. Damaschke, "Wesen," p. 554.

the second floor of the villa, of course, and the rich man who had perhaps tossed aside descriptions of the housing problem in boredom or irritation only a few days before, as if none of this had anything to do with him, learned to think differently as he stood at the sick bed or the death bed of one of his loved ones."[63]

Disease, degeneration, decadence—the popular obsession with these modern ills lent a strong sense of urgency to the League's propaganda, which played on fears of moral corruption as well. Incest was common in the rental barracks, where boys and girls, men and women had to sleep together in a single room, Damaschke claimed, and family life also suffered from the ruthlessness of industrial capitalism, which drove mothers from their homes into the "Molochs" of German factories. The "champions of domestic fortune, the guardians of the future" returned from long hours of such "economically significant" work too exhausted to take on their household duties; the "husband is forced out to the pub—and the children? What does this development mean for them?" The BDB leader answered with yet another barrage of statistics, this time on infant mortality, disease, and juvenile delinquency. "Children sold or given away, children forced to beg, child-beating, starvation, child abuse, baby farming," Damaschke proclaimed, "these are the—by no means isolated—results of our economic conditions, while we at the same time speak so grandly of the 'Century of the Child.' "[64]

The middle ages, by contrast, were portrayed by the land reformer as an idyll of health and prosperity. Before the Thirty Years War and the age of absolutism, the German people had enjoyed the security of native customs and traditions that bound the nation together organically as a social and cultural whole. "The land rights of the middle ages sought to secure free access to nature for all, and thus the possibility of earning a living through free labor," Damaschke asserted, again singling out "Germanic cooperative law" and the *Allmende* for special praise.[65] While the eastern settlements were sparkling examples of land reform's benevolent effects, property relations in Germany's prosperous medieval cities seemed even more enthralling to the BDB leader. "Land speculation in today's sense was unthinkable," he marveled. "It is thus natural that even in the largest cities

63. Damaschke, *Aufgaben,* p. 160.
64. Damaschke, *Bodenreform,* pp. 2–7.
65. Damaschke, *Nationalökonomie,* vol. 1, pp. 85–86.

of the middle ages, there simply were no mass apartment buildings at all."[66] There was also no "women's question," he claimed, since men and women had joined the guilds equally as masters in productive cooperatives that ensured the proud and prosperous medieval artisan good pay, comfortable housing, and a short work day. "And how does it stand after 420 years of wonderful technical progress with the quality of life for the classes who work with their hands?" Damaschke wondered. "Can you even imagine today a decree of the Saxon government, i.e. of the state with the most highly developed German industry, that set the number of courses at lunch and dinner at 'only' four or five?"[67]

Mammonism and the Ugly Jew

Such wistful reminiscences about guilds resonated loudly with the "popular anti-modernism" of German craftsmen who were demanding their reinstatement, just as Damaschke's attacks on "our ruling Mammonistic system" tapped the anti-Semitic undercurrents that nourished the urban artisans' movement at the end of the nineteenth century.[68] Inflating land reform's limited concerns into a sweeping indictment of modern social and economic development, the BDB leader laid blame for contemporary urban blight on "parasitic speculators," "cunning interests," and "usurers," employing vocabulary tinged by association with Adolf Wagner's ugly polemics against Mammonism in the 1870s. In fact, the anti-Semitic scholar had been among the first to call for German land reform, and although Damaschke rejected his radical goals, Wagner remained an outspoken advocate of the BDB. Proudly emphasizing their friendship on frequent occasions, Damaschke also praised Wagner's break with the Association for Social Policy in 1878, which led the economist to Stöcker's Christian Social Party, as a courageous act of defiance against Mammonism.[69]

While distancing himself from the nastier aspects of Wagner's personality, the land reformer did not hesitate to point out Jewish involvement in many of Germany's current problems.[70] Noting a disproportionate pres-

---

66. Ibid., p. 93.
67. Ibid., p. 112.
68. Damaschke, *Bodenreform*, p. 53.
69. Damaschke, *Zeitenwende*, p. 54.
70. Adolf Damaschke, "Adolf Wagner," *Bodenreform* 28, no. 22 (November 20, 1917): 567–73; Damaschke, *Zeitenwende*, pp. 349–55; 1900 BDB congress re-

ence of Jews in the banking and speculative enterprises he despised,[71] he also blamed them for the introduction of interest—or "usury"—that contributed to Germany's fall from grace after the middle ages.[72] Contemporary caricatures from the anti-Semitic press even came to life in Damaschke's autobiography, where an elderly Jewish man is found lurking in the shadows to tempt the honest artisan's son on his way home from school: " 'Learn, my boy, everything you possibly can, sometime or other it will serve you well. Those who can do get rich, get powerful, get honored, can satisfy all their desires, and'—he pointed to a girl who was leaning out of a window—'pretty girls—you can have everything, everything belongs to you, once you've learned something. Learn! Learn!' "[73] The startling appearance of this Shylockian figure in the land reformer's memoirs suggests that he shared the hatred for Jews pervading Wilhelmine political culture at a profoundly personal level. It was in any case certainly intended to appeal to anti-Semites, who were among the groups he specifically mentioned in defining the BDB's "neutral ground" in 1898. Damaschke's wish to reserve space in the new League for these unsavory elements seems also to have been fulfilled, since local chapters of the anti-Semitic German National Commercial Clerks' Unions joined the League in droves during these years,[74] as did the leaders of the intensely anti-Semitic German-Social Party, Friedrich Raab and Count Ernst zu Reventlow.[75] On a trip to Austria sponsored by the Christian Social Party, the land reform leader even managed to convert Karl Lueger, Vienna's notorious anti-Semitic mayor, who not

---

port, *Deutsche Volksstimme* 11, no. 24 (December 20, 1900): 732; Adolf Damaschke, "Der Kampf um Moabit," *Deutsche Volksstimme* 12, no. 22 (November 20, 1901): 677–78; 1908 BDB congress report, *Bodenreform* 19, no. 10 (May 20, 1908): 302; 1910 BDB congress report, *Bodenreform* 21, no. 20 (October 20, 1910): 655–56.

71. Damaschke, *Zeitenwende*, p. 266.
72. Damaschke, *Nationalökonomie*, vol. 1, p. 143.
73. Damaschke, *Leben*, p. 80.
74. See reports on new corporate members appearing under the heading "Aus der Bewegung" in the *Deutsche Volksstimme* (later *Bodenreform*) beginning in 1900; and Berger-Thimme, *Wohnungsreform*, pp. 87–88.
75. BDB annual congress reports in the *Deutsche Volksstimme* and *Bodenreform* from 1900; "Aus der Bewegung," *Deutsche Volksstimme* 11, no. 23 (December 5, 1900): 709; Damaschke, *Zeitenwende*, pp. 223–29; Mosse, *Crisis*, p. 138.

only joined the BDB himself but also promised the corporate membership of his city, which soon followed.[76]

Yet however much he valued the anti-Semites' support, however willingly he flagged their attention with tainted tropes and caricatures, however much he may even have shared their sentiments at some intimate level, Damaschke loudly opposed anti-Semitism and its goals as fundamentally misguided and harmful. Land reform addressed many of the same issues, he insisted, and could perhaps even be expressed in the same terms. But it represented an *alternative,* as the title of Damaschke's first speech to Berlin artisans in 1891 makes clear: "Manchesterism, Anti-Semitism, or Land-Ownership Reform?" "You suppose only the Jews misuse this weapon?" he asked after describing the evils of speculation. Even if they accounted for 99 percent, the other 1 percent would still have to be attributed to Christians, so the problem could hardly be ascribed to some elusive racial characteristics. It was the system that was to blame, not certain kinds of people, and the only way to eliminate speculation was to change the laws that made it possible. "Never yet has an issue of *principles* been resolved by turning it into a *personal* issue."[77] When anti-Semites later tried to use land reform as a platform for promoting their own agenda, the BDB leader again drew a clear line between the two movements. Fighting the views of Raab and Reventlow at a National Social rally in Hamburg, Damaschke demanded and received a resolution publicly denouncing their views in 1898. "How could anti-Semitism help us in this matter?" he asked on another occasion, defending his views on the legal rights of construction workers at a meeting of the Commercial Clerks' Union. "It could only do harm by diverting attention away from the decisive cause of the problem, our false system of land-holding rights."[78]

Jews may have been heavily involved in that system, but they were also at the forefront of efforts to improve it, and Damaschke stressed the "Jewish pride" of pioneers in the German land reform movement, like Flürscheim, Oppenheimer, and Hertzka.[79] If he found Zionism as risky as any "utopian" settlement, the BDB leader also praised the introduction of Mo-

76. Adolf Damaschke, "Lueger und sein soziales Testament," *Bodenreform* 21, no. 6 (March 20, 1910): 152–61.

77. Damaschke, *Zeitenwende,* pp. 258–61; emphasis in the original.

78. Damaschke, *Zeitenwende,* pp. 265–66.

79. Damaschke, "Zionisten": 575–76.

saic law in Palestine, quoting with approval from the *Jewish Review:* "Here
the Jewish people is drawing at the same time on its oldest land codes and
the most modern social movement, land reform."[80] Such glowing reports
did not always receive a positive response, but Damaschke persisted even
at the risk of alienating wealthy patrons. When the wealthy American
businessman Charles Hallgarten threatened to withhold generous financial support unless articles on Zionism stopped appearing in the *German
People's Voice,* for instance, Damaschke refused to comply, despite his
friendship with Hallgarten (who was himself Jewish), and despite the
financial sacrifice it meant for the league.[81] Land reform was not a "personal" matter, and Damaschke welcomed the support of anyone willing to
join in, regardless of the political or ethnic motives involved. In an article
offering testimonials from representatives of a variety of causes, the land
reformer thus chose to follow the words of a Pan-German with those of a
Zionist. "The animosity against us is essentially called forth by social need,"
his Jewish friend explained. "In a nation with healthy social conditions,
where every individual can be secure in his work and happy with his wage,
people are open-hearted and tolerant. Under the constraints of need, each
begrudges the other even a piece of dry bread. At a fully-laid *table d'hôte*
everyone passes the full bowl to his neighbor in a friendly manner,—because of this, land reform is the only way for us to live peacefully side by
side."[82]

"Truly National"

Describing land reform as a path to national salvation, a panacea for modern ills, a weapon against Mammonism and "parasites," Damaschke sent
his message into Wilhelmine political culture piggybacked on powerful
nationalist tropes carrying a vast number of associations, most of which
went far beyond his modest proposals for tax and finance reform. He was
also clearly willing to go far in accommodating these broader interests,
which he legitimated by both welcoming their spokesmen as allies and
stirring up anxieties that sustained their efforts. Yet Damaschke employed

---

80. Damaschke, *Bodenreform,* p. 246.
81. Damaschke, *Zeitenwende,* pp. 414–17.
82. Adolf Damaschke, "Sechzehn Jahre im Dienste der deutschen Bodenreform,"
    Deutsche Volksstimme 17, no. 14 (July 20, 1906): 413.

such language with a distinct purpose of his own, and he loudly repudiated any meanings that thwarted this purpose, even if it meant alienating potential supporters. In other words, he struggled to preserve his claim on what he believed to be legitimate uses of the language of popular nationalism. When anti-Semites challenged this claim, the land reformer responded by marking out the neutral ground they shared in common, but he refused to let the League be dragged one step further onto their terrain. And the same went for other self-appointed guardians of the national heritage as well.

"There is much abuse of the word national in our day," Damaschke complained in the article describing Carpathian settlements as embattled outposts of Germanic culture. "Parties call themselves 'national' parties that oppose all serious efforts at social reform."[83] Such claims amounted to little more than a "convenient slogan," however, and he sharply contested the right of National Liberals and Conservatives to its use. Baron von Stumm was terribly mistaken if he seriously thought national interests would be served by suppressing the working classes, the land reformer wrote in 1897. "[T]he system he represents is a system that must be overcome if a free, happy people is to become Germany's strength and her future," and it was a "high national duty" to oppose the Conservatives' proposals for a repressive law of association. "Let's show that we are truly national!"[84] Turning the tables on Stumm, Damaschke ruled reactionary interpretations of nationalism out of bounds, reserving its language instead as a means to address the concerns of those touched by the social impulse of his generation. After all, according to another article in the BDB journal, the deepest currents of patriotism were probably to be found in German workers, who expressed it as a profound willingness to accept sacrifice for the sake of their proletarian "brothers." Filtered through the distorting lens of Social Democracy, this collectivist ethos needed better focus, the author admitted, but its emotional appeal was much more genuine than the "hurrah-patriotism" of the middle classes, which, despite its flaws, was again merely another expression of the same supra-individual force. Both forms of "patriotism" had their strengths, the one "well-founded" in the people's hearts, the other "ambitious and lofty," and the article concluded

---

83. Adolf Damaschke, "Nationalitätenkampf," p. 468.

84. Adolf Damaschke, "Zum neuen Vereinsgesetz," *Deutsche Volksstimme* 2, no. 10 (May 20, 1897): 167.

with the hope that both forms might blend into a "higher unity," transcending the limitations of each on its own.[85]

Such progressive visions clearly owed much to the influence of Naumann. But the NSV leader had himself begun to stray onto the ground of militant nationalists, and it was in their clash over this issue that Damaschke first defined his own views on the uses and abuses of nationalism with precision. The conflict began in 1897, the same year the land reformer published his patriotic appeals against Stumm, when Naumann heartily endorsed plans for an ominous expansion of the German fleet and even suggested that Germany should be preparing for war with England in what claimed to be a National Social catechism. Outraged, Damaschke spelled out his own "moderate standpoint" on the meaning of 'social' and 'national' as editor of the NSV's only national mouthpiece other than *Assistance*. "The 'German People's Voice' views plans for a substantial strengthening of our fleet much more coolly than other currents in the National Social movement," he declared. While it "fully recognizes the importance of exports for the dynamic ascent of our working class," the paper "always stresses the overriding importance of the domestic market."[86] New colonies and a bigger navy would serve the interests only of a few millionaires, Damaschke complained, and German workers "will have to render taxes in blood and money for all this glitter, but can expect little improvement in their situation." "Issues of domestic policy, questions of social reform have brought us together; they are the unifying bond that holds us close together and through common endeavor will unite us ever more strongly," he concluded. "In issues of foreign policy, though, I think that we should first try together to find some unifying, general principles."[87]

The chance to define this common ground came at the NSV's annual congress in 1897, where Damaschke's analysis of the movement's conflicting national and social priorities added fuel to the dispute between Sohm and Göhre over relations with the proletariat.[88] Many of Göhre's sympathizers approached him during the conflict, praising his articles in the

85. Professor Pfannkuche, "Bürgerliche und proletarische Patriotismus," *Deutsche Volksstimme* 9, no. 14 (July 5, 1898): 406–10.
86. Damaschke, "An unsere Leser," *Deutsche Volksstimme* 2, no. 18 (September 20, 1897): 406–7.
87. Damaschke, *Zeitenwende*, pp. 97–98.
88. Düding, *Verein*, pp. 85–98.

German People's Voice and calling for a resolution that would commit the Association to land reform and thus to its *social* goals. Fearing a split in the movement, Damaschke decided to let tempers cool before elaborating his views in an 1898 pamphlet entitled "What Is National-Social?"[89] Stressing the importance of the NSV's domestic reform program, he now added his own proposals for tax and financial reform to the NSV's demands for increased suffrage, a more liberal law of association, additional workers' protection, and popular education.[90] At the same time, however, the land reformer emphasized that this social agenda in no way marked a departure from the Association's "national" goals, and he went to great lengths to smooth over his differences with Naumann. After all, he argued, military strength *was* a legitimate concern for any patriotic German, and Damaschke even found room in the National Socials' platform for an enlarged fleet—not one to match the strength of France, let alone England, but perhaps of third rank "right behind" the other two world powers.[91] Still, to achieve this goal, the loyalty and cooperation of the German people would be necessary. "Germany's foreign policy as a world power can be carried out only by exerting all the energies of our people," he declared: "Such an exertion is possible, however, only if it is sustained by the understanding of this people in its entirety, and the joyful cooperation that springs from it. It is thus a national imperative to educate the people more and more in this political understanding, and no other way leads there but an arrangement of our domestic affairs that is carried out honestly and in freedom."[92]

Social reform, in other words, made for nationalist "throngs." Battleships and colonies were expensive glitter that added to the misery of the sullen and oppressed masses unless they were sustained by a generous program of domestic reforms that would give the German people the strength, interest, and desire to support not only a thriving domestic economy, but even the most far-flung empire. Seen this way, the movement's national and social goals were pointing in the same direction: "Power and freedom and labor wrought tightly together, *these* provide the foundation on which Ger-

89. Damaschke, *Zeitenwende*, pp. 98–102.
90. Adolf Damaschke, *Was ist National-Sozial?* (Berlin: E. Kundt, 1898), passim.
91. Ibid., pp. 7–8.
92. Ibid., pp. 10–11.

man greatness can be securely built."[93] Here was a platform all of the Association's members could support, whether they were driven by the "politics of misery" or the ruthless calculations of *Realpolitik*. In the process of distancing himself from Naumann's disturbing enthusiasm for military adventures—though without severing his ties to this important ally—Damaschke had thus stumbled upon the magic formula that soon allowed him to portray land reform as Germany's ticket to a "place in the sun."

Land Reform as a "Task of Enlightenment"

> In a time when big business finds so many ways to influence public opinion it becomes the duty of the independent and honest individual to become a power in his own right, capable of serving the cause of organic progress through the quiet, but steady task of enlightenment.
>
> ADOLF DAMASCHKE

Emerging from his clashes with anti-Semites, Conservatives, and imperialists, Damaschke's "truly national" mission preserved the appeal of patriotic sentiments by defining them in the most inclusive terms possible. Equating 'the nation' with 'the people,' a phrase he interpreted as literally as he did 'the Father*land*,' the BDB leader insisted that Germany's security could be assured only by eliminating the suffering of *all* the people, regardless of class, confession, or gender. This very real threat to national interest stemmed from "objective" legal, economic, and hygienic factors, not "personal" enmity, and angry outbursts against Jews or striking workers did no more to confront it than battleships launched against foreign empires. In fact, such acts actually made matters worse, Damaschke argued, by diverting attention away from the modest, carefully targeted reforms that alone offered a practical solution to the country's problems. While he often played on popular manias, the land reformer also sought to dispel irrational fears stirred up by the "dishonesty" of "rhetorical mercenaries and fanatics," which might produce "easy, momentary victories," but which was "poisoning our public life in the most dangerous way." Rhetoric had "always given those who mastered it power over people," Damaschke warned, and he stressed the "heavy responsibility" it imposed

---

93. Ibid., p. 19.

on public speakers in two books devoted solely to questions of political style.[94]

"How is even a strong intellect and good will to distinguish what is true and false, substantial and incidental, in the noise of daily struggles?"[95] Politics seemed like a poor place to look for answers. "It is a crying shame to see the way party life clouds the judgment of men today," Damaschke groaned. "People who regularly hear only one side of things presented by the press, in clubs, in the company of societal intercourse, must at last come to see in the adherents of the opposing parties only bad people or, granting mitigating circumstances, blockheads."[96] Outlining the tasks of communal policy at the turn of the century, he therefore urged "the greatest non-partisanship" in choosing books for public libraries: "anyone in such a reading hall who by chance, perhaps reluctantly at first, picks up an article by the opposing camp and reads it will soon discover that in political, social, and religious matters too 'one man's view is no one's view,' will learn to judge argument and counter-argument independently, will attain a broader perspective and a freer judgment."[97]

Sharing the "unpolitical" views of many of his contemporaries, Damaschke thus defined his cause as a "task of enlightenment" that would liberate the German people from narrow, partisan interests by enabling an informed and rational public to take charge of the nation's future. "Show me a community's school, and I will tell you what that community is worth!" he demanded, condemning the lack of access to free learning materials and the poor hygienic conditions of Germany's public schools.[98] In the BDB's public seminar series and in his two-volume *History of National Economics*, Damaschke also continued his efforts at popular education in hopes of providing his followers with the "comprehensive knowledge" of social conditions they would need to defend the League from political agitators on the right and left. "The land reform movement—despite its inadequate, but now historically given name—will be a social-scientific comprehensive view," he declared in 1899. "It wishes to take its place with

94. Damaschke, *Volkstümliche Redekunst,* pp. 3, 86–87. See also Damaschke, *Geschichte der Redekunst: Eine erste Einführung* (Jena: Fischer, 1921).

95. Damaschke, *Volkstümliche Redekunst,* p. 21.

96. Damaschke, "Sechzehn Jahre," p. 416.

97. Damaschke, *Aufgaben,* p. 38.

98. Ibid., pp. 9, 31.

equal rights next to the old grand views: individualism and communism, and to win respect and authority next to those views and even further beyond."[99] Seeking to preserve what was best in the two progressive ideologies, land reform also sought to transcend their "one-sided" concerns, and the BDB leader devoted considerable space in his critique of modernity to a scathing review of each.

"Neither Mammonism nor Communism"

If on the right Damaschke's "social-scientific" repudiation of partisan dogma denied Stumm's claim to the term 'national,' his unmasking of capitalist greed and hypocrisy produced similar findings on the left. "This view is often unjustly called 'liberal,'" the land reformer concluded in an analysis of "Manchesterism," reducing the creed to a mishmash of select bits of classical economics soured by an unhealthy dose of Malthusian and Spencerian pessimism.[100] Ignoring Adam Smith's warnings about "a class that generally has an interest in deceiving and oppressing the public," the Liberals also overlooked errors in Malthus's faulty extrapolations, which failed to take cultural factors into account. "The wealthy and powerful are satisfied with this wisdom, however, because it absolves those who bear the responsibility for all the blame."[101] Yet the historical guilt of German liberalism was hard to ignore. Playing the card of lost opportunities, Damaschke claimed that the Liberals' rejection of Lassalle's overtures in the 1860s demonstrated a "complete inability . . . to bring about even the slightest advance and security for the idea of freedom."[102] When worker-soldiers returned from the wars of "external unification" a few years later, they found the country torn between a "housing shortage and mass misery on one hand, excessive lust for pleasure on the other" in the Liberal Era.[103] "Our people disintegrated ever more into two nations divided by different world-views and different theories of state, celebrating different festivals,

99. Adolf Damaschke, "Was will die Bodenreform-Bewegung?" *Deutsche Volksstimme* 10, no. 1 (January 5, 1899): 1.

100. Damaschke, *Bodenreform,* p. 18.

101. Damaschke, *Nationalökonomie,* vol. 1, p. 397; Damaschke, *Bodenreform,* p. 24.

102. Damaschke, *Nationalökonomie,* vol. 2, p. 150.

103. Ibid., vol. 1, p. 61.

and carrying different ideals in their hearts," Damaschke sighed.[104] The patriotism of 1871 turned into bitterness, resentment, and Social Democratic agitation, and the cynical defenders of "self-help" had no one to blame but themselves: "To limit the duties of state and community to those of night watchman, 'to prevent gross misdemeanors and disturbing of the peace,' those are the contents of the theory of 'Manchesterism' and where it comes to power its practice as well."[105]

Such views inevitably provoked cries of "Social Democracy in disguise" in some quarters,[106] and Damaschke himself once admitted he was striving "to create a socialism capable of governing in Germany."[107] But the land reformer insisted that the Marxists bore their own share of the blame for the country's current political and social tensions. "They have it easy, as everyone knows: Berlepsch and Puttkamer, Freese and Stumm—*one* reactionary mass!" he grumbled, after Social Democratic leaders refused to join their bourgeois counterparts in a labor-relations initiative that culminated with the founding of the Society for Social Reform in 1900.[108] The demand for a clean separation of the two classes had in fact sparked a quarrel with Mehring that destroyed their friendship shortly after Damaschke began exploring the Wilhelmine reform milieu in the early 1890s, and while he continued to engage in a constructive dialogue with Bebel, Liebknecht, and Auer, the land reformer refused to condone the Marxist strategy of class struggle.[109] The belief in violent revolution was no more realistic than the myopic self-delusion of German liberals, the land reformer argued, and Marxists found themselves in the sad company of utopian dreamers like Saint-Simon and Fourier in his *History of National Economics*, where they chase after fantasies of a socialist paradise rooted in the same yearnings as the "legends of a Golden Age, with which the history

104. Damaschke, *Zeitenwende,* p. 54.

105. Damaschke, *Nationalökonomie,* vol. 1., pp. 448–49.

106. Damaschke, "Kampf um Moabit," p. 676.

107. Adolf Damaschke, "An die Leser!" *Deutsche Volksstimme* 2, no. 12 (June 20, 1897): 230.

108. Adolf Damaschke, "Ein Fehler Berlepschs?," *Deutsche Volksstimme* 10, no. 10 (May 20, 1899): 290.

109. Damaschke, *Leben,* pp. 202–3; Damaschke, *Zeitenwende,* pp. 218–23; Damaschke, "Ignaz Auer," *Bodenreform* 18, no. 8 (April 20, 1907): 216–17.

of every nation begins."[110] Awakening futile aspirations in the lower classes, the spectre of class warfare had also condemned the entire German people to decades of political impotence in the wake of 1848. "Was it any wonder that broad segments of the middle class fled back to the masters of the old system in order to exchange their political freedom for the security of their property?"[111]

Damaschke regretted the absence of Germany's bourgeois revolution as much as any historian in later years, and despite his attacks on Manchesterism he defended personal liberty as the one "great legacy of the liberal era" that had to be preserved at all costs.[112] No friend of the night watchman's state, the land reformer thus found Kautsky's visions of the "future state" even more alarming. "There will be no issue that cannot and will not be brought into some relation to the 'planned regulation' of production," he wrote. "On the *Day after the Revolution* victorious communism will—perhaps not want, but certainly have to—be the end of personal freedom."[113] Even the venerable Germanic tradition of *Allmende* seemed dubious in light of the modern state's powers of intervention, which Damaschke insisted must be curtailed, and he firmly opposed the full-scale reintroduction of communal property. "Given the way things are, after all, the power of municipal bureaucracy would be considerably strengthened, the real or imaginary dependency . . . of large groups of people on city hall and the tendencies that happen to dominate there at any given moment would increase," he observed, "developments that most certainly must give rise to serious reservations of many kinds."[114] Democracy seemed a far more promising way to achieve social justice: "The general interest of the community will remain secure in the long run only when each and every member of the community has the right and the duty to speak out and take action."[115] Denouncing the government's conservative "tutelage" over a powerless Reichstag and Prussia's oppressive three-class voting system, Damaschke called for proportional representation on the basis of universal

110. Damaschke, *Nationalökonomie*, vol. 2, pp. 84, 99–103.
111. Ibid., p. 124.
112. Damaschke, *Zeitenwende*, p. 168.
113. Damaschke, *Bodenreform*, pp. 42–47.
114. Damaschke, *Aufgaben*, pp. 118–19; Damaschke, *Bodenreform*, p. 182.
115. Damaschke, *Aufgaben*, p. 2.

suffrage and the secret ballot.[116] "In an atmosphere of greater political freedom, the developments of the last 70 years would doubtlessly have taken place with less friction," he believed, "and the separation of individual social classes and their cultural values would not have had to take such a harsh and abrupt form—as the example of England proves."[117]

The acrimonious climate of German politics had driven both sides to untenable extremes. While the "Manchester people" approached every issue from a "predator's viewpoint," the Social Democrats were rushing to build "a great society-machine, in which the individual is a cog and nothing more," and neither met the genuine needs of the people, "in whom social and individual elements unite." The "conditions of human coexistence must not be constructed in a one-sidedly individualistic, not in a one-sidedly socialist manner," Damaschke proclaimed: "Not Mammonism and not Communism, but instead social justice and personal freedom!"[118]

"Organic Progress"

Land reform was a "task of enlightenment" not only because it represented a "social-scientific" alternative to the irrational political dogmas of the day, but also because it shared the progressive parties' emancipatory impulse toward "liberty, equality, and fraternity." Despite his jarring contrasts between medieval idylls and current ills, Damaschke fervently embraced what seemed to him the essential promise of modernity. Not ninety years had passed since the first locomotive whistle blew in Germany, the BDB leader had noted in the first lines of "Neither Mammonism nor Communism," yet in that time the nation had transformed the landscape, turning steam and electricity into "our untiring slaves," while "iron serfs" had released the German people from back-breaking tasks of physical labor to enjoy higher culture, recreation, and leisure. If in spite of all this the "misery that destroys body and soul" had yet to "become a shadow of the past as a mass phenomenon," the fault was not in progress, but in the failure to adapt to these new realities in order to realize the vast potential they con-

---

116. Ibid., pp. 4–8; Damaschke, "Vormund?" pp. 225–27.

117. Damaschke, *Nationalökonomie,* vol. 2, p. 124.

118. Damaschke, "Was will die Bodenreform-Bewegung?" p. 3; Damaschke, *Bodenreform,* p. 56.

tained.[119] "New things have come into being—new things must and will come into being!" he insisted, and those who prided themselves in remaining "steadfast" in outmoded ways would be swept aside.[120]

The land reformer thus refused to pander to reactionary agendas, even among the urban artisans whose support he cherished. There was not a craftsman's shop in Germany that would not benefit from the introduction of electric motors, Damaschke wrote, singling out the artisans' movement for particular scolding; "whether or not they are able to make use of the *advantages of modern technology* will be a question of survival for many branches of the handicraft trades." Yet in order to do this, the younger generation needed to attend the new technical colleges, and the campaign to reinstate the masters' traditional monopoly on training apprentices in compulsory guilds was therefore both "injurious" and "short-sighted."[121] As important as the survival of Germany's "modern trades industry" was, Damaschke also realized that the nation's future lay elsewhere: "Anyone who has recognized the importance of the growing industrial population for our national life must also desire the ever greater participation of this abundant segment of our population in our cultural life for nationalist reasons," he proclaimed, echoing Naumann's Darwinian arguments for the new liberalism.[122] "A nation that wants to maintain its position in the struggle of competition cannot engage in the exploitation of its own national strength."[123]

Damaschke's critique of present-day modernity greeted the productive force of commerce and industry, provided that society adapted to it with more efficient forms of labor relations, but—again like the *New German Economic Policy*—it also expressed a firm conviction that the modernity of the future would depart from the nineteenth-century visions of progress in important ways. If "freedom" had been the battle cry of past decades, "socialization" had taken its place in the progressive struggles of the day.[124] A casual phrase in his call for popular education reveals Damaschke's sense

---

119. Damaschke, *Bodenreform,* p. 1.
120. Damaschke, "Unentwegt," *Deutsche Volksstimme* 1, no. 24 (November 22, 1896): 250–51.
121. Damaschke, *Aufgaben,* pp. 81–84, emphasis in the original.
122. Damaschke, *Bodenreform,* p. 169.
123. Damaschke, "Fehler?" p. 291.
124. Damaschke, *Nationalökonomie,* vol. 1, p. 443.

of the shape of things to come more clearly than an explicit definition might—"truly modern, that is social viewpoints."[125] Land reform was not only the most "patriotic" but also "the most modern social movement";[126] and if the communalist impulse of Germanic traditions seemed "reactionary" to the old-fashioned adherents of laissez-faire liberalism, from the perspective of this alternative modernity, it pointed toward a future situated between the extremes of right and left. Describing cooperative credit associations like the Raiffeisen Society as a "modern *Allmende*,"[127] the land reformer also quoted Otto von Gierke in defense of the BDB's campaign for German homesteads. "If the advocates of Germanic law are accused again and again by their opponents . . . of pushing for a return to the justice of the middle ages, they know very well themselves that only *fools* attempt to revive extinct forms of existence," the Berlin professor wrote Damaschke in 1912. "But Germanic law is not dead. It lives and is rich enough in creative energy to bring forth new forms in which the entire content of modern existence can be secured, and in which the goal of *Kultur* can be channeled in the ever deeper and broader current of the future."[128]

The "creative energy to bring forth new life forms" that Gierke discovered in the living tradition of Germanic cooperative law reveals another way in which visions of modernity had advanced beyond the lumbering, mechanical progress of the previous century. As a social theorist of emergent vitalism, the famous law professor helped to disseminate the popular belief in a collective organic life force that Damaschke also used to situate land reform on the cutting edge of future developments. Despite his disdain for the "predator's viewpoint" of Spencerian Darwinism, the BDB leader often turned to naturalistic models such as Friedrich Ratzel's "anthropogeography" as a scientific justification for land reform in the evolutionary struggles of the people, describing the state as an "autochthonous organism" and echoing the Leipzig professor's calls for a "rooting of the nation in the soil through the labor of the individual and the whole on common ground."[129] The "development of modern hygienic science" made it a "duty of communities either to ensure sufficient bathing facilities or

125. Damaschke, *Aufgaben,* p. 37.
126. Damaschke, *Bodenreform,* p. 246.
127. Damaschke, *Nationalökonomie,* vol. 2, p. 419.
128. Damaschke, *Bodenreform,* p. 228, emphasis in the original.
129. Damaschke, "Wesen," p. 554–55.

to bestow ample funding to municipal associations that serve these purposes," he wrote in the *Tasks of Communal Policy,* which demanded a wide range of environmental reforms, including health inspectors and public subsidies for family gardens to ensure the physical and spiritual well-being of the nation.[130] Quoting again from Gierke in the first days of the homestead campaign, the BDB leader appealed to the healing powers of organic reform: "thus we rejuvenate our life force and may hope to remain strong and great enough to prevent the social revolution through social reform."[131]

·　　·　　·

Biological models seemed to represent the wave of the future in Wilhelmine Germany, and Damaschke was hardly alone in promoting "organic progress through the quiet, but steady task of enlightenment."[132] A progressive blend of national economics and biology proved equally alluring to Bäumer, who struggled to integrate women into the "organic community" of the German nation, and who saw "eugenics" as a means to improve the quality of the race. Yet at the same time she warned about the potential for brutal inhumanity lurking in "objective" science and the mechanizing trends of industrial *Zivilisation,* which she feared would strangle the living tradition of German *Kultur.* The daughter of a prosperous bourgeois family, Bäumer expressed aesthetic sensibilities quite foreign to the artisan's son Damaschke, and questions of tactics also kept the two reformers personally worlds apart. But her answers to the social question emerged from the same circles and bore the same stamp—along with similar challenges of interpretation and a fresh perspective on the common milieu in which both lived and worked.

---

130. Damaschke, *Aufgaben,* pp. 29–30, 124, 161–71, 199.
131. Damaschke, "Heimstättenrecht?" p. 91.
132. Damaschke, *Bodenreform,* p. x.

Gertrud Bäumer's New Liberalism
and the Politics of Womanhood

If Damaschke and his "truly national" mission have been forgotten, Gertrud Bäumer figures more prominently in recent histories of women and gender, where her election in 1910 as chairwoman of the League of German Women's Associations (*Bund Deutscher Frauenvereine,* or BDF) often appears as a decisive moment in the bourgeois feminist movement. Mapping out the conflicts between "moderates" and "radicals" that culminated in Bäumer's election, pioneering studies by Richard Evans and Barbara Greven-Aschoff initially described the collapse of the movement's "left wing" in the first decade of the twentieth century as a portentous shift to the right.[1] Evans in particular noted the turn from "liberal individualism," which had inspired a brief, but "genuine liberal revival" under radical predominance at the turn of the century, and both scholars viewed the sudden influx of biological, racial, and "Social Darwinist" themes into feminist views at this moment as an alarming foretoken of things to come.[2] Perhaps most disturbing in this context were the maternalist and "service ideologies" disseminated by Wilhelmine feminists, who stopped demanding emancipation as a natural right and turned instead to strategies focusing on women's contributions to the German nation conceived in terms of "feminine" qualities such as "motherliness" and "caring" that were to heal the physical, moral, and spiritual ills of modernity. The idea of national service merely reinforced militarist traditions that reduced rights to rewards and "dismissed . . . the hope that women could battle successfully

---

1. Richard Evans, *The Feminist Movement in Germany 1894–1933* (London: SAGE, 1976), pp. 150–69; Greven-Aschoff, *Frauenbewegung,* pp. 106–15.
2. Evans, *Movement,* pp. x, 1, 167–68; Greven-Aschoff, *Frauenbewegung,* pp. 105, 267.

against the current of the times," Greven-Aschoff argued, while the "hy-postatization of the concept of womanhood" had its roots in "an under-lying critique of society with features of cultural pessimism that had already come to light before 1914 but did not come into full relief until after the First World War."[3] Finally, in her devastating exposé *Mothers in the Fatherland,* Claudia Koonz asserted that the Nazi idealization of women's domestic roles in fact realized "nineteenth-century feminists' view of the future in nightmare form."[4]

More recently, however, historians have begun to emphasize the ambiv-alence surrounding the collectivist and maternalist politics of the fin de siècle, which were "harnessed to forge improbable coalitions" across the political spectrum in countries as diverse as Sweden and Australia, France and the United States, sustaining reform initiatives that according to Seth Koven and Sonya Michel still "remain important expressions of the sub-versive potential of claims based on the social and economic value of moth-erhood joined to women's freedom to define for themselves their relation-ships to family and work force."[5] Contesting a reactionary trajectory for maternalist discourse in the German case, Ann Taylor Allen has similarly stressed its protean ability to encompass an astonishingly wide range of views and agendas. "In the nineteenth century, the concept of motherhood was constantly developed and reconstituted in different contexts and by different speakers," she argues. "Though never free of constraint, women can thus create alternative views of the world by exposing the contradic-tions and exploiting the unexplored possibilities of dominant discourse."[6] While not losing sight of the dangers lurking in the convergence of eugen-icist and maternalist discourses at the turn of the century, Kathleen Can-ning's pathbreaking study *Languages of Labor and Gender* amply demon-strates how "the focus on women's biological functions, rights, and duties helped to forge bonds across the boundaries of class" in Wilhelmine Ger-many, enabling a "rich array of feminist contributors to the debates" on the social question "to dissect critically and cleverly the disparaging rheto-

---

3. Greven-Aschoff, *Frauenbewegung,* pp. 41, 93; see also Evans, *Movement,* p. 9.
4. Claudia Koonz, *Mothers in the Fatherland:Women, Family, and Nazi Politics* (New York: St. Martin's Press, 1987), p. 31.
5. Seth Koven and Sonya Michel, "Introduction: 'Mother Worlds,' "in Koven and Michel, eds., *Mothers of a New World:Maternalist Politics and the Origins of Welfare States* (New York: Routledge, 1993), pp. 5, 31.
6. Allen, *Feminism,* p. 11; see also pp. 7–8, 230–39.

ric of conservative male reformers" in bourgeois and socialist circles alike. "Feminist activists thus came to occupy a pivotal place within the expanding public sphere and increasingly complex fabric of reform associations between the turn of the century and the First World War."[7]

Far from marking a retreat into the traditional realms of home and family life, maternalist discourse was often translated into calls for "bringing feminine qualities into the public sphere" that created new roles for women as factory inspectors, social hygienists, educators, and specialists in child and juvenile care and thus represented "an important (but subsequently neglected) site of public policy and, ultimately state formation" throughout Europe and the United States.[8] While one scholar has argued that Imperial Germany's "bureaucratic apparatus" presented a "formidable barrier" to such "grassroots pressure," contemporary advocates of feminine anti-politics like Alice Salomon believed that it was precisely in this sphere, among civil servants and other "practical men of the world," that women could achieve the most success.[9] By the end of the nineteenth century, proliferating reform initiatives and associations had in fact fragmented municipal welfare into a bewildering collage of overlapping authorities and projects full of opportunities for Salomon's students, who were alone able to demonstrate the rare professional qualifications needed for positions in a new system of rationalized social and health services that was beginning to emerge—again through private initiatives—before the First World War.[10]

If the focus on motherhood and service in many cases no longer seems to be an unequivocal expression of cultural despair, scholarly recognition of its role in forming modern welfare states has evoked different concerns in the more critical perspectives on the Enlightenment and its legacy of

---

7. Canning, *Languages,* pp. 190, 212.

8. Linda Clark, "Bringing Feminine Qualities into the Public Sphere: The Third Republic's Appointment of Women Inspectors," in Elinor Accampo et. al, *Gender and the Politics of Social Reform in France, 1870–1914* (Baltimore: Johns Hopkins University Press, 1995), pp. 128–56; Koven and Michel, "Introduction," p. 6.

9. Jean Quataert, "Women's Work and the Early Welfare State in Germany: Legislators, Bureaucrats, and Clients before the First World War," in Koven and Michel, eds., *Mothers,* p. 167; Canning, *Languages,* p. 178.

10. Sachße, *Mütterlichkeit,* pp. 70–95, 141–45.

recent years. Although Allen continues to see potential for resisting the dehumanizing impact of instrumental rationality in the bourgeois feminists' ideology of "caring," others have followed Christoph Sachße in finding an "inner contradiction" between the humanistic moral impulses behind the drive for motherhood as a career and the professionalizing side effects that inevitably made the movement a victim of its own success.[11] "The idea of professional helping in a modern society suffered from intrinsic structural contradictions," Young-Sun Hong argues, "because the same modernizing forces which had led to the creation of a vast, highly bureaucratized and rationalized welfare system were destroying those patterns of social interaction in traditional face-to-face communities upon which the idea of social pedagogy as friendly helping was modeled." In their insistence that authentic social work drew its strength from the "vital forces" of maternalist devotion, progressive feminists like Salomon and Marie Baum had correctly diagnosed the crisis of German welfare in the final years of the Republic, Hong believes. "But they failed to realize that the development of the profession was itself an integral dimension of this modernizing process and, consequently, they were mistaken to believe that their idea of helping and the quest for national community could be fulfilled if they could only free social work from these external impediments."[12]

As a major theorist of the politics of womanhood and a leading cultural critic, Gertrud Bäumer lived near the center of the rich and complex world this flourishing scholarship has begun to unfold. "As the essential nature of the technical-capitalist age unmasked itself, the origin, meaning, and purpose of our movement became increasingly clear to us," she later remembered.[13] "We saw a gigantic, automatic mechanism dominating human affairs, everywhere enslaving life, and ever more stealing its personal values from the existence of millions." Yet rather than fleeing into cultural despair, Bäumer encouraged her colleagues to recognize the promise of modern technology, which she believed would bring forth a "bright re-

---

11. Ann Taylor Allen, "The Holocaust and the Modernization of Gender: A Historiographical Essay," *Central European History* 30, no. 3 (1997): 359–64; Sachße, *Mütterlichkeit*, pp. 305–11.

12. Young-Sun Hong, "Gender, Citizenship, and the Welfare State: Social Work and the Politics of Femininity in the Weimar Republic," *Central European History* 30, no. 1 (1997): 15, 18, 20–21.

13. Bäumer, *Lebensweg*, p. 224.

naissance of industry," and endorsed "scientific" demands for "racial reform." Joining the founders of the Progressive People's Party in 1910, the BDF leader tried to extend Naumann's new liberalism to include women as well as workers and to channel their energies into the formation of an efficient and powerful national community. Like Damaschke, Bäumer thus understood her efforts as an "integral dimension" of the "modernizing process" but believed they were guiding it between the extremes of remorseless progress and nostalgic reaction toward alternative modernities, an expectation firmly rooted in the hopes and fears of her generation.

Forged in reformist circles of the spring thaw and tempered by fin-de-siècle clashes between radicals and moderates, Bäumer's new liberalism and politics of womanhood took a salient position in the bourgeois women's movement in 1910. Her early career belongs equally to the histories of German liberalism, the gendering of the public sphere, and the search for alternative modernities, which were so closely intertwined before the First World War. Let us retrace this path, which promises to shed some new light on each, as we continue to explore the possibilities and limits of the world of Wilhelmine anti-politics.

From Family Life to the Life of the Nation

Born in Hohenlimburg, a small city in the Sauerland, on September 12, 1873, Bäumer grew up in a world remote from the rental barracks of Damaschke's youth. Her father, a Protestant minister and a dedicated National Liberal on good terms with Prussian Minister of Culture Adalbert Falk, accepted a post as district school inspector in the Pomeranian town of Cammin when Gertrud was three years old, taking the family from its Westphalian roots to serve as a "pioneer" in Falk's attempts to force reform of religious instruction on *Junker* and peasants in the conservative bastions of the East.[14] While Pastor Bäumer's career was thus enmeshed in the bitter struggles that soon brought an end to the Liberal Era, Gertrud had little exposure to this public strife, which was not allowed to invade the sanctity of their bourgeois home, an idyll of domestic tranquillity as it appears in her memoirs. Instead, the comforting figure of her mother was "present like the sun or the lamp or the four walls . . . It was taken for granted that

---

14. Ibid., pp. 8–10.

she was there, when getting up and washing, for the breakfast milk, the clean shirt, the dry socks, for everything internal and external, from morning until evening. That went without saying, it was a piece of my life."[15] Secure in this environment, she spent her time exploring nature in the surrounding countryside, an experience of almost religious intensity providing the most vivid impressions of her childhood.[16] Yet inevitably the outside world intruded, shattering this interlude of romantic seclusion, and—like Lily Braun in her aristocratic refuge—Bäumer was forced to confront the grim realities of life in Bismarck's Empire.

Exhausted by his battles with the local gentry, Pastor Bäumer finally retreated to western Germany in 1882, where he died a year later at the age of thirty-six, and his young widow took the family home to live with her mother in Halle. For the next six years Gertrud lived under the austere supervision of her maternal grandmother, who presided over an extended family of cousins and in-laws living in the patrician household of a long line of prominent civil servants. Though often critical, Bäumer's memories of this sternly regimented existence foreshadow the social awakening of her generation. "Individualism is excluded there of its own accord," she wrote of the experience. "External and internal order become an almost technical compulsion, like the cycles of nature. It occurs to no one to resist, the structure of life takes on something objective, an obvious certainty, in which caprice has no place and thus does not incite any resistance at all. Therein lies the great power of these very non-personal forms; their yoke is gentle."[17] Bäumer could hardly learn to understand the social question in the private schools to which her grandmother sent her, however, and it was only after the family moved to Magdeburg, where her mother took a job in her uncle's medical clinic in 1888, that she came to appreciate the "factual exclusivity of our previous existence." Shocked by conditions among the working classes of this industrializing city, Bäumer began reading Christian Social literature and taught Sunday School in a local "proletarian congregation" while studying for a career in education.[18]

Despite their distant points of origin, the narratives conveyed by the memoirs of the land reformer and the feminist thus begin to converge

---

15. Ibid., p. 10.
16. Ibid., pp. 11–24.
17. Ibid., p. 55.
18. Ibid., pp. 92–96.

early on. After passing her State Exams in 1890, Bäumer accepted a position at a public school in Westphalia, where the "first phase of heavy industrial development" was introducing the "ugly, bare, smoke-blackened" rental barracks. "Common staircases and toilets made the struggle for customary cleanliness fruitless, the strewing of paper and garbage made the desolate earth around the desolate houses into a shrine of disorder," she wrote of the consequences. "The privacy of the family . . . sank hopelessly into a collective existence. Women grew accustomed to breast-feeding their children on the steps or before the front door, completely out in the open."[19] Listening to arguments between conservative Christian Socials and Liberals committed to self-help, the young teacher began to make sense out of the debates over social policy. While she found the "inflammatory character" of Stöcker's "intense anti-Semitism" repulsive, she was impressed with the "earnestness" of a local speech in which he "blamed bourgeois Christian society for the development of the social question and the increasing strength of Social Democracy," an insight that led her to explore the works of the younger Christian Socials after moving back to Magdeburg-Neustadt to teach in a public girls' school in 1894.[20] Frustrated by the "proletarian animosity and class hatred" of her students' families, Bäumer turned to Naumann and Harnack for a more realistic analysis of the social and economic causes of this tension. And like Damaschke, whose social education was leading him along a parallel route to the same decision in Berlin and Kiel, she soon chose to sacrifice the financial security of a teaching career to devote her energies entirely to the cause of social unity: "I could not just stand there while spiritual and social realities posed their unavoidable questions."[21]

Into the Women's Movement

Bäumer's introduction to the social question coincided with her introduction to the "women's question," and while she gave up teaching to follow Naumann's lead in studying the social sciences, the decision simultaneously spelled her commitment to join the women's movement, which seemed to offer immediate opportunities to begin working for social peace through

19. Ibid., pp. 112–13.
20. Ibid., pp. 120–25.
21. Ibid., pp. 127–34.

practical reform.[22] Refashioning the movement in the 1890s, Wilhelmine feminists looked to the same national economic perspectives young Germans were seeking throughout the reform milieu and saw their efforts as part of the general response to the social question, a link leading representatives of this "new direction" reinforced by taking important roles in key institutions outside the women's movement.[23] Thus, for instance, Elisabeth-Gnauck Kühne defended the interests of female factory workers in detailed studies on the "women's question of the fourth estate" inspired by the younger Christian Socials, regularly spoke at the Protestant Social Congress, and joined Naumann and Göhre as a founding member of the National Social Association.[24] Jeanette Schwerin, who studied national economics at the University of Berlin, was vice-chair of the Society for Ethical Culture, where she founded a Center for Private Assistance aimed at consolidating Berlin's diverse welfare programs, wrote proposals for improving women's working conditions, and helped support the textile workers' strike, while in the BDF she set up commissions for female factory inspectors and the protection of female workers.[25]

It was thus hardly surprising that Bäumer joined the movement at the precise moment she was beginning to read Naumann and his colleagues and deciding to move to Berlin to resume her studies. As a Magdeburg delegate to the General Association of German Female Teachers conference in 1897 (just months after Damaschke made a similar move onto the national stage at Erfurt), Bäumer felt a powerful sense of joining in the patriotic struggle for social unity. "In this meeting, where Bavarian and East

---

22. Ibid., pp. 120–25, 127–34, 178–80.

23. Canning, *Languages*, pp. 137–44; Sachße, *Mütterlichkeit*, pp. 9, 105–25; Greven-Aschoff, *Frauenbewegung*, p. 78; Gertrud Bäumer, "Die Geschichte der Frauenbewegung in Deutschland" in Helene Lange et al., *Handbuch der Frauenbewegung* (Berlin: W. Moeser, 1901), vol. 1, pp. 122–30. Helene Lange, *Lebenserinnerungen* (Berlin: F. A. Herbig, 1921), pp. 228–29.

24. Canning, *Languages*, pp. 158–60; Lange, *Lebenserinnerungen*, pp. 228–29; Göhre, *Bewegung*, p. 162; Ute Gerhard, *Unerhört: Die Geschichte der deutschen Frauenbewegung* (Hamburg: Rowohlt Taschenbuch Verlag, 1990), p. 203; invitation to the NSV founding congress, *Hilfe* 2, no. 42 (October 18, 1896).

25. Sachße, *Mütterlichkeit*, pp. 94, 122–25; "Jeanette Schwerin," *Centralblatt des Bundes deutscher Frauenvereine* 1, no. 10 (August 15, 1899): 33–37; Bäumer, "Geschichte der Frauenbewegung," pp. 121–22; Gerhard, *Unerhört*, pp. 236–38.

Prussian, Westphalian and Saxon were spoken, we experienced our calling and our spiritual existence in a *German* context," she later remembered. "A new meaning flowed into the German anthem as we sang it there: the knowledge that we did not belong to the nation as individuals, but through our common efforts were a complete part of the life of the nation, that in the combined efforts of its energies we had our own purpose, which had grown organically from our womanhood."[26] Bäumer met several leaders of the movement at the Leipzig conference, but she was particularly impressed by Helene Lange, and after moving to Berlin the following year she volunteered to become her assistant.

Weaving together national economic and biological arguments to call for the integration of women's special nature into the public sphere, Lange had done much to revitalize the movement as a moderate voice in the new direction, and by the time Bäumer met her she held seats in the executive committees of the female teachers' Association, the General German Women's Association, and the BDF. Lange's attempt to ground appeals for emancipation in a "scientific" theory of womanhood went back to her famous 1887 *Yellow Brochure,* in which she won national fame by denouncing her male colleagues' perception of women's education as a means to supply German men with scintillating intellectual conversation. After helping to launch the female teachers' Association in 1890 and introducing high school courses for women three years later, the moderate leader founded her own journal, *The Woman,* in which she began disseminating her views in 1893.[27] "National consciousness to this day remains male consciousness. This arises from the simple fact alone that man is never, woman always the object of inspection," she complained. "Man is for himself humanity *par excellence.* He is the bearer of culture, he gives the standards with which woman is measured."[28] Sharing her journal with the popular Darwinists Bölsche and Büchner (who refuted anti-feminist claims about the size of women's brains), Lange argued that the "biological fact" of motherhood as a natural "calling" elicited a "physical and psychological singularity" in women that could substantially improve public life

---

26. Bäumer, *Lebensweg,* p. 141.

27. Allen, *Feminism,* pp. 121–26; Gerhard, *Unerhört,* pp. 146–47.

28. Helene Lange, "Intellektuelle Grenzlinien zwischen Mann und Frau," *Frau* 4, no. 6 (March 1897): 321.

precisely because it eluded male norms.[29] While bearing children was an important contribution, the nurturing energies in feminine nature had potential applications far beyond the home, in social and health services, education, and municipal welfare administration, where women who never became mothers in a physical sense could perform vital functions, and she therefore demanded an "organic division of labor" that would allow "both sexes [to] achieve the free development of their abilities and exercise their full duties in the service of humanity."[30]

Lange's conception of the feminist mission had a deep, though mixed impact on the movement around the turn of the century. On the one hand, her translation of the message of social integration into maternalist terms resonated strongly in radical and moderate circles, both of which were influenced by the socialists of the lectern, the national economic boys, and the progressive circles around Naumann,[31] and it eventually found a place in the BDF's 1907 platform:

> The women's movement wishes to secure for women the free development of all their energies and full participation in cultural life. It recognizes that the sexes differ in nature and in duties, and precisely for that reason it is convinced that culture only becomes richer, more valuable, and more lively when men and women work together more for the solution to all cultural problems. . . . Recognizing that the welfare of the general public can only prosper when all available forces make contributions to it, the women's movement considers it one of its most noble tasks to open the world of public life to the motherly influence.[32]

On the other hand, the radicals soon became impatient with Lange's anti-political approach to women's emancipation, which emphasized the need for professional training and institutional frameworks that would provide

---

29. Ibid., pp. 325–26; Ludwig Büchner, "Das Gehirn der Frau," *Frau* 1, no. 5 (February 1894): 308; Wilhelm Bölsche, "Naturwissenschaft und Mädchenerziehung," *Frau* 1, no. 2 (November 1893): 73–79; Bölsche, "Die Studentin und der ideale Geist unserer Universitäten," *Frau* 1, no. 10 (July 1894): 647–52; Bölsche, "Neue Entdeckungen zur Urgeschichte der Frau," *Frau* 2, no. 1 (October 1894): 11.

30. Helene Lange, "Was wir wollen," *Frau* 1, no. 1 (October 1893): 2.

31. Greven-Aschoff, *Frauenbewegung,* pp. 94–96.

32. Quoted in Gerhard, *Unerhört,* pp. 147–48.

access to influential posts in public administration at the municipal, state, and federal levels without provoking competition with men over existing jobs. While acknowledging the importance of a parallel process of political emancipation, the moderate leader's focus on the narrow details of pedagogical and social reform seemed to be "Sisyphus labor" in the eyes of radicals like Minna Cauer, Anita Augspurg, and Lida Gustava Heymann, who sought to attract attention to the movement's political goals by using more confrontational tactics inspired by the British suffragettes.[33]

Bäumer initially shared this sense of frustration when she arrived in Berlin only to be assigned to research the background on disability insurance for private female teachers, a dreary chore "in which nothing at all could be seen of what obliged me to [Lange] and bound me to her cause." Yet Bäumer was soon convinced that the movement's success depended on knowing the empirical "details of social reality" as well as its "metaphysical depths."[34] Continuing to assist Lange while studying at the Victoria Lyceum and the University, the young activist became her protégé, and from the summer of 1899 the two women lived and worked together, sharing the same "path of life" until Lange's death thirty years later.[35] With the moderate leader's support, Bäumer assumed a prominent role in the movement, joining the executive committee of the female teachers' Association in 1899 and publishing frequently in *The Woman,* for which she gradually took over the editorial duties after the turn of the century. Co-editing a four-volume *Handbook of the Women's Movement* that appeared in 1901, Bäumer and Lange jointly organized panels on pedagogical issues for the International Congress of Women held in Berlin in 1904, and two years later the young star led an important campaign for Prussian girls' school reform that won her the editorship of *New Pathways,* the official newspaper of the General German Women's Association, and a seat on the BDF's executive committee in 1907.

Despite her allegiance to Lange, however, Bäumer continued to share many of the radicals' concerns about propagating the movement's grand objectives, and in exploring possibilities for activism in the movement during these years she tried to define her position in a way that took into

---

33. Greven-Aschoff, *Frauenbewegung,* p. 94; Evans, *Movement,* pp. 88–95.

34. Bäumer, *Lebensweg,* pp. 159–60.

35. Ibid., pp. 161–69; Werner Huber, *Gertrud Bäumer: Eine Politische Biographie* (Dissertation: University of Munich, 1970), pp. 12–15.

account views on both sides. Shortly after joining the BDF leadership, she urged the League to adopt a firm stance in favor of political emancipation,[36] and during the Prussian reform campaign Bäumer worried that the government's offer of a position in the Ministry of Culture would undermine her ability to resist the status quo. "For me it went against the grain at first—to speak with Voltaire—after I had worked so long 'contre le ciel,' now to make myself available 'pour le ciel,' " she confided to Marianne Weber. Considering the possibility "that the whole episode has merely been staged as a *capitio benevelentiae,* so that we will happily swallow the insufficient reform and no one will even think of taking us seriously afterwards," the young moderate eventually decided to accept the post only if she was granted an "independent administrative department."[37] At the same time, she also sought out personal contacts with more radical feminists like Alice Salomon, leader of the Girls' and Women's Groups for Social Work in Berlin, whose work she later described as "a feminine expression of the cosmopolitan intellectual socialism that emerged *Behind the World City*" in the Friedrichshagen colony of playwrights and poets. "They were a step further beyond bourgeois life, the youth of the turn of the century, to whom social literature and art, scholarship, politics, and the social movement had given a consciousness of the social transformations of industrial society," Bäumer wrote in her memoirs, and she never felt entirely at home in the circle.[38] Speaking occasionally at the Groups' meetings, she also enthusiastically endorsed Salomon's Social School for Women, which offered courses on pedagogy, hygiene, national economics, and law, as well as technical and practical fields, and explicitly referred to it as a model when she founded a Social Pedagogical Institute of her own in Hamburg a few years later.[39]

---

36. Protocol of *Gesamtvorstand* meeting, March 16, 1908, Helene-Lange Archiv (henceforth HLA) 71–297[4].

37. Bäumer to Marianne Weber, December 26, 1907, and January 29, 1908; NL Marianne Weber 1, pp. 5–6.

38. Bäumer, *Lebensweg,* pp. 178–79. On Salomon, see Allen, *Feminism,* pp. 208–15; Sachße, *Mütterlichkeit,* pp. 120–25, 141–45.

39. Bäumer, *Lebensweg,* p. 180; "Aus den Bundesverbänden," *Centralblatt des BDF* 9, no. 17 (December 1, 1907): 131; Bäumer, "Das erste Jahr der sozialen Frauenschule zu Berlin," *Neue Bahnen* 44, no. 16 (August 15, 1909): 121–22; "Zur Frauenbewegung," *Frau* 23, no. 9 (June 1916): 566; Bäumer, "Die

Bäumer established closer ties to a similar circle of artists, writers, politicians, and feminists centered around Ika Freudenberg, the founder of the Association for Women's Interests in Munich and Bäumer's closest friend in these years.[40] As a local member of the Abolitionist Federation, Freudenberg had institutional ties to the left wing, and she also took a more strident position on political emancipation than the radicals' Alliance for Women's Suffrage when she demanded universal adult suffrage for both sexes at the 1904 IWC congress in Berlin.[41] Like Salomon, Freudenberg held a dim view of radicals who refused to set aside personal or "ideological" differences in order to work toward common goals, however, and she took pains to mobilize the interests of moderate and even conservative women by founding rural associations devoted to home economics, health, and child care as well as a Housewives' Alliance.[42] Impressed by the cooperative atmosphere in this "most colorful, flourishing, and rich circle of life the women's movement wove together anywhere," Bäumer made frequent trips to Freudenberg's Munich and collaborated with her on projects such as a waitresses' union.[43] Marianne Weber was on intimate terms with Freudenberg in these years, and it seems likely that the mutual friendship of the three women dated back to one of Bäumer's visits to the Bavarian capital, which in turn introduced her to progressive circles around Naumann and the Webers in the liberal Southwest.[44] Both of her friends belonged to local chapters of the National Social Association, as did Elisabeth Jaffé and Marie Baum, a Badenese factory inspector who later helped Bäumer found the Social Pedagogical Institute in Hamburg, and in January

---

Ziele der sozialen Frauenschule und des sozialpädagogischen Instituts in Hamburg," *Frau* 24, no. 6 (March 1917): 338–46; Sachße, *Mütterlichkeit,* pp. 141–43.

40. Bäumer, *Lebensweg,* pp. 180–97; Bäumer to Marianne Weber, October 23, 1907, NL Bäumer 22; Bäumer's letters to Weber 1903–12, NL Marianne Weber; "Ika Freudenberg," *Frauenstreben* 9, no. 2 (January 27, 1912): 7–9.

41. Amy Hackett, *The Politics of Feminism in Wilhelmine Germany* (Dissertation: Columbia University, 1976), vol. 2, pp. 609–610.

42. On Salomon, see Allen, *Feminism,* p. 209.

43. Bäumer, *Lebensweg,* p. 180.

44. Bäumer's heaviest correspondence with Weber coincides with the years of her friendship with Freudenberg, who died in 1912, and letters jointly penned by Bäumer and Freudenberg assume a much more playful, intimate tone; see above, note 40.

1907 the editor of *New Pathways* proudly announced that Weber, Jaffé, and Baum had made the Baden NSV the first "bourgeois party" in Germany to adopt women's suffrage into its platform.[45] A frequent guest at the Webers' home in Heidelberg, Bäumer also had the chance to meet with prominent intellectuals and progressive reformers, including Naumann, Sombart, Georg and Gertrud Simmel, and Edgar Jaffé, who frequented the famous salon after the turn of the century.[46]

Even at the height of conflict in the women's movement, common interests, personal and institutional connections linked Bäumer to radical causes in Munich and Heidelberg, where local activists acknowledged such affinities more easily than national leaders of the "left wing" in the acrimonious environments of Berlin and Hamburg. For that matter, the affinities between moderates and radicals were also evident to Conservatives like Paula Müller, head of the German Protestant Women's League, an organization founded at the instigation of Stumm and his colleagues to counter the influence of "purely humanist, radical, or even anti-Christian elements" in 1899.[47] Enraged by Bäumer's promotion of Prussian girls' school reform as a means to achieve women's entry into public administration, a goal she explicitly linked to Posadowsky's final reform initiatives in the Reichstag, Müller tried to thwart campaign efforts in committee meetings and press polemics.[48] When the Protestant leader prepared to stack an upcoming conference against her, Bäumer feared that "the rose-strewing angelic shows of P[aula] M[üller] and Landmann" would enable the Conservatives to "run off with 'Faust's immortal' " and so urged Marianne Weber to help her enlist the support of "the suffragists proper" in order to bolster "our teachers" and "make ourselves very rigid against the attempts to force us to the right."[49]

In matters of progressive social policy, Bäumer plainly felt she could count on the radicals' support, and the "women's question of the fourth estate" also brought the two wings together against Müller's Protestant

---

45. Gertrud Bäumer, "Die Frauenbewegung an der Jahreswende," *Neue Bahnen* 42, no. 1 (January 1, 1907): 4; on Baum, see Canning, *Languages,* pp. 186–87.

46. Weber, *Max Weber,* p. 408.

47. Reagin, *Movement,* p. 44.

48. Bäumer to Marianne Weber, April 18, 1907, NL Bäumer 22.

49. Bäumer to Weber, September 23, 1907, NL Bäumer 22.

League. Before the 1908 Law of Association sanctioned women's participation in political organizations, Lange's strategy of avoiding friction with
authorities often evoked criticism from left-wing feminists, who decried
anti-political appeals to "public utility" as a ruse to prevent cooperation
with socialists. Yet in fact the moderate leader shared the pages of *The
Woman* with Social Democratic activists and sympathizers like Henriette
Fürth and Jeanette Schwerin and actively encouraged non-partisan organizations of female workers, which she warmly welcomed into the BDF.[50]
The same was true of Salomon, whose efforts in this direction were denounced for similar reasons by Lily Braun, and of Freudenberg, who opposed admitting Social Democratic clubs into the BDF despite frequent
acknowledgment of the Marxists' contribution to the struggle for women's
emancipation.[51] Bäumer too openly defended the legitimacy of the socialist
women's movement.[52] When conservative readers objected to a sympathetic portrait of Bebel in the BDF's *Central Newsletter*,[53] she insisted that
the Social Democratic leader had "pointed out problems, indicated facts,
suggested possibilities that were not seen before" in a defiant review of
Woman and Socialism for *The Woman* in 1913:

> Bebel, of course, interpreted these relationships from a doctrinaire, one-sided
> point of view, which has increasingly been discredited in its essential features
> by the actual course of development. But he directed the attention of thou-
> sands to [these issues] and prevented a purely competitive standpoint from
> becoming the decisive factor, as it has in other employment categories. And—
> something we women should recognize with particular thanks—he dealt with
> problems that were at first difficult and awkward in a manner that was cer-
> tainly rough, but also healthy and *decent* (despite the fact that his theories
> have been subjected to the misuse of erotic exploitation).[54]

50. Greven-Aschoff, *Frauenbewegung,* pp. 88, 92; Evans, *Movement,* p. 52; Helene
    Lange, "Die vierte Generalversammlung des Bundes deutscher Frauenver-
    eine," *Frau* 8, no. 2 (November 1900): 65–70; "Frauenleben und Streben,"
    Frau 8, no. 3 (December 1900): 180–82; Gerhard, *Unerhört,* p. 178.
51. Allen, *Feminism,* p. 210; Hackett, *Politics,* vol. 2, p. 595.
52. Bäumer, "Geschichte der Frauenbewegung," pp. 108–19.
53. Bäumer to Frau M. von der Decken, October 30, 1913, HLA 38–175⁶.
54. Gertrud Bäumer, "Sozialismus und Frauenfrage," *Frau* 10, no. 13 (October
    1913): 9, emphasis in the original.

Observing that Bebel's "doctrinaire, one-sided" position had been "discredited" by recent developments, Bäumer echoed revisionist and progressive critiques of Social Democracy that were part of the common ground moderates shared with the radicals, who had themselves become increasingly frustrated by the socialists' insistence on a "clean break" with the bourgeois feminist movement after the turn of the century.[55] By 1905, when Else Lüders sponsored a radical motion at the BDF's annual congress proclaiming the League's commitment to overcoming class divisions, the two wings had reached full agreement on the issue, and two years later, Lüders's wording was integrated alongside Lange's maternalist formulations into the 1907 statutes.[56]

At the same time, however, Bäumer's remarks about Bebel's "decent manner" and the recent "erotic exploitation" of his theories also pointed to the one area where conflict appeared unavoidable. While both sides shared the progressives' goal of social integration for women and workers, the increasingly brash calls for sexual liberation and free love voiced by some radicals in these years seemed to point in a very different direction. "Unconditional social responsibility . . . and then the individual's right to satisfy his or her sexual needs, that is in itself simply a contradiction," Bäumer argued. "These are two things that, taken in such absolute terms, are mutually exclusive."[57] Far from co-existing peacefully in a single outlook, the "liberal-individualist and social reform/progressive currents" that Greven-Aschoff identified as the defining features of "radical feminism" had come to loggerheads throughout the Wilhelmine reform milieu,[58] as we have seen, and the issue that brought this controversy to a boil in the women's movement was the New Morals.

---

55. Gerhard, *Unerhört,* pp. 179–86; Braun, *Memoiren,* vol. 2, pp. 146–53, 325–35; Irma Jung, *Lily Braun: Eine Revisionistin im Spiegel ihrer Briefe 1891–1903: Untersuchung zur ideologischen Standortbestimmung einer Sozialdemokratin* (Dissertation: Hannover, 1987), pp. 200–14; Hackett, *Politics,* pp. 548–58; Greven-Aschoff, *Frauenbewegung,* p. 101.

56. BDF *Generalversammlung* 1905, "Interpellation Else Lüders," HLA 60–261⁶–262¹.

57. Gertrud Bäumer, "Mutterschutz und Mutterschaftsversicherung," *Frau* 16, no. 4 (January 1909): 198.

58. Greven-Aschoff, *Frauenbewegung,* pp. 106–7.

The "Rotten Mushroom of Subjectivity"

Blending "scientific" concepts of racial hygiene, population policy, "neo-Malthusianism," and sexual psychology with vitalistic themes of "life philosophy," Nietzschean celebrations of radical subjectivity, and current vogues for aristocratic aloofness and *l'art pour l'art*, the New Morals tapped every conceivable fad of fin-de-siècle science and culture to create an explosive mixture of conflicting impulses that was bound to ignite the contradictions between individualist and social perspectives lurking in these "modern" trends.[59] Such tensions had in fact already surfaced in the debates over the abolition of prostitution that led to the crystallization of the left wing at the BDF's congress in 1895. If Hanna Bieber-Böhm's call for discussion of the taboo issue became a rallying point for radicals, her proposals for heightened medical and police surveillance and the "forced internment and education of prostitutes" by the state shocked the majority, who condemned these violations of individual liberty. Bieber-Böhm quickly found herself isolated from the left wing, which continued its campaign outside the BDF in the Alliance of Progressive Women's Associations and the International Abolitionist Federation.[60] Similar divisions were also apparent in the awkward title of the organization radicals founded to spearhead the campaign for the New Morals in 1904, however: the "League for the Protection of Mothers and Sexual Reform" (*Bund für Mutterschutz und sexuelle Reform,* or BfMSR). While the leader of the movement for "protection of mothers," Ruth Bré, hoped to use the BfMSR to push for state-sponsored colonies to provide for single mothers and their offspring (a goal informed by contemporary social and nationalist concerns over the declining birth rate and racial degeneration), "sexual reform" encompassed a rather different agenda.[61] The latter included campaigns for contraception, prevention of sexually transmitted disease, and homosexual rights launched by the "sexologists," a group of physicians and psychologists centered in

---

59. On the New Morals, see Allen, *Feminism,* pp. 149–72; Gerhard, *Unerhört,* pp. 265–73; Evans, *Movement,* pp. 117–36; George Robb, "The Way of All Flesh: Degeneration, Eugenics, and the Gospel of Free Love," *Journal of the History of Sexuality* 6, no. 4 (April 1996): 589–603.

60. Gerhard, *Unerhört,* pp. 235–46.

61. Theresa Wobbe, *Gleichheit und Differenz: Politische Strategien von Frauenrechtlerinnen um die Jahrhundertwende* (New York: Campus Verlag, 1989), pp. 93–137; Allen, *Feminism,* pp. 198–99.

Berlin who had close ties to the Naturalist playwrights and poets of the city and shared their growing preoccupation with the radical, subjectivist philosophies of Nietzsche and Stirner.[62] Hoping to follow Nietzsche in search of "higher, brighter, more joyous culture" through erotic self-expression, Helene Stöcker led the campaign for sexual reform in the BfMSR, which displaced the previous emphasis on motherhood after she took over as the League's chairwoman in 1905.[63] Yet for many radicals the primary reason for dismantling the double standard continued to lie in curbing the social consequences of heightened sexual license already enjoyed by men, not in winning the right to similar excesses for women. As a result, the prominent Abolitionist Anna Pappritz opposed sexual reform from the start, while Bré resigned from the League in 1905, and the Social Democrats Lily Braun and Henriette Fürth followed suit a few years later.[64]

As alarm over Stöcker's message mounted, Bäumer quickly established herself as a leading voice for the opponents of the New Morals by vigorously defending the social impulse behind the new direction both wings claimed to represent.[65] The "idea of freedom" may have been the "palladium of the women's movement in the '60s and '70s," she acknowledged, but now feminists faced a fundamentally new challenge: "to 'politicize' the forces that have in this way been brought to maturity, that is, to make them into organs for the functions of a national whole."[66] There could be no doubt where truly progressive reformers stood in this regard. Naumann himself had "finally and emphatically defeated" the "individualistic view of the social question," though without forgetting "the great and important political mission of liberalism," she reminded her colleagues at the height of the controversy.[67] In fact, as early as 1907, the moderate feminist had begun urging them to see the struggles of the women's movement in precisely the same way:

> what is primarily striven for in the struggle for emancipation is for the time being only one side of the task, though, the one that old liberalism brought

62. Weindling, *Health*, pp. 102–6.
63. Aschheim, *Legacy*, p. 89; Gerhard, *Unerhört*, pp. 265–73; Allen, *Feminism*, pp. 156–63; Evans, *Movement*, pp. 117–20.
64. Wobbe, *Gleichheit*, pp. 102–5.
65. Ibid., pp. 115–22.
66. Gertrud Bäumer, *Die Frau und das geistige Leben* (Leipzig: Amelang, 1911), p. 262.
67. Gertrud Bäumer, "Friedrich Naumann," *Frau* 17, no. 8 (May 1910): 452.

to bear, the liberation of the personality for the possibility of developing individual energy and individual action. There also remains for us besides this necessary struggle for freedom—which is far from over—the task of training for nationhood, training for coordination into the division of labor of the whole, for working together on the cultural tasks of our Fatherland.[68]

Like Damaschke, Bäumer thus reviled Manchesterism and Spencerian Darwinism and looked instead to Naumann's new liberalism and progressive nationalism as she laid claim to a modernity substantially different from that of the previous century: "That Manchester economic liberalism belonged irretrievably to the past was something on which all modern liberals could agree."[69]

Part of nationalism's appeal was its ability to reach more conservative circles, however, and in her confrontation with the radicals, Bäumer did not hesitate to draw on conventional views of home and family life, which she described as the foundation of all social consciousness. As "the spiritual center of the family," women had a special obligation to protect it from "the dangers family life is facing in our modern culture," above all the devastating effect of industrial capitalism, which she depicted in much the same terms as Damaschke using statistics on hygiene and criminality.[70] If the ultimate goal of the women's movement was "to return to the family the forces industrial society had torn away from it" by helping female workers find their way back to "their nearest and actual duty," Bäumer's campaigns for pedagogical reform would further awaken a "spirit of readiness for sacrifice vis-à-vis the whole" by cultivating a "strong and immediate feeling of rootedness in the style and character of the homeland" through a program of "national education for women."[71] Yet in order to

---

68. Gertrud Bäumer, "Die politische und nationale Bildung der Frauen," *Neue Bahnen* 42, no. 12 (June 14, 1907): 91.

69. Huber, *Bäumer*, p. 187. For her critique of Spencer, see Gertrud Bäumer, *Die soziale Idee in den Weltanschauungen des 19. Jahrhunderts: Grundzüge der modernen Sozialphilosophie,* 2nd ed. (Heilbronn: Salzer, 1910), p. 199.

70. Gertrud Bäumer, "Frauenbewegung und Familie II," *Neue Bahnen* 44, no. 2 (January 15, 1909): 10; Bäumer, *Die Frau in Volkswirtschaft und Staatsleben der Gegenwart* (Berlin: Deutsche Verlags-Anstalt, 1914), pp. 14–32, 102–20.

71. Gertrud Bäumer, "Frauenbewegung und Familie I," *Neue Bahnen* 42, no. 1 (January 1, 1909): 5; Bäumer, "nationale Bildung," pp. 90–91.

tap the social energies of this rejuvenated domestic sphere, women needed training in national economics as well as home economics. Despite her defense of the Conservatives' "old morals," the moderate activist also affirmed the movement's commitment to forging careers for women in progressive institutions of the public sphere so that they could "build bridges from the life of the family across to the life of the nation."[72]

The giddy individualism of the New Morals, by contrast, seemed to flee from the new direction's commitment to science and social conscience into the delinquent mania of German Romanticism, which Bäumer repudiated as a "rotten mushroom of subjectivity."[73] Launching a sustained polemic against the influence of Nietzsche and Stirner in *The Woman,* she scorned the fashionable "hyper-modern decadents" of Berlin's salons, where supposed radicals wistfully indulged in fantasies of "a world order that gives 'flowers and sunshine' to every existence" while spending "hours of their lives" remote from any meaningful social activism in the "arrangement of autumn flowers in a vase." True radicalism was certainly not to be found in "free love," Bäumer chided; nor was it "ignited by self-analysis, but instead by submission, reckless, carefree, impulsive submission to grand objectives."[74] In "Psychological Problems of the Present" at the turn of the century, she even detected a cruel and reactionary "tendency to annihilate the weak" in the selfish elitism of those who "seek the source of all life energy within themselves."[75]

Such criticism seems oddly prescient in light of the debates at the annual BDF congress eight years later, where the outspoken sexual reformer Maria Lichnewska demanded that the German Legal Code be revised according to "racial hygienic concepts" in order to permit abortions in cases where "inferior" offspring would be the likely result.[76] While she shared Stöcker's admiration for Nietzsche, however, Lichnewska also agreed with Bäumer's concerns about the social consequences of the New Morals, as indeed did

---

72. Bäumer, "Frauenbewegung und Familie II," pp. 11–12.

73. Bäumer, *soziale Idee,* p. 296.

74. Gertrud Bäumer, "Der moderne Individualismus und die Erziehung," *Frau* 9, no. 6 (March 1902): 323; Bäumer, "Die psychischen Probleme der Gegenwart," *Frau* 7, no. 7 (April 1900): 391.

75. Bäumer, "Probleme," pp. 389–90.

76. Minutes, 1908 BDF congress, HLA 62–262[7]. For an overview of the debate, see Allen, *Feminism,* pp. 190–96; Evans, *Movement,* pp. 134–36.

nearly all of the other participants in the controversy over abortion, which clearly revealed the extent to which Stöcker's radical individualism isolated her even from most "radicals" in 1908. The debate began when BDF chairwoman Marie Stritt proposed a resolution in favor of legalizing abortion. Stritt belonged to the League for the Protection of Mothers and Sexual Reform, and her proposal was eloquently defended by Stöcker in an opening speech that described the measure as a logical correlate to free love and as necessary for the preservation of women's personal freedom and right of self-determination.[77] Subsequent discussion left these remarks unheeded, however, as radicals and moderates alike drew heavily on the "sciences" of racial hygiene and population policy to justify their positions from a social policy standpoint.[78] It seems particularly telling for the circumstances of the debate that the fiercest opposition to Stöcker's views came from Lichnewska, a leading member of the Alliance of Progressive Women's Associations and the Abolitionist Federation as well as the BfMSR, who described the "will to motherhood" as a "duty to the future of the nation." Germany needed "people, indeed many people" to fulfill its "mission to become the first cultural power on earth through the conquest of economic and political domains for ourselves," the longstanding radical insisted. And abortion was therefore acceptable only as a means to improve the fitness of the race.[79] After a long and stormy session, an "overwhelming majority" of the BDF's delegates voted to reject Stritt's proposal, replacing it with a resolution that called instead for an end to prison sentences for abortion and legalization in cases involving rape or a serious threat to the life or health of the mother. In broad agreement with Lichnewska, the assembly also approved abortions in cases where "it can be expected with certainty that the child will enter life severely handicapped either physically or mentally."[80]

---

77. Minutes, 1908 BDF congress, HLA 62–262[8].

78. Ibid. See especially Camilla Jellinek's opening defense of the proposal, in which the issue of "Freiheit der Persönlichkeit" is raised only briefly and late in a speech focusing on questions of racial hygiene and demographic policy. See also Allen, *Feminism*, pp. 193–97.

79. Minutes, 1908 BDF congress, HLA 62–262[8]. See also Evans, *Movement*, pp. 159–67.

80. Minutes, 1908 BDF congress, HLA 62–262[8].

Between Right and Left in 1910

As it emerged from the Breslau debates, the BDF's position on abortion thus reflected a "social reform/progressive current" in the German women's movement that had little to do with liberal individualism and saw the science of racial hygiene as a natural ally. Bäumer, who approached Lichnewska's racial hygienic concepts with caution and helped to soften the wording of the final passage on physical and mental handicaps, greeted this outcome by picking up the polemic against the New Morals with renewed vigor after the congress. Meanwhile pressures for Stritt's removal began to mount in the BDF's executive committee, where the chairwoman's blatant partisanship for Stöcker's unpopular views increasingly alienated other members of the leadership. As early as 1907, local activists in the radical stronghold of Hamburg had looked to Bäumer for support, threatening to discontinue patronage of the BDF *Central Newsletter* edited by Stritt in favor of *New Pathways.* Worried that the chairwoman would blame her for this rebellion, the moderate spokeswoman had counseled against the move, arguing that *New Pathways* "had a completely different purpose, namely propaganda and systematic 'instruction' for all those circles that have not yet arrived at the ultimate issues of the movement and do not know what to make of discussions about free love and neo-Malthusianism."[81] The issue flared up again the following summer, however, and this time Bäumer took a more aggressive stance, attempting to force acknowledgment of Marianne Weber's widely acclaimed *Wife and Mother in the Development of the Law,* in the BDF journal.

Containing a strong defense of conventional marriage and family life as the best environment for raising healthy children, Weber's treatise posed a considerable challenge to Stritt's authority at a moment when she was being confronted by an increasingly restive opposition to her views. The chairwoman, therefore, refused to allow any discussion of the treatise in the *Central Newsletter.* After several unsuccessful attempts to change Stritt's mind, Bäumer appealed to Anna Pappritz, the radical Abolitionist who had opposed the New Morals all along and was eager for a chance to review Weber's book.[82] Pappritz quickly took the matter into her own hands, launching an intensely personal attack on Stritt that flared up

---

81. Bäumer to Marianne Weber, November 3, 1907, NL Marianne Weber 1.
82. Ibid., Bäumer to Weber, June 17 and July 8, 1908.

repeatedly over the next eighteen months and created an atmosphere of mutual hostility and suspicion that made cooperation in the executive committee nearly impossible.[83] BDF Secretary Alice Bensheimer managed to broker an uneasy peace in May 1909, but when the League for the Protection of Mothers and Sexual Reform applied for corporate membership in August, an open clash could no longer be avoided.[84] After only one other member of the executive committee joined Stritt in voting for admission, she retaliated with a denunciatory article published anonymously in the *Central Newsletter* and proclaimed her resolve to bring the matter to the attention of the BDF's General Council in the spring.[85] "There are no chairwomen by the grace of God," Bensheimer warned. And when the isolated leader continued to defy the will of the majority the League Secretary added the threat of her resignation to those of Pappritz, Salomon, and Weber, but Stritt still refused to budge.[86] When the General Council finally met, Lange peremptorily called for an article in the *Newsletter* explaining the leadership's reasons for rejecting the BfMSR's bid for membership. The motion passed, and Stritt resigned on March 11, 1910.[87]

Looking for a successor, leaders on all sides viewed Bäumer as someone capable of restoring an atmosphere of cooperation to the executive committee after years of consumptive acrimony. The outspoken champion of the "old morals" was a welcome change for the Protestant Women's League, which soon gained admittance to the BDF, and Paula Müller greeted her nomination.[88] Yet Bäumer could hardly have represented an ideal choice for the Conservative leader, who had resisted her efforts for Prussian girls' school reform and continued to oppose her views on suffrage and careers for

83. Correspondence of BDF Secretary Alice Bensheimer, March 7, 1909, to March 4, 1910, HLA 3–15[1–2]; see also Evans, *Movement,* pp. 131, 150; Greven-Aschoff, *Frauenbewegung,* pp. 106, 235n113.

84. Bensheimer to Stritt, March 7, 1909; to Forster, Salomon, and Ediger, March 23, 26, 27; to Salomon, September 8; HLA 3–15[1].

85. Bensheimer to Salomon, September 8, 1909; to Stritt, January 14 and 20, 1910; to Salomon, Weber, and Pappritz, January 14; to Hammerschlag, January 26, HLA 3–15[1–2].

86. Bensheimer to Stritt, January 30, 1910, HLA 3–15[2].

87. Minutes, *Gesamtkonferenz* of March 11, 1910; minutes, *Gesamtvorstand* meeting, March 13, 1910; HLA 71–297[5].

88. Bäumer to Forster, June 16, 1910, HLA 3–15[8].

women in the public sphere.[89] After all, Bäumer was among the founding members of the Progressive People's Party in March 1910, a threat to which Müller's patrons in the Conservative Party responded by organizing the German Women's League as a counter to the BDF, which they viewed as an instrument of Naumann's left-liberal fusion.[90] The rush of conservative women to join the League at this time may not have been such a triumph for the right, as some historians have suggested.[91] "The former managers of the [German Women's] League have already said that the League has slipped away from them, and the intention exists to form a new, directly party-political women's group," Bäumer observed in 1913. "For that reason it is probably the right thing if we win influence over the League now. It will simply fall to those with whom it is able to make contact." Facing opposition to her plans to cement this relationship by inviting Müller to join the BDF leadership, Bäumer complained that her colleagues "all have the ridiculous idea that a seat on the Executive Committee is some kind of personal gift, and no one sees the immense tactical importance of binding the Ger[man] Protestant [Women's League] to us."[92]

At the same time, Bäumer also seemed an acceptable, if hardly ideal candidate for the radicals, who in fact submitted her nomination.[93] If she opposed free love and legalized abortion, so did many who had established reputations as leaders of the left wing at the turn of the century but rejected the radical individualism of the New Morals. It was the social impulse that initially inspired radicals and moderates alike to join the bourgeois women's movement, and Bäumer staunchly defended this new direction—against not only Stöcker, but also the Conservatives—in *New Pathways* and *The Woman*. Even the small group of feminists in the shattered left wing who sided with Stöcker and Stritt shared her respect for national economic and social policy concerns. At home with radicals and moderates, liberals and conservatives, Bäumer was thus elected with "by

89. Hackett, *Politics,* pp. 813–30.

90. Gertrud Bäumer, "Der Deutsche Frauenbund," *New Bahnen* 45, no. 3 (February 1, 1910): 18–20.

91. Evans, *Movement,* pp. 198–201; Greven-Aschoff, *Frauenbewegung,* pp. 112–13.

92. Bäumer to Voss, February 5, 1913, HLA 38–174[2]; Bäumer to Müller, June 30, 1914; to Bassermann, July 1, HLA 39–177[1].

93. Bäumer to Weber, May 27, 1910, NL Marianne Weber 1.

far the largest majority" as the BDF's new chairwoman in the summer of 1910.[94]

Liberal Humanism and Eugenics at the Fin de Siècle

If Bäumer's election marked the triumph of the social impulse rather than a victory for conservatism, its implications seem no less troubling in light of the use of racial hygiene and population policy in the debates over abortion that proved to be the turning point in 1908. Both Lichnewska's appeal to enlist "the will to motherhood" in service to a national mission of world conquest and the assembly's agreement on the elimination of "inferior" offspring evoke chilling parallels that situate the League's disregard for individual freedom and self-determination firmly within the context of tragic developments in German history. "In some areas, such as the movement for the protection of mothers, the women's movement undoubtedly prepared the ground in which fascism was later able to thrive," Greven-Aschoff writes. Ute Gerhard similarly finds it "irritating that a concept of race was utilized here that later became a death-bringing, annihilating criterion of selection under National Socialism."[95] Even if one accepts Allen's assertion that the BDF's stance on abortion expressed the "relative advancement and daring" of Wilhelmine feminists and not a "turn to the right," as Evans initially argued, the proclivity toward "disciplined rationality" at the root of these progressive attempts to master the social question appears in this case to have contributed significantly to the modern pathologies that Sachße and others have uncovered in the development of the German welfare state.[96] While stressing the subversive possibilities contained within the "eugenicist consensus," Canning also points out its obvious connections to a radicalized public sphere inhabited by Pan-Germans, Navy Leaguers, and other chauvinistic nationalists on the one hand, and the "programmatic disciplinary claims of social and reproductive hygiene" and infatuation with Foucauldian biopolitics that led "the

---

94. Bensheimer to Bäumer of June 11, 1910, HLA 3–15².
95. Greven-Aschoff, *Frauenbewegung*, p. 105; Gerhard, *Unerhört*, p. 271.
96. Allen, *Feminism*, p. 204; Evans, *Movement*, pp. 157–69; Sachße, *Mütterlichkeit*, p. 86.

state, in coalition with the medical profession" to become "more vigilant in policing women's bodies" on the other.[97]

As a leading representative of the new direction, Bäumer certainly shared her colleagues' enthusiasm for "objective" solutions—especially those drawn from modern biological science—that were to increase the strength and efficiency of the national community by subordinating the egoistic interests of individuals to the needs of the whole. "One believed in science," she later wrote of the optimism that inspired her and other young women to explore rigorous fields of social inquiry at the Victoria Lyceum in the 1890s.[98] Yet Bäumer also firmly believed that the rationalizing impulse of Enlightenment could be reconciled with its humanistic goals of emancipation and social progress. In fact, it was precisely in the life sciences that she saw the greatest potential for resisting the dehumanizing impact of a rigid and inflexible modernity in Wilhelmine Germany. A "precise understanding for the organic" was especially "modern," the moderate feminist proclaimed at the turn of the century, because the advances of biological science had penetrated beneath mere description of physical processes to reveal the "inner pathways and essence of historical development" and the vast "possibilities that lie within the continuity of historical growth."[99] Like many progressive reformers of her day, Bäumer looked to vitalistic conceptions of the organic to restore meaning to the personal struggles of life by dispelling the deterministic nightmare of "mechanistic" nineteenth-century physics. But beyond that she felt that the emphasis on the physical health of human bodies in modern "racial politics" represented an empirical, scientific version of Herder's "humane

---

97. Canning, *Languages,* pp. 172–73, 200–5, 213, 215–16. See also Eley, "Contradictions," pp. 96–103; Anna Bergmann, *Die verhütete Sexualität: Die Anfänge der modernen Geburtenkontrolle* (Hamburg: Rasch und Röhring, 1992), pp. 23–89; Frevert, "Tendency," pp. 320–44; Jürgen Reyer, *Alte Eugenik und Wohlfahrtspflege: Entwertung und Funktionalisierung der Fürsorge vom Ende des 19. Jahrhunderts bis zur Gegenwart* (Freiburg im Breisgau, 1991), pp. 38–41. Reagin similarly portrays the concern with "social poisons" as a means to enforce "bourgeois social and cultural hegemony"; *Movement,* pp. 71–76, 96.

98. Bäumer, *Lebensweg,* pp. 149–50.

99. Gertrud Bäumer, "Moderne Lebensprogramme II," *Frau* 8(1900–1901): 111.

individualism," which had once sustained a more idealistic appreciation for the intrinsic value of human life and human dignity.[100] If Manchesterism had reduced entire classes of people into mere instruments for the pursuit of material gain, the new science of "racial reform" would ultimately restore "the quality of German humanity" to its rightful place as "the final measure of the national economy, social order, and politics," Bäumer predicted a few weeks before the outbreak of the First World War. "In its connection with eugenics, this old ideal [liberal humanism] becomes more corporeal, more concrete. Even now it retains its universally valid, all-encompassing significance. Because the improvement of the race means the improvement of all. Demands of racial politics are by nature democratic inasmuch as they *necessarily* apply to all and cannot be limited to the confines of a single class."[101]

The social and scientific impulses Bäumer claimed to represent repudiated the perceived excesses of liberal individualism and radical subjectivism while seeking to preserve the secular humanist principles at their core. Like the strategies Allen, Canning, and others have begun to uncover, her startling attempt to link eugenics to the "universally valid, all-encompassing significance" of liberal humanism reminds us of the malleability of eugenicist discourse and the gulf separating the world in which its now-suspended meaning was forged from the vastly different historical circumstances that obtained after 1914. Yet the enthusiasms of Wilhelmine feminists and other reformers for racial hygiene and population policy are also linked to the inhuman brutality of the holocaust, as Greven-Aschoff and Gerhard suggest, since they cast an aura of legitimacy around such concepts, a legitimacy they would otherwise never have enjoyed in many circles, and that far outlived the fleeting historical circumstances that initially evoked those enthusiasms. There was nothing inevitable in this development, however, and its appalling outcome—as unthinkable then as it became again after 1945—should not obscure the highly sophisticated awareness of the dilemmas surrounding the relations of science and humanism to progress that informed Bäumer's use of the same language to express the hope for alternative modernities before the First World War.

---

100. For Bäumer's views on Herder, see *soziale Idee,* pp. 27–36.
101. Gertrud Bäumer, "Gedanken zur Jugendbewegung II, *Hilfe* 20, no. 29 (July 16, 1914): 466, emphasis in the original.

"The Improvement of All"

Bäumer's claim that racial politics were "by nature democratic" since they "necessarily" led to "the improvement of all" makes sense only from within the neo-Lamarckian, environmentalist standpoint many progressive reformers continued to defend in these years. Like Damaschke, the BDF leader believed in the creative ability of life—in particular, all *human* life—to adapt and improve with improvements in its surroundings, and she ruled out the pessimistic conclusions of Weismannism, which had yet to succeed in staking an exclusive claim to the legitimate use of such terms. The "racial idea" certainly did not express "any Pan German fantasies of exclusion," the moderate feminist insisted.[102] If she shared her contemporaries' concern over the "decline of energy in the metropolis," Bäumer agreed with the land reformer's claim that degeneration could be quickly reversed by eliminating the unsanitary conditions of the rental barracks, just as employing women outside the home would produce a "beneficial effect for racial hygiene."[103] And by stressing the universalist principles behind such environmentalist "racial reform," she also indicated that "race" for her meant the human race.

Bäumer sharply distanced herself from "Pan-Germans" and others seeking to use the new science to exclude rather than to integrate, but she especially objected to the "crude blather" of racial anti-Semites. "I find it in the general interest of good will very regrettable when such a rude product is actually praised by women," she wrote after the Protestant Women's League published a "ridiculous brochure" by the anti-Semitic poet Adolf Bartels in 1914. The notion "that Germany could regain its health only if it freed itself from Jew-ridden liberalism" was beneath contempt, the BDF leader insisted, and Bartels's recent collection of "German-racist poems with a swastika on it" was "much worse in every way."[104] These remarks may of course express a desire to free liberalism from the taint of Jewish associations, as Evans has pointed out, and Bäumer had in fact confidentially opposed Salomon's nomination as her successor a month earlier on

---

102. Ibid.
103. Bäumer, *Volkswirtschaft*, pp. 20, 302.
104. Bäumer to Bensheimer and Ramsauer, March 17, 1914, HLA 39–176³.

the grounds that "it would be a tactical advantage at the moment if the nominee were not a Jew."[105] Alarmed by attacks from the radical nationalists' League against Women's Emancipation, she rejected the candidacy of a colleague whose work she greatly admired out of tactical considerations. While Bäumer hardly took a courageous stand against anti-Semitism in 1914, however, it is difficult to detect any sympathy for it in her choice, which was no more a "personal gift" to Conservatives than Paula Müller's appointment on the BDF executive committee. On the contrary, there is plenty of evidence that Bäumer consistently opposed racism, especially when it resurfaced in a more virulent form in Weimar. After denouncing the radical nationalists' "repulsive and pharisaical anti-Semitism" as "the socialism of fools" in the Reichstag elections of 1919, she soon joined the Association to Combat Anti-Semitism and later ridiculed the "hysterical rabble-rousers" who were deluded by the "petty bourgeois phantasms of a Hitler" in the Nazis' Beer Hall Putsch.[106] If Bäumer eventually tried to build an alliance between the German Democratic Party and the Young German Order, she rejected the possibility of an Aryan paragraph in the accord.[107] In the summer of 1932, the moderate leader instead called for a "front of women" to resist the "principle of violence" that made fascism an "essential threat" to those who would have to relinquish their "rights and their place at work" if the Nazis took power.[108] Openly depicting her revulsion at Adolf Stöcker's "fierce anti-Semitism" in her 1933 memoirs, Bäumer later argued that she kept her job as editor of *The Woman* and *Assistance* to speak out against Nazi racial policies to those "who have ears to hear."[109] And while there are no independent sources to corroborate her claims of having offered direct assistance to Jewish victims of persecution,

---

105. Evans, *Movement,* p. 200; Bäumer to Bensheimer, January 30, 1914, HLA 39–176[1].

106. Gertrud Bäumer, "Der erste Wahlkampf," *Frau* 26, no. 5 (February 1919): 136; Fricke, *Lexicon,* vol. 4, pp. 375–78; Bäumer, *Grundlagen demokratischer Politik* (Karlsruhe: Braun, 1928), p. 75.

107. Huber, *Bäumer,* p. 384.

108. Gertrud Bäumer, "Die Front der Frauen," *Frau* 39, no. 10 (July 1932): 594.

109. Bäumer, *Lebensweg,* p. 124–25; Bäumer, "In eigener Sache" (typewritten manuscript, Hoover archives, Stanford University), p. 5.

those claims are at least not inconsistent with her statements and actions prior to 1933.[110]

What makes Bäumer's enthusiasm for eugenics before the First World War so startling is precisely the fact that it seemed to her perfectly compatible with the deep commitment to liberal humanism—if not liberal individualism—motivating her efforts to overturn divisive categories of race, class, confession, and gender that stood in the way of social unity. As long as the debates over heredity left open its possibility, this provocative link belonged to a discourse that was up for grabs and could be deployed across a broad range of contested meanings in order to mobilize the social impulse of the generation of 1890 on the left as easily as it was put into play on the right and in the many uncharted spaces in between. The same was true of the language of popular nationalism, which she used alongside appeals to the "old morals" in slogans tinged, occasionally, with chauvinistic undertones. But if she celebrated the nation as the natural locus of collective identity, Bäumer again placed it in the context of universal Enlightenment, drawing on Goethe and Herder to describe nationalism as one stage on the road to "cosmopolitan piety."[111] Returning from the International Congress of Women in the summer of 1914, the BDF leader saw a special role for the women's movement in reaching this ultimate goal and described the "cosmopolitan citizenship of all women" she had discovered at the Rome gathering in much the same way she later remembered the "German context" of her experiences in Leipzig. "Of course—one is never so thoroughly aware of one's own breed as here," Bäumer admitted on the eve of war, "but working in a field of one's own expertise with other nations, growing acquainted with their conditions, views, methods, is an especially effective way to get to know the world, even more so, since the women's question is large enough to include part of the culture of every country."[112]

---

110. Bäumer, "Sache," p. 2.
111. Bäumer, *Idee*, pp. 27–36; Bäumer, *Die Frau und das geistige Leben* (Leipzig: Amelang, 1911), p. 255.
112. Gertrud Bäumer, "Vom Internationalen Frauenkongreß in Rom," *Hilfe* 20, no. 23 (June 4, 1914): 369; see also her description of a trip to England in 1901, *Lebensweg*, pp. 170–74; and her "Eindrücke vom Internationalen Frauenkongreß," *Frau* 11, no. 10 (July 1904): 577–84.

The "Ghastly Calculation" of Population Policy

Like Damaschke, Bäumer thus avoided Naumann's more aggressive nationalism, but in forming her "precise understanding for the organic" she
also borrowed from his "anthropological" approach in order to craft her
message in a way that affirmed her faith in science while at the same time
acknowledging its darker potential. With its "almost ascetically-disciplined
sense for the facts," *The New German Economic Policy* had "loosened up
and broken through the rigidity of economic and social ideas with new,
creative force," the feminist believed. "What was just a theory for Marx—
the materialist view of history—has here become a feeling for life, a way
of perceiving, an ability to see, a new organ for grasping modern reality."[113]
Writing at the peak of the debates over the New Morals, she laid particular
stress on Naumann's recognition of "biological-spiritual forces" as "the
decisive motors of historical development," an insight that enabled him to
uncover countless "links between economic and spiritual facts" and so to
reconcile the subjective need for personal culture with the empirical demands of modern science. Soon after the book appeared, the moderate
spokeswoman met with Naumann to debate its implications for the women's
movement, and a short time later she praised the treatise as "a piece of
our national-economic *reality* . . . in which the seeds of the *future* are already sprouting."[114] Summing up its message in *The Woman*, Bäumer asserted that "the cultural idea of safeguarding the possibility of qualified
labor, i.e. labor rooted in the *personal* sphere, for the largest possible part
of the nation coincides with Germany's economic interest in winning international competition with quality merchandise."[115]

In stressing the confluence of material and spiritual elements in Naumann's sympathetic understanding of the "human life force," Bäumer was
not merely trying to stamp out the "rotten mushroom" of the radicals'
Nietzsche-inspired forays into neo-Romantic subjectivism. At the same
time, she tapped into vitalistic interpretations of biological science circulating in the Wilhelmine reform milieu in order to address concerns of fin-
de-siècle cultural critics, which indeed she shared. "In the language of the

---

113. Bäumer, "Naumann," p. 451.
114. Gertrud Bäumer, "Neudeutsche Wirtschaftspolitik und Frauenfrage," *Frau*
    14, no. 3 (December 1906): 166, emphasis in the original.
115. Bäumer, "Naumann," p. 453, emphasis added.

poet, the artist, the politician, and the philosopher, the same problem appears again and again," she observed in 1909. "It could probably be summed up with this formula: the difficulties of our modern culture lie in the fact that today *Kultur* and *Zivilisation* have fallen into a kind of hostile antithesis."[116] Despite her scorn for Berlin's "hypermodern decadents," the moderate feminist chimed in with her own fashionable laments over the "suffocation" of culture's "higher inner values" under the weight of *Zivilisation,* which she defined as "the perfection of external living conditions, the conquest of time and space and human energy by means of technical inventions." The "modern economic production process" was largely responsible for this loss, she conceded, since its "mechanized tasks" were turning workers' "limbs into machinery belts and their fingers into rasps."[117] In place of the "healthy and rich, deeply-rooted culture" of earlier days, when the master craftsman had worked alongside his apprentices and family in a "closed circle of life" that united aesthetic, technical, and commercial skill in the creation of products distinctively infused with his "harmoniously-developed and well-rounded personality," the utterly desolate phenomenon of the modern mass had appeared, Bäumer sighed: "its type is the stencil of a human being traced by impersonal mechanical labor."[118] The "German of Classicism and Romanticism" had "possessed what is lacking in us today," she sadly concluded: "the interconnectedness of all expressions of his inner personality in certain coherent fundaments of thought and inclinations of the will."[119]

With such sharp contrasts between an "organic" past and a present in which "the individual becomes a cog and part of a machine," Bäumer drew an idyllic portrait of the middle ages similar to Damaschke's in his attempts to appeal to the reactionary sympathies of the urban artisans' movement, and her denunciation of "mechanistic" *Zivilisation* also pandered to the aestheticism and elitism she was attacking elsewhere in her polemics against the radicals during these years. "Never has a culture been so full of ugliness," she complained of the cheap department store displays awakening a base desire for "banal luxury of every kind" in those who

---

116. Gertrud Bäumer, "Die Frauenbewegung und die Zukunft unserer Kultur," *Frau* 16, no. 9 (June 1909): 514.

117. Ibid., p. 516.

118. Bäumer, *soziale Idee,* p. 6.

119. Bäumer, "Zukunft unserer Kultur," p. 514.

could not afford it. Devoid of spiritual content like the "desacralized labor" in the factories that produced them, "proletarian wares" cluttered workers' homes in "coarse imitation" of German high culture, which was thereby being reduced to lifeless external forms.[120] "It is quite remarkable how seldom the outward refinement of our women corresponds to an inner one," the moderate feminist wrote in one of her least sensitive moments. "One need only think of the type of woman one encounters so often in the second class [compartments] of our railways."[121] It was as if "all branches in the organization of industry are joining together in an effective apparatus for the debasement of art."[122] Yet, again like the land reformer, she insisted this was no reason to flee the promise of modernity into solipsistic reveries of cultural despair.

Inflected by contemporary vitalistic discourse, the quintessentially modern science of life seemed to offer potent redemptive capacities in the struggle between the subjective world of living *Kultur*—"healthy," "rooted," "personal," and "spiritual"—and objectified, mechanical forces of *Zivilisation*. Administering to the "biological-spiritual" needs of the people, Naumann's "organic" approach restored corporeal depth to the flattened "stencils" of humanity being stamped out in German factories by protecting the physical health of workers and also by rooting economic life more firmly in the "personal sphere." Technical processes requiring skill and care would inspire "joy in work" in the Werkbund enterprises that Naumann and other progressive reformers were promoting in their campaign for a "spiritualization of German labor" that would release new levels of social energy, strengthening the productive force of German industry while simultaneously bringing quality designs to the masses so that every home might become "a site of aesthetic culture."[123] It was in this sense too that Bäumer hoped the "racial idea" could become a platform for the "new liberalism of the youth." Along with "the Garden City and sports, the immense proliferation of travel and 'tourist' enthusiasts, the invigoration of dance, clothing reform, the whole fresh-air organization of hygiene," the German youth's interest in the science of eugenics seemed part of an "entire

---

120. Bäumer, *geistige Leben*, pp. 298–302.
121. Ibid., pp. 318–19.
122. Ibid., p. 305.
123. Ibid., pp. 305–15; Bäumer, "Naumann," pp. 453–54.

web of modern life reforms,"[124] which she believed had become "strong enough" to sustain "a new health, a new feeling for life" that would sweep away the mechanical wreckage of the nineteenth century, making way for a "bright renaissance" of industry:

> More and more, technology will come to the aid of such life reforms on a broad scale, as we grow out of the black middle ages of industry, with their roaring, smoking, bombastic, crude works piling up in masses, into its bright renaissance: to quieter, cleaner, decentralized methods. How much all this progress benefits human beings, not just the increase of goods, but the enhancement of life, that will depend on the nature of the needs, the force and incandescence of the cultural ideal that compels these means into its service.[125]

Of course, the social application of modern organic science could lead to the same abuses Bäumer condemned in the mechanistic technologies of *Zivilisation,* and she warned against the inhuman consequences lurking in the cool detachment of scientists who systematically severed every emotional bond with the objects of their study in order to treat them with "rational" precision. Such critical distance was not "objective" at all, she argued, but instead mirrored the social distance separating these privileged observers from the fate of the masses in industrial capitalism, which had split economic production into the seemingly isolated components of intellectual and physical labor in much the same way.[126] The distorting effects of such "half-education" were obvious, however, and the BDF leader insisted that scientists needed to complement the purportedly objective analysis of social conditions from a distance with an appreciation for the subjective factors that undeniably played a crucial role in the processes that they were striving to comprehend and manage.

Just a little over a year after her odd celebration of eugenics, Bäumer took an especially vocal stance on precisely this issue when the newly founded Society for Population Policy held a conference on "The Maintenance and Augmentation of Our National Energy" in October 1915. Observing that the Society had allowed only five minutes for discussion of

---

124. Gertrud Bäumer, "Freideutsche Jugend," *Frau* 21, no. 7 (April 1914): 386.
125. Bäumer, "Jugendbewegung II," p. 466.
126. Bäumer, "Zukunft unserer Kultur," pp. 515–16.

the issue "from the woman's point of view," the BDF leader condemned the "ghastly calculation" of its proposal to offer state premiums for child-bearing in order to enhance the production of human material for Germany's defense in future wars.[127] "There is something unfruitful, hope-less—something dead and machine-like in the term" population policy, she fumed. "They want to make that which is fundamental, life itself, into an object of policy proposals, to 'achieve' it from the outside through social contrivances, to produce it experimentally in the social laboratory." Even the "most self-sacrificing, heroic mother" had to be repulsed by the idea "that she should give birth for the battlefield." If German men really wanted to reverse the declining national birthrate, the best way to awaken a desire to bear children in German women was to restore their faith in the future, she argued, and the best way to do that was to create a secure social and economic environment where "the joy at having a child, a hu-man impulse at least as primordial as joy in any of life's other pleasures, can fully develop."[128] Immediately after the conference, the BDF held a congress to establish its own "Guidelines for Population Policy," a nine-page document that included proposals on abolitionism, temperance, ma-ternity and child care, social insurance, increased educational opportuni-ties, and improved working conditions for women.[129] As Bäumer and other feminists defined it in 1915, "population policy" was little more than a scientific label for the same compendium of reforms the women's move-ment had been promoting since the days when it had still conceived its efforts in terms of charity.

"Self-Expression Bound in Rhythm": Liberation and the Life Force

Bäumer's commitment to "scientific" social reform and her anguished cri-tique of Zivilisation were thus closely intertwined, bound together in the curious link she perceived between eugenics and humanism. The new sci-ence of life had resolved the apparent contradiction, she believed, by peer-

---

127. Gertrud Bäumer, "Heimatchronik," Hilfe 21, no. 44 (November 4, 1915): 702; Bäumer, Weit hinter den Schützengräben: Aufsätze aus dem Weltkrieg (Jena: Diederichs, 1916), p. 188.

128. Bäumer, Schützengräben, pp. 188–89, 196.

129. "Richtlinien zur Bevölkerungspolitik aufgestellt vom Bund Deutscher Frauenvereine," HLA 49–223⁴.

ing beneath the externality of its object to discover subjective, "human impulses" at work inside, which could be understood only in their own "fundamental" terms, as ends in themselves. Far from revealing an inhuman essence in modern technologies, "rational" methods that failed to recognize the intrinsic value of human life actually fell short of scientific demands for empirical accuracy in Bäumer's eyes, and denying the validity of such "ghastly calculations" was no cause for cultural pessimism. While she attributed the popular notion of a "hostile antithesis" between *Kultur* and *Zivilisation* to the Aryan mystic H. S. Chamberlain, her own understanding of the concept probably owed more to Sombart, who described modern capitalism as a shift from organic to inorganic material foundations of economic life that shattered the natural bounds of time and space.[130] In the progressive circles where she learned the social question, theories of rationalization, depersonalization, and the "spirit of capitalism" often emerged in the context of a deep commitment to reform that took some of the most impassioned critics of Wilhelmine modernity to the threshold of Social Democracy, as we will see in the next chapter. If the peril of "half-education" drove some German mandarins to follow Langbehn in denouncing modern science, Bäumer used the same language to appeal for direct engagement with the social realities of industrial Germany, and she insisted that the humanists' isolated "enclaves of a highly aristocratic, scholarly and philosophical culture dealing in absolute values" hindered the cultivation of a well-rounded "personality" just as much as the cold detachment of scientific laboratories. "Differences in *education* have an absolutely divisive effect," she complained, "and the inability to create any real understanding between the individual classes of the nation, which is demonstrated again and again in all our social work, is above all connected to the absolutely aristocratic character of all intellectual culture."[131]

Science and the subjective needs of individuals dovetailed neatly in Bäumer's regard for the inner world of human organisms, which also sus-

---

130. Bäumer attributed her notion of *Kultur* to Karl Lamprecht, the renegade cultural historian who, like Sombart, faced conservative harassment because of his perceived affinities to Social Democracy; Bäumer, "Zukunft unserer Kultur," p. 514. On Sombart and Lamprecht, see "Demagoguery in Scholarly Clothing?" and "Academic Freedom in the Stumm Era" in Chapter 4; "Leipzig's Renegades" in Chapter 5.

131. Bäumer, "Zukunft unserer Kultur," pp. 515–16, 518, emphasis in original.

tained powerful appeals for personal emancipation and political rights. Since healthy, organic development occurred only with the free, self-initiated unfolding of internal forces, it could not be compelled from outside through the use of violence. Like the mechanized labor of Manchesterist factories, the crude, repressive policies of Germany's autocratic regime were crippling the life of the people. "This dead, characterless, indifferent state-machine on the one hand—and a glowing, living, energetic nation on the other," the BDF leader enthused on the hundredth anniversary of the "national uprising" against Napoleon. The "glorious" revolt, in which "a nation simply took for itself a power it did not yet legally possess, but for which it was ripe," had nevertheless "succumbed to the Reaction." With a new social political reaction well under way in 1913, she thought it important to remember how easily the healthy impulse toward freedom could be crushed.[132] The rigid discipline of Prussia's "military spirit" merely kept "certain classes" in posts they would lose in "free competition," Bäumer argued when male teachers appealed to the tradition in their objection to women principals in the girls' schools; "a little democratic spirit" in the "chain of command" would do more to inspire the "self-reliant initiative without exception from every single person" that was needed to master the "intellectual task" at hand.[133]

Like Damaschke, Bäumer thus viewed the "nation" as a vast living reservoir of social energy still waiting to be released, but she also believed that this dynamic potential could unfold in a healthy fashion only if the creative striving of all individuals was channeled into the larger life of the social organism. "Over each individual life the rhythm of a living, progressing community holds sway, and each must fit into this rhythm," she wrote, echoing the "energetic" theories of Ostwald and Gierke. "But on the other hand: the perfection of the whole depends on the specific cultivation of individual forces in such a way that every talent is developed and every unique contribution gains full recognition in communal life."[134] While scholars have often depicted such appeals for social liberation as an attempt to "earn" political freedom through the completion of duties, Bäumer

---

132. Gertrud Bäumer, "Liberale Jahrhundertfeier," *Hilfe* 19, no. 8 (February 20, 1913): 121.

133. Gertrud Bäumer, "Der militärische Geist," *Centralblatt des BDF* 11, no. 22 (February 15, 1910): 169–70.

134. Bäumer, *geistige Leben*, pp. 87–88.

depicted both as mutual pre-requisites for achieving a single, infrangible vision of personal self-fulfillment. "It is not—for women even less than for men—a matter of granting rights in the sense of a reward," she explained, defending her calls for "organic democracy" during the First World War. "It is a matter of bringing to life forces that are needed for the tasks of the future, of creating political forms in which the cooperation of all members of the nation can freely develop."[135] There had been "an unleashing of women through luxury, lack of duty, and moody extravagance," the BDF leader admitted, taking a jab at the radicals in 1914, but this cigar-smoking caricature belonged as irretrievably to the past as Manchesterism. "If the women's movement is 'emancipation,' it is so only in the sense that it wanted to give woman the inner possibility of self-determination she needed in a situation that had never existed before, where a new broader sphere of activity filled with freedom of choice and untraveled paths opened itself up to her energy," she insisted. "And in the other sense that it is taking pains to secure a worthy place for this gain in energy within the sum of culture situated beyond physical motherhood and housekeeping duties."[136]

Occupying a privileged site at the intersection of many complex, overlapping discourses in Wilhelmine social and cultural criticism, a "precise understanding for the organic" seemed to reconcile the conflicting impulses of radical individualism and social conscience, humanism and science, *Kultur* and *Zivilisation*, that tore at the women's movement and the wider web of German social and cultural reform at the fin de siècle. Perhaps the best expression of Bäumer's belief in the redemptive quality of organic emancipation came in response to experimental dance techniques developed at the Garden City of Hellerau by Emile Jacques-Dalcroze, an influential modernist who defined rhythm as "the absolute psycho-physical principle" and labeled his work "hygienic for the body as well as the mind."[137] "You could feel almost corporeally the beautiful, harmonious simplification that speaks for the living order of these buildings, which are stark but not cold, objective but not dry and barren," she wrote of her arrival in Hellerau

135. Gertrud Bäumer, "Die Neuorientierung und die Frauen," *Hilfe* 23 (1917): 380.
136. Gertrud Bäumer, "Emanzipation und Emanzipation," *Frau* 21, no. 5 (February 1914): 286.
137. Emile Jacques-Dalcroze, "Die hygienische Bedeutung der rhythmischen Gymnastik," *Gartenstadt* 5, no. 11 (November 1911): 154–55.

after a day of "unrest and fragmentation in the modern bustle" of Berlin. But she was even more impressed with Dalcroze's dances, which seemed perfectly attuned to "liberation—the release of the body to become a willing and pliant organ of the soul." The feeling of emancipation from bodily constraints awakened an "infectiously joyful, relaxed, energetic temperament in the dancers," who were then drawn back together in voluntary submission to the unifying force of the rhythm, Bäumer enthused. "The utterly satisfying element of the dance, self-expression bound in rhythm—as opposed to the one-sided, piecemeal laboriousness of nearly all other forms of intellectual and physical activity—that is the proclamation of the Dalcroze Festivals."[138]

Against Masculine Politics:
Toward a "New Form of Feminine Kultur"

Bäumer owed her contacts in Hellerau to Naumann, who played an important role in making the first German Garden City a success, as we will see in Chapter 5. The year before the Dalcroze Festivals, in 1912, he had asked her to edit the feuilleton section of *Assistance,* and the BDF chairwoman expressed delight at the opportunity to "contribute outside the women's segment" (a reference to the segregated seating to which women were confined at political meetings before the reform of the Law of Association in 1908).[139] Joining Naumann's inner circle, she quickly made personal acquaintances with leading cultural reformers, including Wolf Dohrn, Hellerau's chief administrator and a protégé of Naumann, who issued frequent invitations for her to visit the Garden City and even offered her a job as principal of its school.[140] Yet it was in the sphere of politics that Bäumer initially built her friendship with the progressive champion of new liberalism. Co-chairing a panel on the women's question at the Protestant Social Congress in 1906, she was impressed by Naumann's readiness to accept feminist criticism of his views on the role of women in the new German economy (his "anthropological" analysis had focused on their

---

138. Gertrud Bäumer, "Hellerauer Festspiele," *Hilfe* 19, no. 26 (June 26, 1913): 409–11.
139. Bäumer to Weber, July 13, 1912, BA Koblenz, NL Marianne Weber 1.
140. Bäumer to Dohrn, January 2, 1913, HLA Archiv 38–174¹; Bäumer, "Festspiele" pp. 409–11.

reproductive functions, which he suggested might be impaired by work outside the home). As soon as the new Law of Association made political affiliations possible, she joined the group of National Socials who had followed Naumann into the Radical Coalition after the dissolution of the NSV and was soon appointed to its executive committee.[141]

Hoping to use this "*faute de mieux* party-political location" to push a broader reform agenda, Bäumer instead found herself having to defend the Coalition's stance on women's suffrage during negotiations over left-liberal fusion culminating with the founding congress of the Progressive People's Party in 1910. While the Radicals had already endorsed political equality for women "in principle" two years earlier, the most Bäumer and other women could achieve in the FVP's platform was a call for continued educational reform and new job prospects. "Liberalism bases its program, insofar as it shows any internal unity, on the idea of the individual's free self-determination, the unrestrained development of all national forces," she wrote after the congress. "It is without any doubt illogical and incon-sistent on the basis of this principle not to want women's suffrage. It is a betrayal of liberalism against itself if it avoids the word 'political' in the paragraph on women."[142] Winning a declaration of allegiance to the Co-alition's stance from Radical delegates in 1910, Bäumer kept up pressure on the Progressive majority until women's equality was finally adopted into the party's platform in 1912. Naumann's new liberalism was far more com-promising in its commitment to such "principles" than the BDF leader had imagined, however, and like many contemporaries, she was deeply disillusioned with the results. "Brrr, this Progressive People's Party, the collective energy of the philistines" she wrote to Marianne Weber in 1913. "Politics is no delight, you can believe that." Despite her "impatience and disgust" with the "Radical louts of the old stripe," Bäumer still felt com-pelled to help "the Naumann people" achieve what they could: "How are things ever supposed to get any better unless we actively annoy them?"[143] But while she served as Naumann's "national spokesperson" in the 1913 elections, the progressive feminist seemed to find the signs of renewal at

---

141. Bäumer, "Wirtschaftspolitik," pp. 166–72; *Lebensweg*, pp. 223–25.

142. Gertrud Bäumer, "Die fortschrittliche Volkspartei und die Frauen," *Frau* 17, no. 7 (April 1910): 385–89.

143. Bäumer to Weber, undated, presumably January 1913, NL Marianne Weber 1, pp. 100–1.

Hellerau more hopeful than she did in these discouraging political entanglements.[144]

Increasingly, Bäumer's expectations focused on the "grand party of cultural politics" for a more constructive approach.[145] Long an admirer of the Werkbund, she coordinated the League's 1914 congress with the industrial arts exposition in Cologne, arranging an official BDF exhibit and a public lecture on "The Housewife and the German National Economy."[146] In Garden Cities, rallies of the Free German Youth, Art Education congresses, Wyneken's pedagogical experiments at the Country Home for Education, and the entire range of "modern life reforms" beyond, Bäumer discovered the same desire to avoid the "passionate and egotistical one-sidedness" of party politics, with its inflammatory slogans "designed for the masses," and to "utilize all the technical means that have been achieved for a fuller—and quieter—personal life."[147] Convinced that "our time is ripe for a grand synthesis of social and cultural interests," she sent Weber a proposal for founding a new institution, modeled after the Association for Social Policy, that would transform this remarkable synergy into concrete results. "I don't mean just scholarly," she explained, "but in organizational terms, politically: a community of the kind of people whose political interests in culture" made "social policy" seem "too narrow and technical and old-fashioned." After all, the Association had originally been conceived as a "practically effective form too," Bäumer reminded her friend, and like the socialists of the lectern in the crucial struggles of the founders' years, their generation had an obligation to seize the historic opportunity of the moment in order to build (and this time to sustain) "a new start."[148]

---

144. Bäumer, *Lebensweg,* pp. 259–60.

145. Bäumer, "Zukunft unserer Kultur," p. 519.

146. Bäumer to von Meevissen, April 14, 1913, HLA 38–174⁵; to Meurer, April 3, 1914, HLA 39–176⁵; to von Miesitscheck, November 17, 1914, HLA 39–177⁶.

147. Bäumer, "nationale Bildung," p. 90; Bäumer, "Zukunft unserer Kultur," p. 515; Bäumer, "Freideutsche Jugend," p. 387; Bäumer, "Die pädagogische Sendung des Landerziehungsheims," *Hilfe* 19, no. 40 (October 2, 1913): 634–35. On art education, see Bäumer, *geistige Leben,* pp. 310–13; Bäumer, "Kunsterziehungsfragen," *Frau* 11 (1903–1904): 111–13.

148. Bäumer to Weber, undated, NL Weber 1, pp. 113–14. Archival pagination suggests a date of 1916 for this letter, but its tone and content correspond closely to Bäumer's optimistic articles in *The Woman* and *Assistance* in the

Yet for Bäumer, the greatest hope for anti-political solutions to the social and cultural questions of her day continued to lie in the women's movement. "The entire power and significance of the League rests upon the fact that it melts down extreme political antagonisms in the communality of women's interests. The more it is able to do this, the more perfectly it fulfills its purpose," the chairwoman declared in 1914. "Political neutrality is for us not only a demand of intelligence and foresight, but directly a portion of [our] energy."[149] While she staunchly defended women's right (including her own) to take active roles in party politics, Bäumer found little room for developing a specifically feminine style in this sphere. "Those of us who have already long been working in political associations know how, in times of agitated political struggles, all antagonisms push for the sharpest formulation, how partisan passions blind [us] and encroach on territories one would like to keep free of them," she admitted. "We dare not abandon ourselves to any pipe dreams that women will do it much differently from men."[150] Seeking to ensure that female politicians from all parties had the chance to represent their views at BDF functions, she refused to admit partisan groups into the League and strove to protect it from the encroachment of masculine politics.[151] It was "regrettable when women, in the belief that they must entirely assimilate the forms of public life, accept on their part the usual methods of interest conflicts, when they attempt to match in word and deed the style of the political agitator, whom they take as a model," Bäumer complained, taking a jab at the radicals. "In the long run, they will hold their own in the public sphere only if they make no concessions to a tone that is tailored entirely to the struggle for power."[152] If the BDF was a "political organization," it was only because it "places demands on legislation and administration,"

---

spring and early summer of 1914; see especially "Gedanken zur Jugendbewegung" I and II, "Freudeutsche Jugend;" "Wo steht die Jugend?" *Hilfe* 19, no. 13 (March 27, 1913): 199–200.

149. Gertrud Bäumer, "Das Wesen unserer politischen Neutralität," *Jahrbuch der Frauenbewegung* 3 (1914): 191.

150. Ibid., p. 188.

151. Bäumer to Bassermann, January 16, 1912; to Bensheimer, January 18, 1912, HLA 37–172¹; to Pick-Schenkalowsky, February 6, 1913, HLA 38–171²; *Gesamtvorstand* minutes, March 3, 1912, HLA 72–298¹.

152. Bäumer, *geistige Leben*, p. 295.

like the Society for Social Reform. "But precisely like [the Society] it is unpolitical insofar as it encompasses all parties and may not give its demands any kind of party-political taint or stamp," she insisted.[153] More than just another model institution in the Wilhelmine reform milieu, the League also enjoyed a special advantage in the pursuit of anti-politics. "Because women do not vouch for any one demand they want to achieve, but rather as they fight for that demand they vouch for a new form of feminine *Kultur,* with everything this concept entails, for personal refinement, for a new social development, for a new intellectual self-sufficiency."[154]

In turning to her mentor's theory of womanhood, Bäumer thus carved out a space beyond the acrimonious sphere of masculine politics where the integration of women's liberated energies seemed the key to healing the ills decried by social and cultural critics. As "a front in which *life* was defended against the dominance of means, of the apparatus, of organization," the women's movement had long stood in the vanguard of the struggle against the dehumanizing technologies of mechanistic oppression that had suddenly become the focus of widespread generational revolt.[155] The "essence of organic development" was "deeply and immediately imprinted" on feminine nature, she proclaimed, since as mothers women observed "from quite near at hand how a soul forms itself, how foreign substance slowly becomes one's own, dead matter becomes organic life."[156] Such intimate proximity to the process of human becoming thus endowed women with a special ability to recognize "expressions of personal will, feeling, cognition" in "works of culture," Bäumer argued. "This capacity acts like the special light sensitivity of a photographic plate; it provides a specially tinted image of the world that is the same as the masculine one in its contours, but deviates decidedly from it in its tone, its mental expression." If "modern *Zivilisation,* like the *Zivilisation* of all ages bears the stamp of masculine psyche," the "task of transforming the products of human thought and action, the material of life, back into personal *Kultur,* that can only be done by woman," the BDF leader concluded— "or, to be more circumspect, let us say it cannot be done without her."[157]

---

153. Bäumer, "Neutralität," 190.
154. Bäumer, *geistige Leben,* p. 295.
155. Ibid., original emphasis.
156. Bäumer, "Zukunft unserer Kultur," pp. 522–23.
157. Ibid., pp. 520–22.

. . .

Although scholars often disagree about possibilities for a distinctively "feminine politics" in Wilhelmine Germany, it is hardly surprising to find Bäumer promoting the cultural politics of womanhood in this way at the time.[158] Common ground came at a premium in the struggles between right and left before the First World War, and similar claims could be heard throughout the anti-political milieu in which the BDF certainly had strong roots. Despite their considerable differences, Bäumer's appeals in many ways resemble those of Damaschke, who also used the languages of popular nationalism and cultural despair to present a critique of Manchester liberalism and modern industrial capitalism that was intended to reach a broad audience between right and left. And like the land reformer, she too depicted her movement at the cutting edge in the struggle for an alternative modernity departing from past models in important ways. "The nineteenth century and the twentieth century—but perhaps also the way of man and that of woman," Bäumer speculated, taking an optimistic look ahead in 1911.[159] For both, the conviction that modernity's current ills could be transcended without sacrificing its genuine promise rested on a delicate balance of individualism and socialism, an "organic" synthesis drawn from the contemporary discourses of national economics and biology to resolve urgent conflicts within the generation of 1890. In the next chapter we turn to one of its principal architects, Werner Sombart, whose career illustrates the potential for striking shifts in the tone and complexion of Wilhelmine anti-politics when this synthesis broke down.

---

158. On the disagreement over Wilhelmine feminist politics, see, for example, Greven-Aschoff, *Frauenbewegung*, p. 89; Gerhard, *Unerhört*, pp. 186–87.

159. Bäumer, *geistige Leben*, p. 219.

CHAPTER 4

Werner Sombart's "Anti-Politik" and the Vicissitudes of Socialism "as a Cultural Factor"

"What does Sombart actually want?" Naumann wondered after reading his former colleague's latest work, *Luxury and Capitalism,* in January 1913. "Earlier we all took him for a socialist, and he did nothing to demolish that view at the time, liked to play around with Marxism himself, and already had one foot in the postcapitalist, proletarian world. But that's long over now. If someone mentions socialism to him today, he shudders, because today he thinks of socialism as something monotonous, moralistic and lacking poetry, an organizing of the apathetic for the preservation of mediocrity."[1] Sombart's ennui posed an especially grave threat to Naumann, who was already reeling under the impact of the social political reaction, since the famous scholar was one of the primary architects of the bridge between progressive optimism and cultural criticism that upheld many of his followers—Bäumer not least among them—in the belief that the new technologies of a collectivist social and economic order would enrich personal life along with the life of the nation. Already in his student days, Sombart had pushed for socialism to be "discussed and recognized more as a cultural factor."[2] As a leader of the national economic boys in the 1890s, he insisted that the proletariat's material demands were perfectly compatible with the subjective values of bourgeois culture, urging his contemporaries to accept the transition to industrial capitalism in an appeal so enthusiastic about the possibilities for progress that Max Weber worried that he had abandoned his "relativism" for the "optical illusion" of

---

1. Friedrich Naumann, "Luxus und Kapitalismus," *Hilfe* 19, no. 3 (January 16, 1913): 41.
2. Otto Lang to Sombart, February 6, 1888, NL Sombart 8e.

a "purely technological 'ideal.' "[3] With Naumann's support, Sombart inscribed this vision permanently into the foundations of the Society for Social Reform at the turn of the century, but a few years later he was condemning it himself as a "disgusting cotton-spinner's ideal."[4] Retreating from social activism to cultivate friendships in literary and artistic circles, the economist joined the chorus of lamentation over the depersonalizing forces of mechanistic capitalism, which seemed now to be leading only to a "twilight of the gods."[5] Naumann's pique was understandable. "To hitch him to a social-political or economic party is impossible. He's not serious enough for that, since he can't promulgate a platform for twenty years without unraveling it himself," the Progressive leader bitterly observed. "He doesn't really want to build anything at all, doesn't want to be a statesman or a reformer; he wants to stroll through world and economic history like a museum director."[6] Looking back not long afterwards, the economist agreed: "I, and along with me many, many and not the worst, had succumbed to an absolute cultural pessimism."[7]

Crossing the terrain of Wilhelmine anti-politics in directions even Naumann found hard to predict, Sombart's career took shape in the "field of tension" between "social ethics" and "social technology" that German intellectual and cultural historians have recently begun to explore in the debates of the fin-de-siècle human sciences, and his name often appears alongside those of Weber and Simmel in the latest studies on the rich and complex "diagnosis of modernity" Peukert outlined at the end of the 1980s.[8] Although he was "perhaps the most influential German social sci-

---

3. Weber to Sombart, February 8, 1897, NL Weber 30, vol. 4, p. 54. Weber's comments refer to Sombart's "Ideale der Sozialpolitik," discussed in "The Spirit of Capitalism and the Future of German *Kultur*" in this chapter.

4. Werner Sombart, "Die Bedeutung der syndikalischen Lehren," *Morgen* 1, no. 26 (December 6, 1907): 816.

5. Werner Sombart, *Der Bourgeois: Zur Geistesgeschichte des modernen Wirtschaftsmenschen* (Hamburg: Rowohlt, 1987), p.346; Sombart to Landsberger, November 9, 1913, NL Artur Landsberger.

6. Naumann, "Luxus," p. 42.

7. Werner Sombart, *Händler und Helden* (Munich: Duncker & Humblot, 1915), p. 117.

8. Karl Lichtblau, " 'Alles Vergängliche ist nur ein Gleichnis': Zur Eigenart des Ästhetischen im kultursoziologischen Diskurs der Jahrhundertwende," in Hübinger, Bruch, et al., *Kultur,* pp. 86–121; Gangolf Hübinger, "Die mon-

entist of the first third of the twentieth century,"[9] the national economist remains a shadowy figure today, however, his career tainted by the dark strains of German intellectual development associated with the rise of fascism. Sombart's self-confessed "cultural pessimism," closely tied to a sudden interest in discerning the racial characteristics of Germans and Jews after the turn of the century, the hysterical outburst of wartime xenophia, *Traders and Heroes*, his retreat into transcendental, religious concerns in the 1920s, fascination for neo-corporatism in the crisis years of the Republic, and infamous celebration of German Socialism in 1934 all seem to set him distinctly apart from the progressive search for alternative modernities—or to link him firmly to its malignant pathologies. After 1945 the once-famous scholar thus fell into the obscurity of Germany's unmastered past, only to be rediscovered by liberal historians seeking to reconstruct the decline of the German mandarins in the 1960s and 1970s.[10] On the other side of the Wall, the East German historian Werner Krause neatly characterized him as a "falsifier of Marxism" in the slender volume *Werner Sombart's Path from Socialism of the Lectern to Fascism*, which remained for decades the sole book-length study of his career.[11] Without questioning this trajectory, Jeffrey Herf helped to stimulate a renewed interest in Sombart in the early 1980s by pointing out the complexity of his attitudes toward "technology and the Jewish question," and a more nuanced view of the economist has emerged in the last few years in two new biographies by Michael Appel and Friedrich Lenger.[12] Lenger especially warns against

istische Bewegung: Sozialingenieure und Kulturprediger," in Hübinger, Bruch, et al., *Kultur,* p. 248; Peukert, *Diagnose,* p. 6.

9. Friedrich Lenger, *Werner Sombart 1863–1941: Eine Biographie* (Munich: C. H. Beck, 1994), p. 9.

10. Ringer, pp. 153–57, 183–84, 234–35, 387–89; Arthur Mitzman, *Sociology and Estrangement: Three Sociologists of Imperial Germany* (New York: Knopf, 1973), pp. 32–34, 218–33; Mitzman, "Personal Conflict and Ideological Opinions in Sombart and Weber," in Mommsen, *Contemporaries,* pp. 99–101.

11. Werner Krause, *Werner Sombarts Weg vom Kathedersozialismus zum Faschismus* (Berlin: Rütten und Loening, 1962), p. 167.

12. Jeffrey Herf, *Reactionary Modernism: Technology, Culture, and Politics in Weimar and the Third Reich* (New York: Cambridge, 1984), pp. 132–50; Michael Appel, *Werner Sombart: Theoretiker und Historiker des modernen Kapitalismus* (Marburg: Metropolis, 1992), esp. pp. 25–71, 115–51.

imposing an illusory "telos" on a long and controversial career that might as easily have ended with "the cultural critic and early ecologist who died in 1908 or the worthy Social Liberal of the 1890s."[13] But the political coordinates of cultural despair are too firmly fixed to doubt the direction of the currents into which Sombart plunged by 1913, and a dark cloud hangs over the economist's "appeal to hearken back to the cultural values threatened by capitalist mass society," which entangled him in "the traditional line of the unpolitical man of culture" and "all too clearly" pointed toward the chauvinistic fanaticism of *Traders and Heroes.*[14]

Naumann's anger and confusion hardly suggest that his contemporaries saw any coherence in Sombart's erratic swings of mood, however. As Rüdiger vom Bruch has shown, the economist's appeal also pointed in other directions—toward "political cultivation, civic education, 'Kultur' and cultural politics, professional training and interventions for pluralistic suffrage." The "common denominator" linking these reform efforts to Sombart's "elite/aristocratic consciousness" was a "far-reaching rejection of existing party-political relationships," Bruch argues, and there was thus "no contradiction" if his cultural polemics in defense of *Anti-Politik* "dovetailed with a more general mood of setting out on new departures" in the Wilhelmine reform milieu.[15] This was certainly true of Bäumer's "unpolitical" vision of feminist *Kultur,* which inspired a belief that the time was right for a "new start" at the very moment Sombart was succumbing to cultural pessimism. In fact, her grim views on the "dead husk of mechanized production" made a deep impression on the economist,[16] who had helped inspire them. Despite their strikingly different poses in 1913 Bäumer and Sombart in fact shared much else in common, including a fascination with modern biology, a concern for preserving "transcendental" humanist values, and an awareness of the "contradictions of modernity"— attitudes that did not always mark a turn down the path of radical conservatism—or reactionary modernism—that ended in the brutality of the Third Reich.

---

13. Lenger, *Sombart,* p. 387.

14. Friedrich Lenger, "Die Abkehr der Gebildeten von der Politik: Werner Sombart und der 'Morgen,'" in Hübinger and Mommsen, *Intellektuelle,* p. 77.

15. Bruch, *Wissenschaft,* p. 188.

16. Werner Sombart, *Der Moderne Kapitalismus,* vol. 3, part 2 (Munich: Deutscher Taschenbuch Verlag, 1987), p. 903.

What *did* Sombart actually want? The question remains as vexing today as it was in Naumann's time. Anguish over the ruthless march of progress stands side by side with euphoric celebrations of modern power and efficiency even at the height of Sombart's reformist zeal. Weaving between darkness and light, his path winds through new terrain to reveal some of the richest, but also most disturbing corners in the Wilhelmine reform milieu.

The Ideals of Social Policy

Sombart was born on the family estate in Ermsleben on February 14, 1863 and grew up in affluent circumstances that, though solidly bourgeois, were perhaps as remote from the modest comforts of Bäumer's youth as these were from Damaschke's experiences as a "metropolitan nomad" among Berlin's struggling artisans. "Half agrarian, half industrialist," Werner's father had purchased the estate at a time of rapid turnover in Saxon landholdings during the 1840s and, after building a factory on the premises, he made a fortune in the commercial production of sugar.[17] Like a foil to Rothsattel, the hapless victim of modern capitalism in Gustav Freytag's *Debit and Credit,* Anton Sombart thrived in Germany's vibrant economy at mid-century, soon winning political influence to match his new status as landowner. Elected mayor in 1848, he entered the Prussian Diet by the time Werner was born and also served as a National Liberal delegate in the Reichstag from 1867 to 1878. When Werner was twelve years old, Anton sold the Ermsleben estate and moved to Berlin, where he had begun to play a role in the debates over the social question. A founding member of the Association for Social Policy, the elder Sombart worked closely with Schmoller and Wagner, family friends from early on, and after retiring from politics he focused on securing a viable role for agriculture in industrial, capitalist Germany, experimenting with land reform on a Pomeranian estate purchased in the early 1880s.[18] Werner initially showed little interest in such matters. "The son grew up in wealth, in the life of pleasure of the

17. Franz Boese, *Geschichte des Vereins für Sozialpolitik* (Berlin: Duncker & Humblot, 1939), p. 38. On Sombart's family background, see Lenger, *Sombart,* pp. 27–30; Krause, *Weg,* pp. 13–14; Mitzman, *Estrangement,* pp. 140–45.

18. Mitzman, *Estrangement,* pp. 141–42; Boese, *Geschichte,* pp. 38–39, 52–54; Krause, *Weg,* p. 13.

metropolis, and all the educational means of the day stood at his disposal," Schmoller wrote of Sombart's upbringing in Berlin,[19] and he made use of these opportunities to cultivate his taste for "the Beautiful, the Good, and the True" through a humanistic education that encouraged more interest in Cicero and Schiller than in ideals of social policy.[20] Finishing up at the *Gymnasium* in Schleusingen (where he was sent on account of his delicate health) in 1882, Sombart spent his last summer before college recovering from nervous exhaustion and a vague lung ailment at posh resorts in Switzerland and Italy while his father begged him to keep his expenses under 3000 marks for the year.[21]

A curious mixture of old and new characterized Sombart's adolescence, which blended images of bourgeois self-confidence and the bustle of the founders' years with critical sensitivity to the social costs of prosperity and parvenu pretensions to an aristocratic lifestyle of aloof, cultured refinement. Filtered through his literary and artistic tastes, a gathering awareness of the tensions surrounding Germany's transition to industrial capitalism emerged from these various impressions and may already have surfaced in Sombart's early desire to write a "national-social drama" in which each actor would function as the "representative of a social (or, as far as I'm concerned, psychological) mood."[22] Considering a career more seriously in 1882, the young graduate expressed his frustration with the constraints of Bismarck's Empire in letters to former classmates.[23] "Under this regime I cannot be a princely servant," he wrote, rejecting a career in the civil service, which was currently being purged of its liberal elements. Instead he hoped to use his father's Pomeranian estate to "get into Parliament," where he intended to become "*not* a Social Democrat, but a leftist Progressive man (Richter's Party)," despite his expressed interest in "liberation of the oppressed classes." The "diligent study of political science, social policy, national economics, philosophy . . . and the law" was first necessary to make him "mature enough to be capable of voting in political matters," however, and in the fall of 1882, Sombart consequently enrolled for his first semester at the University of Berlin as a student of Adolf Wagner.

19. Quoted in Lenger, *Sombart,* p. 29.
20. Ibid., pp. 31–32.
21. Ibid., p. 33.
22. Ibid., p. 32.
23. Ibid., pp. 33–34.

"Goethe as Social Democrat"

For the next six years, between frequent stays in Pisa and Rome, Sombart absorbed the lessons of the socialists of the lectern, becoming one of Schmoller's prize students, while he simultaneously indulged his youthful passion for rebellion by exploring Marx's forbidden doctrines and Zola's social realism together with other students who shared his impatience with the regime. "If he would set up a red flag in place of the black and white one, his socialism wouldn't sound so bad to me," Sombart mockingly wrote of Wagner in 1883.[24] While he later described himself as a "blood-red Soc[ial] Dem[ocrat]" in his student days,[25] his enthusiasm for Marx and Zola seems originally to have indicated little more than bored revulsion with the "flatness" of bourgeois life and a provocative nature that later won him a dubious notoriety.[26] Still, these early encounters provided the basis for his friendship with Otto Lang, a future leader of Swiss Social Democracy, with whom he eagerly discussed possibilities for socialism "as a cultural factor" during the 1880s: "With your 'Göthe [sic] as Social Democrat,' you will one day place the crown on your efforts in this direction, upon which I am building very, very much," Lang wrote him in February 1888.[27] By this time, "the delicious one-sidedness" of Sombart's passion for Marx had given way to the "philistrosity" of an incapacitating bourgeois skepticism, however, and he had already named what seemed to him three major weaknesses of Social Democracy: its "brutal manner," its neglect of modern evolution, and—perhaps most revealing of the impulse that had drawn him to it in the first place—its "individualistic" character. The "next goal of our social movement: elevating the lot of the lower classes" should be pursued "not so that millions will be better off as a result," Sombart insisted in May 1887 (anticipating Weber's arguments at the Protestant Social Congress seven years later), "but instead so that the whole gains new forces and evolves further."[28]

Rejection of liberal individualism amid mounting social tension in fact formed the bridge between Sombart's interest in Marx and the older gen-

---

24. Ibid., p. 36.
25. Sombart to Lang, June 21, 1889, NL Otto Lang.
26. Sombart to Lang, September 5, 1886, NL Otto Lang.
27. Lang to Sombart, February 6, 1888, NL Sombart 8e.
28. Sombart to Lang, May 7 and September 30, 1887, NL Otto Lang.

eration's critique of "Manchesterism," which echoed loudly in his earliest work. The young student's first expressions of the social impulse looked to the intimate sphere rather than to politics for the antidote, much like Bäumer's later defense of the "old morals." Writing home from Italy, where he was beginning research on agrarian capitalism in 1884, Sombart used his father's birthday as an occasion to celebrate the "ethical and social" importance of family ties, a constant reminder that individuals were merely "dependent elements of a great social unity."[29] Four years later, the young scholar again stressed the family's importance as a social institution in his first article, which criticized the unrestrained economic developments that were threatening to undermine it.[30] But the clearest indication of Sombart's scorn for the Liberals' "blind idolatry of the individualistic economic principle of our age" came in his dissertation, *On Tenancy and Wage Relations in the Roman Campagna*.[31] Assessing capitalism's cultural impact on the Italian countryside in 1888, he grudgingly admired the "modern luxury" of the *palazzo*, which had ended the earlier "philistinism" of the now "substantially more cosmopolitan, civilized" provincial landowners.[32] Otherwise, however, the effects of capitalist development had been devastating. If "the forest stock was not suffering under the ax-strokes of foreign speculators," this circumstance said more about "the pathetic wood reserves of the Roman Campagna" than about the ruthlessness of modern commercial practices. The latter had, in fact, reduced the region's peasants— proud descendants of "wild tribes in the rugged land of Mars, whose attacks had cost Republican Rome not a little to repel"—to a "broken condition, crushed and enervated by modern culture—here amid the ruins of a powerful great age, on the ruins of Imperial Rome that ruled the world."[33] "[A]bstract/Manchesterist" policies consigned landless day laborers to rootlessness, financial insecurity, and poor hygiene, with alarming consequences for national strength, Sombart complained, and he especially warned against the sale of the Italian *Allmend*: "Italy more than any other country of Europe should be mindful of protecting all institutions that erect a dam against the

---

29. Sombart to his father, September 12, 1884, NL Sombart 8a.
30. Mitzman, *Estrangement,* pp. 143–45.
31. Werner Sombart, *Über Pacht- und Lohnverhältnisse in der römischen Campagna* (Berlin: Ph.D. diss., 1888), pp. 18–19.
32. Ibid., p. 6.
33. Ibid., pp. 10, 39.

complete proletarization of the rural population."[34] Like his father, who was promoting land reform on the family Pomeranian estate with similar arguments, the young economist stressed the racial benefits of the paternalistic land tenure still practiced on the traditional *latifundia*. Unlike the rural proletariat, tenant farmers were "healthy. . . , robust, endowed with a lively spirit and good character; they love their land, their cattle," he observed. "Certainly—their life is not rich in joys and pleasures, but they can at least look trustingly ahead to the coming days; they have a certain security of existence, and this awareness suffices for the undemanding mind of the Italian rural laborer to make him satisfied."[35]

While still informed by Sombart's youthful flair for the dramatic, *Campagna* also marked a departure from his early passion for the revolutionary flourishes of Marx, whom he had once admired alongside Rousseau and Byron. Having learned to appreciate the empirical rigor of his teachers in Berlin, the economist chose instead to adopt the "scientific" categories of Marxist analysis, which now seemed a more substantial contribution, and he warned of the dangers of inflamed rhetoric precisely in terms of culture. "There are elements being preserved in the midst of a cultured nation that are themselves still completely outside the sphere of modern civilization, and they can therefore easily break into that sphere in a destructive manner," he wrote, describing the exploitation of Italian shepherds: "A more suitable avant-garde for a revolutionary army cannot be conceived than these half-barbarians hardened by all sorts of fatigue and hardship."[36] The changing nature of Sombart's relation to Marxism was even more evident in a heated exchange with Otto Lang, who described his own conversion to Social Democracy in almost religious terms in the summer of 1889. "In the name 'socialism' I sum up everything grand, eternal humanity has ever thought," Lang told his friend. "In it I find a description of the most wonderful goals humankind has ever found nobility in pursuing."[37] Scrawling "bravo" in the margins next to the passage, Sombart responded with grave misgivings to this outburst from the person who had taught him "that someone could be enlightened, tolerant, respectable, and still be a Soc[ial] Dem[ocrat]." "I would be happy to find a fresh, gay mood of opposition

---

34. Ibid., pp. 18–19.
35. Ibid., p. 28.
36. Ibid., p. 24.
37. Lang to Sombart, June 27, 1889, NL Sombart 8e.

in my friend, indeed, I would even take encouragement from it," he insisted, but only calculated cynicism or (as he suspected in this case) a desperate urge to flee the frustrations of a professional career could explain Lang's intention knowingly to propagate illusory hopes of violent revolution in workers lacking any "substantial knowledge of the conditions determining the existence of society."[38] The whole point of Marxism was that the material foundations of the social and economic order simply could not be transformed overnight by idealistic fervor. By Marx's own analysis, the conditions required for the transition to socialism did not exist even in an industrialized country like Germany, where vast sectors of the economy remained unaffected by capitalist production. The Party's educated leaders, including Lang, should know better.

Returning to the objections he had raised in 1886, Sombart furthermore criticized the Party's failure to respond to conceptual breakthroughs in social science since Marx's original analysis. While the eighteenth-century ideals of "equality, liberty, human rights and the like" were certainly still important, the younger generation drew inspiration from new sources. "Your party has not even recognized the most eminent idea of the welfare of the species, the actual socialist idea, and can't grasp it," he complained.[39] The one-sidedly individualistic, mechanistic perspectives of the early Enlightenment also blinded Marxists to the "national movement of our day," which belied the notion that class conflict was the *only* agent of historical change. "Cosmopolitanism is completely and entirely obsolete," Sombart informed Lang; "as a principle it has long since been overcome, not only by science, but also by general public opinion." The discovery of evolutionary and psychological forces at work in the collectivist struggles among nations demanded an updated definition of progress, he believed: "The goal of human development would have to be bringing all natural aptitudes of isolated individuals and all functions of the collective organisms to the freest ... development. The individual should 'live life to the fullest,' and humanity should naturally 'live life to the fullest' no less." Concluding the exchange, Sombart underlined his commitment to realizing this goal, not by revolution, but with solid academic scholarship and realistic attempts to answer the social question. "I situate myself on the ground of the present order, which I provisionally acknowledge as the best among many existing

---

38. Sombart to Lang, June 21/25, 1889, NL Lang.
39. Ibid.

ones, but which I want to transform—in the same direction as you—through gradual reform on a peaceful path toward a new, more perfect order."[40]

Despite the vast social distances separating them, by the time he finished his studies in Berlin, Sombart had arrived at conclusions that were again quite similar to those Damaschke and Bäumer reached after exploring the social question a few years later. Blaming "Manchesterism" for the oppression of the proletariat, Sombart defined its costs both in terms of neglected personal needs, physical and spiritual, and in terms of the dangers this suffering posed for the welfare of the nation as a whole, using language that expressed an early concern for race and hygiene. His alternative conception of "progress" also drew heavily on biological, evolutionary discourse. Sombart even pointed to many of the solutions Damaschke and Bäumer later embraced—land reform, a secure home, the gentle yoke of family life—in his earliest writings, which evinced the same communalist impulse to dissolve social tensions all three viewed as the most urgent challenge to Germany's future prosperity. And while it posed far less risk to his financial security, the young economist's commitment to a serious engagement with the social question, and above all with Marxism, soon required painful sacrifices in his professional life as well.

"Demagoguery in Scholarly Clothing?"

Before finishing his dissertation, Sombart had already begun working as a legal representative for Bremen's Commercial Senate in January 1888, and in July he married Felicitas Genzmer, whom he had met at the spas the summer before college and courted on frequent visits to Pisa.[41] While his new job probably played some role in shifting his attention from agrarian to industrial capitalism, he mainly bided his time waiting for an academic post, and in January 1890 the young economist accepted an appointment at the University of Breslau.[42] The move came as a shock to Sombart, who had his hopes set on Berlin, but a thriving circle of progressive reformers soon offered the young couple an encouraging welcome in the provincial outpost shortly after their arrival that summer. Albert Neisser, a derma-

---

40. Sombart to Lang, July 18/21, 1889, NL Lang.
41. Lenger, *Sombart,* pp. 35–36, 38–40.
42. Ibid., pp. 54–56.

tologist who worked on the prevention of venereal disease, was active in city government and helped to launch the racial hygiene and sexual reform movements a decade or so later. Neisser was the center of this circle, and the Sombarts easily befriended the reformer and his wife Toni, who hosted a salon at the Neissers' *Jugendstil* villa. While Felicitas took part in the "Women's Welfare Association," Werner supported Toni's work on peda-gogical and children's issues in the "At Home Club," and he also eventually joined her husband on the Breslau city council, where both men pushed for the expansion of communal property and other land reforms. These efforts were in turn supported by Hans-Georg Kurella, a neurologist who shared Neisser's interest in hygiene and occasionally took Sombart along to meetings of the local National Social Association.[43]

Breslau was also a "bastion of revisionism" in the early 1890s. Sombart took advantage of the remarkable atmosphere of cooperation between "bourgeois" and socialist reformers to make contacts with leading Social Democrats like Bruno Schoenlank and Bebel, who visited the younger pro-fessor's home in these years.[44] Despite their quarrel, he also maintained his ties with Lang and established a close friendship with Heinrich Braun, the Social Democratic editor of *The New Age*. It was in fact Braun who pro-vided crucial encouragement for Sombart's interest in Marx by inviting him to contribute to the *Archive for Social Legislation and Statistics*, which the revisionist socialist founded in 1888 to promote empirical research on the social question.[45] Sombart was delighted with the invitation, which came just ten days after his dissertation defense in November, and a few weeks later he praised the "tendency of the paper" in a letter to Lang expressing his hope that the *Archive* would serve as "the organ for our entire younger generation." Outlining the tenets of "this school—to use that expression—which is still in the process of formation," Sombart included Herkner, Lamprecht, and several others on a list of young schol-ars he believed would join Braun, Lang, and himself in conducting research along the following guidelines: "(1) historical interpretation, (2) Zola-esque/realistic understanding of the present, (3) a state-socialist or even

43. Ibid., pp. 54–56. On Kurella's NSV and land reform activities, see "Aus un-serer Bewegung," *Die Hilfe* 7, no. 9 (March 3, 1901); "Aus der Bewegung," *Deutsche Volksstimme* 10, no. 10 (May 20, 1899): 311.

44. Lenger, *Sombart*, pp. 54, 114.

45. Braun to Sombart, November 27, 1888, NL Sombart 9c.

social-communist (i.e., anti-individualist) way of thinking (along the lines of Rodbertus/Lassalle . . .)."[46] In frequent articles for the *Archive* and the *Social-Political Central Newsletter* Braun founded in 1892, the young economist soon began to elaborate these principles as he continued cultivating reform contacts alongside his new friendship with Heinrich, and later with Lily, in Berlin.

Published in 1889, the first of Sombart's articles read like a call to arms for the national economic boys. If the older generation was content gathering data from official sources "on the sunny heights of advancing production," the "younger men of economic science" understood the need for "distribution statistics" and had dared to venture beyond their comfortable studies "into the factories, workers' apartments, into the field to the day laborers," where they were seeking to learn more about the "lower classes, of whose life and suffering we still have so little secure knowledge," the young rebel proclaimed.[47] Presenting his own "wage-statistical studies," Sombart concluded that Italy's "industrial proletariat is more miserable than any; and what is worse: languishes in deeper misery than its rural population."[48] Besides providing regular installments on working-class conditions in Italy and Germany for Braun's journals, the young professor also began reading his way carefully through Marx. In the winter of 1892–93, he was even bold enough to offer a seminar on the first volume of *Capital* and a few shorter works to a small group of adventurous students at the University of Breslau.[49] Though hardly an endorsement of Social Democracy—like his dissertation, Sombart's articles warned against the spread of "social-revolutionary ideas" to "analphabets still wet behind the ears"—such provocative behavior raised predictable alarms in the tense climate of the early 1890s. After defending Marx from a scathing critique by Julius Wolf, the rebellious scholar soon faced charges by the local press of spreading seditious doctrines.[50]

---

46. Sombart to Lang, January 6, 1889, NL Lang.
47. Werner Sombart, "Lohnstatistische Studien," *Archiv für soziale Gesetzgebung und Statistik* 2, no. 2 (1889): 259–60.
48. Ibid., p. 280.
49. Lenger, *Sombart,* p. 79.
50. Sombart, "Lohstatistische Studien," p. 280; for more reservations about Social Democracy, see Sombart, "Die Hausindustrie in Deutschland," *Archiv* 4,

The polemics began on October 2 with a front-page editorial on "Demagoguery in Scholarly Clothing" in the *Silesian Newspaper*. Describing an alarming trend in this direction among German economics professors more generally, the article noted with horror that even a reliable Conservative like Adolf Wagner had described the Social Democrats' platform as "absolutely open for discussion" and, after leveling its sights on Braun's *Central Newsletter*, finally honed in on Sombart's recent behavior. If the renegade scholar was bold enough to call the Erfurt Platform "beneficial" in a meeting of the Silesian Society for Patriotic Culture, one could only imagine what he was telling impressionable young students, the editors warned, and they closed with a call for official censure of Sombart's work, which was labeled "dangerous to the state."[51] If the desire for social peace had waned at all in Breslau since the February Decrees, this attack visibly revived it among bourgeois and socialist reformers, who responded defiantly. "Leftist Progressives, Center Party, Protestant Ministers and Social Democrats have gone to the barricades for me," Sombart informed Lang not long afterwards.[52] While distancing itself from the professor's "state socialism," the left-liberal *Breslau Morning Newspaper* praised his "work of enlightenment and reconciliation," which sought to restore "the broken connection . . . between a broad segment of our population and the rest of the nation," and condemned the "common arrogance" of those who believed Social Democracy could be dismissed out of hand.[53] For his part, Sombart firmly reasserted his belief that socialism had to be understood objectively if its irrational, revolutionary appeal was to be dispelled. "But precisely this is to be prevented once again," he complained in the *News-*

---

no. 1 (1891): 155–56; Sombart, "Zur Lage der schlesischen Hausweber," *Sozialpolitisches Centralblatt* 1, no. 14 (April 4, 1892): 175–77. The review of Julius Wolf is in *Archiv* 5, no. 3 (1892): 487–98. Wolf is described as a "socialist-killer" in newspaper clippings on his appointment as a "penal professor" in 1897; NL Sombart 41.

51. "Demagogenthum in wissenschaftlichem Gewande," *Schlesische Zeitung* 691 (October 2, 1892); see also clippings from *Schlesische Zeitung* of October 19 and November 4; NL Sombart 37.

52. Sombart to Lang, December 10, 1892, NL Lang.

53. Newspaper clippings, NL Sombart 37.

letter. "The dissemination of such a view . . . is itself already an ill-afforded 'well-wishing' to Social Democracy."[54]

Instead of cowing the younger generation into silence, attacks from Liberals and Conservatives merely strengthened the national economic boys' commitment to what they increasingly perceived as a common cause. "Things have gone much the same for me here as the game they're playing with you in Breslau," Herkner wrote from Karlsruhe on October 17. "I couldn't give even the most harmless lecture in the workers' education clubs or elsewhere, not even so much as an academic inaugural address without . . . immediately being attacked by the organ of the National Liberal Party."[55] The next summer, Schulze-Gävernitz also wrote to express his solidarity. "The *Silesian Newspaper*'s attacks on you vividly remind me of the numerous attacks to which I was subjected: pieces written by editors who depend on big business or by young people anxious about their careers, which are only unsettling in that one can't avoid wasting time on replies to them now and then."[56] While Sombart moved closer to his socialist contacts, renewing his friendship with Lang and spurning the opinion of "respectable people,"[57] Herkner and Schulze-Gävernitz had meanwhile begun considering the possibility of joining the Social Democratic party itself. The idea initially came from Tönnies, who was facing similar frustrations in Kiel, and in December 1893 the famous author of *Community and Society* urged Sombart to join this bold venture in a letter carefully crafted to address his colleague's long-standing reservations about Social Democracy. They would not have to accept "anything that does not appeal to us about the people and their principles," Tönnies assured him; on the contrary, "at a single stroke we will elevate the party from the swamp of half-education in which it is threatening to sink." Similar improvement could be expected in political discourse on the other side of the social divide. "The effect on the middle classes will be colossal," he exclaimed, particularly "among the academic youth," who were just beginning to awaken from "the stifling anti-Semitic dream in which their political

---

54. Werner Sombart, "Demagogenthum in wissenschaftlichem Gewande," *Sozialpolitisches Centralblatt* 2, no. 3 (October 1892): 25–27.
55. Herkner to Sombart, October 17, 1892, NL Sombart 10a, Bd. 4
56. Schulze-Gävernitz to Sombart, July 4, 1893, NL Sombart 45.
57. Sombart to Lang, December 10, 1892, NL Lang.

thought has lain buried."[58] Writing again in January, Tönnies insisted that they had a patriotic duty as scholars "to elevate and support the party that needs elevation and support the most."[59]

Sombart was not about to abandon his foothold in the academy, tenuous as it was, merely to join the "partisan racket," however, and he flatly rejected Tönnies's proposals, arguing that the scholar's real duty was to maintain a critical distance from "everyday politics."[60] As the economist later freely admitted, much of the impetus for the "theory of the value-free nature of national economics" came from the harassment he faced due to his partisanship for the working class.[61] Yet if career anxieties were clearly lurking beneath Sombart's refusal to join the ranks of Social Democracy, the support he received in the *Silesian Newspaper* affair also gave him reason to hope that such "objective" inquiry might indeed calm passions on both sides and prepare the ground for a constructive dialogue with Marxism inside the bourgeois camp. "We are all standing behind you, more than you think," the economist told Lang a year after the polemics in Breslau. But Schulze-Gävernitz had recently convinced him there were better ways to promote the interests of Social Democracy than Tönnies's proposal. "He said to me: what use would it be to the workers' movement if you or Herkner or I or another of us boys went ahead and became a 'comrade,' wrote for the *New Age*, and worked for *Forwards*. None at all," Sombart agreed. "But it might well be of use if German universities were filled with our spirit *by and by*. None of us believes in miracles, after all, but only in slow education and reformation of the minds."[62]

The Spirit of Capitalism and the Future of German *Kultur*

The following year, Sombart gave a clear indication of the "spirit" he and the boys hoped to bring to the university in a review of the long-awaited third volume of *Capital*. Scorning the "piety" in Engels's lax performance

58. Tönnies to Sombart, December 6, 1893, NL Sombart 9f; Sombart to Lang, October 5, 1893, NL Lang.
59. Tönnies to Sombart, January 13, 1894, NL Sombart 9f.
60. Ibid.; Sombart to Lang, December 10, 1892, NL Lang.
61. Sombart, radio transcript, February 14, 1933, NL Sombart 5b.
62. Sombart to Lang, October 5, 1893, NL Lang.

as editor of the posthumous manuscript, he nonetheless believed the new work should prove more interesting to "scholars, theoreticians," since it lacked the "slogans and phrases" that had reduced its predecessors to arsenals for Marxist agitators.[63] Sombart then went on to address the alleged contradictions older economists claimed to have discovered in the earlier volumes, and he proposed an alternative reading of surplus value that reconciled Marx's predictions with current data.[64] The mere possibility of such interpretations proved that "we are not at the end, but just at the beginning of the critique of Marx," he insisted. The older generation would thus have to accept that a definitive "refutation" was impossible: "we younger [scholars] will see to it that your laughter slowly fades."[65] As with the ideas of Quenay, Smith, and Ricardo, "further development" was the only way to get past Marx. What was keeping older scholars from accepting the theory was not contrary evidence, Sombart suspected, but its "extreme objectivity," which he contrasted with the "psychologism" of all other economic schools, "whether they call themselves historical, ethical, organic, abstract, classical or otherwise." Marxist and bourgeois scholars were simply talking past each other: "here two worlds of national economic thought have emerged alongside, almost independently of one another, two kinds of scientific observation that have hardly anything but the name in common."[66] Proposing some "guiding principles for the future critique of Marx," Sombart again called for a constructive dialogue between the two sides and concluded with the hope that "objective" and "psychological" analysis might be reconciled in a new form of analysis yet to be devised.

At the same time, Sombart also built new ties to social reform circles seeking a similar reconciliation beyond the walls of the university. In August 1894 he accepted an invitation to join Viennese reformers in an attempt "to unite bourgeois elements that have sufficient seriousness and understanding for social policy matters, and to introduce social propaganda in bourgeois circles."[67] Working on a handbook and an article, "So-

---

63. Werner Sombart, "Zur Kritik des ökonomischen Systems von Karl Marx," *Archiv* 7, no. 4 (1894): 557–59.

64. Ibid., pp. 571–84.

65. Ibid., p. 587.

66. Ibid., p. 592.

67. Fernstorfer to Sombart, August 25, 1894, NL Sombart 45.

cialism and Communism," the economist became close friends with one member of the group, Otto Wittelshöfer, and frequently returned to Vienna to lecture on reform topics.[68] In Breslau, Sombart spoke on "The Economic Foundations of the Social Movement" at the local Ethical Culture Society in 1895 and successfully ran for the city council for the first time the following year.[69] He also followed the younger Christian Socials with interest. "Protestant ministers" were among his supporters in the "Demagoguery" uproar, and in December 1892 he described Göhre's undercover study of factory workers as "exceptional ... one of a kind and epoch-making."[70] Approached by Naumann's supporters in 1895, he agreed to sign the petition against Stumm's "revolution bill." The following summer Sombart singled out Göhre and Naumann for special praise in his addresses on "Socialism and the Social Movement" at the international Ethical Culture congress in Zurich.[71] As tensions mounted inside the Protestant Congress, he told his father that he agreed "in principle" with the younger Christian Socials but had doubts about Naumann's "practical explications."[72] Admitting that he had "not yet found the right method myself," the economist thus kept his distance from the National Socials' founding congress in November, but he watched the movement's development closely.

To Sombart, scholarship still seemed a more effective means to overcome social tensions than politics. While redoubling his reform efforts, he also continued working toward the reconciliation of the "psychological" and "objective" models he had proposed in his review of *Capital,* and as he did so, the first inklings of "the spirit of capitalism" began to appear in his

---

68. Wittelshöfer wrote eighteen letters to Sombart in the informal form of address between 1895 and 1899, NL Sombart 45. Other members of the circle included Fernstorfer, Elster, and Grünberg, who gave lectures on the "Developmental History of Modern Socialism"; Grünberg to Sombart, October 17 and November 8, 1894; NL Sombart 10a, Bd. 3.

69. Lenger, *Sombart,* p. 56.

70. Sombart to Lang, December 12, 1892, NL Lang; Lindenlaub, *Richtungskämpfe,* p. 78.

71. Mangoldt to Sombart, January 28, 1895, NL Sombart; Lindenlaub, *Richtungskämpfe,* p. 78; Werner Sombart, *Sozialismus und soziale Bewegung im 19. Jahrhundert* (Frankfurt am Main: Europa-Verlag, 1966), p. 105.

72. Sombart to father, August 19, 1896, NL Sombart 8a; Heuss, *Naumann,* p. 115.

writings. The pithy phrase itself speaks to the attempt to mediate between the two "worlds" Sombart had identified (which extended far beyond the academy) in 1894, and the economist clearly placed its origin in this context when he unveiled his theory in *Modern Capitalism* for the first time in 1902. Returning to the distinction between Marx's objective method (which he now termed "strictly causal") and the psychological approach still dominant among bourgeois scholars (now called "teleological"), Sombart insisted in the preface to his great work that neither method provided a sufficient grasp of the dynamics of modern capitalism on its own. The national economists had been unable to recognize the new economic order as such, because the "blindly operating laws of the market" that governed it became visible only "from the perspective of cause and effect." On the other hand, Marxist scholars missed the final cause of economic activity, which was always found in the "motivation of living human beings," and they also tended to conflate the immense heuristic value of abstract regularities with the deterministic force of natural laws.[73] Combining the two approaches, Sombart sought to identify the "motive-series of the leading subjects of the economy" and then to show how "the goals they establish[ed], their aspirations," were objectified in the institutions and practices they constructed to achieve those goals.[74] Once these rationalized structures were firmly in place, he argued, they took on a logic of their own, creating a network of economic relations that could be analyzed only through Marx's "objective" methods. But inside them the subjective intentions of their creators—"the spirit of capitalism"—lived on. Only by keeping a foot in both worlds, Sombart implied, had his analysis finally succeeded in unlocking the secrets of modern economic life.

Though not complete until 1902, his theory on the "genesis of the capitalist spirit" was thus firmly rooted in the middle ground Sombart attempted to stake out between right and left in the early 1890s. In fact, the young scholar had already named its fundamental psychological component—an irrational desire for unlimited profits called the *Erwerbstrieb*, or "drive for acquisition"—while he was still licking his wounds from the Breslau polemics in 1893, the year before his review of *Capital*. After identifying the *Erwerbstrieb* as "the demon of capitalism," Sombart also went on to discuss the "social disciplining" and "subjugation of personal ca-

---

73. Sombart, *Kapitalismus* (1902), vol. 1., pp. xiv–xviii.
74. Ibid., vol. 2, p. 4.

price" he saw at work in the rise of organized labor in the same article, the first of two "Studies on the Developmental History of the Italian Proletariat" published in Braun's *Archive* during these years.[75] "Not until [economic rationalism] fuses into an organic unity with the *Erwerbstrieb* can we speak of the new capitalist spirit in a real sense," the economist would argue in *Modern Capitalism*.[76] But Sombart had already discovered both elements by 1893, and even earlier in his writings, a "calculating" nature appeared as the other essential ingredient of the capitalist psyche. "The entrepreneur calculates, that is his God-given mission," the economist had argued a few months before the *Silesian Newspaper* affair in 1892; "he would be a poor businessman and not do his nation any favors if out of pure philanthropy he" were to abandon this ruthless pursuit.[77]

Over the next five years, as he continued to build a reputation as a practical reformer in progressive circles, Sombart worked out the representative "types" for the social classes he gradually came to see as "carriers" of distinctive psychological motivations, which successively became the ordering principle of economic life as each class assumed a leading role in state and society during a series of evolutionary stages. Discussing the "peculiarities of the type of the entrepreneur and the worker" in 1894, he found a good portrait of the rare "type of the capitalist parvenu" in Zola's Saccard. Still to be encountered in Italy, this "phenomenon from the childhood days of capitalism" had been "more or less overcome" in the more advanced economy of Germany, the economist thankfully observed.[78] Although the project he began the same year on the decline of artisans (as the leading economic subject of the previous era) is often described as the point of departure for *Modern Capitalism*,[79] the "Studies on the Developmental History of the Proletariat" went back at least to 1893, and both projects were bound to the research agenda the young scholar had outlined in 1889. Sombart's "Zola-esque/realistic understanding of the present" is clearly discernible in his continuing scholarship on the working

---

75. Werner Sombart, "Studien zur Entwicklungsgeschichte des italienischen Proletariats," *Archiv* 6, no. 2 (1893): 194–96.

76. Sombart, *Kapitalismus* (1902), vol. 1., p. 391.

77. Sombart, "Hausweber," p. 175.

78. Werner Sombart, "Italienische Briefe (IV)," *Sozialpolitisches Centralblatt* 3, no. 33 (May 14, 1894): 391.

79. Lenger, *Sombart*, p. 118; Appel, *Sombart*, p. 28.

class, which he boldly described as the carrier of the "socialist, communalist" order destined to replace capitalism in his addresses to the Ethical Culture congress in 1896.[80] Unveiling the developmental schema that became the "basic plan" for *Modern Capitalism* the following year, Sombart made the link between his scholarly and reform efforts even clearer in the foundational essay "Ideals of Social Policy."

As Sombart conceived it in 1897, European economic evolution passed through four stages: (1) an "independent economy," governed by the motives of *Junker* and peasants; (2) the artisans' "local exchange economy" of the late medieval and early modern periods; (3) the "capitalist commercial economy" now driven by the subjective interests of the bourgeoisie; and (4) a "socialist economy" of the future, the outlines of which were dimly perceptible in the rising proletariat.[81] While acknowledging the debt this "genetic" model owed to Marx, Sombart hoped the reader of *Modern Capitalism* would recognize the "progress represented by my method" when he introduced it for the second time in 1902. "He will note that the attempt has been made to replace the metaphorical language of Marx with a non-metaphorical designation of concepts, to detach the development process in our social life from the Marxist, inorganic, revolutionary view once and for all by means of an organic, evolutionary view that is more in keeping with modern knowledge."[82] Just as he had proposed in his exchange with Lang, Sombart applied Darwin's "most eminent theory of the welfare of the species" to update Marx's "inorganic" theory, ridding it of the impassioned flourishes of revolutionary rhetoric that were hindering the country's evolution toward socialism. "Why all the acrimony, all the bitterness on both sides, when modern society can also develop without it?!" the economist wondered in 1895.[83] Every piece of scholarship he produced in these years confirmed the integrationist message of his response to Lang in 1889: socialism was coming, but gradually, on the "peaceful path toward new, more perfect forms."

Progress had a price, however, and Sombart also continued to emphasize the cultural costs of European economic development even as he sought

---

80. Sombart, *Sozialismus*, p. 17.

81. Werner Sombart, "Ideale der Sozialpolitik," *Archiv* 10, no. 1 (1897): 1–8.

82. Sombart, *Kapitalismus* (1902), vol. 1., p. 72.

83. Werner Sombart, "Studien zur Entwicklungsgeschichte des italienischen Proletariats," *Archiv* 8, no. 4 (1895): 566.

to smooth its path. "The complete human being has to make way for the career person," he sadly noted, describing the Italian workers' "relinquishment of the activation of personal caprice in the mechanism of production" in 1893.[84] The following year, the young scholar published a series of "Italian letters" in Braun's *Newsletter* that painted an especially dismal portrait of modern life. "Its effect on the land and the people must above all be a leveling one. Ethical idiosyncrasies are not standing up against the onslaught of capitalism, which mercilessly remodels forms of life and customs of life everywhere to suit its uniform needs," he wrote in the first letter.[85] Contrasting the "ugly exterior of the factory compound" with the "majesty" of the landscape of the Italian Alps outside Schio—a "great, fertile cauldron around which the snow-crowned mountain giants group themselves like theater curtains"—Sombart reviled "the rule of atrocious coal" in another letter. But "electro-technology" was quickly "spreading like a sigh of relief through the industrialized countries," he added, and its wholesome influence was obvious in the "splendid buildings" and "broad, airy work rooms" of newer factories elsewhere in Italy. "The old, small establishments are being rapidly transformed and brought up to the heights of technology; new facilities enter life in technical perfection," he raptly concluded. Someday a "liberated humanity" would shudder at the thought of "the rusty first century of capitalism."[86]

Like Bäumer, who also detested "the black middle ages of industry," the young economist thus believed modern science and technology would address the concerns of contemporary cultural critics (including his own) and ultimately even enhance the possibilities for *Kultur* in a "bright renaissance" of the future. Presenting his four-stage model of social progress in his article "Ideals of Social Policy," he firmly denounced the views of Schmoller and other older economists who allowed "instinctive fear of large-scale capitalist development" to cloud their judgment in such matters.[87] The protective legislation proposed by the Association for Social Policy to revive artisan industry sought to restrain vital forces of social and

---

84. Sombart, "Entwicklungsgeschichte" (1893), p. 194.
85. Werner Sombart, "Italienische Briefe (I)," *Sozialpolitisches Centralblatt* 3, no. 28 (April 9, 1894): 326.
86. Werner Sombart, "Italienische Briefe (II)," *Sozialpolitisches Centralblatt* 3, no. 30 (April 23, 1894): 353–54.
87. Sombart, "Ideale," p. 33.

economic evolution that would sustain German prosperity—cultural as well as material—in years to come. However much he might sympathize with the older generation's motives, Sombart denounced the intrusion of "ethical" considerations in formulating "objective" social policy as a grotesque "inversion of the causal relation between economy and morals" that was "by its nature always reactionary." The economic order provided the basis for "all the rest of human existence," not the other way around, he insisted, and "all views concerning the economic system suited to the demands of ethics" could therefore "be derived only from the pre-capitalist, if not the capitalist systems of production." The goal of rational policies had to be the development of more advanced and efficient economic structures, but this was impossible if expectations remained anchored in the past. "[T]he unfolding of productive forces is thereby placed in shackles that prevent the healthy development of economic life," and Sombart therefore demanded the "autonomy of the social-political ideal" from all subjective value judgments.[88]

Like it or not, economic evolution was leading to a socialist order, the germ of which was "carried" by the proletariat, Sombart declared. The "ideal of social policy" thus objectively demanded the protection of this class, not of the artisans. Nor would idealistic notions of social harmony forestall the inevitable, since the "diversity of interests" among the different classes "at a certain point becomes an antagonism of interests that cannot be reconciled," he recognized. "A government that wanted—assuming it was possible—to rule 'above the parties' would either be a government of the zig-zag course. . . , or it would have merely a decorative significance."[89] Yet such harsh realities were no reason for despair. While insisting that his bourgeois readers accept the objective, material demands of social and economic progress, Sombart also insisted that the new structures were perfectly compatible with their cultural values. "In defining the most productive economic system as the ideal of social policy, I set as a target worth striving for an organization of economic life in which the highest productiveness of societal labor comes about"—and, he quickly added—"the possibility is created for society not to work much or to produce a great deal."[90] The rationality of science had nothing to say about the human ends that

---

88. Ibid., pp. 33–36.
89. Ibid., pp. 39–42.
90. Ibid., p. 47.

increased efficiency was to serve, the economist argued, just as Bäumer later proclaimed the autonomy of "the cultural ideal that compels these means into its service." Urging his readers to join him in promoting the social advance of the proletariat precisely "in the interests of the progress of *Kultur*," Sombart offered a list of the personal values he believed "the overwhelming majority of European/American cultured humanity" shared, which "the highest development of productive forces" could easily achieve along the road to socialism:

> Preservation and increase of our modern cultural goods, preservation and consolidation of our status as a national power, at least vis-à-vis the inferior East European and Asiatic nations, natural increase in the population, the dissemination of cultural goods to ever broader segments of the population, the greatest improvement of material existence possible, i.e. the most far-reaching domination of natural forces and the greatest possible relief from the burdens of economic labor.[91]

Social Science and the Social Movement

By 1897 Sombart had poignantly expressed many of the aspirations emerging in Wilhelmine reform circles at the time. Leading the younger generation's critical engagement with Marx, he demanded "objective" recognition of empirical realities and formulated a "scientific" model of progress that foresaw a peaceful transition to socialism through the integration of the proletariat into an inwardly prosperous and outwardly strong Germany. His jarring reference to "inferior East European and Asiatic nations" serves as a disturbing reminder of the diverse meanings contained in the progressive blend of economic and biological discourse at the fin de siècle. If Sombart's view of the proletariat as a "rising class" informed Naumann's democratic anthropology, the aggressive, imperialistic nature of his "subjective" goals suggests a conception of national strength that also came closer to the National Social leader's controversial agenda than those of either Damaschke or Bäumer, though Sombart's attitudes were more complex, as we will see. Well on his way to forming the seminal concept of "the spirit of capitalism," the young economist also undoubtedly helped shape his generation's views on *Zivilisation* and *Kultur* in the early 1890s.

---

91. Ibid., p. 43.

Social and cultural criticism were closely intertwined with scholarly efforts to mediate between worlds divided along lines of class, politics, and generation in Sombart's work of these years. It was not his academic treatise "Ideals of Social Policy" that made his message famous, however, in 1897. Published as *Socialism and the Social Movement,* the young economist's lectures to the Ethical Culture congress had already launched Sombart to stardom in reform circles throughout the country a few months earlier, sealing his commitment to social activism for the rest of the decade.

Addressed to "the warriors themselves, both here and on the other side," the short volume presented the arguments of "Ideals" in a form intended to appeal to partisans in the political struggles of the mid-1890s.[92] Turning first to his bourgeois audience, Sombart explained that the socialist movement was not an expression of malicious caprice, but the "necessary result of a certain series of developments."[93] The proletariat's desire for "eliminating" private property arose from the conditions under which it suffered, and in economic matters a clash with the bourgeoisie was unavoidable.[94] What was more, the workers were bound to win that struggle, since they held the key to the future. There was no sense clinging to "the foundations of the existing social order," which were constantly in flux, and reactionary visions of a return to the feudal past were even more pathetic, Sombart chided, though he gratefully noted that these were finally beginning to wane.[95] In fact, Marx had spoken "one of the greatest truths" of the century when he identified all history as the history of class struggle—but he had spoken only half of this truth.[96] There were *two* poles in human action, the young economist declared, the social and the national, and there was nothing preventing bourgeoisie and proletariat from uniting around the latter, whatever set them apart in economic terms. If the socialist movement had assumed an anti-nationalist posture, the bourgeoisie had no one to blame but itself, Sombart argued, turning to the theme of lost opportunities. "[F]ear of the red phantom" had merely played into Bismarck's hands, he sourly remarked of Lassalle's overtures to the National Association; it was only a matter of time before the Chancellor unleashed his

---

92. Sombart, *Sozialismus,* p. 109.
93. Ibid., p. 17.
94. Ibid., pp. 72–75.
95. Ibid., p. 27.
96. Ibid., p. 15.

"diabolical lust for revenge" on both sides.[97] "Hatred, persecution, suppression are not the appropriate means to awaken joy in the house where
we are to live together with those upon whom everything depends."[98]

No stranger to such harassment, Sombart blamed Liberals and Conservatives for much of the current tension, but he was equally harsh in criticizing the tactics of Social Democracy. "[N]o power on earth, no party,
however revolutionary its demeanor, will be capable of forcing a new social
order upon humanity," he calmly explained, attempting to ease the minds
of his bourgeois listeners as he directed his criticisms across the aisle.[99] If
Marx had made important discoveries, "in substantial points" his theory
went "so far astray that on the whole it can hardly be upheld," the economist believed.[100] Rejecting visions of recovering a lost socialist paradise as
"inconsistent" with an otherwise scientific analysis, Sombart urged Social
Democrats to abandon such rhetoric in favor of the evolutionary perspective, which he insisted represented Marx's "true" position.[101] Competition
and struggle were part of life, the economist concluded; given the right
form, they were invigorating and fruitful. But this was hardly the case in
Germany, where the opposing parties were arming for a conflict that
threatened not only their own survival, but the survival of the nation. "In
the name of culture and humanity," he begged partisans on each side that
"the social struggle not be a struggle to the death, that it be waged with
decent means, not with poison arrows. How far both sides are missing the
mark in this! How hard it is for the one side to stave off bitterness, deceit,
malice, for the other to avoid brutality, ridicule, rape! ... Do we really
believe we give up anything by respecting the decent human being in our
opponents, by surmising that truth and honesty are guiding principles in
the other camp too? I think not."[102]

This impassioned appeal for social peace—or at least sportsmanship—
won an unsurprisingly enthusiastic response from Naumann, coming as it
did shortly after the National Socials' Erfurt congress. "Social Democracy
has yet to understand this, but precisely the Marxist Sombart will be the

---

97. Ibid., pp. 60–61.
98. Ibid., pp. 106–7.
99. Ibid., p. 110.
100. Ibid., p. 68.
101. Ibid., pp. 79–80.
102. Ibid., p. 112.

right man to suggest it," the NSV leader wrote in *The Times* on January 6.[103] More surprising, perhaps, was a friendly review in *Forwards!* It was "an advantage and attraction of Sombart's pamphlet that it is not a Social Democratic book. There are plenty of self-portraits and bourgeois caricatures as it is," the socialist paper had observed already on December 20, 1896. "Sombart has attempted to give us something new: an objective picture. And on the whole he has succeeded sparklingly in this endeavor. Social Democracy has every reason to wish Sombart's book the greatest success, the widest circulation."[104] Conservatives seemed to agree, at least with the last part of the assessment, and Sombart soon found himself embroiled in controversy and his career in jeopardy once more.

Academic Freedom in the Stumm Era

In the months after the publication of Sombart's book, leading Conservatives forced a debate over "academic freedom" in the Prussian parliament, and "socialism of the lectern" suddenly resurfaced as a cause of public hysteria on the right. Stumm led the charge with several tirades in May and June, accusing the younger national economists of having exceeded the subversiveness of their teachers by engaging in "socialistic demagoguery." Private property itself had been called into question, he proclaimed in a garbled reference to *Socialism and the Social Movement*. In order to protect the principle of academic freedom from these displays of open partisanship for Social Democracy, Stumm called for the appointment of conservative academics to keep an eye on the young renegades.[105] These were not empty threats. A "penal professorship" of this sort had already been assigned to Sombart in February, when the "socialist-killer" Julius Wolf won a highly publicized appointment in nearby Greifswald (an ominous gesture, since it was his review of Wolf that helped provoke the uproar over the young economist's "demagoguery" in 1892). And the same month, Max Weber had written to tell Sombart that Baden officials were

103. Friedrich Naumann, "Nochmals Marxismus," *Zeit* (January 6, 1897); newspaper clippings, NL Sombart 38.
104. *Vorwärts* 13, no. 299 (December 39, 1896), 3. *Beilage;* newspaper clippings, NL Sombart 41. See also Bruch, *Wissenschaft,* pp. 145–46.
105. Newspaper clippings; NL Sombart 38.

refusing to appoint him as Weber's successor in Freiburg, despite urgent appeals from the faculty.[106]

Bristling against this renewed assault, Sombart initially enjoyed the role of public martyr. "I drink to free speech at free German universities," he reportedly told a group of Breslau students who gathered to toast him in March, and throughout the spring and summer sympathetic articles in left-liberal newspapers described the attempt "to cripple the effectiveness of the well-known socialist Sombart."[107] Yet he could hardly afford to ignore the animosity of Prussian officials, which threatened to prolong his "exile" in the provinces indefinitely. Though not necessarily caving in to such pressure—an "objective" approach actually required partisanship for working-class interests in the "Ideals of Social Policy"—the young professor warned against the "conflation" of politics and scholarship, thus disappointing rebellious students who had looked to him for encouragement with remarks that in fact signaled his retreat from public activism until 1898.[108] If Sombart signed the petition against Stumm two years earlier, he now remained aloof to the National Socials' publicity campaign in support of the Hamburg strike of 1897–98. Despite Lang's urgent requests, he also refused to attend an international labor protection conference in Zurich, which was strongly supported by the SPD and billed as an attempt to renew the initiative of the February Decrees, the following summer.[109] When Heinrich Braun complained about "all the young social-political professors keeping their distance," the economist significantly observed that "an unfortunate time was chosen," and for the next two years he did not publish another article on reform.[110]

Sombart's unwillingness to put his career at risk demanded awkward sacrifices that strained his friendships in leftist circles. Perhaps the most humiliating instance of intimidation came when he suddenly felt compelled to join the academic campaign for German fleet expansion orga-

---

106. Weber to Sombart, February 8, 1897, NL Max Weber 30, vol. 4. On Wolf, see clippings from *Vorwärts* (February 23, 1897) and the *Berliner Zeitung* (September 23, 1897), NL Sombart 41.

107. NL Sombart 41, newspaper clippings; quotes from the *New Yorker Staatszeitung* (March 14, 1897) and the *Berliner Zeitung* (September 23, 1897).

108. Lenger, *Sombart*, pp. 96–97.

109. Lang to Sombart, June 14 and August 28, 1897, NL Sombart 8e.

110. Braun, *Memoiren*, vol. 2, pp. 190–91.

nized by Schmoller, Brentano, Hans Delbrück, and other prominent professors at the turn of the century.[111] Teased by Heinrich and Lily Braun, Sombart lashed out at the "unfortunate feminist/sentimental streak in Social Democracy" that prevented his friends from realizing what was at stake in the struggle for world power. "Shall the earth belong to us or to the blacks or the Chinese? The answer does not seem difficult to me."[112] What Sombart failed to mention, however, was that his participation had been coerced by Ernst von Halle, a senior colleague who repeatedly tried in vain to recruit him during the winter of 1899–1900, even after using the young professor's well-known reform interests as bait. Halle was a man of some influence, he wrote, and had done his best to win a sympathetic ear in government. "In order to win over the authoritative offices, though, it will take cooperation on the part of adamant representatives of social policy in the present matter."[113] Yet it was only by playing on Sombart's career anxieties that Halle finally succeeded in bringing him on board. Asking the young scholar to speak at meetings scheduled for February 1900, he noted that Schmoller and Friedrich Althoff, who was in charge of Prussian academic appointments, "would place very great importance on . . . you appearing."[114] Althoff had supported the renegade in past brushes with the administration, but Halle implied that his patience was wearing thin. Sombart apparently got the message, since he submitted to joining the ostensibly spontaneous show of support for the fleet.

Sombart's outburst at the Brauns resembled his 1897 remarks about "inferior East European and Asiatic nations" and may well have expressed his genuine enthusiasm for German imperialism. Darwinian struggle, racial mastery, national strength—all appeared in the arguments of radical nationalists as well as in those of reformers like Damaschke and Bäumer, and indeed the two circles often overlapped. As Bruch points out, the fleet question held a "key function" in the agendas of left-liberals as well as reactionaries.[115] Academics participated in the campaign for many reasons, many of them voluntarily. But it seems likely that Sombart's impassioned remarks more accurately revealed the young professor's anger

111. On the campaign, see Bruch, *Wissenschaft*, pp. 66–92.
112. Braun, *Memoiren*, vol. 2, p. 322.
113. Halle to Sombart, December 12, 1899, NL Sombart 10a, vol. 4.
114. Halle to Sombart, February 4, 1900, NL Sombart 10a, vol. 4.
115. Bruch, *Wissenschaft*, p. 81.

at his vulnerability to Halle's machinations. By the time his senior colleagues launched another campaign in 1907, Sombart was prepared to vent
his frustrations openly. "If *Gymnasium* students and young skirts show
interest for the fleet association and join in, then it's certainly not a sign
of growing political interest of any kind, but merely a sign that pubescent
ravings for knighthood and Indian romanticism are momentarily heading
in the direction of sea adventures," he smirked.[116] But the grotesque behavior of academics was another matter. "It makes a shameful impression
on such occasions, when one sees how people are soft-soaped in this terrible way by an arbitrary political wire-puller, people whose deficiencies
are sweating out of their pores and so are good-natured enough to listen
to any banal beer-bench speech as if it were an expression of the highest
political wisdom and to vote without any sense for the 'resolutions' placed
before them."[117] As "unmodern" as the eighteenth-century ideals of liberty,
equality, and fraternity still seemed to him in 1907, the economist greeted
the Social Democrats' continuing appeals to them as a refreshing antidote
to the "chauvinism, militarism, imperialism" of the day.[118] Social reform,
not "sea adventures," was the best way to secure Germany's strength and
prosperity in Sombart's eyes too.

The Society for Social Reform

After the outcry over *Socialism and the Social Movement* died down, Sombart gradually recovered his confidence, and in 1898 he again began publicly promoting a social policy geared toward the proletariat in a lecture
tour on "the protection of the strong."[119] Publishing several articles on
social issues in *Social Praxis,* the official organ of the Institute for Public
Welfare, the economist also joined a new circle of reformers seeking to
build an institutional framework for the mediation of social conflict in
1899. The Institute was headed by Wilhelm Merton, a wealthy Frankfurt

---

116. Werner Sombart, "Unser Interesse an der Politik," *Morgen* 1, no. 2 (June 21,
    1907): 40.
117. Werner Sombart, "Die Politik als Beruf," *Morgen* 1, no. 7 (July 26, 1907):
    199.
118. Werner Sombart, "Der internationale Sozialistenkongreß in Stuttgart I,"
    Morgen 1, no. 11 (August 23, 1907): 324–25.
119. NL Sombart 41, press clippings: *Wiener Tageblatt* (March 24, 1898); *Posener
    Tageblatt* (February 15, 1898); *Leipziger Tageblatt* (February 25, 1899).

industrialist and pioneer in the process of rationalizing municipal welfare services Sachße has described, and its members included leading lights from the Association for Social Policy like Schmoller, Brentano, Max Sering, and Karl Bücher, as well as Sombart's colleague Max Weber.[120] Combining reform attempts with the compilation of statistical material, the Institute set up an Information Office for Workers' Affairs and conducted research on specific issues, including a study on the economic impact of land reform sponsored by the Prussian Ministries of Justice and Finance. While emphasizing its neutrality in political matters, *Social Praxis* initially betrayed the leftist sympathies of its editors, Ignaz Jastrow and Andreas Voigt, but tensions arose when Berlepsch joined the Institute with the intent of promoting "*moderate* reform" after his fall from office in 1896. Under pressure from Berlepsch and Merton, who objected to the editors' more radical views, Jastrow and Voigt were replaced by Ernst Francke after a prolonged struggle that October, and relations between the two wings remained uneasy for the rest of the decade.[121]

Sombart joined the *Social Praxis* circle just as Berlepsch was finally preparing an international initiative to found the workers' protection organization he had put on hold since the February Decrees. With the Prison Bill about to fall, the Free Unions making demands that closely paralleled the reforms endorsed by *Social Praxis*, and the debate over Bernstein's revisionism opening new prospects for Social Democratic cooperation, the time seemed right. On May 3, 1899 leading politicians from the Center, National Liberal, and progressive parties, Protestant and Catholic reformers, and members of the Association for Social Policy met to discuss Berlepsch's plans. Elected to the provisory committee to make arrangements for an upcoming workers' conference, where the organization was to be founded in Paris the following year, Sombart received the task of securing Social Democratic participation, which was deemed vital to the initiative's

---

120. Sachße, *Mütterlichkeit*, pp. 79–95.
121. Handwritten manuscript for a brief history of the *Institut für Gemeinwohl*, NL Berlepsch 3; letters Max Sering to Geibel, December 19, 1896, Voigt to Berlepsch February 9 and October 6, 1897, NL Berlepsch 3–4; see also Ursula Ratz, *Sozialreform und Arbeiterschaft: Die "Gesellschaft für Soziale Reform" und die sozialdemokratische Arbeiterbewegung von der Jahrhundertwende bis zum Ausbruch des Ersten Weltkrieges* (Berlin: Colloquium, 1980), pp. 13–14; Sachße, *Mütterlichkeit*, p. 88.

success.[122] Over a month before the reform congress, at the end of March, he had already urged Braun to "bring your 'rightists' in contact with us leftists from the bourgeoisie."[123] Support for Bernstein among the rank and file should give Braun enough support, Sombart argued, and pressure from the Social Democrats would also allow him to accomplish more on his side. "The radical nature in labor policy is barely represented, by Brentano and myself," the economist wrote his friend two weeks later, and without an extra push from outside the "faint-hearted middle party of Berlepsch/ Schmoller will be given the upper hand."[124] Promoting Sombart's efforts as the beginning of a front "from Berlepsch to Bebel," Naumann heartily agreed with this assessment, but Braun responded with less enthusiasm.[125] The economist's refusal to attend the Zurich conference only a year before cannot have been forgotten, and his friend took the matter up with considerable reluctance. While Bebel's response was mildly supportive, the Party leadership angrily rejected Sombart's confidential overtures with a series of stinging polemics in *Forwards!*[126]

The unexpected harshness of the Social Democrats' refusal to cooperate came as a devastating blow to the Wilhelmine reform milieu. Both Damaschke and Bäumer singled it out as another lost opportunity of historic dimensions, but the incident was especially painful to Sombart, whose efforts to end the fighting "with poison arrows" had finally seemed so close to fruition. "Is this even possible?! Are we dealing with normal, decent people, or with highwaymen?" he asked Braun.[127] It was "a shame for all the good will that has been so uselessly wasted," and he refused to take the blame "if the last bridge is dismantled between Soc[ial] Dem[ocracy] and us. If the gentlemen prefer an open fight—that's fine too. I am prepared for it and will use the opportunity of the conference to say so openly."[128] Sombart refused to abandon the initiative, however, and focused his efforts instead on strengthening the leftist stance in bourgeois circles without the help of Braun's party. Returning to the argument of "Ideals" in several

---

122. Ratz, *Sozialreform,* pp. 29–38.
123. Sombart to Braun, March 30, 1899, NL Sombart 9c.
124. Sombart to Braun, April 12, 1899, NL Sombart 9c.
125. Ratz, *Sozialreform,* p. 38.
126. Sombart to Braun, April 17, 22, 25, May 8 and 13, 1899, NL Sombart 9c.
127. Sombart to Braun, May 16, 1899, NL Sombart 9c.
128. Sombart to Braun, April 17, 1899, NL Sombart 9c.

articles for *Social Praxis,* the economist insisted that the transition to industrial capitalism "means becoming men of culture, plain and simple."[129] In a defiant speech at the Association for Social Policy's annual congress, which was held in Breslau in September 1899, he challenged the older generation's commitment to small enterprise. Department stores, cooperatives, and other large-scale structures were "logical phenomena following from an ineluctable historical development" it was pointless to resist, the young scholar insisted. As a member of a consumer cooperative he could personally vouch for their benevolent influence on the local community. Prompting "loud and sustained applause" from an audience that included his reform contacts from Vienna, Sombart's speech drew fire from Otto von Gierke, the famous professor of "Germanic law," who denounced his views as a threat to the Association's "fundamental orientation," but the economist defended himself with a fierce rebuttal. Schmoller stepped in to smooth things over, closing the proceedings with an explicit recognition of the importance of Sombart's work.[130]

After his humiliating rejection by the Social Democrats, the congress seemed a major victory for the "modern direction in soc[ial] pol[icy]" to Sombart, who touted it as a "turning point in the history" of the Association in a gloating letter to Braun.[131] Buoyed by this success, he took his message to Breslau's local reform community in a series of lectures delivered to an audience he described as "three quarters workers and one quarter bourgeois." Immediately published in the *New German Review,* the addresses were reprinted as *Nevertheless!,* Sombart's second major reformist tract, in 1900. Eschewing his earlier appeals to "the warriors themselves," the economist now called for the "emancipation of the organized labor movement from the tutelage of the political parties." The noisy clashes of Social Democracy had little to do with the interests of German workers, he argued, but once they achieved "self-reliance" the unions

---

129. Werner Sombart, "Entwicklen wir uns zum 'Exportindustriestaate?' " *Soziale Praxis* 8, no. 24 (March 16, 1899): 638; Sombart, "Export und Kultur," *Soziale Praxis* 8, no. 31 (May 4, 1899): 834–40.

130. Boese, pp. 90–92. The argument on cooperatives also appears in Werner Sombart, *Dennoch! Theorie und Geschichte der gewerkschaftlichen Arbeiterbewegung* (Jena: Fischer, 1900), p. 92.

131. Sombart to Braun, October 8, 1899, NL Sombart 9c.

would find "an ally not to be underestimated" in the bourgeoisie.[132] After all, "capitalism and socialism are not mutually exclusive opposites," Sombart proclaimed; on the contrary, "their ideals can be realized very well in one and the same society," which was precisely what the economist predicted: "When I imagine the economic life of modern cultural nations in the twentieth century, I increasingly see it taking shape capitalistically and socialistically at the same time."[133] Promoting the same set of reforms demanded by the *Social Praxis* circle and the Free Unions in 1899, Sombart decried Germany's laws of association as "pitiful and practically beneath the dignity of a modern state" and demanded freedom for workers to develop counterparts to the industrialists' cartels. Once both sides had achieved adequate organization, collective bargaining and smoothly functioning arbitration courts would mediate unavoidable conflicts of interest to the advantage of both sides. The economist believed that a maximum work week and minimum wage would emerge from this fruitful dialogue as some of the first measures benefiting the entire nation as they defused tensions and encouraged the full development of Germany's productive capacity.[134]

The turn of the century seemed an auspicious moment for this new beginning. "May it be an auspicious sign that a morning has now finally dawned that will find living creatures and not phantoms," Sombart wrote, noting the fall of the Prison Bill, and he discerned a new understanding for the needs of organized labor penetrating "ever further into circles of the bourgeoisie." A "peaceful, organic, continuing development of our political life" would soon accompany this process, he hoped, with the "increasing democratization" of a public sphere where workers and employers had equal say in determining Germany's future.[135] At the end of *Nevertheless!*, the economist included a description of the new Union House in Berlin as a "document" illustrating the new possibilities of cooperation. Constructed through the initiative of Leo Arons, a Social Democrat and scholar, the building's food and entertainment facilities were provided by the progressive industrialist Richard Rösicke, who had advised the "Work-

---

132. Sombart, *Dennoch!*, pp. vi, 62
133. Ibid., p. 92.
134. Ibid., pp. 12–13, 23–35.
135. Ibid., pp. 79, 90, 95.

ers' Kaiser" after the Ruhr miners' strike and now belonged to the Institute for Public Welfare. Unlike the artisans' gloomy, cramped guild houses of the past economic age, the Union House was "bright, bold, quickly erected in a few years from sunny blueprints with an extravagant technology, practical, rationalistic to the last corner," Sombart wrote: "a true expression of our clear, all-too-clear, enlightened and sometimes a bit sober times."[136]

Even in launching the most important social policy initiative of his career, the economist could not suppress his misgivings about the cultural impact of the new age. But his overall prognosis was optimistic. Using the same evolutionary schema he sketched out in "Ideals" and would soon elaborate in *Modern Capitalism,* Sombart drew up blueprints for a prosperous future built on cooperation between bourgeoisie and proletariat that guided construction of one of the most prestigious institutions of Wilhelmine anti-politics, the Society for Social Reform, in 1900. At the Paris workers' conference in July, an International Coalition for Legislative Workers' Protection was founded (despite the absence of German representatives from the government or Social Democracy), and the various reform delegations returned to establish national branch organizations at home. In December, the same month Sombart delivered his lectures in Breslau, the Society for Social Reform was founded as the German branch, and he received the task of writing its statutes.[137] After defining the Society's tactics as "enlightenment in person and in writing," Sombart listed "further expansion of legislation in the interest of the working class" and "support for workers' efforts to improve their situation in professional associations and cooperatives" as goals to be achieved via activism in four areas: lecture courses and public meetings, brochures, petitions to the government, legislature, and bureaucracy, and the founding of local branches. Sombart also took the lead in the last area by founding the Breslau Society for Social Reform in March 1901 and writing its statutes, which served as the model for local branches throughout Germany before the First World War.[138]

---

136. Ibid., pp. 117–21.
137. Ratz, *Sozialreform,* pp. 34–35; Sombart to Berlepsch, December 28, 1900, NL Berlepsch 4.
138. "Grundzüge und Satzungen"; "Aufruf zur Gründung des Zweigvereins Breslau der Gesellschaft für soziale Reform"; NL Berlepsch 4; see also Ratz, *Sozialreform,* p. 81.

While Marxist polemics against Sombart intensified in *Forwards!*, the Breslau Society surpassed his highest hopes after the turn of the century, becoming a forum for passionate, but frank debates between bourgeois and Social Democratic reformers at the local level. Catholic and Protestant labor leaders, National Socials (including Hans Kurella, his land reform ally in the city council), and other progressives joined Breslau's "comrades" at the Society's "discussion evenings," where one of the "most zealous debaters" was Paul Löbe, who later became the SPD's Reichstag President in the early Weimar Republic.[139] As chairman, the economist received invitations to meetings of the Breslau SPD, which supported his reform initiatives in the city council, while he in turn encouraged his socialist contacts outside Breslau to participate in the Society's meetings.[140] "Here at the communal level, the seeds of a bourgeois–Social Democratic rapprochement were planted before the First World War," Ursula Ratz has written of such successes, which were repeated on a more modest scale in Berlin, Schwerin, and Königsberg, and eventually spread to the national level, as we will see in the next chapter.[141] After ten years in Breslau, Sombart seemed finally to have established a solid, institutional basis for achieving the goal of social peace.

"Twilight of the Gods"

About a year after the crowning achievement in his reform efforts, Sombart published an impressive synthesis of his scholarly work over the past decade in the first two volumes of *Modern Capitalism*, which might easily be read as a "scientific" vindication of his progressive agenda at the turn of the century. As we have seen, the project of combining "psychological" and "objective" forms of analysis that led to his discovery of "the spirit of capitalism" was deeply intertwined with efforts to bridge the gap between bourgeoisie and proletariat in more direct ways, as was his model of social evolution. Depicting the "gradual becoming" of an economic order over long centuries, *Modern Capitalism* drives home its central message again and again: new systems emerge only from within the established order. Without a well-developed sense of class consciousness (or "spirit") and

---

139. Sombart to Lily Braun, November 11, 1903, NL Lily Braun.
140. Ibid.; see also Lenger, *Sombart,* p. 114.
141. Ratz, *Sozialreform,* pp. 84–85.

concrete structures in place to sustain it, revolution was a chimera, as the German bourgeoisie had discovered in 1848.[142] Instead, businessmen had slowly remodeled the "economic construction" that artisans had once built to suit their needs as the dominant economic subjects of the previous era. Now the bourgeoisie was master and the proletariat merely tenants, but as capitalism moved into its late stages, the working class was busily rebuilding ever more of the "house" to accommodate the next economic order, and Sombart planned to add a third volume describing this gradual transition to socialism.[143]

Modern Capitalism and Its Discontents

Yet if *Modern Capitalism* sustained Sombart's vision of a house where both classes could feel at home, it also supported a less sanguine prognosis. Damaschke and Bäumer may well have drawn the tragic side of their own portraits of modern development from the treatise, which mourned the loss of the medieval artisans' world as an "idyll of peaceful contemplation" crushed under the ruthless march of capitalism and progress.[144] The artisan had once been a "microcosm" of his world, the economist sighed, a model of the fully-developed, well-rounded personality that had become so rare in the modern age.[145] Uniting artistic and technical skill, commercial initiative and organizational talent, the craftsman had lived and worked in the "organic whole" of "familial community," producing quality merchandise that was a "faithful expression of the personality of its creator."[146] Knowledge passed from generation to generation in living form, embodied in the master artisan and inextricable from the practices he had acquired by a lifetime of personal effort.[147] The ordering principle of economic life, "the idea of sustenance," was itself tied to the "corporeal/individual" needs of human beings in this age, Sombart argued, and craftsmen had produced only enough to sustain the family's natural standing.[148] The *Erwerbstrieb* shattered this sheltered and stable community, however, in restless pursuit

---

142. Sombart, *Kapitalismus* (1902), vol. 1, p. 482.
143. Ibid., vol. 1, pp. 72, 654.
144. Ibid., vol. 2, p. 371.
145. Ibid., vol. 1. pp. 84–86.
146. Ibid., vol. 1, pp. 116–18.
147. Ibid., vol. 2, pp. 60–67.
148. Ibid., vol. 1, pp. 86–87, 174, 195–96.

of endless wealth, an abstract goal divorced from all physical or personal needs.

Initially the primitive methods of "robber barons and oppression of peasants, gold-digging and alchemy" that had been used to quench this insatiable desire since ancient times had limited the *Erwerbstrieb*, which would never have grown strong enough on such meagre nourishment to challenge the dominant order. By keeping exact account of all transactions and re-investing profits in rationalized structures designed for the sole purpose of making money, the lowly merchant class had quietly surpassed the spectacular schemes of the rich and powerful, however, discovering the concept of capital and thus the secret to the infinite accumulation of wealth.[149] At the same time, the application of scientific principles turned modern technology into another powerful instrument of the *Erwerbstrieb*. Technical skill was recorded in mathematical formulas and diagrams, losing its bodily connection to the "living personality" of the master artisan to become "objectified as knowledge external to every person applying it, which anyone can understand and attain." Building on the "imperishable property" of this disembodied knowledge, an army of engineers and experts constantly strove to increase productive efficiency and eventually achieved the "objectification of the production process, its complete disconnection from living human beings, its transferal onto a system of lifeless bodies."[150] Like the rational techniques of early modern bookkeepers, the new technology exploded the organic constraints of the human and natural world, and in both cases the economic forces released by the *Erwerbstrieb* took on an objective life of their own, Sombart argued: "Slowly the moloch of business sense stretches out its claws to swallow generation after generation with increasing success."[151]

While capitalist progress was "emancipatory with regard to space as well as time," it demanded terrible sacrifices in human terms.[152] "We have become wealthy because entire races and tribes have died for us, entire regions of the earth have been depopulated for us," Sombart wrote, condemning the Europeans' imperial quest for profits, which had simultaneously brought about the ruthless "depletion of the soil's energies, the

---

149. Ibid., vol. 1, pp. 381–97.
150. Ibid., vol. 2, p. 63; vol. 1, p. 48.
151. Ibid., vol. 1, p. 397.
152. Ibid., vol. 2, p. 43.

exploitation of natural resources, flora and fauna."[153] Capturing the irony of modern development in a series of "antinomies," he observed that the "conquest of matter" had produced the "victory of materialism," just as the "conquest of time" made it all the more precious in the "accelerated lifestyle," the "quicker overindulgence, stress, fatigue" of modern life. "[O]ur systems of philosophy, our artistic styles and trends in literature now change almost as often as our fashions in ties and hats," the economist complained. The extreme rationalism of modern economic practices had ended in the sheer irrationality of consumer capitalism.[154]

Sombart's cultural and environmentalist concerns had blended together with progressive visions of the future to form the characteristic pattern of his complex social criticism from the start, and it should come as no surprise to find them deeply intertwined in the same analytic structure that upheld his reform attempts at the fin de siècle. Nor was he alone in this. As we have seen, hopes for a "bright renaissance" often came packaged in the language of cultural despair at the time. The centrality of both socialism and *Kultur* in Sombart's search for alternative modernities seems difficult to grasp only in light of a historiography that divides Wilhelmine political culture retrospectively into "modernist" and "anti-modernist" camps, so that either the progressive or the pessimist frequently gets lost in recent accounts of *Modern Capitalism*. If Lenger finds cultural concerns "only on the margins" of the work, which Appel similarly situates in Sombart's modernist period, in order to contrast it with a turn to cultural pessimism a few years later, Herf uses the text to illustrate an "uncompromising critique of the economy and culture of capitalism" that set *Modern Capitalism* and *Socialism and the Social Movement* apart from the economist's more nuanced and appreciative views on modern technology in subsequent years.[155] In fact, Sombart saw both threats and opportunities—as well as unavoidable realities—in the dynamic of modern capitalism in 1902, just as he had since his assessments in the late 1880s.

Although the economist had no intention of singing "hymns of praise to modern development and its blessings for the working class," he asserted that "the standard of living has risen quite considerably over the past fifty years" and insisted that Marxists acknowledge that "the terrible times of

153. Ibid., vol. 1, p. 348.
154. Ibid., vol. 2, pp. 68–87.
155. Lenger, *Sombart*, p. 136; Herf, *Modernism*, p. 134.

want and misery are over for broad sections of the proletariat."[156] Despite his tragic portrait of the craftsmen's decline, Sombart also dismissed the "circus criers at the artisans' congresses" who were demanding a return to the guilds, much as he had rebuked the clinging fears of the older generation of national economists.[157] "Today's artisan trade, to the extent that it is not a phony artisan trade without apprentices, ekes out its existence as long as legislation allows it to exploit immature labor forces to a greater extent than capitalist industry," he scorned, "and as long as society does not see to it that the present system of exploiting apprentices, which signifies the complete bankruptcy of industrial training, makes way for a form of instruction better adapted to the times."[158] It was only a matter of time before the last artisans hiding in the cellars of capitalism "die out and even the rooms they lived in will be furnished in the style of the whole house and occupied by the new generation."[159] What that "style" would be was difficult to say, but Sombart found hope in the very technology he also found so disturbing: "the same science that has toppled us from the long-occupied throne of rule and exposed us in our complete nothingness, has simultaneously shown us . . . how we can get over that imaginary and lost rulership by attaining anew a real rulership."[160] It was "exciting to observe how quickly our taste is transformed along with the transformations of technology," he enthused, describing promising signs of a partnership between art and industry. "I see future generations, after long years of deprivation, once again finally leading a life that is saturated with beauty and comfort. A generation will arise that will let a world of comfort and beautiful forms spring forth from the fullness of wealth that grows up around it in extravagant measure—people whose delight, whose joy in life has once again become a natural companion on their earthly pilgrimage; people with refined senses, with an aesthetic appreciation of the world."[161]

For all the bleakness of *Modern Capitalism*, Sombart still glimpsed possibilities for "socialism as a cultural factor" when looking ahead in 1902. Continuing his effort to realize this vision in the Society for Social Reform,

---

156. Sombart, *Kapitalismus* (1902), vol. 2, pp. 268–69.
157. Ibid., vol. 1, p. 646.
158. Ibid., vol. 2, p. 582.
159. Ibid., vol. 1, p. 654.
160. Ibid., vol. 2, p. 67.
161. Ibid., vol. 2, pp. 312, 317–18.

he also supported new causes, including Garden Cities and the Werkbund, after the turn of the century. Attending the 1904 Congress for the Protection of Cottage Industry Workers, which was held at Arons's Union House and sponsored by the Free Unions, Sombart joined Francke and other members of the Society for Social Reform in a gesture of solidarity that turned out to be the crucial beginning of a cautious rapproachement between bourgeois and socialist reformers before 1914.[162] "There are still well-meaning people who believe they can improve the lot of workers without increasing the efficiency of labor," he complained, reporting on the congress in *Social Praxis*. "But in the long run, the highest principle of social reformers must always be to configure the organization of labor so that the optimum productivity is attained."[163] Promoting the Society's goals in a flurry of pamphlets that again included extremely pessimistic formulations side by side with calls for progressive reform the same year, Sombart insisted that "[t]he elimination of these societal ills is considered necessary not only in the interests of the working class itself, but just as much in the interest of the entirety of the nation, and the healthy progress of cultural development."[164] As head of the Breslau Society he published a recent resolution endorsing several land reform and other measures promoted by Damaschke in these years—housing inspection, construction ordinances, a communal annexation policy, the preservation and increase of communal property holdings, the taxation of undeveloped property, public low-interest credit, an excise tax on land sales, and a federal housing law—and despite a perceptible stalling of the reformist impulse at mid-decade, the economist insisted that "no standstill must come about" in the protection of organized labor.[165] But the clearest indication of Sombart's continuing resolve to find realistic solutions to the social question was his decision to join Max Weber and Edgar Jaffé as the new editors of the *Archive*, which Braun was forced to sell for financial reasons in 1904.[166]

---

162. Ratz, *Sozialreform*, p. 194.
163. Werner Sombart, "Zum allgemeinen Heimarbeiterschutz-Kongress," *Soziale Praxis* 13, no. 23 (March 3, 1904): 597.
164. Werner Sombart, *Die gewerbliche Arbeiterfrage*, 2nd rev. ed. (Berlin: G. J. Göschen'sche Verlag-shandlung, 1912), p. 37. See also Sombart, *Gewerbewesen*, 2 vols. (Leipzig: G. J. Göschen'sche Verlagshandlung, 1904).
165. Sombart, *Arbeiterfrage*, pp. 97, 148–54.
166. "Geleitwort," *Archiv* 19, no. 1 (1904): i–vii.

It was in the refurbished journal, renamed the *Archive for Social Science and Social Policy*, that Weber published his famous studies *The Protestant Ethic and the Spirit of Capitalism* between 1904 and 1907, and it seems appropriate to conclude our discussion of *Modern Capitalism* by considering the careers of the two reformers and cultural critics in the years leading up to their collaboration. Both had come to the social question through an interest in agrarian questions, Weber through his work on inner colonization in the early 1890s, and Sombart through his research on the Roman Campagna, inspired by his father's land reform experiments almost a decade earlier. Both had begun to work out "developmental" schema and representative "types" at almost the same moment, around 1893, in an attempt to diagnose Germany's social and economic transformations that coincided with a deepening personal involvement in reform initiatives, Weber at the Protestant Social Congress, Sombart in progressive circles in Breslau, Vienna, and Zurich.[167] While Sombart watched the National Socials' founding congress from a safe "scholarly" distance, his more famous colleague took part in the opening debates but withdrew after his warnings about the "politics of misery." In 1897 Weber then suffered a nervous collapse that left him incapacitated for the crucial half-decade in which Sombart defiantly promoted the cause of rising proletariat as "the protection of the strong," helped to found the Society for Social Reform, finished working out his synthesis of bourgeois and Marxist scholarship in his theory of "the capitalist spirit," and published the results of all of this effort in the two thick volumes of *Modern Capitalism.* As Weber gradually recovered the same year, 1902, he supported Naumann's campaign for a "renewal of liberalism" and drew together the circle of progressives and intellectuals around his Heidelberg salon that included both Sombart and Bäumer as well as Simmel, who had just published his own critique of modern rationalization and depersonalization in *The Philosophy of Money* (1900).

While Weber insisted his own interest in the capitalist spirit went back to 1897, he acknowledged his debt to Sombart for developing the concept, and in pursuing it he crossed the same intersection between progressive reform and cultural criticism, though Simmel's increasing influence may have attracted Weber to the more pessimistic side of Sombart's theory,

---

167. On Weber's developmental models, see Scaff, *Fleeing*, pp. 41–52.

placing him at a greater distance to social activism in the early 1900s.[168] Inspired by Tönnies's analysis of the rationalizing process in the transition from community to society, which had also influenced Sombart, Simmel had looked not to Social Democracy, but instead to the radical subjectivism of *Schopenhauer and Nietzsche,* seeking "to re-create the aesthetic as a genuine sphere of redemption bearing cosmic significance." Weber was strongly impressed by the "psychologism" of Simmel's sociology and lent an increasingly sympathetic ear to the fashionable aestheticism of the turn of the century, but like Sombart he concluded that "ecstatic rapture" offered no escape from the harsh realities of "objective culture."[169] While following Simmel in exploring Nietzsche, he also joined the critical dialogue with "Marx's historical materialism" Sombart had opened in Breslau a decade earlier.[170] Both perspectives were indispensable, the two national economists agreed, and despite concern for the future of personal *Kultur,* they reaffirmed their commitment to a scientific understanding of the empirical foundations of the modern world in 1904.

Announcing that the *Archive* would continue to promote the same orientation as it had under Braun, the new editors asserted three basic truths about the modern world: (1) that capitalism "can no longer be wiped from the face of the earth and therefore must be accepted," since "no path now leads back to the patriarchal foundations of the old society"; (2) that "whether we wish it or not," the previous system "will make room for new ones that are capable of adapting to the altered conditions of economic life," and therefore "especially that the integration of the proletariat, once this class was produced by capitalism, became an unavoidable problem for all state policy"; and (3) "that the reconfiguration of society" had to take the form "of a gradual, 'organic' transformation of historically received conditions and institutions in which the assistance of scientific knowledge concerning the historically given situation was indispensable."[171] A clearer statement of the younger generation's social impulse is difficult to imagine.

---

168. Lenger, *Sombart,* pp. 130–34; Appel, *Sombart,* pp. 14, 121–24.
169. Scaff, *Fleeing,* pp. 104–8, 134–38; Lichtblau, "Alles," passim.
170. Mitzman, *Cage,* p. 182.
171. "Geleitwort," p. iv.

Cultural Despair

Privately, however, there were signs that Sombart's commitment was starting to fade. Coaxing him to attend the cottage industry congress in February 1904, Lily Braun had to remind her friend that "social policy is, after
all, your first love" and cautiously inquired "if on this occasion you will
... descend from the heights of cultivation to the depths of politics."[172]
Although he gave in and also agreed to rescue the *Archive* that year, the
economist stubbornly refused to keep the Brauns' *New Society* afloat in
1906, despite Tönnies's desperate appeal for help; and the following year
he broke with his socialist friends entirely.[173] After Posadowsky's fall to the
Bülow Bloc, the prospects for reform seemed so hopeless in 1907 that
Sombart could no longer bring himself to write on such a "thoroughly
boring" topic and asked Jaffé to take his name off the *Archive*.[174] Jaffé
dissuaded him by agreeing to do all the editorial work, but Sombart tried
to wriggle out of even this nominal association with such "shallow and
hucksterish" work the following year in letters to Weber, who responded
to his friend's desire for escape with skepticism. "You want to write 'personal' books. I am convinced that personal character (which you quite
certainly possess in strong measure) always comes out when it is *uninten-
tional,* and *only* then," Weber argued. "What you are intentionally dis-
playing to the public as 'self' has ... thoroughly typical qualities and very
few personal traits" and would do little to enhance Sombart's reputation:
"everyone merely has the impression of it having to do with one of the
many representatives of the usual aestheticism and the typical aristocratism
that goes with along them."[175]

Weber apparently found this impression misleading, but what lay behind
it was characteristically difficult to judge. Career frustrations certainly had

---

172. Braun to Sombart, February 23, 1904, NL Sombart 9d.
173. Tönnies to Sombart, March 18 and 20, 1907, NL Sombart 9f; Braun, *Memoiren,* vol. 2, p. 501; Braun to Sombart, April 9 and 16, May 2, 1909, NL
Sombart 9d.
174. Jaffé to Sombart, April 24, 1907, NL Sombart 17; see also Jaffé's letters of
June 19, 1907, February 19, 1908, February 15, 1912, and January 13, 1913.
175. Weber to Sombart, July 16, 1908, NL Max Weber 30, vol. 7, emphasis in the
original.

much to do with Sombart's withdrawal from his reform commitments in these years. In 1906 he finally escaped his "exile" in Breslau, but the renegade was not allowed to lecture in his new post at Berlin's Commercial College, where he joined Jastrow (the "radical" editor of *Social Praxis*) and other suspicious academics in a "salon des refusés."[176] Nor had *Modern Capitalism* done much for his career. "Major influence in the discipline has not been forthcoming," one colleague wrote three years after its publication. Among economists, only Schmoller wrote a thorough review of his former student's work, which he criticized for neglecting "psychological" and historical factors in an essentially materialistic analysis that relied solely on objective causal explanations, despite the conceptual smoke screen of Sombart's "spirit of capitalism."[177] Historians showed more interest, debating the study's merits at their annual conference in 1903. Having recently defended the field from Lamprecht's subversive "cultural history," Hans Delbrück, Georg von Below, and Felix Rachfahl now attacked *Modern Capitalism*, which seemed to pose a similar threat of "sociologization." Delbrück lashed out with particular acerbity against Sombart's admitted debt to Marx: "whoever wanders onto the treadmill of that pseudo-thinker doesn't find his way back to real scholarship so easily," the influential editor of the *Prussian Yearbooks* scowled.[178] Battering Sombart's scholarly reputation in a relentless polemical assault lasting for several years, the powerful academic crushed the economist's hope of returning to the University of Berlin just at the moment when he retreated from social reform, and it was after Delbrück's latest attack that he asked to have his name removed from *Archive*'s masthead. "[H]ow can you say: 'completely ruined externally'! Is a full professorship everything!?" Weber chided in the same letter that tried to dissuade Sombart from abandoning scholarship for the sake of cultivating a more distinctive persona. "Toss this strange mood, I'd like to say: *Weltschmerz*, behind you!"[179]

His academic career apparently in ruins, Sombart flaunted the very image of recklessness that Delbrück and others had drawn. One student remembered him in these years as a "combination of man of the world and

---

176. Appel, *Sombart*, p. 15.
177. Ibid., pp. 39–41.
178. Lenger, *Sombart*, p. 126–27; Appel, *Sombart*, pp. 41–47; Max to Alfred Weber, January 30, 1907, NL Weber 30, vol. 7.
179. Weber to Sombart, July 16, 1908, NL Weber 30, vol. 7.

artist, . . . and though not supposed to be a poet, he went driving in Byronic fashion with the handsomest opera singer, sat lolling in his seat at concerts passing his delicate hands through his long black hair."[180] Bored by the Brauns' prosaic interests, Sombart moved into the circles of Berlin high society, meeting Walter Rathenau, the well-known industrialist and patron of literature and the arts whose *Critique of the Times* he strongly influenced, and other prominent figures of artistic and literary fame, including Max Liebermann, Hugo von Tschudi, Hugo von Hofmannsthal, and Hermann Bahr.[181] This change of venue was undoubtedly eased by the friendships Sombart had made in the Friedrichshagen circle, central to the worlds of both reform and *Kultur,* beginning around the turn of the century. It was probably at the Neissers' salon that Sombart first met Gerhart and Carl Hauptmann in Breslau, where the brothers had grown up with Alfred Ploetz, a pioneer of racial hygiene who also belonged to the Friedrichshagen circle.[182] The renegade economist became especially close friends with Carl, who had abandoned a career in science to explore Nietzschean subjectivism and art, seeking to emulate his famous brother by writing mawkish plays depicting the virtues of homeland and "peasant" life.[183] It is difficult to say whether, or precisely when, the dubious tastes of his new comrades began to erode Sombart's earlier commitments, since the Naturalists maintained steady ties to reform circles—Heinrich and Lily Braun were also close to Haupt-mann, as was Tönnies—but his friendship with Carl peaked between 1902

---

180. Emil Ludwig, quoted in Mitzman, *Estrangement,* p. 224.

181. Lenger, *Sombart,* p. 183. For Sombart's influence on Rathenau, see Hans Dieter Hellige, "Rathenau und Harden in der Gesellschaft des Deutschen Kaiserreichs: Eine sozialgeschichtlich-biographische Studie zur Entstehung neokonservativer Positionen bei Unternehmern und Intellektuellen," in Hans Dieter Hellige, ed., *Walther Rathenau, Maximilian Harden: Briefwechsel 1897–1920* (Munich: Müller, 1983), pp. 34, 92–100; Hartmut Pogge von Strandmann, ed., *Walther Rathenau: Industrialist, Banker, Intellectual, and Politician: Notes and Diaries, 1907–1922* (Oxford: Clarendon Press, 1985), p. 123.

182. Carl Hauptmann to Sombart, March 1, 1900, printed in Carl Hauptmann, *Leben mit Freunden: Gesammelte Briefe* (Berlin: Horen-Verlag, 1928), p. 62; on the Hauptmanns' friendship with Ploetz, see "The Court of the Muses" in Chapter 5.

183. Lenger, *Sombart,* pp. 163–86; Mitzman, *Estrangement,* pp. 224–25. Hauptmann's letters to Sombart are published in his *Gesammelte Briefe;* see also Sombart to Lily Braun, February 23, 1907, NL Lily Braun.

and 1907, a period coinciding with his descent into cultural pessimism. Purchasing a "hut" in Schreiberhau around 1905, Sombart frequently joined Hauptmann, Bölsche, Wille, and others to exchange "heretical opinions" at the mountain retreat, where they sought "to shake off convention even more."[184]

Around the turn of the century, the economist had also begun an affair with Marie Briesemeister, the wife of a well-known Viennese opera singer, which sparked emotional and violent quarrels that shattered his marriage to Felicitas in these same years and eventually became "one of the essentially deciding motives" for his move to Berlin in 1906.[185] Hauptmann served as liaison for the affair, which was intimately connected to Sombart's attempt to create a new self-image, and the economist privately dedicated his first "personal book" to Briesemeister after it appeared in 1903. Passionately composed in only three months, *The German National Economy in the Nineteenth Century* seemed "from an artistic standpoint" his "most successful—a work of a single stroke," the economist believed.[186] The book opens with an invitation addressed informally to his "dear girlfriend" to take an imaginary journey through the wilds of Germany as it appeared in 1800. While joking about the poor roads and endless customs barriers, Sombart expressed clear nostalgia for the "old German *Kultur,* as it is still preserved in its broad outlines at the beginning of the 19th century," which "had really and truly sprung up out of the forest; the murmuring stream, the rustling oak tree are the sensual images of the German life of comfort, which, in the very days that we're traveling through the German lands in spirit, put forth the wonderful 'blue flower' of Romanticism."[187] Contrasting the melodic song of the night watchman with the tram conductor's shrill whistle, Sombart found a perfect symbol for the change in social relations.[188] If he had celebrated the aesthetic potential of modern industrial production the year before, by 1903 the economist lamented the "character of our technology, the character of our social life next to each other in great stone ravines and on hills of stone and glass," which he now

---

184. Hauptmann to Sombart, June 4 and November 18, 1905, January 16, 1906; Hauptmann, *Briefe,* pp. 136–37, 141, 146.

185. Sombart to Lang, July 29, 1906, NL Lang; Lenger, *Sombart,* pp. 172–74.

186. Sombart to Lang, December 23, 1904, NL Lang.

187. Werner Sombart, *Die deutsche Volkswirtschaft im neunzehnten Jahrhundert,* 4th ed. (Berlin: Brandi, 1921), p. 11.

188. Ibid., pp. 19–20.

held responsible for the "mountain of dead matter" that "towered up between us and the living nature in which God placed us at creation, lending our spiritual life its characteristic stamp. Thus a new basis for culture is created: pavement," Sombart sneered; "a new culture has emerged from it: the Asphalt Culture."[189]

In an elegy to Briesemeister's Vienna written four years later, the economist revealed the implications of his "development into a man of culture" over the past decade in *The Morning*, a "Weekly Journal for German *Kultur*" he founded together with some new friends in Berlin high society—Hofmannsthal, Richard Strauß, Artur Landsberger—while pulling away from the *Archive* in 1907.[190] "Ten years ago I still found it ridiculous that Vienna didn't have a nightlife or any streetcars and wasn't growing by 100,000 inhabitants a year," Sombart admitted. "Since then everything has turned into its opposite for me."[191] The more efficient, large-scale structures he had once seen as an objective means to enhance personal culture now seemed to be destroying what little remained. "What is threatening our culture is the overrating of the massive, the big, the purely quantitative. The overrating of technical means," he insisted. After all, New York had ten times as much noise and traffic as Berlin and could boast of amusement parks and restaurants that were ten times as big. "And what is New York? A desert. A great cemetery of culture. Shall humanity end up there?!"[192] It was time to renounce "progress" along with the "idea of utility" he had vigorously defended just three years earlier (and a year after *The German National Economy*) in 1904. "If only the entire hollowness of this idol 'progress,' before which capitalism forces us on our knees, were recognized," Sombart wailed. "While we should proselytize with all our might: we don't want to pray to your 'progress,' which makes us neglect our old saints. Which is the destroyer of the best values. Because with a callous hand—filled only with the idea of utility—it gropes inside the organic creation of humanity that has grown up over the centuries."[193]

Thwarted in his career, disgusted with the Liberals' 'mating' with Conservatives in the Bülow Bloc, unable to escape his own wrecked marriage, Sombart also used his brief tenure as *The Morning*'s social science editor

---

189. Ibid., p. 415.
190. On Sombart's relation to *The Morning*, see Lenger, "Abkehr," pp. 62–64.
191. Werner Sombart, "Wien," *Der Morgen* 1, no. 6 (June 19, 1907): 172.
192. Ibid., pp. 173–74.
193. Ibid., p. 174.

to explain "The Departure of the Well-Educated from Politics" in a series of extraordinarily bleak articles on German public life and the prospects for *Kultur* in the modern world. Describing the social "type" of the educated bourgeois, he drew a caricature that in many ways resembled a self-portrait: "He believes that all values finally rest upon and are rooted in the personal," the economist wrote; "he loves to go around with real women, who let him experience the whole person, because she [sic] is not crippled by a straight jacket of professional or likewise incomplete activities." Unlike Sombart, the educated man was solitary and introspective and seldom went to the theater, but he did share the flamboyant scholar's hatred for "the outward accomplishments of modern culture, above all, technology."[194] Given better circumstances, cultivated Germans could still rightly feel a "moral duty" to engage in public life, however, as they had in the 1860s and 1870s, when there had been a chance to achieve something significant.[195] But everyone knew that Germany's present constitution was a sham, once the Liberals had fled "behind the Prussian bayonets again and again," and the appalling "insincerity" that had become "an especially characteristic feature of our public life" more than justified the educated man's current disgust for politics.[196]

Finally venting his frustration over the "political wire-pullers" behind the academics' fleet campaign, Sombart also lampooned German politicians who fooled themselves into believing that they could make a difference. "For us the road to power goes via the post of the *Landrat* or the lieutenant," he wrote, echoing Karl Kraus's ridicule of Viennese Liberals in an analysis that compared the Reichstag to a comic opera: "While the 'people's representatives' dutifully drag their sacks to the mill down in the pit, the ruling caste looks down at their bustle from above with a benevolent-sympathetic smirk that says as much as: well done; but your path will never lead up here to us. The parliamentarian always remains second rate."[197] No wonder German Liberalism had grown tired of "waiting for

194. Werner Sombart, "Politik und Bildung," *Morgen* 1, no. 3 (June 28, 1907): 68–69.

195. Werner Sombart, "Die Abkehr der Gebildeten von der Politik," *Morgen* 1, no. 16 (September 27, 1907): 479, 481–82.

196. Werner Sombart, "Die Elemente des politischen Lebens in Deutschland," *Morgen* 1, no. 9 (August 9, 1907): 258; Sombart, "Vom Stil des politischen Lebens in Deutschland," *Morgen* 1, no. 8 (August 2, 1907): 225.

197. Sombart, "Elemente," p. 257.

the prince who will come to her rescue" and had thrown "herself into the arms of the first best thing to run across her path," while the enchantment of Social Democracy transformed the opposition into a "grief-stricken, nagging, a real dragon with bad manners."[198] Embodying "half the spirit of the nursery, half that of the barracks," the government's "tutelary policies" annulled the "far-reaching rights of the populace" granted by the constitution at every turn, Sombart insisted, and the slogans of German politicians were equally divorced from the realities of life.[199] "Think of expressions like these: defense of national honor; bread-profiteering; coal baron; enemy of the Empire; class justice; militarism; exploitation; *Kulturkampf*; clericalism; party of revolt," he wrote: "all expressions that for any reflective person are completely without any meaning." By reducing complex thoughts into "pill-form," professional politicians merely assisted in the "process of mechanization" that was taking over all the other spheres of modern life. "The living dies and the dead alone lives on."[200]

Coupled with his retreat from activism, such breathtaking displays of cynicism certainly give the impression that Sombart had embraced the "usual aestheticism" of the day, just as Weber warned, and historians have often pointed to them as signs of his flight into "voluntaristic" or "kitsch-Nietzschean models of entrepreneurial and national heroism."[201] But the economist also ridiculed the fashionable "coffee-house *Übermenschen*," and even in his most desperate moments he refused to indulge the fantasies of "impotent aesthetes" who dreamed of transforming society through a sudden change of consciousness.[202] Much as he had done after Lang's ecstatic conversion to Social Democracy in 1889, Sombart insisted that it was "childsplay to make demands without knowing the conditions to which they were bound" when he introduced his agenda as *The Morning*'s social science editor in 1907. "Only the sociologist can speak about cultural problems today, and even then only if he precisely understands the conditions of economic life as a result of his own scholarship and observation."[203] If

---

198. Sombart, "Abkehr," p. 481.
199. Sombart, "Stil," pp. 224–25.
200. Sombart, "Politik als Beruf," pp. 197–98.
201. Mitzman, *Estrangement*, pp. 225–33; Mitzman, "Conflict," p. 100. See also Appel, *Sombart*, pp. 165–75.
202. Sombart, "Politik und Bildung," p. 69.
203. Werner Sombart, "Kulturphilosophie: Ein Programm von Werner Sombart," *Morgen* 1, no. 1 (June 14, 1907): 2, 4.

the economist sympathized with the syndicalists' wish to defeat the "forces of state-centralization that are destroying humanity and the bureaucratization of our entire life," Sombart also recognized that France needed the systems of transportation and communication these developments had made possible in order to survive.[204] Georges Sorel's belief in a "fabulous creature who finds himself in a state of ecstasy from morning to night" and could somehow replace modern institutions with the force of *élan* was a "starry-eyed fantasy" leading "directly to la-la land."[205] There were no easy answers for Sombart, who had fallen victim to cultural *despair* in the truest sense of the word.

This profound loss of faith sharply distinguishes the *Morning* polemics from Sombart's earlier writings, which affirmed the possibility of reconciling *Kultur* and progress, and also from the later euphoria of his wartime pamphlet *Merchants and Heroes*—despite Lenger's attempt to draw an "unbroken" line between them.[206] "Who would have suspected we would once again emerge from that swamp?" the economist wrote Landsberger in August 1914.[207] Once the Social Democrats joined Conservatives and Liberals in the "civic peace," German political culture seemed to be opening up to reveal exciting possibilities, and participation in public life again became a "moral duty" for the scholar, who responded by promoting his old ideals in *Merchants and Heroes*: "A powerful state armored in steel and in its protection a free, strong nation are the ideal."[208] Grounding his vision in an "organic-objective" model he traced back to Lassalle, Sombart insisted that economic life be "arranged so that the organism of the German national economy thrives: but the German national economy is only there to serve the state." Because it relied on the vitality of the people, this uniquely "German idea of the state" did "not allow the individual to be consumed," he argued, but instead "reconciled" parts and whole so that "every individual, in proportion to his strengths and abilities, takes part in the administration of the commonwealth."[209] Returning to his earliest cri-

---

204. Sombart, "syndikalischen Lehren": 817–18.
205. Werner Sombart, "Die Erziehung zum Sozialismus," *Morgen* 2, no. 1 (January 3, 1908): 7.
206. Lenger, "Abkehr," p. 77.
207. Sombart to Landsberger, August 29, 1914, NL Landsberger.
208. Sombart, *Händler*, p. 124.
209. Ibid. On Lassalle and the "organic-objective" state, p. 76.

tiques of Manchesterism, the economist praised the outlawed Social Democrats of Bismarck's Empire as "heroes," but he hoped that today's socialists would not fall back into the Marxist error of sacrificing the organic forces of national development to narrow class interests. "[A] party is not a living whole as a nation is, in which all the life currents of individuals flow together and from which every individual takes back the values of life," Sombart maintained, echoing Bäumer's celebration of social energy and its rhythms. "It is a dead organization that does not live its own life."[210]

Sombart's observation that "the living dies and the dead alone lives on" stands in marked contrast to the optimism he expressed about the healing powers of organic life force in *Merchants and Heroes*. In his last works before the War, vitalistic discourse offered no hope of escaping the "constricting embrace" of mechanistic capitalism, and instead of redeeming socialism "as a cultural factor," collectivist forms of economic organization seemed to lead "ever deeper into the snares of false powers" that would achieve the complete "leveling of bourgeois civilization."[211] Describing the type of "the bourgeois" in 1913, Sombart concluded that human striving was now utterly superfluous in modern economic life. If the "heroes" of capitalist enterprise (he included both Englishmen and Germans in this prewar definition) still poured their souls into the pursuit of profit, they could spare themselves the trouble. A prefabricated "system" of corporate growth would do the work for them: " 'it' plans; 'it' keeps the books; 'it' calculates; 'it' determines wage contracts; 'it' saves money; 'it' registers, etc. It confronts the economic subject with self-aggrandizing violence," Sombart wrote; "it demands from him, it forces him. And it does not rest; it grows; it perfects itself. It lives its own life."[212] The "Conquistadors" of capitalism's early years had wound up as the "salaried officials" of a leviathan no one could control, and the prognosis for the future looked grim.[213] "Perhaps the giant, once he has become blind, will be condemned to pulling the democratic cart of *Kultur*. Perhaps too it will be the twilight of the gods. The gold will be returned to the currents of the Rhine. Who knows?"[214]

---

210. Ibid., pp. 111–12.
211. Sombart, radio speech transcript, pp. 235–36.
212. Sombart, *Bourgeois*, p. 333; on the English, see pp. 208–9.
213. Werner Sombart, "Der kapitalistische Unternehmer," *Archiv* 29, no. 3 (November 1909): 729.
214. Sombart, *Bourgeois*, p. 346.

Science and Humanism at the Crossroads

> *Man is linked to the chain of generations by the spirit,*
> *not by the blood.*
>
> WERNER SOMBART

If the "twilight of the gods" remained Sombart's final word on modern society before the First World War, it did not express a decision to flee from the constraints of science into Nietzsche-inspired fantasies of voluntaristic life philosophy. On the contrary, despite his posturing in the face of Delbrück's attacks, he spent most of his time working on a massive research project intended to answer his critics' objections by providing a more rigorous empirical foundation for the revised edition of *Modern Capitalism* that finally appeared in 1917. Exploring a bewildering range of factors—from military expenditure to the demand for luxury goods—Sombart produced a series of minutely detailed studies on isolated causal chains contributing to the emergence of the capitalist spirit, which he planned to array "horizontally" next to each other in a more compelling defense of his thesis.[215] While the 130 pages he devoted to the medieval transport system still impressed Fernand Braudel as a "classic work" sixty years later, the sheer quantity of material Sombart amassed effectively blocked its reception among contemporary scholars, who preferred Weber's decision to approach the analysis of the capitalist spirit on a more theoretical plane.[216] "What all hasn't Sombart brought up in turn as a reason for the emergence of modern capitalism," one reviewer jeered. "This no doubt justly provoked some head-shaking and gave grounds to the complaint that everything possible and much more besides could be held accountable."[217] The torrent of empirical data Sombart published after 1911 thus merely strengthened the impression of frivolity he had encouraged upon arriving in Berlin, and it was after reading one of these studies that Naumann vainly tried to guess his intentions in 1913. "When the present becomes too normal and shallow for him, he flees into the wonders and magnificence of the past," the progressive reformer snorted, "and roots around in old trunks after the favorite clothes of pretty grandmothers."[218]

---

215. Appel, *Sombart,* p. 51.
216. As Appel argues; ibid., pp. 50–64, 266–69.
217. Ibid., p. 50.
218. Naumann, "Luxus," pp. 41–42.

By far the most controversial study at the time, *The Jews and Economic Life* has also understandably done the most damage to Sombart's historical reputation. David Landes asserts that the book "should have been dismissed out of hand as a pseudo-scholarly hoax, a pedantic effort to confer, by the lavish use of footnote references, an academic respectability on errant nonsense already current in plain German terms,"[219] and Mitzman similarly cites it as evidence that Sombart had fallen into "the trap of *völkisch* sentimentalism."[220] Given his simultaneous plunge into cultural despair, such assessments seem particularly well justified. The economist's decision to expose the biological roots of the capitalist spirit in alleged Jewish racial characteristics at a moment when the "Jewish question" was making headlines in the daily press was hardly coincidental. Indeed, Sombart's conclusions on intermarriage and the place of Jews in the public sphere set precedents that undoubtedly played a role in the formulation of Nazi racial policies. The execrable nature of the study stands beyond doubt. But few social scientists would have been willing to dismiss it as a "pseudo-scholarly hoax" at the fin de siècle—when racial theory was taken quite seriously—least of all in progressive circles, where Weber himself understood racial hygiene to represent "scientific sociology."[221] Among German women's activists, only Conservatives dismissed such views "out of hand," preferring to indulge their anti-Semitism with more potent doses of Bartels's Aryan mysticism. As we have seen, a "modern" biological approach seemed an indispensable ally for progressive and leftist reformers at the time.

In fact, Sombart's use of Darwinian and racial concepts in studying capitalism went back to his early attempts to correct the overly "individualistic" tendencies of Social Democracy by applying the "actual socialist idea" of evolutionary theory in the 1880s, and it was clearly evident in his celebration of technological progress in the "Ideals of Social Policy," which warned of the threat from "inferior" Eastern peoples. Discussing promising trends in "racial hygiene," the economist had cited a study by John Haycraft that had been recently translated by his land reform ally on the Breslau city council, Hans Kurella, along with the work of Alfred Ploetz, the Hauptmanns's friend and a regular guest at the Neissers' villa in these years. While

---

219. Quoted in Herf, *Modernism,* pp. 135–36.
220. Mitzman, "Conflict," p. 100.
221. See "Human Economics" in Chapter 5.

he scorned Otto Ammon's round-head/long-head theory along with the popularized versions of other "dilettantes," Sombart respected his friends in the medical profession, whose ideas he described as "exceedingly worthy of attention."[222] It is thus not entirely surprising that, facing accusations of scholarly laxness and reliance on "that pseudo-thinker" Marx, the economist later decided to complement his theory of *classes* as "carriers" of economic motives with a consideration of *race* as another isolated causal series that might provide a more solid, empirical explanation for the psychological predispositions of leading economic subjects that he was trying to establish as the driving force of economic evolution. "Obviously, under the influence of the natural sciences, our eye has been sharpened for seeing the qualities of the blood in human beings," Sombart explained in 1912; "we have become more conscious, more distinguishing in our perception, more critical in judging human differences. We see in a single case more individual characteristics based on qualities of the blood than the men of the 'Age of Enlightenment,' or even the men of the Paulskirche."[223]

Yet there was obviously more at stake in the economist's decision to spend two years studying *Jewish* racial characteristics. Lenger is certainly correct in asserting that Sombart's interest in racial theory was closely linked to his plunge into cultural pessimism after the turn of the century.[224] The dilemmas of racial hygiene mingled progressive hope with cultural fears in Naturalist circles, often with deeply ambivalent results. Sombart's first sustained attempt to apply racial categories appeared in his "personal" portrait, *The German National Economy in the Nineteenth Century*, at the same time he was cultivating his friendship with Carl Hauptmann. Yet the economist's sketch of German and Jewish racial types certainly did not portray the "Nordic nations" in a flattering light. A "physiological freshness" and "greater capacity for bodily performance" were the Germans' most appealing features in the economist's eyes, but their "strong sense of duty" was more significant for his decision to include them in the category of "overdetermined capitalist nations."[225] "[I]n such a country, God knows, there is nothing better to do than one's damned duty," Sombart groaned.

222. Sombart, "Ideale," p. 24.
223. Werner Sombart, *Die Zukunft der Juden* (Leipzig: Duncker & Humblot, 1912), p. 51.
224. Lenger, "Abkehr," p. 77.
225. Sombart, *Volkswirtschaft*, pp. 101–2.

Contrasting da Vinci's prolific genius with Kant's categorical imperative, he traced the Germans' self-discipline to their "lack of sensual/artistic abilities" and "talent as partial human beings," which also explained the country's economic success. The "type of German nature" was the "social component-person," Sombart argued: "our capacity for subordinating ourselves to a larger whole, a powerful organization so that we function like cogs in a mechanism and a tremendous increase in the effectiveness of [the nation's] energy emerges from the collaboration of many."[226] But capitalist enterprise required more than disciplined rationality. Lacking in the plodding Germans, the crucial *Erwerbstrieb* was supplied by Jews, in whom Sombart identified a strong personal will and determination in pursuit of "individual profit" as decisive racial characteristics. By an act of historic providence, the borders of the new German Empire encompassed the perfect mixture of both races, producing a nation possessed by the capitalist spirit, the economist claimed. The presence of Jews was thus "one of the greatest advantages this country has with regard to ethnicity," and he flatly stated that Germany's rise to world power would never have occurred without them.[227]

By the time Sombart published *The Jews and Economic Life* in 1911, however, he had reversed the roles of each "race" in the symbiotic emergence of German capitalism. Emphasizing the "entirely tentative state of anthropological/biogenetic science," the economist repeatedly observed that nothing was known with certainty about relations between the "somatic" and "psychic properties of human beings," and he prefaced his work by insisting that, even if such knowledge became available in the future, it could never legitimate attempts to rank Jews or any other race "higher" or "lower" than another.[228] "Nowhere . . . has subjective judgment achieved as much mischief, nowhere has it obstructed knowledge of objective realities as much as it has in the area of the 'racial question,' and most especially in the area of the so-called 'Jewish question' "[229] Using the new discipline as a prop for crude political agendas, H. S. Chamberlain and others had rendered the terminology of racial science nearly unusable, so that Sombart felt compelled to coin new words—replacing 'racial' with

---

226. Ibid., pp. 106–9.
227. Ibid., pp. 112–21.
228. Sombart, *Juden und Wirtschaft*, pp. xi–xiv, 381, 385.
229. Ibid., p. xi.

'nationish' (*völkisch* with *volklich*), for instance—in an awkward attempt to distance himself from such "dilettantes." Much as he had in 1903, the economist also stressed the benevolent influence of Jews on economic life. "Like the sun, Israel rose over Europe: where it arrived, new life sprang forth, where it departed, everything that had previously blossomed began to molder."[230] The source of this vital energy was no longer the impassioned "teleologism" of the *Erwerbstrieb*, however, but instead the rigid discipline imposed by a religion based on the abstract notion of a "contract" with God. The elements Weber had identified in the *Protestant Ethic* (which Sombart himself had once found in Kant's categorical imperative) were in fact borrowed from "the Jewish religion," the economist now argued. "Holiness in a word means: rationalization of life. Means replacing natural, instinctive, creaturely existence with conscious, purposeful, moral life."[231] The artificial, abstract, rational qualities of the "Jewish spirit," which had evolved over thousands of years of adaptation to the harsh, unforgiving climate of the desert, were fundamentally foreign to the natural instincts of Europeans, who had faced more immediate and concrete, personal challenges in the fertile Northern woods. "Desert and forest, sand and swamp: these are the great oppositions," Sombart wrote, and it was in the fruitful "cultural mating of oriental and Northern peoples" in modern times that he discovered the "world-historical significance of the Jews."[232]

Sombart's anguished renunciation of rationalizing "progress" as a "destroyer of the best values" during these same years gives his revised appraisal of the "Jewish spirit" a decidedly anti-Semitic subtext, as Herf persuasively argues, and when the economist first presented his findings in a public lecture tour, many contemporaries interpreted his message in precisely this light.[233] "[E]ven the most dogged opponents of the Jews have not dared to level such summary incriminations up until now," the anti-Semitic publicist Theodor Fritsch mirthfully reported in *The Hammer*, while the Berlin *Citizen's Newspaper* found it "quite clear that these con-

---

230. Ibid., p. 15.
231. Ibid., pp. v, 242–43, 265.
232. Ibid., pp. 403, 421–22.
233. Herf argues that *The Jews and Economic Life* translates Tönnies's categories from social to racial terms by telling the story of the transition from Christian "community" to Jewish "society"; pp. 136–37.

clusions can only point in the direction of anti-Semitism."[234] Yet many on both sides also read his criticism of Chamberlain and descriptions of the Jews' invigorating effect on economic life in the opposite direction. While the virulently anti-Semitic *German High Guard* denounced the economist as a "praiser of Jewishness," the *Jewish Review* reported that a Zionist community in Leipzig was taking up a collection in his name for a "Herzl Forest" in Palestine.[235] *The Jews and Economic Life* evoked a similarly ambivalent response. While the American Jewish Historical Society bestowed an honorary membership on Sombart in recognition of the book's merits, and Ludwig Feuchtwanger also described the work as "a document of fair, penetrating understanding for Jews" the Alliance against Jewish Arrogance was equally pleased, inviting him to repeat his lectures for the benefit of its members.[236]

Facing charges of "cowardice," the economist took it upon himself to publish a "confession" clarifying his views on *The Future of the Jews* in 1912. "What a terrible gap would open up in the world of humanity if this breed were to vanish!" Sombart wrote, praising Heine's "wonderful melancholy" as an example of the Jews' cultural contributions, which now reappeared alongside a positive economic influence as one of their most desirable racial traits. "Colorful is what the world should be. And it is a pity when any plant species, however invisible it might be, when any species of animal, however unimportant, dies out. We should be afraid of nothing so much as the impoverishment of the world and the forms of life. And in humanity, this wish must . . . intensify into a passion."[237] After launching into this rhapsody on the multiplicity of life, however, the economist turned his long-standing concerns over cultural and environmental devastation into a tirade against the assimilationists in the "Jewish liberal press," who were suppressing the Zionists' efforts to preserve a distinct ethnic identity and threatening to cause the "extinction" of the race by encouraging young Jews to "relinquish individual characteristics" for the sake of "social mimicry."[238] Even if assimilation were desirable, "the difference in the blood

---

234. Press clippings, NL Sombart 28.
235. Ibid.
236. Ibid.
237. Sombart, *Zukunft der Juden,* pp. 55–57.
238. Ibid., pp. 38–40, 59–64.

between [Jews] and the 'Aryan' tribes is obviously too great" for a "melding" of the two races, Sombart argued, since German/Jewish marriages produced "intellectually and morally unbalanced" offspring, "who are either morally corrupt or come to an end in suicide or mental derangement."[239]

Having thus provided an argument that would later reappear as justification for the Nuremberg laws against racial intermarriage, Sombart went on to advocate the Jews' exclusion from broad regions of the public sphere. The prominent role of Jews in Eastern Europe and the United States did much to explain the more extreme anti-Semitism in those societies, and therefore it was best to keep them out of the Officer Corps, public administration, and academia, as well as other areas where conflict was likely, he argued, particularly at a time of growing public awareness of racial difference.[240] Despite his high words of praise for the Jews, the economist thus anticipated many of the Nazis' racial policies, lending the appearance of scientific legitimacy to anti-Semitic stereotypes while simultaneously feeding the contemporary fears of racial and cultural degeneration. "I wish in the interests of the German nation's soul that it be liberated from the constricting embrace of the Jewish spirit so that it can develop in purity once more," Sombart wailed. "I wish the 'Jewification' of so many extensive areas of our public and intellectual life would cease: for the salvation of German culture, but just as much for the salvation of the Jewish."[241]

This tirade against "Jewification," like Sombart's plunge into cultural despair, sets the economist far apart from Damaschke and Bäumer, who shared his respect for the "science" of racial hygiene, but rejected the solutions proposed by radical anti-Semites and saw "race" as a category that broke down segregating barriers of class and confession. While Damaschke also believed that Jews had achieved a disproportionate influence in German society and was personally perhaps more inclined to accept the anti-Semitic caricatures in the press, he refused to turn an "issue of principles" into a "personal issue," just as Bäumer ruled out any connection between "Pan German fantasies of exclusion" and "the universally valid, all-encompassing significance" of eugenics. A strong commitment to the

---

239. Ibid., pp. 42–45, 52.
240. Ibid., pp. 16–27, 48–50, 83–86.
241. Ibid., p. 58.

neo-Lamarckian, environmentalist position in the debates over heredity sustained both reformers' optimistic faith in the organic world's dynamic ability to resolve the conflicting impulses of the day—individual and social, material and spiritual, humanist and scientific—as it had for Sombart earlier in his career, and would again in *Merchants and Heroes*. But in 1912 the economist had grown "more critical in judging human differences" that now seemed permanently fixed in "qualities of the blood" and no longer saw the possibility for solutions of any kind.

Far from a flight into life philosophy, Sombart's plunge into cultural despair was in fact closely related to the waning credibility of vitalism in scientific circles. With his connections to Neisser, Kurella, and Ploetz, the economist quickly learned of the triumph of Weismannism, and its pessimistic conclusions clearly informed the bleak tone of his writing after the turn of the century. In *The German National Economy,* Sombart had already announced that "the theory of the life force" had been stamped out once and for all in the early nineteenth century and that science had worked steadily toward the "destruction of nature's soul" ever since.[242] While the death of the life force became a powerful theme in Sombart's cultural criticism—in the same volume, he lamented the "mountain of dead matter" separating modern man from "living nature"—it had a devastating impact on his attitudes toward social reform. *The Jews and Economic Life* included a sharp attack on the progressive "milieu fanatics" who clung to outdated environmentalist theories; and in *The Bourgeois,* the economist spelled out the biological underpinnings of his own grim prognosis for the future quite explicitly. "[W]ithout a doubt, Lamarckism corresponds to a 'liberal' (or Social Democratic) view of the world, which always has a tendency toward improving the world, just as a consistent Weismannism is the scientific correlative of 'conservative' views," the economist recognized. But "the pure 'Lamarckists'" were "in the process of dying out" as a result of "the present state of biological research," and even the noblest of personal motives could not be permitted to obscure the results of objective inquiry. "That the great mass of mental states is founded on properties of the blood, and that these properties and not the milieu essentially determine the mental activities of human beings is to my knowledge no longer contested by any serious researcher," he conceded. "It will

---

242. Sombart, *Volkswirtschaft,* pp. 139–40.

suffice if the author professes himself to be an adherent of the anti-Lamarckist view."[243]

Yet Sombart stopped short of declaring support for Weismannism in 1913. While rejecting the "milieu fanatics'" claims that eugenics could actually *reinforce* humanistic values, he was also unprepared to sacrifice the latter to the ruthless demands of science. "These ideals of humanity impose duties on us all as human beings (I would like to add: on all creatures), duties of love, of mercy, of good will," he proclaimed in *The Future of the Jews.*[244] As important as racial categories might be, they did not in any way diminish the validity of "humanitarian ideals" as universal guidelines of moral behavior. Jews were "fellow human beings, despite all opposition of the blood," the economist wrote, encouraging gentile readers to form friendships that would allow both races to see past their differences. "One should never forget that everything that is said about national character and national oppositions always applies only to the great multitude. Individuals will always find their way out of different groups to personal friendship. And at a certain level of humanity, group instincts and national peculiarities disappear entirely." Nor was race any more important in determining political loyalties.[245] One could also be "self-consciously Jewish and a very good German (as a citizen of the state) at the same time," Sombart argued. "Why should a Jew who feels himself to be a Jew not have his full share of German spirit?"[246]

In racial matters as in so much else, subjective, humanist values represented Sombart's last refuge from an "objective" reality that seemed to grow increasingly harsh and uncompromising as science destroyed his hopes for reconciling these two worlds, and the economist's "development into a man of culture" left little room for doubt where his sympathies would lie if forced to choose between them. In fact, this commitment to the "transcendental" ideals of liberal humanism repeatedly inspired Sombart to take a firm stance against Nazi racial policies after 1933. Although Herf has suggested that *German Socialism* "continues what was his central contribution to reactionary modernism, that is, the translation of the language of social theory into the language of race," Sombart stridently opposed all

---

243. Sombart, *Bourgeois*, pp. 370–71n 246; *Juden und Wirtschaft*, p. 388.
244. Sombart, *Zukunft der Juden*, p. 89.
245. Ibid., pp. 89–90.
246. Ibid., pp. 76–77.

attempts to apply racial science to the problems of social policy in the 1934 treatise.[247] Echoing Bäumer's objections to the "ghastly calculation" of population policy, he asserted that the most effective way to encourage "the will to multiply" was to ensure "mother and child are brought into favorable living conditions. A healthy social order . . . is the only and in any case the best condition for the rearing of healthy offspring."[248] While repeating his arguments for the exclusion of Jews from the public sphere to prevent "social anti-Semitism," Sombart explicitly rejected claims that such policies had any foundation in the alleged racial characteristics of Jews or would improve economic life. In fact, the "Jewish spirit" was itself not Jewish. "[T]he biggest finance magnates in the world are very much of Aryan blood, and many of the great stock market and speculation scandals are attached to non-Jewish names," he observed, repeating Damaschke's argument against making economic policy a personal matter.[249] Denouncing "the route of selection or extinction" for this reason alone, Sombart fought harder on ethical grounds, insisting that "our present-day religious and moral feeling would protest against it." Racial science could never determine which characteristics were desirable human qualities. "[W]ho vouches for the fact that all racy [*rassigen*] people are worthy people, and that worthy people can only be racy people?" the economist wondered. "An urgent warning must be made not to believe we can derive our values from nature."[250] If he had frowned on inter-racial unions because they allegedly produced "intellectually or morally unbalanced" offspring, Sombart now dismissed the regulation of marriage on racial principles as a dubious practice at best, arguing that most geniuses had been " 'ill' in a biological sense." It was not merely a matter of protecting geniuses, however. "Do we know the mission of idiots on this earth?" he demanded, revealing the nature of his recent interest in Dostoevsky. "In

---

247. Herf, *Modernism*, p. 150.

248. Werner Sombart, *Deutscher Sozialismus* (Berlin: Buchholz und Weißwange, 1934), pp. 188, 199.

249. Ibid., pp. 194–95. While Herf finds evidence of Sombart's implicit "belief in biologically based racism," in this argument, it seems important to note that the economist used it as a point of departure for an extended diatribe against Nazi racial policies that explicitly refutes the validity of such views; cf. Herf, *Modernism*, p. 149.

250. Sombart, *Deutscher Sozialismus*, p. 197.

earlier times, the village idiot was taken for a kind of saint. And are not qualities perhaps developed in the 'healthy' through their dealings with the feeble-minded that we must take for granted as especially worthy? Should one deny that the most delicate emotions are aroused in parents when handling an idiotic child? The exclusively naturalistic treatment of these problems always conceals a danger. Therefore, the greatest of all possible caution is called for."[251]

In 1939, Sombart again firmly ruled out the application of natural science to solve the problems of human society in his last published work, *On the Human Being,* which desperately strove to establish the transcendental qualities that set humanity apart from the animal world. "No human being without spirit, no feeling, no action without spirit. The human being is woven into spirit," he proclaimed. "We can speak of an omnipresence or ubiquity of spirit in human existence."[252] The "naturalistic" perspective could not even explain why a human should be a person if a dog was not, the economist scorned.[253] While he had accepted the idea that mental states were "founded on properties of the blood" in 1913, Sombart now indignantly rejected the idea. "What is that supposed to mean: someone is born to be a criminal, is a *deliquente nato,* brings with him the capacities that make him predisposed to becoming a criminal?" he irritably demanded. "What nonsense to speak of a 'technical predisposition' or even of a 'gift for invention!' "[254] Returning to the environmentalist standpoint, the aging scholar declared that the fin-de-siècle debate between vitalists and mechanists had remained unresolved and insisted that "spirit and nature are equally involved in the construction of personality."[255] The proponents of "eugenics" had "dared to interfere in the natural course of human development and to eliminate influences they consider detrimental (hereditary illnesses)," but their narrow, physical approach could never touch (or improve) human essence, which existed "only in man's mysterious interpen-

251. Ibid., p. 199.
252. Werner Sombart, *Vom Menschen: Versuch einer geisteswissenschaftlichen Anthropologie,* 2nd ed. (Berlin: Duncker & Humblot, 1956), p. 21.
253. Ibid., p. 26.
254. Ibid., p. 423.
255. Ibid., p. 430. Sombart specifically mentions the dualistic vitalism of Hans Driesch in making his assertion about the unresolved debates; ibid., pp. 414–15.

etration with spirit," Sombart concluded: "Everything biological is always just an ingredient."[256]

Sombart, Naumann, and the Fight for Anti-Politik

Sombart's refusal to allow science to challenge the humanistic values of his *Gymnasium* education, his avowal of transcendental idealism and renewed faith in the voluntaristic principles of vitalism—qualities often deemed suspect by historians of "anti-modernism"—thus led him to condemn the notion of "life unworthy of life," creating an unbridgeable gap between his views and those of Nazi policy makers at a time when such criticism required courage. While similar attitudes informed his cultural pessimism before the First World War, the economist was still unprepared to abandon his discipline's claim to the status of social "science" in the attempt to found a purely "humanistic anthropology" in 1914.[257] The prestige of biological sciences and his own youthful belief that the conditions of the material world could be changed to enhance the quality of life were still too close for him to neglect the importance of empirical research in the formulation of an "objective" social policy. But the debates over heredity seemed settled, the constraints of public life firmly locked in place, the dictates of modern social and economic development a "hated necessity." Repelled by the "guardians and grail-keepers" of the "new world" and unable to find a way "back to the old," Sombart lost hope in scholarly solutions while at the same time rejecting the "starry-eyed fantasies" of the "coffee-house *Übermenschen*," and so he privately retreated from the Wilhelmine reform milieu into the "grand, grand realm in between, where the freest live."[258]

Such open betrayal of the social impulse destroyed Sombart's friendship with the Brauns and angered many of his former colleagues in progressive circles, above all Naumann, who had consistently supported his reform initiatives since *Socialism and the Social Movement*. Picking up the "gauntlet" Sombart had thrown down in a derisive article, "Politics as a Vocation,"

---

256. Ibid., p. 431.
257. The subtitle of *On the Human Being*.
258. Letter from Sombart to Lily Braun reprinted in the *New Community*, 1906; NL Sombart 9d. The passage describes Braun's relation to Social Democracy but more accurately reflects Sombart's own stance at the time.

the "professional politician" vented his frustration in an open letter to *The Morning* in 1907. Sombart had once come close to becoming a political leader himself but had since "taken a fright," Naumann argued, and after defending his own efforts to mobilize the masses, the Progressive leader offered to discuss the real reasons behind his former colleague's sudden change of heart but insisted that all dialogue was pointless until the latter revealed the extent of his "anti-politics."[259] In response, Sombart angrily spurned the suggestion that cowardice had motivated his "departure from politics," insisting that Naumann was the one who had really changed. Even if "the slime-waves of politics have drained off you," their traces remained clearly visible, the economist snarled: "When you pass over problems more easily than before; when you arrange the facts more capriciously; when you treat objectively insignificant things with stress and emphasis, only because they play a coincidental role in the politics of the moment." Thanking Naumann for coining the phrase, Sombart promised to entitle his next major work *Anti-Politik,* in which he intended to demonstrate that "politics is frightfully overestimated in its significance for the fashioning of human existence."[260]

Although the book never appeared, Sombart spelled out his understanding of the term 'Anti-Politik' over the next few months as he developed his critique of Wilhelmine political culture in *The Morning*. It was time to stop blaming every personal problem on the government, which was "without significance for the essential nature of our life up to a certain, very expansive limit," he wrote, and despite its "tutelary policies" the economist even managed an ironic defense of the regime: "it's so nice and orderly that it's a joy to behold, it can't be bribed and has many another good quality." But the most important developments of public life were beyond the government's reach in any case. While artistic and cultural currents flowed outside "the official bed," capitalism continued to thrive, taking over ever more regions of the public sphere against the wishes of the ruling classes. The same was true of organized labor, which relied on self-help in many cases, and intellectual life could certainly sustain a healthy life independently of official culture: "My God: we don't need state universities

259. Friedrich Naumann, "An Herrn Professor W. Sombart," *Morgen* 1, no. 13 (September 6, 1907): 384, 387.
260. Werner Sombart, "An Friedrich Naumann," *Morgen* 1, no. 14 (September 13, 1907): 416, 420.

and the Academy in order to do scholarship and art."[261] Beyond the oppressive grasp of the regime, the anti-political world of social and cultural reform offered plenty of room to make valuable contributions toward the improvement of life. "[W]hoever feels the drive to work practically for the common good finds thousands of opportunities to do so in the clubs and cooperatives: starting with nurseries and kindergartens and going as far as construction cooperatives, popular education clubs, and settlements," Sombart wrote in another article:

> And if he wants to work for the propagation of ideas, then there are again enough opportunities outside the political treadmill: he can promote the ideas of the Society for Social Reform, can roll up his sleeves in clubs named after their goals, in clubs for housing reform, land reform, animal rights, the prevention of venereal disease, fish-breeding, bee-keeping, and for thousands of other useful things. The best thing here is a practical approach, but at the very least you need a knowledge of the field, and to limit yourself respectfully to the specific area in which you have assembled expertise and experience. Thus the stupid phrase, the shallow and snide know-it-all who is at home in politics, can be avoided here.[262]

Withdrawal from politics did not mean that Sombart and others like him had become "weary souls" who had lost the desire to work toward a better future, he insisted. "Oh no, ladies and gentlemen! We do not feel tired at all. We take joy in our existence and want to build as long as there is daylight, each according to his talents and powers." Official channels and political parties were simply not the best outlets for that urge, which could be satisfied only in "living works, in working from person to person."

Despite such assurances, however, Sombart *was* a "weary soul" in 1907. Lenger is largely correct in asserting that the defiant endorsement of antipolitics "cannot have convinced even its author."[263] If he recommended the Society for Social Reform to his readers as a viable forum for constructive action, the economist had ceased to play an active role in it himself since 1904, when he reluctantly attended the cottage industry congress at Lily Braun's urging, and nine years later he resigned even his nominal

---

261. Sombart, "Abkehr," pp. 482–83.
262. Werner Sombart, "Wir müden Seelen," *Morgen* 1, no. 17 (October 4, 1907): 514.
263. Lenger, "Abkehr," p. 72.

membership on its Executive Committee.[264] After his move to Berlin, he no longer led the discussion evenings of the Breslau branch, nor was he promoting land and housing reform with the help of his progressive allies on the city council. While he joined the League for the Protection of Mothers and Sexual Reform to promote the campaign for preventing sexually transmitted diseases along with Neisser and Ploetz, Sombart withdrew his support in 1908. "There are two kinds of people, those who believe in solutions and those who do not," he explained. "I stand on the ground of the latter."[265] An inactive member of the Garden City Society, he briefly reasserted his belief that the Werkbund could elevate the tastes of the bourgeoisie and develop higher forms of cooperative organization in 1908, but two years later he quit that movement as well.[266]

Yet the observation that anti-politics failed to convince "*even* its author" is also misleading, since it suggests a lonely and desperate appeal, and as Bruch has shown, Sombart's defense evoked considerable resonance in contemporary reform circles.[267] Nor should this reaction come as a surprise. After all, the economist was simply mouthing familiar arguments that the generation of 1890 had heard since its youth, and even in his most despairing moments, Sombart expressed them more poignantly than most of those who repeated them with conviction. Hope as well as despair might be hiding beneath this commonly shared language, as we have seen, and given the remarkable similarity in surface appearance, how was one to tell the difference? Damaschke and Bäumer certainly continued to believe in anti-politics, promoting Sombart's message fervently throughout these years. And beyond them, an entire milieu of intellectuals and activists did the same.

---

264. Ratz, *Sozialreform*, p. 64.
265. Evans, *Movement*, p. 124.
266. Werner Sombart, *Kunstgewerbe und Kultur* (Berlin: Marquard & Co., 1908), pp. 109–10, 117–18; Campbell, *Werkbund*, pp. 30–31.
267. Bruch, *Wissenschaft*, pp. 185–90.

CHAPTER

·

5

The Wilhelmine Reform Milieu

With Naumann's untimely repudiation of *Anti-Politik* and Sombart's resonant response in 1907—the year of the Liberals' disastrous "mating"
with Conservatives in the Bülow Bloc—we have come full circle, returning to the "professional politician's" bizarre collision with Posadowsky's
New Course and to the lessons it held for socially conscious men and
women in the broader context of the Wilhelmine reform milieu.[1] In charting three separate paths to anti-politics, the preceding case studies brought
much of this terrain into sharp relief from the perspective of individual
reformers. Starting with Damaschke's exploration of Berlin in the spring
thaw, we encountered progressively more of the circles, movements, and
institutions that comprised this anti-political landscape—socialist editors,
social drama and popular education, natural health and medicine, Ethical
Culture, the Friedrichshagen circle, national economic boys, Christian and
National Socials, and, of course, land reform. Bäumer's attempt to steer a
course between radicals and moderates in the bourgeois women's movement covered much of the same ground but revealed different facets—
Salomon's links to the "humanitarian socialism" of Friedrichshagen, for
instance—while also opening up new terrain to view: Freudenberg's Munich, the National Social feminists of the liberal Southwest, the Webers'
salon, and a whole series of cultural reforms, Garden Cities and Werkbund,
art education, the youth movement, and clothing reform. Many of these
causes were also explored by Sombart, who combined interests in land
reform and Garden Cities with an early commitment to improving labor
relations and also briefly took up the radical feminists' struggle for sexual

---

1. See "Posadowsky's Lessons" in Chapter 1.

reform as he made his own ties to Friedrichshagen and the circles of Berlin's cultured elite. All three reformers thus learned to diagnose the ills of Wilhelmine modernity and mobilized support for their solutions while building successful careers within this densely interwoven network, which deeply informed the hopes, fears, and expectations of many in the generation of 1890, creating a common *habitus* that lent a discernible coherence to their visions of the future and rendered them accessible to their contemporaries. Each reformer's path constructed that common world along different lines, however, and only after careful examination does a precise sense for the potentialities contained within this complex set of relations become possible in individual cases. From Damaschke's finely tuned conception of his "truly national" mission to Bäumer's celebration of eugenics and Sombart's faltering yet sincere defense of anti-politics, the idioms of Wilhelmine political culture carried nuances that were heard and understood by contemporaries to convey meanings far removed from those associated with the discourses of popular nationalism, biologism, and cultural pessimism in later years. Without first sampling this terrain up close with a few detailed examples, the broader resonances, patterns of association, and thumbnail sketches of other careers mapped out in the following exploration of the Wilhelmine reform milieu can have little concrete meaning. The case studies will thus provide constant and necessary points of reference as we return to assess the possibilities and limits of the search for alternative modernities in this broader context.

Resonating powerfully in diverse circles of reformers who had reached many of the same conclusions regarding the corrosive futility of politics and the perfidy of German liberalism, Sombart's clash with Naumann serves as a case in point, since it foregrounds regions of Wilhelmine political culture that appear quite familiar on the surface—the "unpolitical German," the "failure of liberalism," the complicitous flight into aestheticism and neo-humanist idealism—but which on closer inspection reveal widespread opposition to the regime and a firm resolve to transform the status quo quietly through effective action in areas of personal "expertise and experience." If Sombart had lost faith in solutions, he did not "leap from despair to utopia across all existing reality," and his defiant call to anti-politics still breathed convictions won over years of struggle, convictions that continued to inspire others to "roll up their sleeves" and undertake "living works" beyond the sphere of official culture. Neither Damaschke's refusal to follow Naumann from socialism to liberalism nor his withdrawal from politics after 1903 signaled resignation on the part of the land reformer; and even Bäumer, who worked with Naumann in the Progressive People's Party, criticized the workers' pastor for "wasting energy" in the "pettiness" of the "parliamentary racket."[2] The decision to join the "diabolical" game of politics, which set "bourgeois against worker, worker against bourgeois, the farmer against both, and both against the farmer," was in fact tantamount to "desertion" in the eyes of many of Naumann's friends and colleagues, who were committed to a more constructive approach.[3] The men and women "of the most diverse political leanings" who "worked peacefully together" building Garden Cities certainly had no intention of "uselessly wearing down [their] energies in the political and economic struggle."[4] Introducing a new journal significantly entitled *The Deed*, which would soon lead cultural reformers in the campaign to democratize Prussia's suffrage laws and which greeted the Social Democrats' stunning electoral victory a few years later, the Monist Ernst Horneffer spoke for many when he spelled out his goals in 1909: "Salvation can only come from the 'unpolitical.' "[5] The common thread in these disparate efforts was a "rejection of existing party-political relationships" that evoked not despair, but exhilaration, a "mood of setting out on new departures," as Bruch demonstrated in his pioneering study on *Academic Politics in Wilhelmine Germany*.[6]

Recent scholarship has in fact charted possibilities for effective opposition to the established order in many unsuspected regions of Wilhelmine political culture, challenging the image of a society in abject submission to reactionary authorities described by liberal historians (following leads from Thomas and Heinrich Mann) in the 1960s.[7] While explorations into

2. Gertrud Bäumer, "Friedrich Naumann," undated manuscript, NL Bäumer 19, p. 2.

3. Franz Staudinger, "Gartenstadt und Genossenschaft," *Gartenstadt* 3, no. 2 (January 1909): 25. "Desertion" is Willy Hellpach's term, quoted in Conze, "Naumann," p. 355. See also Göhre, *From Socialism to Liberalism*.

4. Hans Kampffmeyer, *Die Gartenstadtbewegung* (Leipzig: Teubner, 1909), pp. 59, 88.

5. Ernst Horneffer, "Unsere Ziele," *Tat* 1, no. 1 (April 1909): 4.

6. Bruch, *Wissenschaft*, p. 188.

7. See especially Nipperdey, "Untertanengesellschaft?"; Evans, "Untertanengeist."

the subversive side of German cultural politics at the fin de siècle still remain in the early stages,[8] this historiographical reassessment has focused more extensively on two areas that are helpful in fixing the coordinates of the reform milieu in relation to the Wilhelmine political system: (1) the "technocratic anti-politics" and rationalizing "governmentalist" movements described by Peukert, Weindling, Bruch, Sachße and others; and (2) "integral nationalism" and the "German-national public realm" mapped out somewhat earlier in pathbreaking works by Eley and Chickering. Given the deep strains of humanist cultural criticism that at times made them indistinguishable from the pundits of anti-modern despair, Damaschke, Bäumer, and Sombart hardly evinced the "fantasies of omnipotence" Peukert saw as a decisive characteristic of progressive reform circles at the turn of the century, but they certainly contributed to the "network of social-scientific theories and methods on the one hand and social institutions and practices on the other that were set up to solve the 'social question' " and played a crucial role in modernizing German social and health services, particularly at the municipal level, in these years.[9] All three reformers shared the common belief that social and economic development could be "managed" within limits defined by the empirical complexities of the modern world and the demands of ethics in order to realize the potential of technological progress for bringing about a genuine improvement in the quality of human life through heightened productive efficiency. And they also looked to science to circumvent the acrimony of politics by substituting economic and "biological values where hitherto the categories of political economy and civil society had predominated."[10]

Following the example set by the Association for Social Policy, land reformers, feminists, the Society for Social Reform, and other social activists undertook detailed research and analyses of current issues under deliberation in parliament, exercising an indirect, but substantial influence on public policy through technical proposals backed by claims of specialized expertise. Model institutions were another important avenue of Wilhel-

---

8. Recent scholarship on German feminism is a noteworthy exception; see the introduction to Chapter 3. For promising signs, see the essays in Hübinger, Bruch, et al., *Kultur.* See also Jelavich, *Munich;* Fritzsche, *Berlin;* Applegate, *Nation;* Rollins, *Vision.*

9. Peukert, *Diagnose,* pp. 106–11.

10. Weindling, *Health,* pp. 19–20.

mine anti-politics. The private centers for welfare administration founded by members of the *Social Praxis* circle in Frankfurt and the Ethical Culture society in Berlin pioneered the new comprehensive approach to municipal services based on the "scientific penetration of social problems and corresponding systematic knowledge of those charged with their treatment" that began replacing paternalistic and charitable institutions before the First World War, as Sachße has shown. The city planners, architects, and engineers of German Garden Cities also worked closely with local municipalities, tackling a variety of technical and aesthetic challenges in the attempt to construct viable alternatives that eventually transformed modern urban landscapes in significant ways.[11] Private seminars and training programs geared to civil servants and municipal administrators represented a third important method of influencing policies through unofficial channels—again, drawing on precedents set by the socialists of the lectern—an especially effective tactic for feminists, who used expertise to carve out an exclusive field of action in the burgeoning sphere of local health and social services, and for land reformers. Mayors, municipal officials, and city council members figured prominently alongside academics and professionals in Damaschke's League, which often used such personal connections to gain the desired result behind the scenes. After a visit to the salon of a high-ranking naval officer led to Tirpitz's personal intervention in the campaign for colonial reform, the BDB leader even used a contact in the Imperial entourage to slip a pamphlet to the Kaiser himself, who showed promising signs of interest but balked at reading the longer, statistic-laden treatise *Land Reform.* "It can hardly be imagined today what the will of the Kaiser meant in the pre-war era," Damaschke later remembered, "and how the entire higher civil service, whatever it may have thought at heart, was thoroughly governed by the will of this one man."[12]

To a considerable degree, Wilhelmine anti-politics depended on peculiarities of German constitutional history—powerful bureaucracy, impotent Reichstag, strong municipal governments that remained "bastions" of progressive liberalism due to a highly restricted local franchise—which sustained the curious space, neither public nor private, inhabited by the reform milieu. Yet the technocratic impulse was also a common feature of

11. Sachße, *Mütterlichkeit,* pp. 79–95, esp. p. 89. On The Garden City movement, see "Naumann's Successes" in this chapter.

12. Damaschke, *Zeitenwende,* pp. 235–49.

the industrializing democracies to the West, including the United States, where attempts to solve the social question blended with "strong professional aspirations" to inspire a remarkably similar configuration of circles and movements to fight interest politics with technical expertise. "Joining doctors in public health campaigns, were social workers, women's clubs, and teachers who specialized in the problems of youth," Robert Wiebe has written of the American progressive milieu in these years; "lawyers who drafted highly technical bills; chambers of commerce that publicized and financed pilot projects."[13] Nor were the tactics of German reformers limited to undemocratic means. As we have seen, Damaschke, Bäumer, and Sombart all supported the push for "democratization" after the turn of the century, and the same methods used to reach bureaucratic elites were also applied to reach the masses: social seminars, public education, "university extension" programs, lecture circuits, and petition drives. In the campaign for a national capital gains tax on land values, for example, Damaschke's movement organized between 800 and 900 public meetings, circulated 600,000 fliers, and collected 145,768 signatures on petitions endorsed by organizations representing a total membership of 730,000.[14]

While anti-political institutions that focused on areas of specialized technical expertise like the Society for Social Reform attracted a small following of individual members, more broadly based movements like the League of German Land Reformers and the League of German Women's Associations achieved levels of support similar to other groups seeking to mobilize grassroots support through non-partisan appeals to integral nationalism (see Table 5.1).

As we have seen, the integrationist message of the Wilhelmine reform milieu was by no means equivalent to the "radical nationalism" Eley and Chickering have identified as a significant force in the rapidly expanding public sphere of late Imperial Germany. Regarding the fleet campaign with "cool reserve," rejecting "Pan-German fantasies of exclusion," actively fighting against anti-Semitism, Damaschke and Bäumer used similar tropes to promote moderate reforms that appealed to movements comparable in size to those on the radical right. They also drew support from the same social strata of "new arrivals"—teachers, professionals, and civil

---

13. Robert Wiebe, *The Search for Order, 1877–1920* (New York: Hill and Wang, 1967), p. 128.

14. BDB congress report, *Bodenreform* 22, no. 12 (June 20, 1911): 375–76.

Table 5.1 Approximate memberships, 1912

Organization	Individual	Corporate	Representing
Society for Social Reform	1,300	232	1,500,000
League of German Land Reformers	33,800	728	800,000
League of German Women's Associations	280,000	2,200	500,000
Pan-German League	17,000	N/A	N/A
Colonial Society	41,163	N/A	N/A
Society for the Eastern Marches	53,500	N/A	N/A
Navy League	320,174	N/A	776,613
Defense League	33,000	N/A	N/A

Sources: Ratz, *Sozialreform,* p. 49; Berger-Thimme, *Wohnungsreform,* p. 86; Evans, *Movement,* pp. 193–95; Gerhard, *Unerhört,* p. 170; Eley, *Reshaping,* p. 366. The official figure for the BDF was 328,000; Gerhard, *Unerhört,* p. 205.

servants—who were eager to assume "custodial roles" as the guardians of Germany's cultural traditions in the German national public sphere.[15] White-collar workers and teachers accounted for approximately one-third of the women's League's members, while a social analysis of the first 1,000 BDB members reveals a strong presence of teachers, technicians, civil servants, and professionals alongside "Bildung und Besitz" and more traditional representatives of the national heritage (see Table 5.2).

Perhaps most interesting is the co-existence of workers, nobles, and agrarians in the land reform movement, a characteristic further borne out by the social composition of the League's Executive Committee, in which labor secretaries and cooperative leaders gradually increased in numbers to become the third largest group, after intellectuals (with professors and teachers almost evenly divided) and municipal officials by 1912 (see Table 5.3). Leaders of the anti-Semitic German National Commercial Clerks' Unions accounted for a substantial number of these secretaries, but they also included representatives of both Protestant and Catholic workers. While the radical right-wing leaders of the Christian Social Party joined the Executive Committee, Bebel and Auer repeatedly tried to win Damaschke over to the SPD, which had inserted a land reform plank in its Erfurt

---

15. Chickering, *Men,* pp. 108–29.

Table 5.2 BDB social composition: first 1,000 members

Technical professions	59
Professionals	127
Teachers	192
State and municipal officials	169
Students and academics	77
Publicists and artists	61
Industrialists and businessmen	160
Blue- and white-collar workers	37
Agrarians	80
Clergy	39
Officers	20

Source: Based on figures given in Berger-Thimme, *Wohnungsreform,* p. 88.

Program of 1891, and the League reported its first Social Democratic life-time member in 1905.[16]

The territory of broadly based organizations in the Wilhelmine reform milieu thus clearly overlaps with the "new terrain" of populist nationalism that has been thoroughly charted in recent years—Bäumer, it will be remembered, also took pains to include the right-wing Protestant Women's League into the BDF, while the radicals organized female white-collar workers who increasingly fell under the spell of the Commercial Clerks' Unions. But the milieu also transcended deep divisions in German political culture produced by the very radicalism of chauvinistic and imperialist nationalism, which often proved to be the opposite of an "integrating" force, as Helmut Smith has shown in his study of *German Nationalism and Religious Conflict.*[17] Here again the sphere of anti-politics crosses into regions that are currently the focus of intensive scholarship on the fragmentation, or "pillarization," of Imperial German society, which has followed in the wake of M. Rainer Lepsius's classic analysis of the "social-moral milieu" as a vehicle for political mobilization that simultaneously blocked effective democratization of German political culture. Defined as "social units formed by a coincidence of several structural dimensions

---

16. Damaschke, *Zeiten-wende,* pp. 218–19; Damaschke, "Auer," pp. 216–17; "Aus der Bewegung," *Deutsche Volksstimme* 16, no. 4 (February 20, 1905): 118.

17. Smith, *Nationalism,* pp. 84–102, 118.

Table 5.3 BDB Executive Committee social composition, 1899–1912 (%)

Occupation	1899	1901	1903	1906	1908	1909	1910	1912
Labor/coop secretaries	6.3	10.0	15.6	9.0	9.3	10.8	11.8	13.6
Intellectuals	25.0	23.3	26.7	22.0	16.7	14.8	25.5	23.3
Municipal officials	—	—	—	9.0	8.3	13.7	10.0	14.6
Other civil servants	—	—	—	6.5	4.6	5.0	4.0	4.0
Professionals	37.5	20.0	22.0	10.4	6.5	10.8	7.8	10.7
Industry/commerce	25.0	20.0	13.3	17.0	9.3	10.0	10.0	6.0
Members of parliament	—	6.7	6.7	7.8	5.6	4.0	5.0	4.0
Clergy	6.3	6.7	4.4	4.0	5.5	5.9	3.9	4.0
Nobles/officers	—	13.3	9.0	11.7	8.3	7.8	7.0	6.8
Women	—	—	—	—	21.3	16.7	14.8	11.7

Source: Compiled from Vorstand lists in BDB annual congress reports in *Deutsche Volksstimme* and *Bodenreform.*

Notes: The sudden drop in figures for most groups after 1908 is due to the admission of women into the BDB after the reform of the Law of Association; occupations for women are in most cases not provided on the lists.

such as religion, regional tradition, economic position, cultural orientation, [and] class-specific composition of intermediary groups," Lepsius's milieus divided German society into "highly closed," self-contained worlds, preventing contact and communication at the level of everyday life that might have allowed the development of common discourse and dispositions across increasingly politicized lines separating Protestants, Catholics, workers, and feudal aristocrats, to which Shulamit Volkov has added a fifth milieu of urban artisans.[18] Extreme social and political polarization was perhaps the most pervasive, salient fact of life in the Empire—it was this side of the "social question" that prodded Damaschke, Bäumer, and Sombart to action—and exploration of Lepsius's milieus has contributed substantially to our understanding of its central dynamics. Yet by focusing primarily on the extensive networks constructed along these lines, this scholarship also tends to render invisible the personal and institutional

---

18. M. Rainer Lepsius, "Parteisystem und Sozialstruktur: zum Problem der Demokratisierung der deutschen Gesellschaft," in Gerhard Ritter, ed., *Deutsche Parteien vor 1918* (Cologne: Kiepenheuer & Witsch, 1973), pp. 68–69, 77; Volkov, *Rise,* pp. 298–99. The term 'pillarization' is used by Gangolf Hübinger, *Kulturprotestantismus,* pp. 2–3, 305–9.

connections that run across them, and it was precisely such contacts that sustained the Wilhelmine reform milieu.

The social question itself evoked a common discourse and dispositions linking Lepsius's isolated social worlds, where it was universally perceived as a significant problem, and led to the construction of parallel organizations that were often inspired by the same principles. Founded in 1890, the Protestant Social Congress and the People's League for a Catholic Germany represented competing but parallel responses to the spring thaw, just as the spontaneous growth of Protestant and Catholic labor organizations in the 1880s vied with Social Democratic unions to tackle the challenge of social and economic transformations, and all three were strongly influenced by the socialists of the lectern.[19] While very much at home in the "Protestant-liberal milieu" Gangolf Hübinger has recently examined, Wilhelmine progressive reformers reached beyond it by appealing to the common interest in social problems and rejecting the "sharper key" of populist rhetoric. Catholic labor leaders were especially strongly represented in the *Social Praxis* circle and the Society for Social Reform, which brought Franz Hitze, Franz Brandts, August Pieper, and Carl Trimborn together with Protestant leaders like Adolf Stöcker, Ernst Francke, Wilhelm Kulemann, and Naumann in an institution that was supported by Protestant Workers' Associations and Christian Unions and that also won the endorsement of the Free Unions as well before the First World War.[20] The growing number of labor secretaries in the land reform League's Executive Committee also included prominent Catholics alongside leaders of Protestant labor and the Commercial Clerks' Unions: Franz Behrens, Monsignor Werthmann, head of the Charity Alliance for Catholic Germany, and Reinhard Mumm, General Secretary of the Ecclesiastical Social Conference, from 1908. Perhaps the most startling indication of the permeable confessional boundaries in progressive circles came with Elisabeth Gnauck-Kühne's conversion at the turn of the century, after which the National Social feminist went on to found the Catholic Women's League of Germany while continuing to play a role in the BDF, and she later joined the German Society for Sociology, which contemporaries saw as an "essentially Jewish" enterprise due to the

---

19. Hübinger, *Kulturprotestantismus*, pp. 25–33; Nipperdey, *Geschichte*, pp. 439–40, 462–66; Göhre, *Bewegung*, pp. 105–19.

20. Ratz, *Sozialreform*, pp. 17, 29, 36–39, 46, 61–62.

Table 5.4 Berlin municipal elections results, 1901

Occupation	Damaschke	Glocke (SPD)
Workers	189	2,061
Artisans	175	152
Professionals	62	17
Civil servants	726	44

Source: Damaschke, "Der Kampf um Moabit," *Deutsche Volksstimme* 12, no. 22 (November 20, 1901): 681–82.

involvement of other central figures of the reform milieu such as Franz Oppenheimer.[21]

The barriers surrounding Social Democracy were by far the most difficult to break down, and despite concentrated efforts, Wilhelmine reformers achieved only modest successes in forming alliances with the other mass movement in Imperial Germany, at least at the institutional level. As we have seen, the failure of Sombart's overtures to the left in founding the Society for Social Reform came as a crushing blow to many. And while Clara Zetkin's "clean break" with bourgeois feminists eventually discouraged even the radicals' attempts to bridge the gulf, Bebel's stern condemnation of revisionism at the SPD's Dresden congress in 1903 and the purge of moderates from the Social Democratic press two years later contributed to the ebb in reformist momentum at mid-decade as much as the disillusioning experience of the Bülow Bloc did in 1907.[22] Even before this, Damaschke's campaign in Berlin's municipal elections in 1901 gave clear indications of the failure to reach the rank and file of a working-class constituency (see Table 5.4).

Yet Damaschke maintained cordial relations with Bebel, whose salon he frequented alongside those of high-ranking navy officers in these years, and he also kept up his friendships with the rebellious socialists of Friedrichshagen, Bruno Wille and Paul Kampffmeyer—the brother of Garden

---

21. Gerhard, *Unerhört,* pp. 205–6; Dirk Käsler, "Das 'Judentum' als zentrales Enstehungs-Milieu der frühen deutschen Soziologie," in Klingemann, *Rassenmythos,* pp. 50–79.

22. Stanley Pierson, *Marxist Intellectuals and the Working-Class Mentality in Germany, 1887–1912* (Cambridge, Mass.: Harvard University Press, 1993), pp. 162–83.

City Society president Bernard Kampffmeyer—with whom he had collaborated in workers' theater and popular education in the early 1890s. Moving in the same circles as Wille, Kampffmeyer, Heinrich and Lily Braun, Eduard David, and Wolfgang Heine, progressive reformers and academics in fact achieved more success among revisionist intellectuals who shared many of the same convictions about the integrative potential of cultural politics and who, although forced underground after 1905, influenced the SPD's orthodox leaders considerably before the First World War.[23] At the grassroots level, bourgeois feminists proved remarkably successful in reaching the working class with the anti-political conception of social motherhood, which was thoroughly absorbed into the Social Democratic women's movement.[24] Although failing to make alliances at the national level, the Society for Social Reform managed to break down barriers of mutual fear and suspicion on both sides in local branches like Breslau too. Discussing common problems and making personal contacts, Wilhelmine social and cultural reformers indirectly contributed to the atmosphere of cooperation and new willingness of young Germans to experiment with Socialist coalitions in state governments, but as Beverly Heckart has shown, the National Liberals' resistance to social reform and aggressive nationalism prevented the formation of a federal Grand Bloc.[25] Of course, the Cartel of Productive Estates, Delbrück's mocking announcement of a "reasonable" social policy in 1913, and vocal opposition from radical Social Democrats the following year represented serious setbacks for the Society for Social Reform. Yet through its resolute agitation against the "standstill" in social policy caused by the Liberals' "master-in-one's-own-house" attitude, the Society nevertheless succeeded in winning a resolution endorsing cooperation with bourgeois reformers as "expedient for workers' interests" at the Free Unions' Munich congress in June 1914.[26] In general, Bruch's conclusions about academic politics may also speak for Wilhelmine anti-

23. Pierson, *Intellectuals,* pp. 14–89, 110–12, 130–31, 153–56.
24. Christiane Eifert, "Coming to Terms with the State: Maternalist Politics and the Development of the Welfare State in Weimar Germany," *Central European History* 30, no. 1 (1997): 27; Susanne Rouette, "Mothers and Citizens: Gender and Social Policy in Germany after the First World War," *Central European History* 30, no. 1 (1997): 63–64.
25. Heckart, *Politics,* pp. 274–87.
26. Ratz, *Sozialreform,* pp. 214–38.

politics in relation to the working-class milieu: while helpless to prevent the coming of war, it likely made a "substantial contribution to the accord between bourgeoisie and Social Democracy that took wholesome effect" in later years.[27]

The Wilhelmine reform milieu did not erase the sharp divisions that were part of everyday life in the Empire, nor was it free from the dark potential scholars have uncovered in the radical nationalism, rationalizing utopias, illiberalism, and cultural despair of the fin de siècle. Crossing boundaries between populists and technocrats, neo-humanist idealists and empirically minded scientists, Protestants and Catholics, workers and aris-tocrats, the space of anti-political social and cultural reform existed along-side familiar regions of Wilhelmine political culture, or better yet it over-lapped them, intersecting with the territory of each but co-extensive with none. And while by no means diminishing these other regions, it consti-tuted a substantial presence in Imperial Germany in its own right, revealing a widespread search for alternatives that cannot be found solely by tracing the outlines of these other milieus. The reform milieu becomes visible only by examining the matrix of shared issues and objectives that lent it coher-ence, the "structuring structure" of a common *habitus* that opened up this space and was in turn reproduced and sustained by the discursive networks, institutions, and practices that it helped to inspire. In one way or another, each member of the milieu interacted with this matrix, which included concerns for the impact of capitalism and industrialization, the purposive application of modern science and technology, the need for social order and efficiency, the creation of an integral national community, the main-tenance of humanistic values, and a predilection for organicist models of development and synthesis. This is not to say that each member shared an interest in all of these issues. As we have seen, individual reformers chose to concentrate their efforts in different areas. Yet within this matrix, dis-cussion of each component came to be dominated by the discourse of an alternative modernity, which emerged from the common experiences of the generation of 1890, circulated through personal and associative ties, and, once its structures had gained sufficient currency, established its own boundaries on the complex map of divided loyalties in Imperial political culture.

---

27. Bruch, *Wissenschaft,* p. 422.

Shared concerns and recognizable coherence hardly made the terrain of anti-politics devoid of conflict. The focus on specific problems and the tendency to rely on claims of professional expertise that characterized the milieu often caused friction, especially when a movement claimed to represent *the* solution to Germany's social problem. Thus, for instance, Damaschke had no patience with organizations like the Ethical Culture Society, which he could not convince of the importance of his cause, and his drive to make land reform the National Socials' defining quest sparked anger in the NSV leadership, where others resented his intrusions.[28] Specialization could also lead to squabbles over territory. While Bäumer's League eventually endorsed the creation of a women's association inside the BDB (in which Else Lüders, a prominent radical, played a central role), the land reformers' venture into feminist territory initially sparked a hostile exchange between the two organizations that permanently soured relations between Damaschke and Bäumer.[29] A few years later, land reformers responded to unwelcome competition with equal force. When the Garden City Society began billing efforts to construct "the land reform city of the future" and promised to fulfill all of Damaschke's demands "in a single stroke," BDB leaders repudiated such claims, fearing they would siphon off "outstanding intellectual and financial forces that could accomplish great things for the larger movement," and an open conflict at the 1909 land reform congress ended with a resolution condemning the Garden City movement.[30] The newcomer persisted, however, and by 1911 Damaschke

---

28. See "Onto the National Stage" in Chapter 2.

29. "Aufruf zur Gründung einer Frauengruppe für Bodenreform," *Deutsche Volksstimme* 11, no. 15 (August 5, 1900): 433–37; "Für unsere Frauengruppe," *Volksstimme* 11, no. 20 (October 20, 1900): 599–601; "Aus der Bewegung," *Volksstimme* 11, no. 23 (December 5, 1900): 714; "Aus der Bewegung," *Volksstimme* 12, no. 2 (January 20, 1901): 55–56; Adolf Damaschke, "Endlich ein rechtsfähiger Körper für unsere Bewegung," *Volksstimme* 15, no. 6 (March 20, 1904): 145–47; BDB congress report, *Volksstimme* 15, no. 22 (November 20, 1904): 667; "Frauenleben und -streben," *Frau* 8, no. 7 (April 1901): 440; 1903 BDF congress report, HLA 59–260²; Damaschke, *Zeitenwende*, p. 458.

30. Bernhard Kampffmeyer, "Die Bodenreformstadt der Zukunft," *Deutsche Volksstimme* 15, no. 21 (November 5, 1904): 656; "Vor zehn Jahren," pp. 160–62; Adolf Pohlman, "Letchworth, die erste Gartenstadt," *Bodenreform* 18, no. 24 (December 20, 1907): 748–49; BDB congress report, *Bodenreform* 20, no. 8 (April 20, 1909): 211–58.

relented to endorse Hellerau as the "embodiment of practical land reform."[31] Nor were disputes over territory the only source of discord in the reform milieu. Competing claims of representational authority often combined with tactical questions to produce bitter in-fighting between rival groups, as we saw in the case of radicals and moderates in the women's movement. The clash between land reformers and the Garden City Society was also fueled by tactical disputes. While Damaschke considered federal legislation the only means to truly systemic reform, Garden City leaders insisted that the state was too weak to break the resistance of capital and that settlements offered a more immediate way to accomplish their goals in any case. In practice, though, the construction of Garden Cities required state and municipal legislation, while land reform benefited from model projects demonstrating the usefulness of its proposals, and the two causes eventually found a basis for cooperation. And however bitter personal antagonism between the two wings of Wilhelmine feminism might have been, they still came together in local centers like Munich and beyond the women's movement in Ethical Culture meetings, the Society for Social Reform, the German Society for Sociology, and later even in the National Women's Service. Disputes over territory and tactics did not demolish the anti-political discursive network, and in the end they actually enriched it. Naumann, who continued to work as personal liaison and organizer in the milieu long after his quarrel with Sombart—although he could expect no support for his political agenda in these quarters—supplies perhaps the strongest evidence of the network's resiliency.

This tangled web of crisscrossing paths meeting at odd junctures in unexpected antagonisms and alliances comprised the fabric of Wilhelmine anti-politics, woven from the matrix of aspirations and concerns outlined above, in which no single set of social, economic, or cultural criteria alone determined the overall pattern. What held the milieu together was relationships: relationships to the practices and institutions of social and cultural reform, to the discourse of alternative modernities, to the space of anti-politics. These connections existed at various levels and to varying degrees of intensity, but the individuals who forged them can be recognized as members of the milieu, in much the same way that Wittgenstein argued that chess and solitaire can both be recognized as games. Damaschke, Bäumer, Sombart, and the others shared the resemblances of a family—albeit a quarrelsome one—and in moving from biography to prosopography, this

---

31. BDB congress report, *Bodenreform* 22, no. 12 (June 20, 1911): 337–38.

chapter seeks to flesh out its portrait by exploring the contrasts and resonances among a diverse array of careers that intersected in the educational
centers, associative ties, and institutions that sustained the search for alternative modernities before the First World War. Based on an analysis of
some four hundred individuals who participated in the same movements
and wrote for the same journals as our three central figures, this tour stops
only at a few sites where relationships appear densely bundled, but even
so, the cast of characters will seem exasperatingly large to anyone unfamiliar with the world of Wilhelmine reform. Yet God is in the details. Even
a cursory glance at the names associated with the various settings will
suffice to gain a strong sense for the intricate connections among the lives
of these reformers, where the concrete possibilities and limitations of the
milieu alone reside. Every effort has been made to offer at least a brief
identification of rarely mentioned individuals at every instance of their
appearance, and the strong narrative flow with which the data has been
infused will, I hope, make its assimilation painless, allowing the reader to
achieve a vivid impression of the texture that draws these nodal points of
contact together into a not-overly coherent whole.

Learning the Social Question

The generation of 1890 saw itself as living through a "turning point in the
times," an epochal caesura at which rapid transformations in the social,
economic, and political structures of the new Empire could lead either to
progress or to ruin. While the outbreaks of violence in the Ruhr and disease
in Hamburg confirmed the threatening side of modernity, many young
Germans brandished them as signs of the need for change to realize modernity's potential. The February Decrees and the lapse of the Anti-Socialist
Laws offered hope for a "New Course" in social relations, and those seeking
to realize that promise found teachers eager to guide them in the search
for new solutions, above all in the sciences of national economics and
biology, which had come to dominate German social thought after the
founding of the Empire. From the "socialists of the lectern" they learned
to understand the economy as an integrated whole and to grapple with the
socialist critique of capitalism and the question of the state's role in regulating economic life. From biologists they not only learned how to prevent
the spread of infectious disease, but perhaps more importantly they heard
the message of progressive evolutionism as an alternative to the pessimistic
creed of Spencerian Darwinism. The unresolved debates over heredity in

particular absorbed the attention of this generation, which understood them as bearing directly on the prospects for social reform. Many came to grasp the significance of economics and biology for answering the social question by attending public lectures and reading popularized versions of Marx's and Darwin's theories in the press, but many also learned the social question at the university. At centers of learning in Berlin, Munich, Jena, Leipzig, Breslau, and beyond, an increasing number of students absorbed ideas and made personal connections that shaped the reform milieu in important ways.[32]

The University of Berlin: Center of Centers

Of all these centers, Berlin was undoubtedly the most prominent. From the turbulent founders' years onward, the booming Imperial capital had become a focal point for discussions of the social question, and two of the most prominent socialists of the lectern, Gustav Schmoller and Adolf Wagner, were stars at the University. In lectures and seminars, Schmoller combined emphasis on empirical research with a psychological approach, defining the "reciprocal interaction" between "individual cells" and the "central organ" of the nation's economy as a "real totality," while he encouraged students to seek an "alliance between the monarchy and the workers' world."[33] Wagner promoted state socialism by delivering a sharp critique of liberal economics and presented national economics as a specifically "German" field aimed at "achieving recognition for the social-economic and social-judicial standpoint."[34] Outside academia, both professors helped make Berlin a "political, intellectual, publicity, industrial, and administrative center" for the circles of economists, civil servants, and business leaders who met regularly in the Wednesday Society, the Central Association for the Welfare of the Working Classes, and other organizations.[35] The German capital was no less important as a center for the study

---

32. On the explosion in German university enrollments, see Jarausch, *Students*, pp. 23–77.

33. Gustav Schmoller, *Grundriß der Allgemeinen Volkswirtschaftslehre* (Leipzig: Duncker & Humblot, 1901), vol. 1, pp. 5, 10–26, 99–111; Schmoller, *Die soziale Frage: Klassenbildung, Arbeiterfrage, Klassenkampf* (Munich: Duncker & Humblot, 1918), p. 648.

34. Adolf Wagner, *Lehr und Handbuch der politischen Oekonomie* (Leipzig: C. F. Winter'sche Verlagshandlung, 1892), vol. 1, pp. 5–36, quotation p. 25.

35. Bruch, "Sozialreform," p. 85; Bruch, *Wissenschaft*, pp. 249–53.

of biology, where Emil du Bois-Reymond and Rudolf Virchow had played prominent roles in the debates over the social meaning of Darwinism. With Friedrich Althoff's generous financial support, du Bois-Reymond's Physical Institute and Virchow's clinics provided the university research facilities in which the causes of diseases such as tuberculosis, diphtheria, and pneumonia were discovered in the 1880s.[36] Student enrollment grew from three thousand to nine thousand between 1878 and 1910, while the University's budget increased six-fold in the same years. With Wagner, du Bois-Reymond, and Virchow serving as rectors, Berlin exerted a magnetic pull on young Germans looking to economics and biology for answers to the social question.[37]

Sombart, as we have seen, studied national economics under Schmoller and Wagner at the University of Berlin, and while Bäumer was unable to study the social sciences, she had ample opportunity to hear the lectures of Wagner, who impressed her as a "prophet and signpost for the actual essence of the times to come."[38] Even the artisan's son Damaschke, for whom the University was beyond reach, established a close friendship with the famous state socialist, who became an avid supporter of the land reform League in the 1890s. Many other young reformers and activists shared the formative experience of Wagner's and Schmoller's lectures. Among those to pass through the university were the national economic boys Tönnies, Herkner, Schulze-Gävernitz, and Karl Diehl, and future leaders of the sociological Society Oppenheimer, Kurt Breysig, Franz Eulenburg, Rudolf Goldscheid, and Heinrich Waentig. Members of the *Social Practice* circle and the Institute for Public Welfare—Jastrow, Jaffé, Nathaniel Brückner— and other labor relations leaders, like Hermann Pachnicke, also attended the seminars of Wagner and Schmoller, as did prominent members of several other movements: Georg Obst and Waldemar Zimmermann from the land reform League, Franz Staudinger of the cooperative movement, the founder of the Social School for Women Alice Salomon, the sexual reformer Helene Stöcker, and Naumann's future associates Theodor Heuss and Paul Rohrbach. While focusing on the social sciences, these students also had the chance to attend du Bois-Reymond's enormously popular

---

36. Weindling, *Health*, p. 160.
37. Michael Doeberl et al., eds., *Das akademische Deutschland* (Berlin: C. A. Weller Verlag, 1930), vol. 1, p. 78.
38. Bäumer, "Heimatchronik," *Hilfe* 22, no. 5 (February 3, 1916): 76.

courses on "physical anthropology" and "recent findings of natural sciences," which routinely attracted 10 percent of the entire student body.[39] The students of du Bois-Reymond and Virchow also played prominent roles in the reform milieu. Future leaders of the racial hygiene movement—Alfons Fischer, Ludwig Woltmann, Albert Fischer, Alfred Grotjahn, and Carl Flügge—studied biology and medicine in Berlin, as did others who later turned to cultural interests: Naturalist playwright Gerhart Hauptmann, National Social poet Ferdinand Gregori, Paul Schultze-Naumburg of the historical preservation movement, and Hermann Cohen from the Society for Ethical Culture.

Berlin's students of economics and biology did not move in separate circles but instead recognized a common orientation, exploring the connections between their fields of study and absorbing the currents of nationalism and socialism that pervaded instruction in the human and natural sciences beyond their specific areas of focus. Thus, for example, the national economist Tönnies investigated the relations between biology and the social sciences in a series of studies on criminology and later defined social reform as the "best eugenics." Biology student Alfred Grotjahn described himself as "the first medical socialist of the lectern" and frequently visited Tönnies after the economist took a post at Kiel, where the two spent their evenings discussing reform and politics.[40] Grotjahn's identification with the national economic boys was more than idle talk. Like Tönnies, Herkner, and Sombart, the medical student made close contacts with revisionist socialists like Heinrich Braun and toyed with the idea of joining the SPD, only to distance himself from the party in later years because he could not endorse its rejection of nationalist principles.[41] This dual commitment—most clearly expressed in Naumann's National Social Association—emerged from the classrooms of German universities, where students

39. Ruff, *du Bois-Reymond*, pp. 72–73.

40. Cornelius Bickel, "Tönnies' Kritik des Sozialdarwinismus: Immunität durch Philosophie: Die Auseinandersetzung mit der Krupp-Preisfrage von 1900," in Klingemann, *Rassenmythos*, pp. 174–81. Weindling, *Health*, pp. 221–22; Klaus Christian Köhnke, "Wissenschaft und Politik in den Sozialwissenschaftlichen Studentevereinigungen der 1890er Jahre," in Othein Rammstedt, ed., *Simmel und die frühen Soziologen: Nähe und Distanz zu Durckheim, Tönnies und Max Weber* (Frankfurt: Suhrkamp, 1988), p. 326.

41. Weindling, *Health*, pp. 119, 218.

had the opportunity to hear inspiring lectures from virulent proponents of both nationalism and socialism. This was particularly true of Berlin, where Treitschke, Mommsen, and Gierke promoted competing visions of national strength and unity,[42] while socialism found diverse spokesmen in the Christian Social leader Adolf Harnack,[43] the founders of the Ethical Culture

42. Treitschke's conservative, anti-Semitic nationalism sparked conflict with Schmoller (Gustav Schmoller, *Über einige Grundfragen der Sozialpolitik und der Volkswirtschaftslehre* [Leipzig: Duncker & Humblot, 1904], pp. 1–211, esp. 14–26), but also with Mommsen, who was affiliated with the Progressive party and promoted a culturally based nationalism in his *Roman History*, which presented a thinly veiled contrast between the youthful virility of the German nation (in the guise of Greece) and the corrupt stagnation of France (as Rome); Theodor Mommsen, *Römische Geschichte*, 3 vols. (Berlin: Weidmann, 1854–56). Despite Gierke's increasingly fanatical Prussian nationalism, his theory of Germanic cooperative law inspired leaders of the cooperative movement like Staudinger and Oppenheimer to pursue a synthesis between individualism and socialism in a decentralized federal state based on traditions of Germanic community; John D. Lewis, *The Genossenschaft-Theory of Otto von Gierke: A Study in Political Thought* (Madison: University of Wisconsin Press, 1935).

43. Harnack was appointed to the University of Berlin in 1888 over the objections of the Supreme Council of the Evangelical Church, belonged to the Wednesday Society, moved in the same circles as Schmoller and Mommsen, and helped Naumann found *Assistance,* later serving as Chairman of the Protestant Social Congress between 1903 and 1911; Wilhelm Pauck, *Harnack and Troeltsch: Two Historical Theologians* (New York: Oxford University Press, 1968), pp. 4–41; Fricke, *Lexikon,* vol. 3, pp. 376–78; Gerhard Besier, ed., *Die Mittwochs-Gesellschaft im Kaiserreich: Protokolle aus dem geistigen Deutschland 1863–1919* (Berlin: Siedler Verlag, 1990), pp. 15, 187, 263; Historische Kommission bei der Bayerischen Akademie der Wissenschaften, ed., *Neue Deutsche Biographie* (Berlin: Duncker and Humblot, 1953–1998), henceforth *NDB,* vol. 5, pp. 688–89. Stressing the impact of capitalism on the Church, Harnack promoted its "social mission," working in the popular education movement as a member of the Society for Ethical Culture and supporting women's drive to gain access to the university; Adolf Harnack, *Essays on the Social Gospel* (New York: G. P. Putnam's Sons, 1907); Harnack, *Thoughts on the Present Position of Protestantism* (London: Adam & Charles Black, 1899); Harnack's frequent contributions to *Ethische Kultur,* vols. 1–4; Winfried Döbertin, *Adolf von Harnack: Theologe, Pädagoge, Wissenschaftspolitiker* (New York: Peter Lang, 1985), pp. 177–205. As President of the Kaiser Wilhelm

movement Friedrich Wilhelm Förster and Georg von Gizycki,[44] and the Social Democrat Leo Arons, who instructed students in physics until he was expelled from the University in 1899.[45] While the radical nationalist Association of German Students followed Adolf Stöcker in tackling social problems with virulent anti-Semitism, the "varieties of nationalism" circulating in Berlin allowed for more serious engagement with socialism at German universities than historians often suggest, and in the 1890s, social-science and biology students explored common interests in Marxism, reform, and nationalism in the Social Scientific Student Union.[46]

Attracting a balance of students from medicine, economics, law, and political science, the Union was founded in 1894 and promoted an integrationist message of social unity, sponsoring lectures by older scholars such as Brentano, Max Sering, and Carl Lamprecht, as well as younger economists and sociologists who had themselves been students only a few years before—Sombart, Tönnies, Jastrow, Max Weber, Paul Barth, and Georg Simmel.[47] Many of the Union's members were affiliated with Social Democracy, and they also invited non-academic spokesmen such as Naumann and the Friedrichshagen socialist Bruno Wille to promote a more accommodating view of the workers' movement. Such an open display of sympathy for socialism was dangerous, however. Less than a year after its founding the Union was disbanded because of harassment from conservative students, university administrators, and the police. Only the intervention of Adolf Wagner, who strongly defended the students' right to engage in an open dialogue with Marxism and reinstated the group upon becoming rector in 1895, saved it from permanent banishment.[48] Such conflicts played a direct role in the renewed controversy over "socialism of the lectern" that

Society, Harnack also assisted Althoff in securing funds for biological and medical research facilities and clinics; Pauck, *Harnack,* p. 12; Döbertin, *Harnack,* pp. 183–84; Weindling, *Health,* pp. 240–41.

44. Georg von Gizycki, *Grundzüge der Moral: Gekrönte Preisschrift* (Leipzig: Wilhelm Friedrich Königliche Hofbuchhandlung, 1883); Gizycki, *A Students' Manual of Ethical Philosophy* (London: Swan Sonnenschein & Co., 1889).

45. Lindenlaub, *Richtungskämpfe,* vol. 2, p. 147; Weindling, *Health,* pp. 34–35.

46. Jarausch, *Students,* pp. 345–63; Bruch, *Wissenschaft,* pp. 170–74.

47. Köhnke, "Wissenschaft," pp. 312, 315, 332.

48. Ibid., pp. 311–18, 322; Adolf Wagner, *Die akademische Nationalökonomie und der Sozialismus* (Berlin: Becker, 1895).

led to Sombart's withdrawal from activism in 1897, and Bruch argues that such pressure put a definite end to the "fleetingly blossoming swamp flower of 'socialism of the educated' " by the turn of the century.[49] Yet the experience of political suppression seems only to have strengthened the bonds between students and teachers in the Social Scientific Union, who joined fourteen years later to found the German Society for Sociology. Many of the same individuals also contributed to *The Socialist Academic*, which was founded in 1895 at the initiative of Berlin university students and was remarkably successful in promoting a synthesis of nationalism and revisionist Marxism in its new guise as the *Socialist Monthly* after the turn of the century.[50]

Among the Union's members was Franz Oppenheimer, a central figure in the land reform, Garden City, and cooperative movements, who later gained prominence as one of the "most outstanding German sociologists before 1933."[51] After studying under du Bois-Reymond in the 1880s, Oppenheimer practiced medicine in the Polish provinces of East Prussia and the poorer districts of North Berlin until the "Medusa's face of the social question" compelled his return to the university, where he studied national economics under Wagner and Schmoller in the mid-1890s.[52] Training in medicine and economics was essential for an adequate understanding of the problems of modern industrial capitalism, Oppenheimer believed, and in 1896 he published the first of two massive studies on the "physiology and pathology of the social body."[53] Revealing the "purely mechanical laws" governing the self-regulation of the "social organism," the

49. Bruch, *Wissenschaft*, pp. 145–46, 172.

50. Köhnke, "Wissenschaft," p. 332; Pierson, *Intellectuals*, p. 102–10, 206–12. See also Roger Fletcher, *Revisionism and Empire: Socialist Imperialism in Germany, 1897–1914* (Boston: Allen & Unwin, 1984), pp. 66–79.

51. Volker Kruse, "Von der historischen Nationalökonomie zur historischen Soziologie: Ein Paradigmenwechsel in den deutschen Sozialwissenschaften um 1900," *Zeitschrift für Soziologie* 19, no. 3 (June 1990): 150.

52. Oppenheimer, *Erlebtes*, pp. 70, 93–103.

53. Franz Oppenheimer, *Die Siedlungsgenossenschaft: Versuch einer positiven Überwindung des Kommunismus durch Lösung des Genossenschaftsproblems und der Agrarfrage* (Leipzig: Duncker & Humblot, 1896). The second study appeared two years later; *Großgrundeigentum und soziale Frage: Versuch einer neuen Grundlegung der Gesellschaftswissenschaft* (Berlin: Deutsche Verlags-Anstalt, 1898).

economist-physician diagnosed "atrophy" of German agriculture as the root cause of the "social illness," which was ruining the health of the population in the "glowing molochs" of the cities and causing unbearable social tensions.[54] The conservative Junker of the Eastern provinces who were forcing agrarian labor off land they had obtained through "political rape" might be blamed for this problem, but Oppenheimer rejected such an explanation as superficial. As a "grateful student of Marx," he recognized that the capitalist system was responsible, not individuals: "Humans flow from areas of higher economic pressure to areas of lower economic pressure along the line of least resistance."[55] The "unpolitical" healing powers of the "settlement cooperative," which would produce areas of low economic pressure in the countryside, were the recommended "therapy."[56] Once planted, Oppenheimer's settlements would literally suck the insides out of the capitalist economy, breaking down the oppressive structures of the present system to make room for a "society of the future," which would be based on the traditions of Germanic law: "productive cooperatives will be integrated into settlement cooperatives, these into associations, [and] the associations of the highest order into the 'state system.' "[57]

Oppenheimer's bizarre mixture of Darwinism, Marxism, and Germanic ideology seems baffling to the modern reader, but it made perfect sense to the members of the Wilhelmine reform milieu, who produced similar schemes in abundance. The Jewish economist-physician, who became close friends with the anti-Semitic Adolf Wagner and described himself as a disciple of Eugen Dühring, went on to a career that was as strange—and successful—as his theory of the settlement cooperative.[58] With support

---

54. Oppenheimer, *Siedlungsgenossenschaft,* pp. 3, 418–19; *Großgrundeigentum,* p. 445.

55. Oppenheimer, *Großgrundeigentum,* pp. 9, 32, 46, 477–78. Siding with Lamprecht in the "methodological dispute," Oppenheimer defined the "heroic view" of history as the final obstacle to the political emancipation of the oppressed; ibid., p. 221.

56. Oppenheimer, *Siedlungsgenossenschaft,* pp. 302–3.

57. Oppenheimer, *Großgrundeigentum,* p. 504. Oppenheimer's developmental scheme relies heavily on Gierke's *German Cooperative Law;* see also Lewis, *Theory,* pp. 28–35.

58. Despite attacks from the Association of German Students, Oppenheimer spoke warmly of Wagner and notes that in the 1890s, nearly all of Dühring's

from Wagner and Schmoller, Oppenheimer obtained a Ph.D. in national economics at the University of Berlin, where he took a post as sociology professor in 1917 before accepting a chair at the University of Frankfurt two years later.[59] Outside academia, he continued promoting the settlement cooperative. A leading activist in the Garden City Society, Oppenheimer also designed the first Zionist settlements in Palestine, and in the 1920s he received federal grants to build a successful settlement in East Prussia, where he moved after retiring from Frankfurt University in 1929.[60] When the Nazis deprived him of his emeritus status and liquidated his settlements, Oppenheimer was driven to emigrate in 1938, despite his intense nationalism. After helping found the *American Journal of Economics and Sociology* with the support of his land reform contacts, he died in the United State in 1943.[61] At a celebration of Oppenheimer's one-hundredth birthday at the Free University of Berlin in 1964, the former Minister of Economics and current Chancellor Ludwig Erhard testified to the lasting impact of his former teacher, whose "liberal socialism" had inspired Erhard's own "social liberalism": "As long as I live, I will not forget Franz Oppenheimer! I will be happy if the social market economy—as perfect or imperfect as it might be—continues to bear witness to the work, to the intellectual stance of the ideas and teachings of Franz Oppenheimer."[62]

Munich's "Colorful Circle"

Vying with Berlin as a center of learning, the "cultural capital" of Germany's new Empire proved fertile ground for similarly diverse contacts. While the "colorful circle" of artists, writers, National Socials, and feminists in Freudenberg's Munich offered Bäumer escape from the tense political climate of Berlin, the artistic impulses emanating from Schwabing also drew many future leaders of the Garden City Society and Werkbund to the Bavarian city. Here Theodor Fischer and Bruno Paul trained as

---

followers were Jewish; Oppenheimer, *Erlebtes*, pp. 77, 136–37, 140, 154–55, 206.

59. Ibid., pp. 202–3; "Franz Oppenheimer," *NDB*.
60. "Oppenheimer," *NDB*; Oppenheimer, *Erlebtes*, pp. 169–74, 210–16.
61. "Oppenheimer," *NDB*; Oppenheimer, *Erlebtes*, pp. 7, 266–67, 271–76.
62. Oppenheimer, *Erlebtes*, pp. 5–6. Erhard claimed that he had only one picture on the wall of his study—Franz Oppenheimer's.

architects, and Paul Schultze-Naumburg came to study art and history after giving up his medical studies in Berlin.[63] Yet Munich was also a center for the study of biology, and other members of the Garden City movement, like Alfons Fischer, studied medicine at the University, where Max von Gruber set up his Hygiene Institute in the 1890s.[64] Like Fischer, Gruber promoted Garden Cities and land reform while assuming a lead role in the racial hygiene movement, and Fischer became a member of the Munich branch of the National Social Association, to which Freudenberg also belonged.[65] Naumann, who met Oppenheimer at the Berlin Social Scientific Union and became a major presence in the Bavarian capital in these years, thus had ample opportunity to make connections with leaders who later came together in two of his most successful initiatives of anti-political reform, Garden Cities and the Werkbund.[66]

Among these contacts was Wolf Dohrn, whom Naumann chose to become the Werkbund's first Secretary and who later invited Bäumer to Hellerau as the Garden City's chief administrator.[67] The son of prominent marine biologist Anton Dohrn, Wolf had come to Munich to study under Lujo Brentano, and it was as students of the famous economist that Naumann met him and his friend Theodor Heuss in the 1890s. As we have seen, Brentano had rejected the state socialism and "social monarchy" of Wagner and Schmoller two decades earlier, when he joined with them to found the Association for Social Policy, but he gradually moved closer to

---

63. See articles on these individuals in the *NDB* and *Reichshandbuch der deutschen Gesellschaft: Das Handbuch der Persönlichkeiten in Wort und Bild* (Berlin: Deutsche Wirtschaftsverlag, 1931), henceforth *RHB;* Campbell, *Werkbund.;* Kristiana Hartmann, *Deutsche Gartenstadtbewegung: Kulturpolitik und Gesellschaftsreform* (Munich: Heinz Moos, 1976).

64. Weindling, *Health,* p. 226.

65. BDB annual congress report, *Deutsche Volksstimme* 16, no. 20 (October 20, 1905): 619–20; *Bodenreform* 20, no. 15 (July 20, 1909): 546–54; Max von Gruber, "Gartenstadt und Volksgesundheit," *Gartenstadt* 5, no. 10 (October 1911): 125–26; Weindling, *Health,* p. 219.

66. Cf. Heuss's claim that Naumann "entered into a new circle of people" with the founding of the Werkbund; *Naumann,* pp. 224–25.

67. Friedrich Naumann, "Wolf Dohrn," *Hilfe* 20, no. 7 (February 12, 1914): 111; Klaus Dohrn, *Von Bürgern und Weltbürgern: Eine Familiengeschichte* (Augsburg: Neske, 1983), pp. 249–53; Campbell, *Werkbund,* p. 20; and "Against Masculine Politics" in Chapter 3.

the position of his Berlin colleagues in the 1880s. Greeting the New Course with enthusiasm, Brentano argued that fear of change represented the only real danger in the coming decades, and as one of the most outspoken advocates of social reform in the 1890s, he urged young Germans to embrace the rapid social and economic transitions. In addition to Dohrn, Heuss, and Naumann, the economist's students in these years included labor relations leaders Ernst Francke of the *Social Practice* circle and Adam Stegerwald, the General Secretary of the Catholic Labor Unions from 1903 to 1919, who later served as chairman of the German League of Labor Unions in Weimar.[68] Both Francke and Stegerwald were active in the Society for Social Reform, which promoted Brentano's goal of establishing the rights of organized labor. Other members of the Society who studied under Schmoller and Wagner also spent time in Brentano's seminars: Nathaniel Brückner of the *Social Practice* circle, for example, and Adolf Dominicus, who made a successful career as municipal reformer and become mayor of Berlin-Schöneberg in 1911.[69] Members of the sociological Society like Herman Kantorowicz and Heinrich Waentig—who became a national economics professor himself, joined the Garden City Society, and served as a Social Democratic deputy in the Prussian parliament—also studied in Munich, as did the writers and activists Artur Landsberger and Erich Lilienthal, who had ties to Berlin's Friedrichshagen circle.[70]

Heuss and many of Brentano's other students supported the National Socials in Munich, and the prominent economist helped strengthen Naumann's conviction that positive relations with the Social Democratic party were necessary, serving as liaison with Georg Vollmar when the workers' pastor came to Munich looking for guidance in the early 1890s.[71] Joining his younger colleague Max Weber, Brentano encouraged Naumann during the conflict with conservative agrarians in the Protestant Social Congress that led to the formation of the National Social Association as well.[72] The Munich economist's position on unions was formally adopted by the As-

---

68. *NDB*, vol. 5, p. 326; *RHB*, vol. 2, p. 1831; Fricke, *Lexikon*, vol. 2, pp. 92–96, 729.

69. *NDB*, vol. 4, p. 67; *RHB*, vol. 1, p. 225.

70. *NDB*, vol. 11, p. 127; *NDB*, vol. 13, pp. 515–16; *RHB*, vol. 2, pp. 1122, 1967–68.

71. Heuss, *Naumann*, p. 176; Sheehan, *Brentano*, pp. 143–147.

72. Sheehan, *Brentano*, p. 133; Conze, "Naumann," pp. 356–57.

sociation, and it was largely Brentano's influence that guided Naumann into the Radical Coalition after the National Socials disbanded in 1903.[73] The *New German Economy,* which had such an enormous impact on Bäumer and many others in the Wilhelmine reform milieu, emerged from Naumann's collaboration with Brentano and the national economic boys Sombart, Max Weber, and Schulze-Gävernitz.[74] The close cooperation of the economist and the "professional politician" continued until 1908, when the Bülow Bloc destroyed their friendship. Even Brentano, who had encouraged the shift from socialism to liberalism, found Naumann's political compromises too much to bear.[75]

The strong links between national economics, socialism, and organic cultural reform that attracted so many students to Munich did not prove as fragile, however. Long after the break, Naumann's contacts with Brentano students like Heuss and Dohrn bound him to the reform milieu and ensured his support for anti-political projects like Hellerau and the Werkbund. Another such contact was Ernst Jäckh, who built a career that was as impressive as Oppenheimer's and, while showing some parallels to the economist-physician, illuminates the diverse potentialities emerging from the search for alternative modernities.[76] Jäckh studied in Munich at the same time as Heuss and Dohrn and established a close friendship with Naumann around the turn of the century. As editor of the *Neckar Newspaper,* the former student promoted the Württemberg branch of the land reform League and Naumann's election campaigns between 1902 and 1912, when he became Secretary of the Werkbund, following in Dohrn's footsteps.[77] As president, Jäckh later organized a Werkbund exhibit on the "new

---

73. Sheehan, *Brentano,* pp. 144, 151–52.

74. Heuss, *Naumann,* p. 190.

75. Sheehan, *Brentano,* pp. 168–70.

76. *NDB,* vol. 10, pp. 264–66; Campbell, *Werkbund,* pp. 34–35, 201–5; Ernst Jäckh, *Kiderlen-Wächter: Der Staatsmann und Mensch* (Stuttgart: Deutsche Verlags-Anstalt, 1924), 2 vols.; Jäckh, *Das größere Mitteleuropa* (Weimar: G. Kiepenheuer, 1916); Jäckh, *The New Germany* (London: Oxford University Press, 1927); see also Jäckh's frequent contributions to *Assistance* beginning in 1910.

77. Jäckh belonged to the Württemberg BDB's Executive Committee along with Gottfried Traub, another of Naumann's associates; "Aus der Bewegung," *Bodenreform* 21, no. 2 (January 20, 1910): 61.

age" that portrayed organic synthesis as the essence of modern life in the last years of Weimar. At the same time that he was assuming a leading role in anti-political cultural reform, he also established a career in the Foreign Office. Naumann had introduced his friend to Kiderlen-Wächter while Jäckh was working at the *Neckar Newspaper,* and the latter was soon sent on missions to negotiate economic relations with Turkey. After publishing plans for the Berlin-Baghdad railway in 1909, he helped Naumann develop his views on a Central European economic and political union during the First World War, while propagating a "German-Turkish Brotherhood in Arms." After the war, Jäckh accompanied the German delegation to Versailles and assumed a post in the presidium of the National Economic Council during Weimar, using his post to found the National Keeper of Art *(Reichskunstwart),* a cultural reform institution named after Ferdinand Avenarius's journal of the art education movement. Failing to stave off the Nazis' co-optation of the Werkbund, Jäckh went into voluntary exile in 1933 and helped build an alliance between Turkey and Britain, where he headed the Near East division in the Ministry of Information after 1939. After the Second World War, he moved to America and spent the last years of his life working as unofficial liaison between Washington and Bonn and setting up an Asian studies institute at Columbia University.

Leipzig's Renegades

While Leipzig fell behind the rapidly growing universities of Berlin and Munich after the 1870s, it is difficult to overstate its importance as a center of learning for the generation of 1890. Adorned by Friedrich Preller's murals and Max Klinger's sculpture, the University of Leipzig drew on the rich artistic resources of nearby Dresden (and later Hellerau), combining the cultural attractions of Munich with the synthesis of biological and social sciences that drew students to Berlin.[78] As the "hub of the Pan-German League" and headquarters of the radical Social Democrat Bruno Schoenlank, the city also contained the extremes of nationalism and socialism in an intensely political community that included leading members of the National Social Association such as Rudolf Sohm as well.[79] The

---

78. Doebel, *Deutschland,* vol. 1, p. 302.

79. Roger Chickering, *Karl Lamprecht: A German Academic Life (1856–1915)* (Atlantic Highlands, N.J.: Humanities Press International, 1993), p. 398.

University itself maintained close ties to Leipzig's municipal government, particularly the medical faculty, which created the first German chair in hygiene and established a major presence in the city with its hospitals and clinics.[80] A center of the medical reform movement led by Virchow in 1848, Leipzig pioneered the cooperation of state, university, and private sector in the 1850s and 1860s, tackling immediate social and health issues through the training of an expanded research staff in practical techniques and the development of Carl Ludwig's innovative physiological institute.[81] The Leipzig women's clinic was expanded three times in the final third of the century, and the University also set up an Institute for Syphilis and Skin Diseases and a clinic for nervous disorders. Most important, however, the University established a reputation for allowing innovative interdisciplinary cooperation among biologists, psychologists, national economists, historians, and artists.[82] That reputation, well-deserved, was sustained by a closely knit circle of renegade scholars: Wilhelm Ostwald, Wilhelm Wundt, Karl Lamprecht, Friedrich Ratzel, and Karl Bücher.[83]

Ostwald and Wundt, who were the first to arrive in Leipzig, began exploring relations between biology and social science in the early 1880s. Ostwald, a chemistry professor, developed the "energetic theories" that not only strongly informed the optimism of Damaschke and Bäumer about possibilities for an organic synthesis of individualism and socialism, but also inspired attempts to synthesize organic compounds that led Fritz Haber to revolutionary breakthroughs in thermodynamics and Robert Bosch to construct a "technocratic, industrial-scientific lifeworld," crossing professional and social boundaries to integrate the expertise of managers, engineers, and skilled labor at the BASF plant in Ludwigshafen.[84] Ostwald's ideas also influenced sociologists like Rudolf Goldscheid, the author of

---

80. Doebel, *Deutschland,* vol. 1, p. 303.

81. Timothy Lenoir, "Science for the Clinic: Science Policy and the Formation of Carl Ludwig's Institute in Leipzig," in Lenoir, *Instituting,* pp. 96–130.

82. Doebel, *Deutschland,* vol. 1, p. 303.

83. For an excellent description of this circle, see Smith, *Politics,* pp. 204–18. See also Chickering, *Lamprecht,* pp. 288–97; Günther Buttmann, *Friedrich Ratzel: Leben und Werk eines deutschen Geographen* (Stuttgart: Wissenschaftliche Verlagsgesellschaft, 1977), p. 77.

84. Timothy Lenoir, "Practical Reason and the Construction of Knowledge: The Lifeworld of Haber-Bosch," in *Instituting,* pp. 217–38, esp. p. 235.

Human Economics, who joined Ostwald in the Monist League to promote the "energetic imperative": "waste not energy, exploit it!"[85] While Wundt avoided the notoriety of Ostwald, who left academia to promote monism from his "Energy House" in the countryside in 1906, the physiological psychologist sought to discover scientific laws determining human behavior in a voluntaristic synthesis of humanism and positivism that inspired both Emil Kraepelin's hereditarian foray into forensic psychology and the cultural therapies advanced by revisionist socialist Willy Hellpach, who hoped to use pedagogy to eliminate the "hystericizing germs" causing the proletariat's "childhood illness" of revolutionary Social Democracy.[86] The collectivist impulse of Wundt's work also brought him close to Lamprecht, whose "analytical assault on freedom and individuality" led both left and right to suspect an underlying sympathy for Social Democracy.[87]

More than anyone else in the circle, Lamprecht was responsible for Leipzig's reputation of harboring renegade academics. In his attempt to introduce "cultural history" to the German university, the Leipzig scholar suffered a systematic assault on his scholarly reputation not unlike that experienced by Sombart in Breslau.[88] Even his participation in the fleet campaign and membership in the Pan-German League did not shake the impression of subversive political intentions attached to Lamprecht's focus on the life of the masses, but in keeping with the explicitly anti-political theme of his subject matter he remained aloof from overt political action.[89] After the scholar's signature on the petition against Stumm's revolution bill caused

---

85. Chickering, *Lamprecht*, p. 296; Gasman, *Origins*. On Goldscheid, see "Human Economics" in this chapter.
86. Chickering, *Lamprecht*, pp. 175, 204; Eric Engstrom, "Kulturelle Dimensionen von Psychiatrie und Sozialpsychologie: Emil Kraepelin and Willy Hellpach," in Hübinger, Bruch, et al., *Kultur*, pp. 164–89.
87. Chickering, *Lamprecht*, pp. 175, 204.
88. On this depressing display of academics wielding "axes and knives," see ibid., pp. 146–283; Bruch, *Wissenschaft*, pp. 364–79.
89. Chickering, *Lamprecht*, pp. 399–404; Karl Lamprecht, "Die Entwicklung des wirtschaftlichen und geistigen Horizonts unserer Nation," in Gustav Schmoller, Max Sering and Adolf Wagner, eds., *Handels- und Machtpolitik: Reden und Aufsätze im Auftrage der "Freien Vereinigung für Flottenvorträge,"* vol. 1 (Stuttgart: J. G. Cotta'sche Buchandlung Nachfolger, 1900), pp. 39–62. Lamprecht quit the Pan-German League about the time of its drift to the radical right in 1908; Chickering, *Men*, pp. 229–45.

a local uproar in 1895, he limited his engagement to articles in cultural magazines like *The Keeper of Art* and Sombart's journal, *The Morning*, expressing the integrationist message of the milieu.[90] At the university, Lamprecht collaborated with Wundt, seeking to discern the laws governing "socio-psychic life," and developed an "evolutionary," "genetic," or "morphological" methodology resembling Sombart's.[91] Attempting to achieve a synthesis between individualism and socialism, Lamprecht defined the "progressive emergence of individuality out of collective restraints" as a central theme of modern history.[92]

Friedrich Ratzel also explored the laws of "man's determination by nature," developing the new science of "anthropogeography."[93] Ratzel's approach, which explored the "reciprocal interaction" between "organisms and their environment," combined the study of anthropology, zoology, and phytology and depended on the close "intellectual collaboration" of Lamprecht, Wundt, Ostwald, and Bücher.[94] At the center of Ratzel's theory of national and social evolution was the concept of "living space" *(Lebensraum)*. Although the Leipzig geographer did not coin the term, he was its most influential advocate prior to the Nazis, and even his admiring biographer admits that the language of Ratzel's works could easily have "misled" later generations.[95] This is something of an understatement, since Ratzel idealized the German peasant as the backbone of the nation and defined the national community's relationship to the soil as so close "that both become one and can no longer be thought of as separated from each other without [the nation's] life passing away."[96] Claiming that "the strug-

---

90. Perceiving a "new idealism" that would heal Germany's social and political divisions, Lamprecht also found signs of hope in many of the same economic developments Sombart championed in his early years—cooperatives, cartels, trade unions, and social reform; Chickering, *Lamprecht*, pp. 401–2.

91. Ibid., pp. 177, 202.

92. Ibid., p. 204.

93. Smith, *Politics*, pp. 140–46; Buttmann, *Ratzel*, p. 66.

94. Friedrich Ratzel, *Anthropogeographie* (Stuttgart: Verlag von J. Engelhorn, 1899), vol. 1, pp. 8–10 and passim.

95. Buttmann, *Ratzel*, p. 66; Chickering, *Lamprecht*, p. 289; Smith, *Politics*, pp. 219–33.

96. Smith, *Politics*, pp. 129–39; Friedrich Ratzel, *Politische Geographie oder die Geographie der Staaten, des Verkehrs und des Krieges* (Munich: R. Oldenbourg, 1903), p. 6.

gle for space" was a "universal fact of life," the anthropogeographer especially stressed the significance of the "border as peripheral organ of the state."[97] "Once the land, the space is full," the situation was "conducive to the growth" of nations, he wrote. Just as northern animals had driven back those of the South, "the races and nations belonging to the northern regions of the earth are everywhere spreading out over the southern regions" of the human world. As chairman of the local German Colonial Society, Ratzel thus strongly defended overseas and internal colonization, comparing Germany, which was "growing eastward," with the United States, which was expanding to the West.[98] Ratzel's aggressive imperialism must have met conflicting responses in the reform milieu, as Damaschke's clash with Naumann over the National Socials' foreign policy objectives suggests, yet both reformers were influenced by Ratzel's organicist theory of the state.[99] Ratzel himself openly promoted land reform in his works, and Damaschke proudly repeated his definition of the state as an "organism rooted in the soil," as we have seen.[100] The anthropogeographer's strong emphasis on environment was also more generally in tune with the reformist impulse of the day. Specifically rejecting the importance of skin color, body size, and the shape of the skull as racial characteristics, Ratzel viewed such differences as the fleeting result of a historical process of transformation and insisted that increased contact among the world's populations via commerce and colonial expansion would restore humanity to its original, homogenous state: "The unity of the human race is based upon the unity of the species."[101] Ratzel's environmentalism also led him to reject Darwinism and to attack the racial theories of Gobineau and Chamberlain.[102] For those who saw social reform as the "best eugenics," Ratzel served as both mentor and ally.

The last to fall in with Leipzig's interdisciplinary scholars was Karl Bücher. After holding posts in Basel and Karlsruhe, the national economist joined

---

97. Ratzel, *Anthropogeographie*, vol. 1, p. 244.

98. Ratzel, *Geographie*, p. 123.

99. Gebauer, "Staat"; Paul Weindling, *Darwinism and Social Darwinism in Imperial Germany: The Contribution of the Cell Biologist Oscar Hertwig (1849–1922)*, (New York: Fischer, 1991), p. 265.

100. Ratzel, *Geographie*, pp. 51–52. See also "Organic Progress" in Chapter 2.

101. Ratzel, *Anthropogeographie*, vol. 1, pp. 41–65; vol. 2, pp. 577–85.

102. Ibid., vol. 1, p. 88. See also Smith, *Politics*, pp. 146–49.

Ostwald, Wundt, Lamprecht, and Ratzel in 1892, applying psychology and physiology to the study of economic "evolution." Like Ratzel and Ostwald, Bücher promoted land reform, and his theory of rhythm as the unifying force in organic motion influenced the educational reform activities in nearby Hellerau, where it made a lasting impression on Bäumer.[103] According to Bücher, the body provided the "technical means" for translating the subjective will of individuals into the collective force of economic activity. Studies of production had revealed that "the corporeal task of the worker" could be reduced to "simple muscular movements," and the economist believed that rhythm provided the key to understanding the origin of these basic components of the labor process.[104] Rhythm, which "originates in the organic nature of human beings," had been the underlying "economic principle of development" since the earliest days of social labor, he argued.[105] Analyzing the work songs of "primitive peoples" in Africa, Asia, and the "cultured nations" of Eastern Europe and Germany, Bücher showed how the "collection of uniform labor accessible to rhythmatization at specific points of concentration" had gradually evolved into the "workshops of the professional laborer" and made possible "the great technical progress of the last centuries and of our present 'age of machines.' "[106] Yet despite this potential, Bücher shared Bäumer's and Sombart's concerns regarding the destructive effects of the "new labor rhythms," which made machines the masters of men rather than the other way around. In studies such as *Work and Rhythm* and *Industrial Evolution,* Bücher gave "practically important tips for the technical configuration of the labor process" that could lead "technology and art once again to a higher rhythmic unity, which restores the joy to the spirit and harmonious training to the body, in which the best among the primitive peoples excel."[107]

The creative interdisciplinary environment sustained by the Leipzig circle attracted many students who later assumed leading roles in the Wil-

---

103. BDB congress report, *Deutsche Volksstimme* 12, no. 24 (December 20, 1901): 751–53. Dohrn, who brought Dalcroze to Hellerau, drew heavily on Bücher in his own book on rhythm; August Horneffer, "Jacques-Dalcroze in Hellerau," *Tat* 4, no. 3 (June 1912): 127.
104. Karl Bücher, *Arbeit und Rhythmus* (Leipzig: Teubner, 1902), p. 22.
105. Ibid., p. 398.
106. Ibid., p. 417.
107. Ibid., pp. 419–421; Karl Bücher, *Industrial Evolution* (New York: Holt, 1901).

helmine reform milieu. After studying medicine and working as an assistant in Wundt's laboratories, Robert Sommer worked on physiological psychology in Berlin, joined in the racial hygiene movement, and helped found the German sociological society.[108] Ferdinand Avenarius—whose brother Richard spent the 1880s in Zurich trying to discover the "biological foundation of aesthetic processes"—also started out as a medical student in Leipzig before switching to art history.[109] Lamprecht, Ratzel, and Bücher all tried to integrate artistic elements into their scholarship and may well have supported such a move, which was certainly greeted by Alfred Lichtwark, Avenarius's fellow student at the university. It was in Leipzig that the future leaders of German cultural reform met and Avenarius developed his interest in socialism.[110] Another leader of popular education, Gerhart von Schulze-Gävernitz, studied national economics here before going on to found the university extension movement, promote Ethical Culture, sign the petition against the revolution bill, and help Naumann found his short-lived daily, *The Times*.[111] Other economics students at Leipzig included Christian Klumker, who ran as a National Social parliamentary candidate in 1903, later becoming a professor of public assistance and social policy at the University of Frankfurt; and Hans Köppe, a member of the land reform League, who emphasized that human beings were the "foundation of our national economy" as Marburg economics professor and promoted collective wage negotiations as a means to defuse class conflict.[112]

The diverse potentialities contained within the potent mixture of economics, biology, nationalism, socialism, and artistic enterprise that drew so many to Leipzig is perhaps best illustrated by the career of Max Mau-

---

108. Julius Pagel, *Biographisches Lexikon hervorragender Ärtzte des 19. Jahrhunderts* (Berlin: Urban & Schwarzenberg, 1901), p. 1619.

109. Kratzsch, *Kunstwart*, pp. 60–61; "Ferdinand Avenarius," *NDB*.

110. See "Cultural Reform" in this chapter.

111. *RHB*, vol. 2, p. 1729; Düding, *Verein*, pp. 43, 157–64; Gerhart von Schulze-Gävernitz, "Die gegenwärtigen Mittel zur Hebung der Arbeiterklasse in Deutschland," *Ethische Kultur* 3, no. 18 (May 4, 1895): 137–39; Fricke, *Lexikon*, vol. 2, p. 591.

112. *NDB*, vol. 12, pp. 144–45, 369–701; Hans Köppe, "Die Bodenreform als Sozialpolitik," *Bodenreform* 22, no. 14 (July 20, 1911): 447–54.

renbrecher.[113] While still a student, Maurenbrecher began his rapid rise in the National Social Association, introducing Lamprecht to Naumann and nearly convincing his teacher to endorse the movement at its annual convention in 1902.[114] Like many others, he refused to follow Naumann into the Radical Coalition when the NSV disbanded, choosing instead to join the SPD "for nationalist reasons." While continuing to support the Society for Social Reform, of which he was a founding member, and Ostwald's Monist League, Maurenbrecher remained in the Social Democratic Party until 1913, when his nationalism eventually led to a break with the orthodox leadership. During the First World War he moved to the radical right, joining the Fatherland Party and the Pan-German League, and after the war the former National Social served briefly as a parliamentary representative of the German Nationalist party before retiring from politics in 1921. For the last nine years of his life, Maurenbrecher worked as chief editor of the intensely anti-Semitic *German Newspaper* and died far from his progressive origins in 1930.

Jena's "Upward-Striving"

Although small and pitifully funded, the University of Jena also drew students interested in solutions to the social question that incorporated the latest advances of science and technology. It was here that Haeckel launched his campaign to bring Darwinism to the German schoolroom in the 1860s and 1870s, and university curator Moritz Seebeck continued to seek out young talent on the cutting edge of biological research in the following decades.[115] This "notorious group of Darwinists" joined "progressively minded" Jena intellectuals to form a circle of scientists, philosophers, and humanists similar to the one in Leipzig.[116] Next to Haeckel, the most prominent member of the group was his friend Ernst Abbé, who taught physics at the university. Abbé developed the precision optics that paved the way for the revolution in microscopics, facilitating Haeckel's

---

113. Marlies Jansen, *Max Maurenbrecher: Der weltanschaulich-politische Weg eines deutschen Nationalisten 1900–1930* (Munich: dissertation, 1964).

114. Chickering, *Lamprecht,* p. 404.

115. Weindling, *Darwinism,* pp. 192–93.

116. Ibid., p. 261.

embryological research as well as breakthroughs in detecting infectious bacteria, so that Helmholtz tried to lure him to Berlin in the mid-1870s.[117] The optics technician's ties to the local community were strong, however, and he chose to remain in Jena, where he served as a leader of the Progressive Party, endorsed housing reform, juvenile care, and popular education, and contributed generously to land reform.[118] The Progressive leader won national prominence for his innovative approach to labor relations and was among the signatories of the petition against the "revolution bill," but establishing the Carl Zeiss Foundation was undoubtedly his most significant achievement in social reform.[119] After rising from the rank of manual laborer to sole owner of the Jena Optics Manufactory, Abbé created the Foundation to protect factory workers through measures including an eight-hour day, profit sharing, and pensions, and its statutes limited the salary of the corporation's chief executive officers to no more than ten times the average worker's wage.[120] Surplus profits went to the University and the municipal government, which were to use them to finance free popular education. As with Damaschke, Abbé's motives derived not only from his own experiences among the lower classes, but also from a conviction that unbridled capitalism represented "an enormous disadvantage for the nation in economic terms." Conducting studies on energy utilization at the Zeiss factory, the physicist discovered that repeated use of "the same muscle groups, the same nerve centers" resulted in fatigue and "what is referred to in machines as energy consumption for idling." An eight-hour day was thus not only more humane but also more efficient, he argued. It was the responsibility of employers to achieve an optimum balance between "energy expenditure and replacement" and to "compen-

117. *NDB*, vol. 1, p. 3; Weindling, *Darwinism*, pp. 38–39.

118. Felix Auerbach, *Ernst Abbé: Sein Leben, sein Wirken, seine Persönlichkeit* (Leipzig: Akademische Verlagsgesellschaft, 1918), p. 443; BDB activities report, *Deutsche Volksstimme* 10, no. 6 (March 20, 1899): 183; Wilhelm Rein, "Ernst Abbé," *Hilfe* 10, no. 4 (January 29, 1905): 7–8.

119. Ernst Abbé, "Welche soziale Forderungen soll die Freisinnige Volkspartei in ihr Programm aufnehmen?" in Abbé, *Sozialpolitische Schriften* (Jena: Fischer, 1906), pp. 1–56; Abbé, "Motive und Erläuterungen zum Entwurf eines Statuts der Carl-Zeiss-Stiftung," in *Schriften*.

120. Abbé himself refused to accept any other title than that of an "ordinary official 'member of the executive board' "; *NDB*, vol. 1, p. 3.

sate for the utilization of national energy, just as they have an amortization quota for the wear and tear on machines." Much like Bücher's "practical tips" in nearby Leipzig, Abbé's Foundation contributed to the new science of work Rabinbach has described, providing a powerful argument for reformers who wished to promote their efforts as social policy rather than charity: "Not crutches for the weak, but a shield and armor for the strong!"[121]

The Jena circle also included a prominent representative of organicist state theory, Oscar Hertwig, who taught biology at the university until receiving a post at the University of Berlin in 1888, and the neo-Kantian advocate of "physiological pedagogy" Wilhelm Rein. A former student of Haeckel, Hertwig gradually distanced himself from Darwin's theories for the same reasons as Ratzel in Leipzig. Stressing environmental factors, the biologist insisted that natural selection was not enough to explain evolutionary development, and he sharply attacked the Spencerian Darwinism that increasingly soured the debates over heredity after the turn of the century. Like Bücher, Hertwig viewed industrialization as organic development and believed that the "age of science had of necessity to become the age of 'cooperative Gemeinschaft [community].' "[122] Claiming biology as a replacement for party politics, like Bäumer Hertwig believed organic division of labor would preclude conflict and promoted the "physiological integration" of women into the public sphere. Yet the biologist also demanded the maintenance of Kantian humanitarian values, and in this his laws of organic development clearly reflected the influence of Wilhelm Rein.[123] A professor of education, Rein signed the petition against the revolution bill along with Abbé and became a leading member of both the National Social Association and the land reform League.[124] Describing the

---

121. Georg Hohmann, "Das sozialpolitische Erbe Ernst Abbes," *Hilfe* 12, no. 37 (September 16, 1906): 4–5.
122. Weindling, *Darwinism*, pp. 261–292, here p. 261.
123. Ibid., p. 290. Hertwig's six laws included association ("individuals, both cellular and human, formed a higher being"); division of labor; physiological integration; equality of parts; correlation of parts (mutual dependence); and multiplicity of causes (individuals must be assessed in the context of their environment).
124. "Erklärung gegen die Umsturzvorlage." See Rein's frequent articles in *Deutsche Volksstimme* and *Bodenreform*. Rein also belonged to the Executive Committee of Avenarius's Dürer League; Kratzsch, *Kunstwart*, p. 466.

NSV's synthesis of nationalism and socialism as "people's politics" aimed at the "totality of ruling, propertied, and upward-striving" classes, he had begun promoting popular education as a means for social integration in the late 1880s, wrote the National Socials' policy on school reform, and was a major theorist of the university extension movement Schulze-Gävernitz launched in Freiburg.[125] Rein's "pedagogical system" emphasized the need for a strong grounding in science, which he described as an important source of the "social current" of the times. While national economics and sociology provided a necessary grasp of the laws governing the "complicated [social] organism," biology offered guidelines for the inclusion of exercise "based upon anatomical and physiological principles" in the curriculum in order to "render the body pliant and as capable as possible for intercourse with the outer world."[126] Physiological psychology was also uncovering "regularities of intellectual life" teachers could not afford to ignore, Rein observed, acknowledging the work of his Leipzig colleagues, but an exclusively "physiological pedagogy" was unattainable, since science could never explain ethical choices, and he rejected the attempt to prove that individuals "only meant something in quantity and organization, that man was a product of [social and economic] conditions" as the basic flaw in Marxist theory.[127] In order to improve social conditions, "character and sacrifice" were needed, Rein insisted: "the ethical culture of the will must be regarded as the highest purpose of education." On the basis of Kantian ethics, the Jena pedagogue defined five "ideas" constituting a comprehensive system of social education: inner freedom, completeness ("many-sidedness in energy, concentration, and progress of the will"), goodwill, mutual recognition of rights, and equity ("impartial adjustment of the relations between human right and wrong").[128] Bäumer and others like her

125. Wilhelm Rein, "Volkspolitik nicht Massenpolitik," *Hilfe* 4, no. 31 (July 31, 1898): 5–6. "Zweiter nationalsozialer Delegiertentag," *Hilfe* 3, no. 41 (October 10, 1897): 5–6; Kratzsch, *Kunstwart*, pp. 331–32.

126. Wilhelm Rein, *Pädagogik in systematischer Darstellung* (Langensalza: Beyer & Söhne, 1911), pp. 44, 65; Rein, *Outlines of Pedagogics* (Syracuse, N.Y.: C. W. Bardeen, 1893), p. 184.

127. Rein, *Pädagogik*, pp. 51, 64–66.

128. Rein, *Outlines*, pp. 73–76.

who respected science but recognized its limits, could count on Rein for support.[129]

Like students in Berlin, Munich, and Leipzig, many of Jena's students assumed important roles in the Wilhelmine reform milieu in the 1890s. Herman Lietz became an instructor at Rein's People's University before moving to Berlin, where he joined the Friedrichshagen circle and taught at Wyneken's Country Home for Education in the poor districts of North Berlin.[130] Ernst Harmening worked as a lawyer in Jena after finishing his studies, joined the local Ethical Culture Society, and founded a left-liberal newspaper with Abbé's financial support.[131] Harmening also belonged to the Executive Committee of the land reform League, and from 1890 to 1893 he served as a Reichstag deputy of the Progressive People's Party.[132] The national economic boys came to Jena as well, including Tönnies and Karl Diehl, who established a reputation as the "most important authority on socialism, communism, and anarchism" next to Sombart.[133] Like the Breslau economist, Diehl viewed Bernstein and the revisionists as a sign of hope and demanded continued social legislation "[r]egardless of the growth or decline of Social Democracy" in lectures to Rostock's Social Scientific Union.[134] Perhaps remembering Rein's lessons in Jena, Diehl also rejected the authoritarian ideal of the Marxist future state and emphasized the importance of the "free personality" for the economic vitality of the nation.[135]

---

129. Damaschke, who also began his career as a teacher, endorsed Rein's system as well; Adolf Damaschke, "Eine lebendige Ethik," *Bodenreform* 21, no. 22 (November 20, 1910): 735–37.

130. *NDB*, vol. 14, pp. 543–44; Lunn, *Prophet*, p. 141.

131. Rudolf Eckart, *Lexikon der niedersächsischen Schriftsteller von den ältesten Zeiten bis zur Gegenwart* (New York: Georg Olms, 1974), p. 84; Auerbach, *Abbé*, pp. 443–50; see also Harmening's frequent articles in *Ethische Kultur* from the early 1890s.

132. Report on the DBB meeting of April 2, 1898, *Deutsche Volksstimme* 9, no. 7 (April 5, 1898): 196; BDB congress report, *Deutsche Volksstimme* 10, no. 20 (October 20, 1899): 629; Damaschke, *Leben*, p. 235.

133. *NDB*, vol. 3, p. 644.

134. Karl Diehl, *Über Sozialismus, Kommunismus und Anarchismus: Zwölf Vorlesungen* (Jena: Gustav Fischer, 1906), pp. 89–107, 212–28, quotation p. 227.

135. Ibid., p. 39.

Breslau and Beyond

The site of Sombart's provincial "exile," Breslau was hardly a center for the study of national economics until the renegade critic of modern capitalism began conducting his seminars on Marx there in the early 1890s. While pet projects of the social science faculty were allowed to wither from financial neglect, the University's medical institute received generous funding, again largely as the result of Althoff's support.[136] Expanding its clinical facilities, the university also constructed research institutes for botany, physics, and zoology between 1888 and 1908. As the director of Breslau's dermatology clinic, Sombart's friend Albert Neisser conducted research on gonorrhea and syphilis that strongly influenced the young generation of racial hygienists, and he later became the president of the German Society for the Prevention of Sexually Transmitted Diseases.[137] A Progressive deputy in Breslau's municipal government, Neisser maintained close ties to Abbé, while hosting a circle of scientists, intellectuals, and reformers not unlike those in Jena and Leipzig at his *Jugendstil* villa.[138]

The familiar constellation of biology, economics, and social reform sustaining the collaborative efforts of Sombart, Neisser, and Kurella in Breslau attracted young, socially conscious Germans to the University of Breslau. These included Alfred Ploetz, who grew up here with the brothers Hauptmann, combined the study of medicine and national economics, and later influenced Sombart's studies on race as a leader of the racial hygiene movement. It was in Breslau that Ploetz and the Hauptmanns swore a midnight oath of brotherhood in 1879, founding the League to Reinvigorate the Race. This early interest in biology led the three friends first to ties with Haeckel and Jena's student scientific society, then to Karl Kautsky's work on population growth, which in turn inspired an "interest in Marx and scientific socialism."[139] While Carl became a chemistry professor before joining his brother Gerhart in Friedrichshagen, Alfred continued his medical and economic studies in Breslau and later in Zurich, where he joined

---

136. Doebel, *Deutschland,* vol. 1, p. 103.
137. Weindling, *Health,* pp. 169–70, 181.
138. Lenger, *Sombart,* pp. 54–58.
139. Weindling, *Health,* pp. 63–68.

the group of socialists and feminists around Richard Avenarius, the promoter of biological aesthetics, and visited Bebel at his lakeside villa.[140] Still pursuing the League's visions of racial redemption, Ploetz even went to America to learn about utopian colonies, visiting the settlement projects outside Chicago and making friends with socialists in Springfield and New York.[141] While the young medical economist maintained his contacts with Bebel during the 1890s, it is telling that racial theories began to supplant Ploetz's socialist orientation during his stay in the United States.[142]

The attempt to fuse biology and social science in answer to the social question evoked intense exploration of the troubled relation between science and humanism at German universities, as it did in our case studies—Ratzel's insistence on the unity of the human race in Leipzig and the determined neo-Lamarckism and Kantian idealism of Hertwig and Rein in Jena each bear witness to it. But perhaps more than anyone else, Ploetz personified the struggle to resolve what seemed to him a fundamental conflict between the "terrible law of nature" governing the Darwinian struggle for survival and the ideals of "liberty, equality, [and] fraternity." Seeking to discover the "laws of variability" governing human destiny in order to subordinate them to the "power of man," Ploetz increasingly turned to Weismannism and "scientific" definitions of race that ruled out all hope for environmentalist solutions, and he eventually saw direct manipulation of genetic material at the cellular level as the only way "to break out of the . . . vicious circle in a humane manner." While he came to oppose social reform and promoted selective breeding as a "successful union of socialist/humanitarian demands with those of racial hygiene," many of Ploetz's friends and colleagues strongly disagreed. The "Hamlet conflict"—as he referred to it—would be resolved only in the battles to institutionalize racial hygiene and sociology as academic disciplines.[143]

---

140. Ibid., p. 70; Becker, *Geschichte*, p. 61.

141. Weindling, *Health*, pp. 69, 76.

142. Ibid., p. 123; Becker, *Geschichte*, p. 61.

143. Becker, *Geschichte*, pp. 91–95; Ploetz, "Der Konflikt zwischen Individualhygiene und Rassentheorie," in Altner, *Darwinismus*, p. 123; and "Human Economics" in this chapter.

Our tour of universities where the generation of 1890 learned to debate such issues could continue. At centers of learning in Freiburg, Heidelberg, Karlsruhe, Tübingen, Strasbourg, Cologne, Bonn, Göttingen, Marburg, and Halle, future leaders of the reform milieu had similar opportunities to discuss the relations of the natural and human sciences to social problems in circles that included biologists, economists, and humanists. Beyond the borders of the new Empire, young students also gathered in Zurich, Basel, and Vienna, establishing friendships and contacts that slowly wove together to form a discursive network sustaining the search for alternatives. The tradition of combining study with travel encouraged this process, so that university-educated members of the milieu generally spent time in at least two of these centers, and many leaders at considerably more. Heinrich Herkner—a national economic boy active in the Association for Social Policy, Protestant Social Congress, and Societies for Social Reform, Garden Cities, and German sociology—studied in Berlin, Leipzig, Freiburg, Strasbourg, and Vienna. Occasionally, future colleagues followed the same circuit of learning, such as Society for Social Reform leaders Nathaniel Brückner and Adolf Dominicus, who studied in Berlin, Munich, Strasbourg, and Heidelberg. When students became professors, they continued cultivating this network of relationships in places like Freiburg, where Herkner taught national economics and Schulze-Gävernitz launched his university extension movement, and Heidelberg, where the former students of Weismann built their "phalanx" of racial anthropologists and Max and Marianne Weber hosted gatherings of progressives, economists, sociologists, and feminists to which Bäumer, who lived in Berlin, gained entry through Freudenberg in Munich. Rather than continuing this survey, however, let us now turn to social circles outside the academy, where former students and others built more associative ties in a network that was truly national—if not international—in its dimensions.

Social Circles

"These things, so to speak, were 'in the air,' " Anton Erkelenz later wrote of the common fin-de-siècle belief that capitalism was evolving toward an economic system capable of synthesizing individualism and socialism. "None of us believed the social order as it was then had to remain that way forever," he remembered. "We knew that everything human was subject to the mutations of time and life. We wanted to fuse freedom and constraint in a comprehensive plan."[144] The people Erkelenz described had not learned the social question at the university, but were among the "upward-striving" Wilhelm Rein hoped to unite with *Bildung* and *Besitz* in pursuit of "people's politics." They were workers trying to bring the Social Democratic, Protestant, and Catholic unions into an alliance with the Hirsch-Duncker Workers' Associations in support of the Progressives' election campaign in 1904. While he had scarcely heard of Naumann at the time, Erkelenz's initiative in launching this grassroots drive won the attention of the "party politician" who quickly mobilized financial support from railroad magnate Charles Hallgarten, Damaschke's former patron of land reform.[145] At a single stroke, Erkelenz found himself plugged into a network of movements and circles that included academics and business-men, bourgeois politicians, artisans—and workers. Within a few years, the Hirsch-Duncker secretary had joined the executive committees of Damas-chke's League, the Society for Social Reform, the League for the Protection of Mothers and Sexual Reform, and the National Association for a Liberal Germany, and he later went on to lead the "Naumann wing" of the German Democratic Party together with Bäumer in the Weimar Republic.[146]

Erkelenz was not the first to join the milieu from outside the academy. While Damaschke's training as a teacher may have introduced him to Rein's pedagogical system, his social education began in the rental bar-racks and continued in meetings of "United Christendom" and Ethical Culture, in campaigns for the protection of construction workers and natural health, where the artisan's son experimented with solutions to the social question, making friends who later supported him in the land reform League. Women too had until recently been excluded from the university, and if Bäumer had been able to study there, many other women got their

---

144. Anton Erkelenz, "Autobiographische Niederschrift," NL Erkelenz 103, pp. 28, 37.

145. Naumann to Hallgarten, October 16 and November 21, 1905, NL Naumann 147.

146. *NDB,* vol. 4, p. 591; BDB congress reports, *Deutsche Volksstimme* and *Bod-enreform* from 1904; Society for Social Reform, Ortsgruppe Berlin, "Arbeits-programm, Geschäftsbericht und Mitgliederverzeichnis" 1909, NL Sombart 19; Fricke, *Lexikon,* vol. 4, pp. 87–89; Evans, *Movement,* pp. 122, 136; Fricke, *Lexikon,* vol. 1, pp. 575, 606; Huber, *Bäumer,* pp. 100–139; Bäumer to Er-kelenz, January 15, 1934, NL Erkelenz 139. Erkelenz joined the SPD in 1930.

start in the same circles as Damaschke. At times, differences in education could lead to tension. "The highest regards for 'studied' women. We blazed the trails for them and we're blazing them further," Bäumer's moderate mentor Helene Lange wrote in her conflict with the radicals. "But we reject academic half-education, which is already characterized as such by making itself into an absolute value, most vehemently."[147] Damaschke too felt defensive about colleagues who "shook their heads" at his rustic "passion," and Theodor Heuss remembered the embarrassment of former National Socials when the land reformer's name came up in conversation.[148] Yet for outsiders in Wilhelmine political culture, the thick web of reformist circles provided contacts just as student life did for others, preparing the ground for specialized professional institutions and umbrella organizations that crossed traditional barriers, if not completely dissolving them.

Popular education offered another, increasingly important alternative to university studies. Here workers themselves provided the model with night classes and socialist youth groups, which focused much more on professional training and cultural literacy than on Marxist indoctrination.[149] While respecting the autonomy of Social Democratic organizations, bourgeois reformers readily acknowledged their debt to these attempts at self-education, which inspired them to pursue Rein's goal of social integration through pedagogical means.[150] Offering courses on philosophy, national economics, constitutional law, history, technical fields, and natural science, Schulze-Gävernitz's university extension program hoped to improve the expertise of leaders in organized labor and created a forum where academics and workers, civil servants and artisans, men and women could learn the social question together.[151] From the early 1890s, the move-

---

147. Helene Lange, "Zielbewußt," *Frau* 6, no. 3 (December 1898): 133.

148. Theodor Heuss, *Erinnerungen 1905–1933* (Tübingen: Wunderlich, 1963), pp. 34–35.

149. Lidtke, *Culture*, pp. 162–89.

150. Reinhard Buchwald, "Sozialdemokratische Bildungsarbeit," *Tat* 6, no. 14 (1914): 77–83; see also Kratzsch, *Kunstwart*, pp. 331–32.

151. Schulze-Gävernitz, "Mittel," pp. 149–52. Like Sombart, Schulze-Gävernitz hoped such knowledge would discourage labor leaders from subscribing to "the 'chiliastic' elements of the future state" as "social aspirations that can not be demonstrated."

Table 5.5 Free University of Frankfurt student body

Occupation	%
White-collar workers	37
Blue-collar workers and artisans	15
Engineers and technicians	13
Military officers and high-level civil servants	19
Teachers	8
University students	4

ment rapidly grew in size, posting major successes after the turn of the century.[152] The Free University in Frankfurt am Main, for example, boasted a staff of 80 instructors and a student body of 19,800 by 1913.[153] Of these students, 40 percent were women, a remarkably even gender distribution compared with formal university education, and the group's social composition crossed class lines in much the same way as broadly based movements like the land reform League (see Table 5.5). If the ideas of social unity were "in the air" in Düsseldorf, institutions like the Free University in Frankfurt could take credit for doing their part in fanning the breeze.

In addition to reform gatherings and popular education, political events could also lead to associative ties, as Erkelenz's case goes to show. The Ruhr miners' strike of 1889 had a galvanizing impact on the generation of 1890, as the strikes of Hamburg dock-workers and Berlin textile workers had seven years later, but Stumm's revolution bill is by far the most impressive example of this catalytic effect, and in fact it proved to be a defining moment in the coalescence of the reform milieu. Uniting those who had been inspired by the New Course, the campaign against Stumm's bill not only evoked Naumann's reminiscence of the "unforgettable" February Decrees but also collected signatures of reformers with "a major reputation as theoretical or practical social policy experts" on a petition that reads like a membership list for the Executive Committees of the National Social Association, land reform League, the Societies for Social Reform, Garden

---

152. Bruch, *Wissenschaft*, pp. 262–64.
153. Wilhelm Müller, "Der Rhein-Mainische Verband," *Tat* 6, no. 14 (1914): 89–93.

Cities, and German Sociology, as well as other organizations central to the reform milieu (see Table 5.6). Organized by Karl von Mangoldt, who went on to become a leader of the Garden City Society, Dürer League, and forest preservation movement, the campaign provided an opportunity for members of local circles from all over Germany to express solidarity in the desire for social peace.[154] And just as it had for the Social Scientific Union in Berlin, the attempt at political suppression—which again involved Baron von Stumm—reinforced the common identity of a diverse group of individuals who later joined in major institutions of Wilhelmine anti-politics.

The reform milieu grew together in complex, intertwining relationships to overlapping circles spread out over the territory of the new Empire, and at times it grew by fits and starts. The nationwide discursive network came together like a jig-saw puzzle, where circles that formed locally and movements inspired by common experiences formed the interlocking pieces. In the case studies, we have already discovered some of the more important of these pieces, in points of mutual contact for Damaschke, Bäumer, and Sombart, which will serve as orientation for the following exploration of the milieu through its associative ties.

"The Court of the Muses"

"They were a feminine expression of metropolitan, intellectual socialism that came up 'behind the world city' in [the works of] Richard Dehmel and Hauptmann, Bölsche and Wille, the brothers Hart, and Käthe Kollwitz," Bäumer wrote of Alice Salomon and the Girls' and Women's Groups for Social Work, which she described as "the origin of modern social careers for women."[155] Though hardly remembered for engagement with practical dimensions of social reality, the Friedrichshagen circle exerted a magnetic pull on young, empirically minded reformers who personified the milieu's professionalizing, technocratic impulse. While Bäumer viewed the "New Community" and the Naturalists' "modern programs for life" with skepticism, many of her notions about organic synthesis derived from Bölsche, who actively supported Wilhelmine feminism and contributed to

---

154. German Garden City Society membership list, *Gartenstadt* (1909); Karl von Mangoldt, "Großstadt und Waldschutz," *Hilfe* 16, no. 17 (May 1, 1910): 265–67; Lindenlaub, *Richtungskämpfe*, vol. 1, p. 78.

155. Bäumer, *Lebensweg*, pp. 178–79.

Table 5.6 Signatories, petition of protest against the "Revolution Bill"

Signators	Location	Affiliations
Academics		
Mentors:		
Lujo Brentano	Munich	VFSP, GFSR, FV
Gustav Schmoller	Berlin	VFSP, IfG, GFSR
Adolf Wagner	Berlin	VFSP, ESK, BDB, GFSR
Karl Lamprecht	Leipzig	DGfSoz, Dürer League
Ernst Haeckel	Jena	Monist League, GfRH, BFMS
Wilhelm Rein	Jena	BDB
J. v. Lehman-Hohenberg	Kiel	BDB, NSV, DGG, Egidy Movement
Generation of 1890:		
Werner Sombart	Breslau	VFSP, GFSR, DGFEK, DGG, BFMS, DGfSoz
Ferdinand Tönnies	Kiel	VFSP, BFSP, BDB, DGFEK, GFSR, DGfSoz
G. v. Schulze-Gävernitz	Freiberg	VFSP, DGFEK, ESK, GFSR, FVP
Heinrich Herkner	Karlsruhe	VFSP, DGFEK, ESK, GFSR, DGG, DGfSoz
Max Weber	Freiberg	VFSP, ESK, BFMS, DGfSoz
Paul Natorp	Marburg	DGFEK, Dürer League, DGfSoz
Factory owners		
Ernst Abbe	Jena	DGFEK, BDB, FVP
Heinrich Freese	Berlin	DGFEK, ESK, BDB, GFSR
Richard Rösicke	Berlin	BDB, GFSR, FV
Other non-academics		
Friedrich Naumann	Berlin	VFSP, ESK, NSV, BDB, GFSR, DGG, FV, FVP
Paul Göhre	Frankfurt	ESK, NSV, SPD
Martin Rade	Marburg	ESK, NSV, DFG
Otto de Terra	Berlin	NSV, BDB
Ludwig Quidde	Munich	BDB, DGG, DFG, FVP
Theodor Zollmann	Halle	BDB, DGG
Wilhelm Kulemann	Bremen	ESK, GFSR, DGG, NLP
Ernst Francke	Munich	ESK, IfG, GFSR
Moritz von Egidy	Berlin	Egidy movement, DGFEK, BDB, DFG

Source: "Erklärung gegen die Umsturzvorlage," *Hilfe* 1, no. 9 (March 3, 1895): 3–4.

Abbreviations: BDB: League of German Land Reformers; BfMS: League for the Protection of Mothers and Sexual Reform; BFSP: Bureau for Social Policy; DFG: German Peace Society; DGFEK: German Society for Ethical Culture; DGfSoz: German Society for Sociology; DGG: German Garden City Society; ESK: Protestant Social Congress; FV: Radical Coalition; FVP: Progressive People's Party; GfRH: Society for Racial Hygiene; GFSR: Society for Social Reform; IfG: Institute for Public Welfare; NSV: National Social Association; SPD: Social Democratic Party; VFSP: Association for Social Policy.

The Woman in the 1890s. Damaschke nearly gave up his career to develop his "poetic talents" in Friedrichshagen and helped Wille found the Free University, while Sombart made friends with Carl Hauptmann, Bölsche, Wille, and Landsberger, with whom he founded *The Morning*. Creating more than thirteen different associations and circles at the end of the nineteenth century, the Berlin Naturalists in fact stood near the center of the Wilhelmine reform milieu, and they were masters in the art of building discursive networks.[156]

These networks provided access to the avant-garde, including the pioneers of expressionism—Franz Wedekind, Edvard Munch—and the first, innovative leaders of modern architecture and design, Peter Behrens and Henry van de Velde.[157] Actively disseminating ideas "for modern life and the evolutionary struggle of our time," the Friedrichshagen circle helped found the Free Stage, where Gerhart Hauptmann made his debut, and a journal of the same name that published leading representatives of modernist and futurist literature—Hugo von Hofmannsthal, Arthur Schnitzler, August Strindberg, Thomas Mann, Hermann Hesse, and Gabriele d'Annunzio.[158] But *The Free Stage* went far beyond aesthetics. Later renamed *The New Review,* the journal contained sections devoted to the "women's question," the "school question," "sociology," "medicine," and "natural science" and also solicited contributions from land reformers (Lehmann-Hohenberg, Harmening, de Terra), feminists (Helene Stöcker, Käthe Schirmacher), national economists and sociologists (Sombart, Herkner, Simmel, Breysig), and others promoting social reform. The influential and the wealthy also belonged to the circle. Maximilian Harden, editor of the controversial paper *The Future,* had "daily contact" with Hauptmann, Dehmel, and Wille, as did Walther Rathenau, owner of the General Electric Company.[159] Like the progressive industrialists Abbé and Freese, Rathenau used his position to promote reform. Consulting with Oppenheimer on plans for a work-

156. Günther, *Gruppenbildung*, passim.
157. Harry Graf Kessler, *Walther Rathenau: Sein Leben und sein Werk* (Frankfurt: Fischer, 1988), p. 57; B. Uwe Weller, *Maximilian Harden und die "Zukunft"* (Bremen: Schünemann Universitätsverlag, 1970), p. 65.
158. Authors listed in this paragraph were published in *Freie Bühne* (later *Neue Rundschau*) in its first ten years.
159. Kessler, *Rathenau*, p. 57.

ers' housing settlement at his factory, he supported Damaschke's League while also maintaining close ties to Berlin's revisionist socialists, including Willy Hellpach, and Sombart's friends, Heinrich and Lily Braun.[160] It was through Friedrichshagen connections that Sombart met Rathenau, who took a strong interest in national economics and developed his own ideas about "organized capitalism" with the help of Sombart and Max Weber.[161] If Rathenau's *Critique of the Times* not only promoted an organic syn- thesis of "freedom and constraint" but also responded to recent concerns about racial degeneration, it was no doubt largely due to the influence of another frequent guest in Friedrichshagen, Alfred Ploetz.[162]

It was not for nothing that Heinrich Hart described "technology, science, and the 'social movement' " as the sources of the Naturalist impulse.[163] Bölsche was by far the most successful popularizer of Darwin in Germany before the First World War, and the Hauptmanns were in close contact with Haeckel when they grew up together with Ploetz in Breslau, as we have seen.[164] Gerhart Hauptmann's first major success in "social drama," *Before Sunrise,* in fact largely echoed the dilemmas being fought out inside the mind of his boyhood friend. The similarities between Ploetz and Alfred Loth, the tragic hero of Hauptmann's play, are difficult to overlook, as Peter Becker has pointed out: both have contacts in Jena, have traveled to America, and have similar personal histories.[165] Like Ploetz, Loth also stud- ied national economics, and it is while conducting a study of a mining region in Silesia that he falls in love with the young Helene Krause, whom he is determined to save from the alcoholic haze of her parents' country

---

160. Rathenau later abandoned Oppenheimer's proposals due to Social Demo- cratic opposition; Strandmann, *Rathenau,* pp. 141, 144, 157; Hellige, "Rath- enau," pp. 129–30, 136.

161. Hellige, "Rathenau," pp. 34, 92; Strandmann, *Rathenau,* pp. 142–43. Rath- enau also took courses from Schmoller and was strongly influenced by Adolf Wagner.

162. Walther Rathenau, *Zur Kritik der Zeit* (Berlin: Fischer, 1912), pp. 95–157.

163. Pascal, *Naturalism,* p. 59.

164. Kelly, *Descent,* passim. Wille's proposal for a new SPD platform in 1892, which called for the creation of a "social aristocracy," echoed the ideas of another popularizer of Darwin, Ludwig Büchner; Weindling, *Health,* p. 78.

165. Becker, *Geschichte,* pp. 98–99. Loth's full name is also an anagram of Ploetz's.

inn.[166] A "complete abstinent," Loth further recites the arguments of Gustav von Bunge, the temperance leader who had strongly influenced the young members of the League to Reinvigorate the Race in Breslau.[167] "My struggle is a struggle for the happiness of all," he tells Helene early in the play, and the hero initially expresses his firm belief in the possibility of achieving this goal through social reform: "I would have to see around me neither sickness nor poverty, neither serfdom nor meanness."[168] While such sentiments certainly express the socialist idealism of Ploetz's early days in Breslau and Zurich, there is another character in Hauptmann's play who more strongly resembles the future racial hygienist of the 1890s. Ploetz may have studied national economics, but he became a physician and, like Dr. Schimmelpfennig, gradually convinced himself that an improved environment could offer no escape from the hereditary effects of "drunkenness and incest."[169] It is the doctor who persuades Loth to abandon his foolish plan to rescue Helene, ridiculing his need for "faith, love, [and] hope," and the play ends with Helene's "unbroken screams" fading into the background as the hero slips quietly away to find shelter in Schimmelpfennig's home.[170]

For Hauptmann, the outcome of his friend's "Hamlet conflict" was obviously tragic, and Bölsche, the popularizer of Darwin, censured Loth's behavior as "cruel, selfish and scientifically mistaken."[171] Yet despite such

---

166. Gerhart Hauptmann, *Vor Sonnenaufgang: Soziales Drama* (Frankfurt am Main: Ullstein, 1982), p. 19.

167. Ibid., pp. 27–28.

168. Ibid., p. 41.

169. Ibid., p. 82, 88.

170. Ibid., pp. 87, 95.

171. Weindling, *Health,* p. 89. Bölsche addressed the issue frequently in the *Freie Bühne* and the *Neue Rundschau,* where he published articles on "Moderne Medizin" and "Lombroso" (1890), "Der Jugenduntericht und die Tatsachen der Embryologie" (1891), "Der Humanität im Kampf mit dem Fortschritt" (1896), "Bazillus-Gedanken" (1899), and "Neue Kämpfe um Darwin" (1902). Hauptmann also dealt with the degenerative effects of alcohol in "Carnival," a short story published in 1887, which contains images that reappear in the social criticism of Damaschke and Bäumer. Especially striking is a moment when the Kielbocks, an alcoholic couple, subject their infant son

misgivings, the Naturalists continued to welcome Ploetz's visits to Friedrichshagen, publishing his essays in *The New Review* together with those of other Berlin doctors who were laying the groundwork for racial and social hygiene as academic disciplines, including Albert Moll, who set up a clinic for nervous disorders and conducted research on sexual psychology after finishing his studies at the University of Berlin.[172] The sexologist Magnus Hirschfeld, who also joined the "New Community" out in Friedrichshagen, worked closely with the sexual reformer Helene Stöcker, launching a petition to repeal the laws against homosexuality that bore the names of prominent members of the circle like Gerhart Hauptmann and Wedekind, but also those of the Social Democratic leaders Bebel and Kautsky, as well as another of the Berlin doctors who maintained close contact with the Brauns and other revisionist socialists, Alfred Grotjahn.[173] Grotjahn, in turn, was a close friend of Oppenheimer,[174] the economist-physician and author of the theory of settlement cooperatives, who went in and out at Friedrichshagen and was the brother-in-law of Richard Dehmel.[175]

Along with Damaschke, Oppenheimer provided Friedrichshagen's closest link to another group of reformers who settled "behind the world city"

Gustavchen to the "atmosphere of schnapps and beer vapors, dust and cigar smoke" at a country dance, the mother sitting on the front steps to nurse him at "her panting breast, sweaty from drinking and dancing, which he greedily sucked dry" before falling into a "death-like, leaden sleep." While he thus points to environmental factors, Hauptmann also seems to question the potential of social reform, since the Kielbocks' behavior appears determined by natural inclination rather than by economic need; Gerhart Hauptmann, "Fasching," in Gerhart Hauptmann, *Auswahl für die Jugend* (Berlin: Verlag Neues Leben, 1962), pp. 96–97, 105, 113–14.

172. Alfred Ploetz, "Rassentüchtigkeit und Sozialismus," *Neue Rundschau* (1894); Albert Moll, "Die Psychologie des Fanatismus," *Neue Rundschau* (1894).

173. Grotjahn, whom we encountered in the Social-Scientific Union, was inspired to a career in social medicine by Hauptmann, Zola, and Hertzka's "Free Land" movement. Among other Social Democrats with whom Grotjahn kept in touch was Leo Arons, the physics instructor expelled from the university in 1899, who ran the Union House Sombart admired in *Dennoch!*; Weindling, *Health*, pp. 126, 221.

174. Weindling, *Health*, p. 119.

175. Oppenheimer, *Erlebtes*, pp. 107–129, 154–55.

in order to found the Orchard Colony of Eden. While the vegetarianism and prohibitions on alcohol and tobacco at Eden were too restrictive for Oppenheimer to consider joining, both he and Damaschke played active roles in the first "land reform cooperative," which inspired the Berlin Naturalists' decision to found the Garden City Society in 1902.[176] On fifty-five hectares to the north of Berlin, Eden's colonists built 189 homes and supported themselves by selling apple butter and other products to health food outlets known as "reform stores."[177] A commercial success, Eden is still in existence today.[178] The colony's restrictions on personal lifestyle prohibited membership in political parties, but the settlers subscribed to "all leanings, from the swastika to extreme communism."[179] The founder of Eden, Bruno Wilhelmi, was himself inspired by Egidy's vision of "United Christendom" and joined other high-ranking officials of the colony in the Executive Committee of Damaschke's land reform League.[180] A sterling example of practical anti-politics, the settlement was affiliated with popular education, feminism, and the peace movement, in addition to promoting its ideals of vegetarianism, abstinence, and animal rights.[181] Eden, in short, was a gateway from social reform to "life reform."

Life Reform

The term "life reform" first gained currency in the circles we are exploring sometime in the mid-1890s and referred to a broad spectrum of movements seeking alternative modernities.[182] Initially confined to a small group

---

176. Ibid., p. 160; Damaschke, *Leben*, p. 275; Hermann Krecke, "Grundsätze und Entwicklungsanfänge der Bodenreformgenossenschaft Eden," *Deutsche Volksstimme* 10, no. 16 (August 20, 1899): 490–93.

177. Hartmann, *Gartenstadtbewegung*, p. 35. On Eden's products, see advertisements and inserts in early issues of *Die Gartenstadt*.

178. Although its existence seems uncertain after the collapse of East German communism; Gabriele Riedle, "Paradies sucht Zukunft," *Die Zeit* 38 (September 11, 1992).

179. Oppenheimer, *Erlebtes*, p. 161.

180. Mosse, *Crisis*, p. 111; BDB congress reports from 1899, *Deutsche Volksstimme* and *Bodenreform*. The BDB sponsored day trips out to Eden, which Damaschke endorsed as "a significant social-political experiment"; "Aus der Bewegung," *Deutsche Volksstimme* 10, no. 11 (June 5, 1899): 343.

181. Krecke, "Grundsätze," pp. 490–91.

182. Wolfgang Krabbe, *Gesellschaftsveränderung durch Lebensreform: Strukturmerk-*

of advocates, it became increasingly popular after 1910, when clubs began renaming themselves to include the phrase as good publicity in their titles, eventually becoming a fad that, like the Garden Cities, was used as an advertising gimmick for commercial enterprises with little interest in social or cultural reform.[183] Bäumer's vision of a "bright renaissance of industry" and Sombart's list of anti-political causes both indicated a consciousness of common orientation among these movements, and they specifically named many of the causes Wolfgang Krabbe has identified as defining the parameters of genuine life reform: temperance, "body maintenance," gymnastics and sports, natural health, nudism, settlements, vegetarianism, animal rights, land and housing reform. A "quasi-religious structure of mentality" distinguished the central core within this diverse field of activism from life reform's "periphery," which according to Krabbe consisted of the League of German Land Reformers, Garden City Society, and housing reform.[184] While there was no sharp line separating scatterbrained dreamers from practical reformers interested in professional, scientific solutions, Krabbe's analysis provides a useful way to conceive the relationship of Damaschke, Bäumer, Sombart, and other social reformers to the broad range of movements we will briefly examine below. Life reform constituted the periphery of the anti-political milieu.

Situated at the permeable boundary between these worlds was the temperance movement and its leader, Gustav von Bunge, whom Loth quotes in *Before Sunrise*. Bunge combined racial and economic arguments to demonstrate that alcoholism was as destructive to the national community as it was to individuals, and his book *The Alcohol Question* sold 220,000 copies before the First World War.[185] Inspired by Bunge, the Hauptmanns and Ploetz founded an International Association to Combat Alcohol Consumption in 1890 with the help of Sombart's friend from college, the socialist Otto Lang.[186] The temperance movement, which helped to define the community of life reformers in Eden, also sparked an interest in social medi-

---

male einer sozialreformerischen Bewegung im Deutschland der Industrialisierung-speriode (Göttingen: Vandenhoeck & Ruprecht, 1974), p. 12.
183. Ibid. See also Erich Lilienthal's amusing satire, "Die 'Gartenstadt' Berlin-Wilmersdorf," *Hilfe* 17, no. 36 (September 7, 1911): 564–65.
184. Krabbe, *Lebensreform*, p. 13.
185. Ibid., p. 161.
186. Weindling, *Health*, pp. 70–71.

cine, and it was here that Ploetz and other hygienists like Alfred Grotjahn made their start.[187] Other leaders of the reform milieu were actively involved in the movement as well. Damaschke, who described the degenerative effects of the "poisonous" alcoholic teas used in working class families to lull children to sleep, promoted temperance in the pages of the land reform journal, as did several of the other leaders of the movement, and Bäumer saw herself as a "fellow soldier in the movement against alcoholism."[188] Like the new science of eugenics, temperance was an issue on which radicals and moderates could agree; Maria Lichnewska, whose racial hygiene arguments proved so convincing in the debates over abortion at the BDF's Breslau congress in 1908, presented proposals designed to limit access to alcohol in local communities, while Ottilie Hoffmann led the League's Temperance Commission and spoke at the national Congress of Anti-Alcoholics in 1903.[189] The Christian Social and Egidy movements, Societies for Ethical Culture and Garden Cities, and other anti-political organizations added their support to the common fight against alcoholism, which included bourgeois and workers' clubs boasting memberships of 86,000 and 45,000 respectively in the decades around the turn of the century.[190] Inside the Social Democratic party, the small but vocal German

187. Ibid., p. 72.
188. Damaschke, *Leben*, pp. 231–34. Other BDB leaders promoting temperance included Krecke (a high-ranking official at Eden), Otto de Terra, Dr. Roese (who organized the 1903 Anti-Alcohol Congress), and J. Bergmann. On Bäumer: BDF congress protocol, 1908; HLA 62–268².
189. "Ottilie Hoffmann," *Centralblatt des BDF* 7, no. 8 (July 15, 1905): 57–58. See also Gerhard, *Unerhört*, pp. 174–75; Allen, *Feminism*, pp. 224–25; Reagin, *Movement*, pp. 80–81.
190. The Christian Socials' Inner Mission helped found the German Association against the Misuse of Alcoholic Beverages in 1883; Weindling, *Health*, p. 176. On the Egidy movement, see activity reports in *Ernstes Wollen*. Prominent temperance spokespersons addressed Ethical Culture meetings. August Forel, for example, spoke on "The Alcohol Question as a Social-Ethical Question" in the Munich chapter of the Society in 1895; "Deutsche Gesellschaft für ethische Kultur," *Ethische Kultur* 3, no. 35 (August 31, 1895): 279. Bunge joined the Garden City Society, as did Ploetz, Max von Gruber, and several other racial hygienists who supported the temperance movement, and an "anti-alcoholic Garden City" was founded in Sindelfingen in 1913; Karl Bittel, "Eine deutsche Reform-Gartenstadt," *Die Gartenstadt* 7, no. 6 (June,

Workers' Abstinence League pushed through an anti-alcohol resolution that also included demands for land and housing reform, an eight-hour day, and "hygiene of workplaces and methods of work" in 1907, but the issue remained controversial among the rank and file, and attempts to organize a "liquor boycott" made little headway.[191]

While temperance was promoted by major institutions devoted to social reform, it also belonged to the larger natural health movement, part of life reform's "inner circle," which viewed personal changes in diet and dress as an effective alternative to public policy, encouraging the "privatization of the social question."[192] Here too, Damaschke, Bäumer, Sombart, and others from the milieu joined in. Eden's statutes included severe restrictions on personal habits of consumption, and natural produce from its orchards found its way beyond the settlement's confines through a thriving chain of health food stores still to be found throughout Germany, which trace their origins back to the 1890s. While Damaschke and Oppenheimer helped put Eden on the map, Sombart supported the Association of German Reform Houses in later years, and as editor of *Nature's Doctor,* the land reformer played a leading role in the movement for natural medicine, which shared this interest in diet and also included members of both core and periphery.[193] Social Democrats were a significant presence in the leadership of the Association for Natural Health Care Damaschke joined in 1892, as we have seen. Defending the environmentalist stance in 1909, the revisionist Eduard David also promoted the "hygienic factors water, air, and sunshine," and the socialist workers' Alliance of Associations for the People's Health combined interests in social hygiene and natural health, sports and nudism, growing steadily to a membership of 11,640 by 1914.[194] On the other side of the divide, the German League of Associations for a

---

1913): 117–18. The German Association against the Misuse of Alcoholic Beverages reached peak membership in 1896; the Knights Templer, mainly an organization for workers and artisans, had 45,000 members in 1911; Krabbe, *Lebensreform,* pp. 41–46.

191. Franz Walther et al., *Sozialistische Gesundheits- und Lebensreformverbände* (Bonn: Dietz Nachfolger, 1991), pp. 181–96, esp. pp. 191–92.

192. Krabbe, *Lebensreform,* p. 15.

193. Newspaper clipping, *Würzburger General-Anzeiger* (August 22, 1939); NL Sombart 2/o.

194. Walther et al., *Lebensreformverbände,* pp. 21–42, 69.

Natural Lifestyle and Healing claimed 148,000 members and 3.3 million marks in fixed capital and assets a year earlier.[195] The debates over heredity played themselves out in the movement for natural medicine, and the extensive network of tuberculosis sanatoria that were established beginning in the 1890s testified to the commitment of doctors, feminists, and social workers to the environmentalist approach espoused by such organizations.[196]

Clothing reform also sought to improve the environment in a very immediate and personal sense. Drawing on hygienic principles, the movement's leaders insisted that dress too was more than a matter of personal taste, since clothing had a direct impact on the "health of the nation," and by transforming the textile industry "with regard to social and artistic considerations," reform-minded consumers boosted the nation's "economic life" as well. Clothing reform, in short, represented "a special kind of cultural politics."[197] It was also largely a politics of womanhood. While Ploetz and the Hauptmanns had already begun wearing "reform clothing" in the 1880s, by the time the movement came into its own after the fin de siècle, its focus had sharpened, as discussed in *The Culture of the Female Body as the Basis for Women's Clothing*.[198] Leaders of cultural reform, like Paul Schulze-Naumburg, Richard Riemerschmid, and Bernhard Pankok, furnished the designs, and Bäumer, who worked together with them in the Werkbund and Garden City movements, specifically included clothing reform in her ideas about a new style of feminine politics. By 1909 the German Alliance for Improvement of Women's Clothing had chapters in twenty major cities throughout the country.[199]

In addition to its emphasis on diet and dress, the natural health movement also sought to create a clean and secure environment on the greener

195. Krabbe, *Lebensreform*, pp. 142–44.

196. See "Experts and Officials" in this chapter.

197. Prospectus for *Die Neue Frauenkleidung*, the journal of the German Alliance for Improvement of Women's Clothing, insert in *Die Gartenstadt* 3(1909). See also Krabbe, *Lebensreform*, pp. 108–11.

198. The title of Schultze-Naumburg's 1905 book on clothing reform; Erich Viehöfer, *Der Verleger als Organisator: Eugen Diederichs und die bürgerlichen Reformbewegungen der Jahrhundertwende* (Frankfurt am Main: Buchhändler-Vereinigung, 1988), pp. 36–38.

199. See note 202.

outskirts of German cities. First devised by a Kiel physician in the early 1860s, the Schreber Gardens that rapidly spread throughout Germany were part of a broadly based movement that included both bourgeois and working-class organizations and solicited support from the land reform and women's movements.[200] While Damaschke praised the Schreber Garden as a healthy environment for working class families, German feminists lent their assistance to the "exclusively proletarian" arbor colonies that began cropping up haphazardly during the acute housing shortage after the Franco-Prussian War.[201] By the mid-1890s there were 45,000 gardens in such colonies in Berlin alone, but the workers tending them found themselves at the mercy of leaseholders trying to force the sale of alcoholic concessions on the tenants. If the Berlin municipal government passed protective ordinances by 1910, the women's movement could claim credit for helping to popularize their cause. In 1905 the Patriotic Women's Association founded the first in a network of Red Cross Workers' Gardens intended for "the refreshment of the laborer and his family in healthy air," recuperation of those suffering from "lung illnesses," the provision of alternatives to the tavern as a source of recreation, the sale of garden produce, which would lead to "increased contentment through an improved economic situation," and a "strengthening of a sense of family and family life."[202] The small urban gardens were thus part of a natural health movement that pursued its objectives not only for the sake of personal fulfillment but also to ensure the physical and socio-political "health of the nation." Led by Schulze-Naumburg, the League for the Protection of *Heimat* sponsored environmentalist initiatives that similarly combined subjectivist concerns with "scientific" legitimation, drawing on proto-ecological developments in botany and zoology as well as the professionalizing impulses of modern city planning in attempts to improve the quality of urban life that were by no means equivalent to neo-Romantic "hostility to the metropolis," as William Rollins has shown.[203] While Schulze-Naumburg's League was a "middle-class, white-collar affair," the forest protection movement cut across social and political lines more easily in seeking

200. Martin Kleinlosen and Jürgen Milchert, *Berliner Kleingärten* (Berlin: Arno Spitz, 1989), pp. 16–17.
201. Ibid., pp. 18–22, 29–32.
202. Ibid., pp. 30–32.
203. Rollins, *Vision,* pp. 14–18, 146–60.

to preserve the greenbelts around major German cities, attracting "scholars, artists, public figures from the President of the Prussian House of Lords to August Bebel, clerics, military officers, civil servants ... [and] nearly 500 of the most prominent names from Greater Berlin," as Karl von Mangoldt (author of the petition against Stumm) reported of a rally promoted by Naumann's *Assistance,* Damaschke's League, and the Garden City Society in 1910.[204]

The German youth movement, in which Bäumer detected hopeful signs for "the beginning of a very significant and far-reaching return of life" in her bizarre celebration of eugenics and liberalism in 1914, offers a final example of interaction between social and life reforms in the search for alternative modernities.[205] Like the colonists of Eden, the Free German Youth placed severe restrictions on the personal lifestyle of its members, who were forbidden to consume alcohol and tobacco.[206] The *Wandervogel* and the Free German Youth epitomized the back-to-nature longings of life reformers in general, which even found expression in the upper-middle-class flight to suburban villas in places like Grünewald, but again parallel movements indicate a similar impulse in Social Democratic circles.[207] Bölsche's handbooks on hiking and the outdoors served as guides for the socialist Friends of Nature, as did Haeckel's work on evolution.[208] Pedagogical reform was another area in which the milieu's interests intersected with the youth movement, bourgeois and socialist alike. Gustav Wyneken,

---

204. Ibid., p. 103; Mangoldt, "Waldschutz," pp. 265–67. See also "Aus der Bewegung," *Bodenreform* 18, no. 11 (June 15, 1907): 335; Erich Neuhaus, "Ein Berliner Waldschutztag," *Bodenreform* 20, no. 3 (February 5, 1909): 70–75; Prospectus for Hermann Kötschke's *Die Berliner Waldverwüstung und verwandte Fragen,* insert in *Die Gartenstadt* 4, no. 4 (April 1909).

205. Bäumer, "Jugendbewegung I," p. 449.

206. Peter Stachura, *The German Youth Movement, 1900–1945* (New York: St. Martin's, 1981), p. 22; Walter Laqueuer, *Young Germany: A History of the German Youth Movement* (London: Routledge and Kegan Paul, 1962), p. 45.

207. Eberhard Bohm, "Wohnsiedlung am Berliner Stadtrand im frühen 20. Jahrhundert: Das Beispiel Frohnau," *Siedlungsforschung, Archäologie-Geschichte-Geographie* 1 (1983): 125–26.

208. Kelly, *Descent,* p. 134; Lidtke, *Culture,* p. 64; Laqueuer, *Germany,* pp. 67–69. On the Friends of Nature, see Walther et al., *Lebensreformverbände,* pp. 241–91.

the innovative leader of the Country Home for Education whom Bäumer praised as a pioneer in techniques to emancipate individual energies for collective cultural strivings, was a central figure in the youth movement. While Rein's former student Hermann Lietz taught at Wyneken's school, Ludwig Gurlitt, a founding member of the *Wandervogel* who also joined Ostwald's Monist League, was among the first to introduce the organic rhythms promoted by Bücher and Dalcroze to the German classroom.[209] With points of contact throughout the milieu in Friedrichshagen, Jena, Leipzig, and Hellerau, the youth movement gained pledges of support not only from Bäumer but also from Gerhart Hauptmann, Naumann, and Ferdinand Avenarius—one of Germany's leading cultural reformers.[210]

Cultural Reform

Welcoming back-to-nature ascetics, abstinents, anarchists, "friends of peace and land reformers, modern pedagogues and women's rights activists," the Berlin salon of Moritz von Egidy hosted one of the earliest circles in which cultural reform was discussed as the basis for national unity in the 1890s, as we have seen.[211] United Christendom inspired not only the leader of Eden's life reform community, Bruno Wilhelmi, but also vocal advocates of eugenics as "biological politics" like Heinrich Driesmanns.[212] Egidy's success thus illustrates the effectiveness of a common cultural orientation in bringing together social and life reformers of all leanings in a way that would have been impossible in the political sphere. Damaschke and Lily Braun both belonged to this circle, as did other prominent social reformers: the moderate Regine Deutsch wrote for its journal, *Earnest Desire,* which also promoted the efforts of radicals like Helene Stöcker and Else Lüders (a leader of the women's club in Damaschke's League), and National Socials Hellmut von Gerlach and Adolf Harnack were involved with the movement

---

209. Stachura, *Movement,* p. 25.
210. These three joined Wyneken, Natorp, and others at the Free German Youth's rally at the Hohe Meissner in 1913; Laqueur, *Germany,* p. 34.
211. See "Into the Spring Thaw" in Chapter 2.
212. Heinrich Driesmanns, "Eugenik," *Tat* 5, no. 2 (May 1913): 179–84. Driesmanns was Egidy's biographer and a leader of the movement.

as well.[213] The brothers Hart, Bölsche, Oppenheimer, and above all Gustav Landauer were also close to Egidy.[214] Landauer, who joined the Friedrichshagen radicals Wille and Türk in attempting to rejuvenate Social Democracy in 1890, impressed the former cavalry officer with his "romantic socialism" to the point that Egidy became a defender of German anarchism.[215] The possibility of such contacts also encouraged Georg von Gizycki and Wilhelm Förster, the two Berlin professors who founded the German Ethical Culture Society in 1892.

Sharing Egidy's desire to harness the integrative force of moral and aesthetic values, Gizycki and Förster rejected his religious orientation and looked instead to science in defining the "ethical cultural of the will" Rein described as the ultimate aim of his pedagogical system in Jena. Building on the bridge between national economics and biology that sustained the non-partisan cultural politics of the reform milieu in so many areas, the Ethical Culture Society's synthesis of Marx and Darwin attracted a group of individuals as impressively diverse as Egidy's circle in support of popular education, women's rights, cooperatives, temperance, animal rights, and the campaign to end the tradition of dueling. Bäumer's mentor, the moderate Helene Lange, was among the Society's founding members, who also included the socialist feminists Lily Braun and Jeanette Schwerin. Damaschke too joined the movement in its early years, and Sombart delivered his famous speeches published in *Socialism and the Social Movement* at the International Ethical Culture Conference in Zurich in 1895. Perhaps meeting in the Society for the first time, many prominent members of the milieu went on to work together in organizations like the League of German Women's Associations, the land reform League, and the Societies for Social Reform, Garden Cities, and German Sociology. In addition to Gizycki, Braun, Schwerin, and Förster, members of the Ethical Culture's executive committee in these years included national economic boys—Tönnies, Jastrow, and Jaffé—the Friedrichshagen Darwinist Bölsche, and Ernst Har-

---

213. Gerlach spoke at its meetings; see, for example, *Ernstes Wollen* 3, no. 51 (October 22, 1901): 240. Harnack supported the movement from a distance; Driesmans, *Egidy*, p. 85.

214. Driesmans, *Egidy*, p. 84; Oppenheimer, *Erlebtes*, pp. 154–55; Lunn, *Prophet*, pp. 139–41.

215. Lunn, *Prophet*, pp. 139–41.

mening of the Jena circle. The society's journal published still more prominent activists: Ludwig Büchner, the Darwinian proponent of women's rights
and "social aristocracy," radical women's activists Minna Cauer and Marie
Stritt, land reform leaders Flürscheim, Freese, and Abbé, Franz Staudinger
of the cooperative movement, Friedrichshagen writers Bruno Wille and
Erich Lilienthal, Naumann's mentor Lujo Brentano, Schulze-Gävernitz, another of the national economic boys who launched the university extension
movement, and of course Naumann himself.[216]

The cultural ideal of organic socialism promoted by the Ethical Culture
society also pervaded Ferdinand Avenarius's influential journal, *The Keeper
of Art,* as well as his synthesis of social and cultural reform movements,
the Dürer League. Avenarius had switched from medicine to art history as
a student in Leipzig, where he had been deeply influenced by competing
currents of nationalism and socialism in the intense political atmosphere
of the city, as we have seen. After completing his studies, the former medical student founded the *Keeper* in order to educate popular artistic tastes
while simultaneously "stressing socialist ideas in accordance with the convictions of myself and my colleagues." While the journal cited Sombart
and Herkner in support of these convictions, it more frequently relied on
Damaschke's more popular works, which also included a *History of National Economics,* and Avenarius joined the land reform League's executive
committee in 1910.[217] The *Keeper* had close personal ties to Naumann's
Assistance, and several years earlier the art historian openly greeted the
crossover in readership between the two journals: "Wherever there is spirit
and life, we wish to look in that direction, be it to the right or the left, be
it behind or in front of us."[218] On the left was Avenarius's colleague Franz
Diederichs, the Social Democratic editor of the *Dresden Workers' Newspaper* who later edited the feuilletons of *Forwards!,* as well as the non-

---

216. See reports in *Ethische Kultur* 1, no. 38 (1893): 305, and 2, no. 32 (1894):
   366. For contributors and causes, see numbers for the 1890s. Many of these
   names are also listed as belonging to the journal's "circle of colleagues" in a
   supplement to vol. 6, no. 1.
217. Kratzsch, *Kunstwart,* pp. 103, 261; Viehöfer, *Verleger,* pp. 94–95; Lulu Strauß,
   ed., *Eugen Diederichs: Leben und Werk* (Jena: Eugen Diederichs, 1936), p. 43;
   BDB congress report, *Bodenreform* 21, no. 21 (October 20, 1910): 651–53.
218. "Allerlei," *Hilfe* 7, no. 31 (August 4, 1901): 15.

Marxist socialists Bölsche and Wille.[219] The *"Keeper of Art* circle" was in fact centered in Friedrichshagen, though the art historian lived in Dresden, and it may have been there that Avenarius first encountered the ideas of Damaschke and Sombart. Attacking the "petty officer's tone" of employers' relations to workers and the "incomplete democratization" of the German public sphere, the *Keeper* also popularized the milieu's integrationist message through cultural means in serialized *Heimat* novels that focused on the life of the lower classes and served to strengthen democratic convictions in Diederichs's feuilletons as well.[220] Combining the "biological aesthetics" of his brother Richard with the Darwinism and national economics of his colleagues in Friedrichshagen, Avenarius emphasized organicism as much socialism. The former medical student published articles demanding the institutionalization of hygiene as a branch of the civil service, while also promoting life reforms such as temperance, vegetarianism, and body maintenance.[221]

The land reform, cooperative, popular education, and women's movements received similar attention in *The Keeper of Art,* and the increasingly diverse circle of activists around the journal led Avenarius to the idea of establishing a formal link among his colleagues. Founded in October 1902, the Dürer League expressed the common orientation of its members on an institutional basis, focusing attention on aesthetic education and the preservation of natural and historical monuments.[222] Along with supporting his college friend Lichtwark, who sought to use modern media to bring art to the masses and promoted a revival of provincial artistic traditions as director of the Hamburg Art Hall, Avenarius especially endorsed the efforts of Schulze-Naumburg's *Heimat* movement, which combined a commitment to environmental protection with a diverse range of reform interests, from the preservation of local customs and artifacts to Garden Cities, tourism, hiking, *Heimat* literature, and land reform.[223] The Dürer League's broad synthesis of social, cultural, and life reform movements achieved remarkable success in soliciting support from individuals and organizations throughout

219. Kratzsch, *Kunstwart,* p. 11; Viehöfer, *Verleger,* pp. 94–95; Strauß, ed., *Diederichs,* p. 43.
220. Kratzsch, *Kunstwart,* pp. 293–94.
221. Ibid., pp. 119–20, 182–84.
222. Ibid., pp. 134–42; Rollins, *Vision,* pp. 83–84.
223. Rollins, *Vision,* passim; see also Applegate, *Nation,* pp. 59–107.

the reform milieu and across the political spectrum. By 1912 its Executive Committee included the former National Social leaders Naumann and Damaschke, Social Democrats Eduard Bernstein and Franz Diederichs, the racial anti-Semite Adolf Bartels, racial hygienists Max von Gruber and Hans Driesmans, the cultural historian Karl Lamprecht, Jena pedagogue Wilhelm Rein, Bäumer's friend Marianne Weber of the BDF, and Avenarius's friend from Friedrichshagen, Wilhelm Bölsche. Among the Dürer League's corporate members were the German Garden City Society, the Frankfurt Free University, clubs devoted to popular education and life reform, and student and teacher associations.[224]

Avenarius was not the only one to make plans for such a synthesis. As we have seen, Bäumer's contacts with the Garden City Society, Werkbund, and youth movement inspired her hopes that the "time was right" to found a cultural forum modeled on the Association for Social Policy in 1914. A similar scheme was presented by Eugen Diederichs, the owner of a Jena publishing house and a skillful organizer of cultural movements. Another close friend of Avenarius, Diederichs had taken part in Friedrichshagen's attempts to establish an alternative community along the lines of Eden, which eventually culminated in the German Garden City Society. Choosing the Jena of Haeckel, Abbé, and Rein as his headquarters, the financially independent reformer set out to promote social and cultural movements without regard to profit at the fin de siècle, publishing the works of his friends in Friedrichshagen. These publications included Bölsche's *Behind the World City,* Dohrn's *Garden City,* Schulze-Naumburg's treatise on clothing reform, and a series of workers' biographies collected by Paul Göhre, the National Social leader who later joined the SPD and began his career by describing his experience in *Three Months as a Factory Worker.*[225] While Diederichs endorsed both social and cultural reform, his own interests tended toward the quasi-religious mentality Krabbe identified as defining the parameters of life reform's inner circle, and he also printed deluxe editions of Lagarde's works, a series on medieval German mystics, Bergson, and Driesch (the neo-vitalist proponent of "entelechy"), alongside literature pertaining to the Nietzsche cult. Acquiring Ernst Horneffer's *The Deed,* which promoted popular education and democratization in addition to Monism, the publisher significantly expanded his repertoire in

---

224. Kratzsch, *Kunstwart,* pp. 336–38, 466.
225. Viehöfer, *Verleger,* pp. 13–15.

1912, and the next year he used the journal to unveil a "Program for the Future" that proposed to consolidate social and cultural reform activities in a new "German People's Council." Diederichs took the Werkbund, rather than Bäumer's Association for Social Policy, as a model for the institution, which was to enable "personal contact and a close association of creative forces in all areas." Its Central Committee was to include departments for popular education, legal and social reform, the religious movement, school and university reform, historical preservation, and "anti-politics." Claiming the support of "men from the most diverse political parties," the publisher closed by insisting that his idea was a serious plan for practical cooperation, "not a utopia."[226]

Diederichs's defensiveness indicates the weakness of a proposal that saw the "life of the spirit" rather than "material civilization" as the "common thread of all efforts at reform" in Wilhelmine Germany.[227] While many shared his belief in the autonomy of humanistic ideals, Diederichs's apparently low regard for economics and natural science put him at odds with the milieu's goal of reconciling the two cultures within an alternative modernity. Rein's system may have been founded on Kantian "ideas," but the Jena pedagogue also took pains to incorporate the latest findings of science, which sustained the progressive "social current" of the day. Despite her laments over the fate of personal *Kultur*, Bäumer did not reject the outward accomplishments of *Zivilisation* but instead looked for a synthesis of both built on the foundations of a new German economy. Rejecting the critical, empirical impulse of his generation, Diederichs's initiative evoked skepticism from Naumann and the national economic boys—Sombart, Tönnies, Weber—who attended one of his "cultural congresses," but without much enthusiasm.[228] Idealism that was not firmly grounded in the material world had little impact on the reform milieu, and plans for the People's Council were quickly shredded in angry disagreements among the proponents of environmentalist and hereditarian eugenics.[229]

---

226. Eugen Diederichs, "Ein Deutscher 'Volksrat,' " *Tat* 5, no. 1 (April 1913): 43–44.

227. Ibid., p. 40.

228. Marianne Weber, *Weber,* p. 647.

229. See, for instance, Driesmans, "Eugenik": 179–84; Karl Hauptmann, "Eine eugenetische Maßnahme," *Tat* 5, no. 2 (May 1913): 184–85.

The Politics of Illusion?

With his "almost ascetically-disciplined sense for the facts," Naumann offered a striking contrast to Diederichs, and his message resonated much
more strongly in the Wilhelmine reform milieu. Describing "human life
force" as the "foundation of the national economy," his proposal for a *New
German Economic Policy* skillfully blended the discourses of biological and
social science, which had come to pervade discussions of the social question, not only at the university, but in social circles and movements beyond as well. It was from Naumann that Bäumer first learned to grasp
the concrete, corporeal significance of "the materialistic view of history,"
and his "organic," or "anthropological" analysis of "biological-spiritual
forces" as decisive "motors of the historical process" echoed views in the
Leipzig circle—Ratzel's "anthropogeography" as well as the physiological
psychology, cultural history, and economics of rhythm developed by
Wundt, Lamprecht, and Büchner—and in the Social Scientific Union,
where the erstwhile National Social met Berlin's socialist students of medicine and economics. Brentano and the national economic boys—Sombart, Schultze-Gävernitz, and Max Weber—also collaborated on the *New
German Economic Policy*, as we have seen. Despite his quarrel with Sombart, Naumann understood the dynamics of anti-politics far better than
Diederichs, who remained on the milieu's periphery, while the progressive leader stood (alongside Friedrichshagen) very close to the center. Indeed, we have encountered Naumann and his colleagues at every turn: in
the case studies, at the centers of learning, and in circles of social, cultural,
and life reform.

Like the Berlin Naturalists, the workers' pastor had impressively mastered the art of building discursive networks. Founded in the wake of the
younger Christian Socials' clash with Conservatives in the Protestant Social
Congress and the campaign against Stumm, the short-lived National Social
Association was by far the clearest and most memorable expression of the
younger generation's commitment to the message of social integration proclaimed in the February Decrees, and it created one of the densest tangles
of crisscrossing paths, personal and institutional ties in the entire web of
Wilhelmine anti-politics.[230] Land reformers, feminists, economists, labor

---

230. On the NSV, see "From Christian to National Social" in Chapter 1.

leaders, pedagogues, physicians, and artists came together in the Association, which enjoyed the support or active membership of leading figures in the reform milieu, starting with Damaschke, the NSV's vice-chairman after 1901. Several members of the land reform League's Executive Committee joined the National Social movement—Adolf Pohlman, the BDB's vice-chairman, temperance leader Otto de Terra, Hermann Francke of the Protestant Workers' Associations, and Lehmann-Hohenberg, leader of the German People's League and Damaschke's patron in Kiel. While Bäumer and Lange stood close to the Association in Berlin, Elisabeth Gnauck-Kühne joined, as did Bäumer's friends Ika Freudenberg, Marianne Weber, and Marie Baum, with whom Bäumer later founded the Social School for Women in Hamburg. Sombart too followed the movement with interest, praising Naumann and Göhre in *Socialism and the Social Movement*. Weber, Brentano, and Schulze-Gävernitz supported the National Socials, along with the economist-physician Oppenheimer, Jaffé of the Societies for Ethical Culture and sociology, Wilhelm Rein in Jena, Avenarius of the Dürer League and the *Keeper of Art*, Naumann's fellow students in Munich, Heuss, Dohrn, and Jäckh. The common link between all was Naumann himself.

The National Social experiment may have abruptly ended with "the politics of illusion," but the strength of the milieu that came together behind it had never been in the realm of politics. Rejecting Weber's cool calculation of political interests, the NSV's founding delegates had decided to create an "Association" rather than a party, as we have seen, and many agreed with Damaschke that Reichstag elections were a poor indication of success or failure in 1903. Naumann's increasing preoccupation with imperialistic foreign policy and electoral strategy had diverted attention from social concerns that formed a stronger basis for the movement's solidarity. It seemed to make more sense to abandon politics than to destroy an institution that had in fact achieved a great deal. The NSV brought people together. Many joined Damaschke's land reform League as a result of the personal contact the Association afforded, and many more would work together to build the institutions and practices of reform as a professional, rather than a political occupation after the National Socials disbanded. For these men and women, inspired by the vision of a reformed national community based on social justice, personal freedom, and economic vitality, Naumann's illusion had become reality on an immanently practical and fundamentally anti-political level.

Wiring the Network

The generation of 1890 learned the social question together. At universities in Berlin, Munich, Leipzig, Jena, Breslau, and beyond, and in social circles that met in Friedrichshagen, Eden, and Egidy's open home, at congresses of the Ethical Culture Society, Dürer League, and the NSV, an extensive milieu of intellectuals and activists, workers and aristocrats, artists, scientists, humanists, civil servants, physicians and lawyers, feminists, and others discussed possibilities for creating a new synthesis of economics and biology that could guide Germany beyond present ills toward a future at once modern and human. Such discussions often produced heated arguments about the nature of both problem and solution at the turn of the century. Was environment or heredity the decisive factor in shaping future generations? Was state intervention the best means to effect change, or self-help through private initiative? Did radical agitation or carefully formulated statistical analyses do more to gain the ear of those who made the decisions? How were the conflicting Enlightenment impulses of social progress and scientific and technological advance to be reconciled? It is difficult to find two reformers who entirely agreed on any of these questions, let alone on all at once. Taken together, though, they formed an anti-political matrix of concerns and issues that reinforced the associative ties and discursive networks of the Wilhelmine reform milieu even as participants in these discussions angrily disagreed.

But anti-politics was more than idle talk. The members of the milieu built and continued to build—clubs, associations, institutions, vehicles for collective action in areas of shared interest. In the case studies we have seen how education and personal contacts led Damaschke, Bäumer, and Sombart to construct or to remodel institutions in areas of specialized interest: the League of German Land Reformers, the League of German Women's Associations, the Society for Social Reform. Concentrating their efforts in these specific areas, all three reformers also participated in the broad range of circles and movements examined in this chapter, each according to a set of experiences and inclinations that reflected his or her individual path through the milieu. The same was true of others as well. Thus, for instance, Tönnies's interest in national economics, socialism, and eugenics found expression in his signature on the petition against Stumm and in his membership in the land reform and Dürer Leagues, the Societies for Ethical Culture, Social Reform, and German Sociology. Hellmut von Gerlach's path from right to left took him through much of the same territory—he signed Mangoldt's petition and joined the land reform League and the Society for Social Reform as well—but it also led to other causes with which the national economist had no affiliation—the Protestant Social Congress, National Social Association, feminist and peace movements. Gnauck-Kühne shared Gerlach's ties to the Protestant Social Congress, National Socials, and feminism, joined Tönnies in the Dürer League and German Society for Sociology, and pursued other interests of her own by helping to found the Catholic Women's League. The milieu was a web spun out of distinctive sets of intertwining relationships, and its complexity reflected both the diversity and the commonalties of the men and women who wove it together.

The impulse to build and participate in these institutions was also inseparable from the professional aspirations motivating the generation of 1890. Commitment to anti-politics was in part a conviction that expert knowledge was a more desirable basis for public policy than the tactical ploys of party politicians, and Wilhelmine reformers saw opportunities for themselves as well as for the nation in establishing the framework for a non-partisan decision-making process. Professional training was to enhance the competitiveness of German industry, the mediation of social conflict, and the "health of the nation"; public and private institutions were to administer the policies of the newly trained experts; and both were to provide credentials, jobs, and status—first and foremost for those who built them, but also for the upward-striving who would follow in their footsteps. The strength of the anti-political milieu lay in quietly laying the foundations of an alternative modernity, not in the politics of illusion, and it was in fact here too that Naumann achieved what were arguably his most impressive and lasting successes.

Naumann's Successes

In 1907, the same year Naumann unmasked Sombart's "anti-politics," he also helped found the German Werkbund, a professional organization committed to the practical engagement of non-partisan technical experts in the search for alternative modernities. Attending a national crafts exhibition in Dresden, the former National Social met with Karl Schmidt to discuss plans for restoring the links between art and industry, a development Bücher was promoting in nearby Leipzig and Sombart had optimistically forecast in his critique *Modern Capitalism*. Schmidt was owner of the Dresden Workshops, the center of Germany's arts and crafts movement, which was largely inspired by Ruskin and Morris in England and had grown steadily since the 1890s.[231] The belief that mass production had seriously diminished the quality of modern design was common to both countries, but Schmidt and others leading the German movement rejected their British counterparts' nostalgia for pre-industrial modes of production, insisting that the only hope for restoring artistry to architecture and interior design lay in modern technology and would have to be realized within the existing capitalist order.[232] In order to make quality merchandise accessible to the masses, artists would need the help of factory owners and businessmen to harness the awesome productive force of German industry in pursuit of this goal. Greeting Naumann, who had published his *New German Economic Policy* a year earlier, Schmidt, Muthesius, Theodor Fischer, Bruno Paul, Henry van de Velde, Peter Behrens, and other leaders of the industrial arts movement seized on his plan as an opportunity to achieve precisely this sort of cooperation. Founded on October 5, 1907, the Werkbund strove for a "spiritualization of labor" that would enhance the personal lives of workers, countering the crass materialism and shoddy products Sombart, Bäumer, and other cultural critics found so distressing, but without giving up the benefits of modern technology and in the end actually enhancing the efficiency of the German economy.[233]

Naumann's engagement with anti-politics thus actually intensified after his clash with Sombart. While he may not have "entered a new circle" with the founding of the Werkbund, as Heuss claimed—the "professional politician" had opportunities to meet the leaders of the movement in Munich and through contacts with Rathenau and the Friedrichshagen circle, and he had promoted the goals of modern architects as early as 1899, arguing that "the new style must have iron bones"—but it was certainly a significant new commitment to cultural reform.[234] Here too Naumann played the role of linchpin, linking Werkbund architects and designers to other circles, appointing Dohrn and Jäckh as secretaries of the new organization

231. Kampffmeyer, *Gartenstadtbewegung,* p. 52; Campbell, *Werkbund,* p. 20; Sombart, *Kunstgewerbe,* pp. 54–125.

232. Campbell, *Werkbund,* p. 3.

233. Ibid., pp. 9–10.

234. Heuss, *Naumann,* p. 219.

and introducing Bäumer to its leaders, with whom she worked to coordinate the women's League congress and the Cologne industrial arts exhibition of 1914. Although publicly embroiled in a feud with Naumann, Sombart was among the Werkbund's first members, and Damaschke echoed its attacks on "handicraft romanticism," while Schultze-Naumburg, leader of the *Heimat* protection movement, was a founding member.[235] On their part, the designers and architects in Naumann's new circle had their own manifold connections to the social circles in Friedrichshagen, Jena, and so on. The Werkbund pursued its anti-political goals in two ways. Lobbying industry and state officials for support at the production end, Naumann and his colleagues stressed the economic advantage to be gained in the world market by improving the quality of German merchandise. At the same time, the Werkbund held seminars for commercial retailers modeled after the popular education movement, and launched publicity campaigns to create a market for its products. While improving the quality of life for the lower classes remained the ultimate goal, the sale of more expensive products would first have to stimulate the establishment of new commercial centers of quality production, and at first the Werkbund's efforts to educate popular tastes focused on the bourgeoisie. Yet training in the new techniques would also raise wages and self-esteem for the skilled labor in these new workshops, the movement's leaders argued, by rescuing workers from the mindless, mechanized tasks on drab assembly lines that were producing little of real value.[236] Combining the professional aspirations of the reform milieu with its social and cultural impulses, the Werkbund was a model of practical anti-politics.

If the goal of social unity through improved quality of life for all proved to be elusive, the Werkbund achieved considerable successes in other ways. The organic functionalism developed by Muthesius and his fellow architects paved the way for the Bauhaus, where van de Velde and other leaders from the Werkbund defined the new institution's objectives in much the same way, while Jäckh's National Keeper of Art brought the movement's agenda into the sphere of official policy-makers in the Weimar Republic.[237]

---

235. Campbell, *Werkbund*, p. 25.
236. Ibid., pp. 18, 42–46.
237. Hans-Joachim Hubrich, *Hermann Muthesius: Die Schriften zu Architektur, Kunstgewerbe, Industrie in der 'Neuen Bewegung'* (Berlin: Mann, 1981),

Unable to stave off co-optation by the Nazis, the Werkbund later suffered the fate of many institutions created by the Wilhelmine reform milieu after 1933. Becoming both tool of Nationalist Socialist cultural policy and an influence on programs for "Beauty of Labor" and "Strength through Joy," the Werkbund's leaders severely compromised the integrity of the organization, which collapsed along with the Third Reich in 1945. Yet still Naumann's institution persisted. Rebuilt in 1947, the Werkbund continues to exist in Darmstadt today, where it has recently expanded its activities to include environmentalism and urban planning.[238] The leaders of the movement could hardly have guessed what success would mean, however, when they laid plans for a permanent institution to realize visions of a very different future in 1907.

At the very moment the Werkbund was being conceived, many of its founding members were preparing to launch a construction project that soon gave this vision concrete form—the Garden City of Hellerau, Naumann's second major success in the world of Wilhelmine anti-politics. While the progressive politician helped raise the one million Marks that put Hellerau on its feet, the German Garden City Society had been founded five years earlier in Friedrichshagen.[239] As we have seen, the Berlin Naturalists' circle was involved in the Eden Orchard Colony and had also attempted to found a communal settlement of its own. When the experiment failed, the group took encouragement from developments in England, where Ebenezer Howard had recently brought together a small band of land reformers and other activists to make what seemed a more promising start, founding the first Garden City Association in 1899.[240] Blending the environmentalist and communitarian impulses that inspired a coalition of British temperance and public health movements not unlike the one forming in Germany, Howard's plans won the support of "pragmatists" and "pro-

pp. 74–75, 151; Frank Trommler, "The Creation of a Culture of *Sachlichkeit*," in Eley, ed., *Culture*, pp. 465–86.

238. Campbell, *Werkbund*, pp. 246–85.

239. Hartmann, *Gartenstadtbewegung*, p. 46; Kampffmeyer, *Gartenstadtbewegung*, p. 52; "Vor zehn Jahren," pp. 160–62.

240. Stanley Buder, *Visionaries and Planners: The Garden City Movement and the Modern Community* (New York: Oxford University Press, 1990), p. 78.

fessionals," and by 1902 the Association appeared to be moving rapidly toward practical success.[241] After hearing about the movement, the Friedrichshagen circle called a meeting of the New Community for September, at which Heinrich Hart announced the creation of a "new foundation from the life and spirit of our times," the German Garden City Society. By harnessing modern technology, Hart told the audience of approximately 350 intellectuals and activists, the Garden City would "satisfy all needs with regard to hygiene, aesthetics, [and] spatial expansion," providing a space where all "reform ideas of the day, whether they extend to social, ethical, or cultural areas, can come to fruition in the most secure and prosperous way."[242]

Coming from the "court of the muses on Lake Müggel," such assurances of the Garden City's viability hardly seemed convincing, as historians have been quick to point out. Thus Christianne Hartmann has argued that Friedrichshagen's "mystification of the entire social situation" kept the circle from facing the realities of Wilhelmine society, while Stanley Buder's comparative study of Garden City movements in Europe and America found that "Germany did not offer a political or social soil conducive to nurturing the movement's ethos as contrasted to its technical offerings."[243] Despite these compelling explanations for its failure, however, the German Garden City movement in fact turned out to be a remarkable success. The "dreamers" of Friedrichshagen may not have been effective in working with stone, but they knew how to build networks, as we have seen. In addition to Hart, Bölsche, and the painter Fidus, the Society's founding committee included Damaschke and Oppenheimer, who were committed to practical social reform, and among the Naturalists' contacts to the avant-garde were Peter Behrens and Henry van de Velde, two of the Werkbund's founding members who helped design the plans for Hellerau five years later. If they refused to engage in a "dialectical analysis" of their society, the writers and artists of Friedrichshagen understood the anti-political space that existed within it well enough to know that a lack of democratic rights, deplorable as it was, did not constitute an insurmountable obstacle to practical success. After all, it was in the "soil" of anti-politics that both

241. Ibid., pp. 70–80.
242. "Vor zehn Jahren," pp. 160–62.
243. Hartmann, *Gartenstadtbewegung*, p. 16; Buder, *Visionaries*, p. 136.

the "ethos" and the "technical offerings" of the movement had grown from the start.

Like the Werkbund, the Garden City Society manifests the confluence of social and professional aspirations that came together in the generation of 1890. While the Society initially publicized its efforts in the *Tall Guard,* a cultural magazine devoted to popular education and "social justice," after gaining enough funds it founded *The Garden City,* which rapidly established itself as a professional journal after 1907.[244] Publishing detailed street plans and blueprints, proposals for revising local tax codes and property laws, and reports on ongoing projects to connect new settlements to the transit and sewer lines of nearby cities, the editorial staff included economists and sociologists, including Sombart, Oppenheimer, and Mangoldt, the racial hygienists Ploetz, Grotjahn, and Gruber, architects Muthesius, Riemerschmid, and Taut, and a long list of engineers.[245] These technical and socio-economic experts also worked alongside professional social reformers: Bäumer and Marie Baum from the feminist movement, Damaschke, Pohlmann, Lehmann-Hohenberg, and Otto Jackisch from the land reform League, cooperative movement leader Franz Staudinger, and many more.[246] As a result of this collaboration, nine Garden Cities and four Garden Suburbs were built throughout Germany before the First World War, and three more were in advanced stages of planning.[247]

Built with financial backing from Naumann and Karl Schmidt, owner of the Dresden workshops, the model inspiring this boom in Garden City

---

244. See *Gartenstadt* issues 1907–10.

245. "An den Leser," *Gartenstadt* 2, no. 6 (May 1908): 41.

246. See membership lists published in *Gartenstadt;* Marie Baum, "Mutter, Kind, und Wohnung," *Gartenstadt* 2, no. 5 (April 1908): 33–34; Franz Staudinger, "Gartenstadt und Genossenschaft," *Gartenstadt* 3, no. 2 (January 1909): 22–24.

247. See the reports "Aus der Bewegung" in *Die Gartenstadt* from the years 1909–14. The Garden City Society's journal reported Garden Cities near Karlsruhe, Wandsbeck, Wedau (near Duisburg), Obereßlingen, Magdeburg (Hopfengarten Reform), Essen (Margarethenhöhe), Merseburg, and Nuremberg. Garden suburbs were discussed in Leipzig (Marienbrunn), Hagen, Berlin (Grünau), and Mannheim (Skopau). The Garden City of Munich appeared to be on the verge of construction in 1914, and other preparations were reported in Bonn and Braunschweig.

construction was Hellerau, which General Secretary Hans Kampffmeyer billed as "a new type of city" designed to address "a number of national economic, hygienic, and cultural problems" by implementing land and housing reform, "guaranteeing advantageous conditions for industry and handicrafts, and permanently [securing] a large portion of its terrain for gardens and agriculture."[248] Staudinger's cooperatives were "the technical transformer through which the capitalist economy [became] a communal economy" at Hellerau, where "an exaggerated emphasis on individualism" was also discouraged by the aesthetic expression of "human beings as social creatures" in the architecture of homes arranged in such a way as to create an "organic whole."[249] It was in Germany's first Garden City that Muthesius sought to implement his theories about architectural rhythm and Dalcroze emphasized the "hygienic importance of rhythmic exercise."[250] Marie Baum used statistics on infant mortality to contrast Hellerau's healthy environment with the "rental barracks" of the city, and others called for public health offices and the erection of a "National Hygiene Museum" for the "people's enlightenment."[251] The latter proposal appears to have been realized when the joint congress of the League of German Land Reformers and the Garden City Society coincided with the National Hygiene Exhibition in nearby Dresden, which was turned into a permanent museum.[252] Women were encouraged to participate in communal government as housing inspectors, and Hans Kampffmeyer adopted Lily Braun's proposals for multiple-family household cooperatives for use in Hellerau.[253] Other communal institutions included laundry and consumer cooperatives, a health food restaurant, municipal swimming pools and sports facilities, a community hall, and a library. There was always room for "more

248. Kampffmeyer, *Gartenstadtbewegung*, p. 10; Kampffmeyer, "An den Leser," *Gartenstadt*, first (undated) issue.

249. Paul Behrens, "Die Gartenstadtbewegung," *Gartenstadt* 2, no. 4 (March 1908): 27.

250. Jacques-Dalcroze, "Bedeutung"; see also note 107.

251. Baum, "Mutter," p. 33; Artur Luerssen, "Gesundheitsämter für die Gartenstädte," *Gartenstadt* 4, no. 6 (June 1910): 61–64.

252. BDB congress report, *Bodenreform* 22, no. 12 (June 20, 1911): 337–419; Weindling, *Health*, p. 144.

253. Kampffmeyer, *Gartenstadtbewegung*, pp. 90–96. On Braun's proposals, see Braun, *Memoiren*, vol. 2, pp. 301–3, 323–33; Allen, *Feminism*, pp. 167–68.

economy" in the efficient configuration of space at Hellerau,[254] where everything worked in tandem. Nowhere was the web of intertwining personal, professional, and institutional relationships of the Wilhelmine reform milieu woven as tightly as in the first and most prominent Garden City.

Like the Werkbund, Hellerau still exists today, if only as a suburb of Dresden, where it escaped the destruction of the fire-bombing in 1945. Appropriated by the Nazis, Hellerau's tightly knit community experienced the same fate as Naumann's other success, but the Garden City Society too lives on in a radically altered form.[255] Encouraged by the development of Garden Suburbs, Kampffmeyer went on to make a career as a city planner, taking a position as settlement advisor in Vienna after the First World War before moving to Frankfurt am Main, where he served as General Secretary of the International Housing Association until his death in 1932. Still in Frankfurt, the Association helped to create the concentric rings of new communities surrounded by parks and fields that has become a familiar pattern in Germany and far beyond.

Experts and Officials

While Hellerau was an impressive example of the anti-political approach to communal administration, it did little to alleviate social problems in existing cities, and it was largely for this reason that Damaschke resisted an open affiliation between the land reform League and the Garden City movement, which he quietly supported in hopes that it would demonstrate the effectiveness of his ideas. Model institutions like Hellerau and Eden could be useful, Damaschke believed, but in order to root out the economic and hygienic causes of the social question, federal social legislation and nationwide municipal reform was necessary. The League of German Land Reformers thus provided state and municipal bureaucrats with detailed statistical analyses of economic factors involved in land reform and used extra-parliamentary means to draw attention to its proposals for reforming local, state, and federal tax structures regarding capital gains, excise, and

---

254. Leberecht Migge, "Mehr Ökonomie," *Gartenstadt* 4, no. 10 (October 1910): 109–13.

255. Hartmann, *Gartenstadtbewegung*, p. 97; Buder, *Visionaries*, pp. 151–52.

unused land.[256] In accusing Damaschke of reducing Henry George's grand ideals to "a bourgeois tax matter," Oppenheimer was thus criticizing a trend toward professionalization apparent in his own career, as we have seen, and the land reform leader in fact promoted an extensive package of municipal reforms to complement his demands for tax reform. Based on a systematic survey of mayors' concerns throughout Germany, Damaschke's *Tasks of Communal Policy* presented a reform agenda covering a broad spectrum of issues and goals in the matrix of Wilhelmine anti-politics:[257]

Education	Free learning materials
	School doctors
	Improved hygienic conditions of classrooms
Employment	Non-partisan, municipal employment agency,
	leading to the creation of a National Employment Agency
Housing	Zoning ordinances
	Central housing agency
	Separate ownership of land and buildings
Health and hygiene	Official housing inspectors
	Municipal baths, in accordance with the
	"development of modern hygienic science"

With the exception of the changes in property laws, each of these proposals required the employment of professional social workers as municipal officials. Land reform sought to ease social tensions by providing careers as well as homes for the "upward-striving."

Major institutions of the reform milieu took steps to train such professionals. In 1893, as the popular education movement led by Schulze-Gävernitz and Rein was gaining momentum, the Protestant Social Congress held its first specialized courses on social policy matters in Berlin. Attended by five hundred theologians, teachers, lawyers, and civil servants, the courses included lectures on national economics, industrial policy, "The German Workers' Movement," and social legislation, which became the

---

256. See Chapter 2, note 43.
257. Damaschke, *Aufgaben*, pp. 57–58, 161–80, 199.

models for similar programs in Breslau, Halle, Limburg, Karlsruhe, and the Rhineland, as well as for the Association for Social Policy's seminars, first held in conjunction with the Protestant Congress in 1894–1895.[258] In addition to supporting Frankfurt's Free University, the Institute for Public Welfare set up a permanent Academy for Social and Commercial Sciences in 1901 and an Information Center that was later turned into a Social Museum and archival center.[259] Damaschke's land reform League also joined in on this "task of enlightenment." While the BDB leader's *Tasks of Communal Policy* went through ten editions by 1922 and his *History of National Economics* thirteen editions, the BDB's central library contained works on economics, municipal administration, zoning law, factory inspection—as well as reports on tax proposals and parliamentary debates—published by leading socialists (both Marxist and academic), sociologists, and progressive reformers: Friedrich Engels, Karl Kautsky, Ferdinand Lassalle, Heinrich Freese, Elisabeth Gnauck-Kühne, Ernst Harmening, Franz Oppenheimer, Ernst Abbé, Schmoller, and Wagner.[260] Beginning in 1911, the League also held its own weekend seminars, at which civil servants, municipal officials, labor leaders, and a growing number of female social workers learned about Damaschke's program for municipal administration and land reform (see Table 5.7).

While the overall success of this campaign is difficult to gauge, the presence of mayors and municipal administrators in the BDB Executive Committee and as speakers at its annual congresses, as well as the corporate membership of numerous German municipalities in the League, indicates that the program was not without effect. At the land reformer's sixtieth birthday celebration in 1925, Dr. Koch claimed that "we mayors, the entire younger generation, have all absorbed infinitely much from Damaschke" and particularly stressed his "social" influence in the area of "economic law."[261]

As we have seen, German feminists were even more involved in the drive for professionalization. Emerging from charity work and popular education initiatives in the early 1880s, the Pestalozzi-Froebel House in Berlin

---

258. Bruch, *Wissenschaft*, pp. 264–66.

259. Sachße, *Mütterlichkeit*, p. 89.

260. Damaschke's land reform "bible," *Die Bodenreform*, went through twenty editions; Berger-Thimme, *Wohnungsreform*, p. 90. For the BDB's library catalogue, see the regular installments in *Deutsche Volksstimme* and *Bodenreform*.

261. Erman, *Bekenntnis*, pp. 18–19.

Table 5.7 Attendance at BDB seminars

Occupation	1911	1914
Civil servants	45	118
Mayors and municipal representatives	23	40
Architects, engineers, technicians	17	41
Commerce and industry personnel	19	19
Union and cooperative secretaries	5	11
Academics and professionals	13	24
Male and female teachers	99	47
Male and female university students	21	71
Editors, journalists, writers	4	45
Artisans and white-collar workers	9	26
Clergy	1	6
Women with no occupation indicated	7	47
No occupation indicated	—	138
Total	263	643

Source: Bodenreform 22, no. 10 (May 20, 1911): 281–82, and 25 (May 5, 1914): 264.

became an important center for developing this impulse, rapidly branching out to encompass a broad range of activities involving social work and training, much like Jane Addams's Hull House in the United States, where it in fact received international recognition at the Chicago World's Fair of 1893. The Pestalozzi-Froebel House inspired Lange's famous Yellow Brochure and petition for women's educational reform in 1887, as well as the more ambitious women's high school curriculum that she introduced a few years later. In the early 1890s, the school developed training courses in collaboration with the Girls and Women's Groups for Social Work, then led by Ethical Culture activist Jeanette Schwerin, who founded Berlin's Center for Private Welfare and was succeeded by Alice Salomon after her death in 1899.[262] The same year, the Groups held their first annual training course in social work, which included courses on children's education, poor relief, and national economics, and eventually led to the founding of Salomon's permanent Social School for Women in 1908, with a curriculum specifically geared toward the production of professional female social workers (see Table 5.8). Providing professional accreditation for po-

---

262. Sachße, *Mütterlickeit,* pp. 114–31.

Table 5.8 Curriculum of Alice Salomon's Social School for Women

First year	Hrs/wk	Second year	Hrs/wk
Scholarly fields		*Scholarly fields*	
Educational theory	2	National economic theory	2
Influence on the life and		Civic studies and family law	2
work of important pedagogues	1	Social ethics	1
Hygiene	1	Pedagogy	1
National economic theory	1	Social hygiene	1
Civic studies	1	Introduction to pedagogical	
Introduction to social and		and social literature	1
pedagogical literature	1		
Technical fields		*Technical fields*	
Manual dexterity	2	Introduction to the problems	
Manual work	2	of social work	1
		Theory and history of poor-law	1
		administration and public relief	
		Theory of juvenile care	1
Practical fields			
Work in kindergarten	4		
Cooking and domestic occupations	4		
Total	19		11

Source: Sachße, *Mütterlichkeit,* pp. 142–43; see also Allen, *Feminism,* pp. 212–15.

sitions in health, housing, and juvenile care administration, Salomon's curriculum became the model for other institutions. The Protestant Inner Mission, where Naumann got his start, founded its own the following year, and by 1914 there were fourteen Social Schools for Women in Germany, helping to ensure that "the newly emerging fields of work" in rationalized municipal administration Sachße described "were exclusively occupied by women" before the First World War.[263]

Among those following Salomon's example was Bäumer, who joined with Marie Baum (the Garden City hygienist who had pushed for women's suffrage in the Baden National Social Association in the 1890s and joined

---

263. Ibid., p. 145; see also Reagin, *Movement,* pp. 113–16.

the Society for German Sociology) to found a Social Pedagogical Institute and Social School in Hamburg during the First World War. Offering majors in "Careers Connected to Professions and Financial Gain," "National Health," "Juvenile Care," and "General Welfare," the Hamburg program included required courses on "The Development of Heavy Industry and the Workers' Question," "Hygienic Enlightenment of the Nation," "Labor Market and Employment Agencies," and other topics mirroring Bäumer's critique of modern capitalism that were intended to allow women to achieve status and security while working toward the construction of a healthy and integral national community.[264] As chairwoman of the League of German Women's Associations, Bäumer also presided over an organization that pushed the drive for professionalization and contributed to the process Canning described, by which feminists "came to occupy a pivotal place within the expanding public sphere" and influenced the formulation of public policy before 1914. Using maternalist discourse to "build bridges from family life to the life of the nation," the League sent petitions to state and federal governments demanding reforms of the Prussian law of association (which excluded women from both political and social political activity), women's voting rights in workers' councils, the certification of female hospital workers after three years' training, the "purposeful interaction" of administrators, doctors, nurses, and male and female hospital orderlies, female factory and housing inspectors, and women's access to the communal school administration.[265] In 1907, the League's Executive Committee furthermore published a resolution defining the "Principles and Demands of the Women's Movement," which included the following proposals:[266]

- The admission of women as fully authorized members of poor relief and orphanage facilities;
- The allocation of women (teachers and mothers) to school administration and supervision;

---

264. Bäumer, "Ziele": 338–46.
265. HLA. Petitions on the Law of Association (44–196[1]), on the workers' councils (50–229[2]), on hospital personnel (49–223[3]), on female factory inspectors (50–229[2]), on housing inspectors (49–223[3]), and on access to communal school administration (53–271[1]).
266. "Grundsätze und Forderungen der Frauenbewegung"; BDF *Gesamtvorstand* resolution, May 13–15, 1907.

- Collaboration of the female sex in communal and state housing inspection and maintenance;
- Utilization of female forces in the areas of health, alcoholic, and prison care, and in police maintenance;
- Elevation of women to the administrative offices of the insurance system and occupational interest groups;
- Collaboration of the female sex in legal counsel, above all in advocacy, as well the office of jurors;
- Admission of women to higher posts in the civil service.

The Society for Social Reform also worked to establish semi-public institutions and training programs. With financial backing from Wilhelm Merton, head of the Institute for Public Welfare, who founded Frankfurt's Center for Public Assistance and supported the Free University and Garden City movement, the Society created a Berlin Bureau for Social Policy that offered continuing education programs and lecture series and set up an office for legal counsel in order to coordinate data collected by organized labor, cartels, and government. Described as a "General Staff for securing the logistics of bourgeois social reformers," the Bureau consolidated a corps of professional labor relations experts and "very quickly became a significant point of contact" with workers' organizations that helped lay the foundations for the "civic peace" of 1914 and anticipated the triangle of decision-makers behind German economic policy in later years.[267] Like Naumann's successes and Oppenheimer's "liberal socialism," the dream of "organized capitalism" lived on—in the consultations between the leaders of business, unions, and government that still seemed to be the wave of the future not so long ago in West Germany's highly coordinated economy of the 1980s.[268]

Working in a broad field of professional activities that included both private and public initiatives, the reformers of Wilhelmine anti-politics influenced official policy through unofficial channels, using specialized seminars, model institutions, statistical archives, petition drives, and protests to in-

---

267. Bruch, "Sozialreform," pp. 136–37; Ratz, *Sozialreform*, pp. 71–76.
268. See for example "Das Ende des Laissez-Faire," *Zeit* (June 1992). Since the end of the Cold War, the article argues, communism and capitalism have ceased to be useful points of reference for describing the "directed" economies of Germany and Japan, which represented models for an efficient and productive "third way."

form public administration with the discourse of alternative modernities in significant ways. While such efforts could at times lead directly to the creation of major laws and institutions—such as the federal capital gains tax, the land reform provisions in Weimar's constitution, the National Keeper of Art, the International Housing Association, and so on—the milieu's success usually took less spectacular, but ultimately far more substantial and pervasive forms found in the ordering of expert knowledge and information necessary for the resolution of policy debates through detailed statistical analyses and pre-defined options ready to hand, in training the dispositions of generations of bureaucrats and policy makers (including the "social liberalism" of West Germany's Minister of Economics Ludwig Erhard), in populating the rapidly expanding sphere of public administration with professionals seemingly made to order, above all at the municipal level. During the Wilhelmine period, this approach was especially successful in establishing practices and institutions that allowed young men and women to confront the social question while simultaneously making careers for themselves in two areas: labor relations and public health.

As we have seen, the solution of "workers' protection" endorsed by Wilhelm II in the February Decrees had themselves been worked out by labor relations experts, progressive industrialists, and local administrators, and among the first institutions established by the New Course were the parity-based arbitration courts Berlepsch introduced in 1890.[269] Intended to mediate social conflict between organized capital and organized labor, the arbitration courts had been proposed by the socialists of the lectern in the 1870s and formed the core of Sombart's program for the Society for Social Reform. Although the courts' verdicts fell short of the economists' hopes for a neutral instrument for economic coordination, the Society supported the institution's continued development.[270] In 1901, the year after Sombart published *Nevertheless!*, a federal law required that the courts be set up in cities with a population larger than twenty thousand, and while the BDF's demands for including women in the courts remained unheard, the construction of a national network of social institutions had begun, which would eventually allow both men and women to make ca-

---

269. Bruch, "Sozialreform," p. 83.
270. Steinmetz, *Regulating*, pp. 132–33.

reers in the search for social unity. The New Course also brought a reform of the Industrial Code in 1891 that included requirements for written work regulations and workers' councils, much like the "factory constitutions" implemented by Abbé and Freese, and extended the obligatory employment of factory inspectors, which had earlier been limited to heavy industry, to encompass most firms, and increased the legal powers of these officials. Factory inspection remained a matter for states to decide until 1918, however, and although Prussia implemented the measures included in the reform of the Industrial Code, growth in the civil service remained limited in this area. By 1912 there were still only 328 state-employed factory inspectors in the entire country.[271]

If demands for the inclusion of women in the arbitration courts fell on deaf ears, feminists were more successful in shaping the development of regulations and institutions governing female workers' protection. As Canning has shown, the arguments and studies of economists, sociologists, racial hygienists, and progressive reformers strongly informed public debates over female factory labor at the turn of the century. While Heinrich Herkner opposed women's employment in industry, other leaders of the milieu including Lily Braun, Adele Schreiber, Henriette Fürth, Minna Cauer, Alice Salomon, Bäumer's ally Marie Baum, and—initially—Naumann himself defended the rights of female workers, eventually winning confirmation in the factory inspectors' report of 1901, which framed the complex negotiations that led to a revised industrial code seven years later, together with the provisions and language of the code Berlepsch hammered out in defining the New Course in 1891. Deeply inscribed with the eugenicist discourse circulating in the milieu, the result was a compromise that "partially fulfilled some of the key demands of both feminists and eugenicists," such as a ten-hour day (eight hours on Saturdays), the extension of medical coverage and maternity benefits, and a ban on work by pregnant women and new mothers in the weeks surrounding childbirth, which confirmed the centrality of Wilhelmine reformers in the formation of public policy as well as the ambivalent direction of "reproductive hygiene" we encountered in the debates over abortion.[272] The BDF's "principles and demands" also found a receptive audience at the municipal level, where

---

271. Ibid., p. 133–37.
272. Canning, *Languages,* pp. 170–215, esp. p. 211.

some twelve thousand women were employed as administrators in areas including housing inspection, infant care centers, alcoholic clinics, school and child-labor boards between 1899 and 1913.[273]

Municipal government played an active role in work-related issues more generally, as well as becoming an important site for the development of institutions devoted to health and hygiene. The employment agencies Damaschke included in his *Tasks of Communal Policy* were the creation of the local administrators and officials responding to his survey, who also launched unemployment insurance programs and public works projects.[274] In order to counter the "crises" economists like Sombart spent so much time studying, two hundred German cities hired between fifteen thousand and twenty thousand unemployed workers in the recession of 1908–09 alone. As we have seen, Wilhelm Merton's private initiatives in Frankfurt led to the development of a comprehensive and rationalized approach to health and social services at the municipal level, while German medical officers assumed executive powers in local government in order to coordinate sanitation, disease prevention, and health education.[275] At schools set up in Wiesbaden, Strasbourg, Halle, Leipzig, and Hamburg, municipal accreditation of social health officials became a reality, and the doctors Damaschke demanded began appearing in German schools during these years as well.[276] As centers of the medical reform movement, university clinics and research facilities in Leipzig and Berlin worked in tandem with city and state officials in the same effort. After Robert Koch succeeded in producing tuberculin in 1890, for instance, Berlin allocated 150 beds in its hospitals to facilitate development of a treatment program, while the Prussian government rushed to support his Institute for Infectious Disease.[277] The Imperial capital's network of public clinics—Oppenheimer discovered the "Medusa's face of the social question" in the 1890s—also expanded rapidly in this period, from a mere 26 in 1904 to 1,145 ten years later, and became the envy of municipalities in Germany and far beyond.[278]

---

273. Steinmetz, *Regulating,* p. 200.

274. Ibid., pp. 178–82.

275. Weindling, *Health,* pp. 216–17.

276. Ibid., pp. 213–16.

277. Ibid., pp. 163–64.

278. Ibid., p. 180.

As in the formulation of labor policy, much of the impetus for this boom came from the reform milieu, which exerted pressure on state and federal governments as well. Arguing that hygiene was a means to increase "the capacity of service" of both individuals and state, the National Society for Public Health formulated a biological version of the integrationist message promoted by socialists of the lectern, Christian Socials, and the Association for Social Policy in the 1870s, which also informed the language of the February Decrees, as we have seen. Later, the German Association of Midwives won support from the League of German Women's Associations, Progressive People's Party, and Prussian Medical Advisory Committee, with the result that the Ministry of the Interior decreed a set curriculum for the training and accreditation of midwives, a reform of their fee structures, and an official textbook for standard instruction.[279] In 1902 Sombart's friend, the Breslau dermatologist Albert Neisser, joined Albert Blaschko, one of the Berlin doctors associated with the Friedrichshagen circle, to found the Society to Combat Venereal Diseases, which distributed pamphlets demanding sex education and insurance coverage for sexually transmitted diseases, eventually winning the ear of Bülow, who backed their efforts with grants from the Prussian and federal governments.[280]

Not all reformers greeted such cozy ties with Imperial authorities, which were a source of controversy within the milieu. Koch's Institute in Berlin, for instance, evoked opposition from a colleague at the University, Ernst Leyden, who spearheaded the campaign for open-air tuberculosis sanatoria run by municipal, rather than state officials. Here distrust of the state dovetailed with neo-Lamarckian resistance to the new science of bacteriology, which appeared to reinforce Weismann's theory of hard heredity in its early years. Leyden's crusade was taken up by the Society for National Hygiene and the Patriotic Women's Leagues, which were promoting the environmental approach by setting up a network of Workers' Gardens in the city during these years as well. While the debates over heredity remained a bone of contention, opinions on the role of the state could change. When Prussian and Imperial authorities offered to join Berlin's city government in support of the Empress Auguste Victoria House, the

279. Ibid., pp. 194–96.
280. Ibid., pp. 181–82.

coalition of doctors, hygienists, and feminists behind the campaign eagerly accepted. Providing training for women as professionals specializing in infant hospital care, the Victoria House integrated both demands and discourse of Wilhelmine feminism into a federal institution, describing mothers as the "source of national strength," while the sanatoria campaign went on to establish the most tuberculosis clinics of any city in the world by 1910.[281] Regardless of unresolved tensions, the generation of 1890 built and kept on building in matters of public health right up to the First World War.

"Human Economics"

In Hellerau's tightly woven web of activities, members of the milieu could see a microcosm of the reformed national community they strove to create through an interlocking network of professional social-political institutions. Whether it was a matter of private initiative or public service, the success of these efforts depended on their ability to establish an intricate net of mutually interacting relationships like the one in Hellerau, reformers believed, to bring together the multitude of individual activities in an efficient and functional "organic whole." National economics had provided one compelling paradigm in support of such visions since the 1870s, and the prestigious biological sciences took their place alongside it in the following decades. The generation of 1890 looked to both for answers to the social question. Indeed, some socially conscious students even combined them in a double major, like Alfred Ploetz and Franz Oppenheimer. It seemed only natural that these young reformers should try to create a new academic discipline from the synthesis of economics and biology, a discipline that could legitimate the search for alternative modernities as well as professional careers in a new science of "human economics." Our examination of the infrastructure built to sustain the Wilhelmine reform milieu concludes by taking a look at two such attempts: the institutionalization of racial hygiene and sociology as academic disciplines. Emerging from bitter strife among competing factions, both illuminate the quarrelsome rivalries that quickened efforts to stake out new territory on the expanding terrain of anti-politics as well as a deep awareness of the tensions between science and humanism we encountered earlier. Yet they also highlight the

---

281. Ibid., pp. 164–67, 177, 203–6.

common ground on which these struggles occurred—the impulse to answer the social question not by fleeing modernity, but by resolving its contradictions, which drove the milieu together in founding institutions that would soon leave that original terrain far behind.

As an academic discipline, racial hygiene was largely a creation of the Berlin doctors associated with Bölsche, the Hauptmanns, and the other writers and artists of Friedrichshagen. While Ploetz pursued his double major, several other members of the group were among the socialistic students of medicine and economics in Berlin's Social Scientific Union, where they heard lectures by Sombart, Tönnies, Brentano, and Naumann, mingling with political scientists and law students sharing an interest in combining nationalism and organic socialism in a progressive synthesis. Alfred Grotjahn, the "medical socialist of the lectern" who talked politics with Tönnies in Kiel and maintained close ties to the Brauns in Berlin, was part of this circle, as was Ludwig Woltmann, who joined the Social Democrats, helping to define the Party's stance on socialized medical care, while Kautsky published favorable reviews of his work in *The New Age*.[282] Together with Oppenheimer, Blaschko, Hirschfeld, and Moll, Ploetz, Grotjahn, and Woltmann shared the socialistic and professional interests that bound the Berlin doctors closely together during the 1890s, but the debates over heredity and the social question shattered these ties at the turn of the century. Far from being a product of collegial effort, racial hygiene was born from the struggle for existence among competing visions of the new science and its social meaning.

"What do we learn from the principles of evolutionary theory with regard to the domestic political development and legislation of states?"[283] It was this question, posed in 1900 by the industrialist Alfred Krupp, that sparked the controversy among the erstwhile friends. Inspired by Haeckel, his "intellectual mentor," Krupp offered prizes for the best answer in an essay contest that solicited responses from leading academics and physicians, most of whom proposed some form of state socialism, but there was less agreement about its scientific foundations.[284] First prize went to

282. Ibid., pp. 119, 221.
283. Erhard Stölting, "Die anthroposoziologische Schule: Gestalt und Zusammenhänge eines wissenschaftlichen Institutionalisierungsversuchs," in Klingemann, ed., *Rassenmythos*, p. 137.
284. Weindling, *Health*, p. 117; Bickel, "Kritik," p. 174.

the hereditarian advocate of selectivist eugenics Wilhelm Schallmayer, who sided with Koch against the campaign for open-air sanatoria and condemned the "disastrous effects of hygiene and pity," but the award drew fire from Woltmann, recipient of Krupp's third prize and a target of Schallmayer's polemics against environmental reform. Emphasizing the "complex interaction of heredity, environment, climate, national history and economics" in the struggle for survival among the peoples of Europe, Woltmann's "anthroposociology" echoed Ratzel's anthropogeography, but instead of greeting humanity's return to racial unity, he insisted on preserving the purity of Germanic blood from the homogenizing forces of commerce greeted by his colleague in Leipzig.[285] To Schallmayer and Grotjahn, anthroposociology sounded more like mysticism than science, and Krupp's jury also criticized Woltmann's entry for its lack of scientific discipline. Yet another group rallied to his defense, however: the notorious Freiburg "phalanx" of racial anthropologists, including the future Nazi theorist Fritz Lenz, Otto Ammon, author of the round-head/long-head theory rejected by Ratzel and ridiculed by Sombart, and Eugen Fritz.[286]

Virulent anti-Semites and enthusiastic supporters of the Pan-German and Navy Leagues, these former students of Weismann had wandered from a "scientific" preoccupation with racial degeneration to the Aryan mysticism of Richard Wagner, Chamberlain, and Gobineau, and they seem like strange allies for the Social Democrat Woltmann, whose credibility they did little to improve, but he accepted their support all the same. Still, it was Woltmann who first tried to institutionalize racial hygiene—or "anthroposociology"—as a scholarly discipline. Although the attempt to "reconcile Marxism with Aryan mysticism" doubly removed him from the academic community, Woltmann founded the *Political-Anthropological Review* in 1901 in order to establish the presence of his field at the university and to assert its primacy over all other social sciences.[287] Winning two

---

285. Weindling, *Health*, p. 119; Stölting, "Schule," pp. 140–48. The jury of the contest included a national economist (Johannes Conrad), a historian (Dietrich Schafter), and a biologist (Heinrich Ernst Ziegler); Stölting, "Schule," p. 137.
286. Weindling, *Health*, pp. 96–112, 119, 162, 188; Stölting, "Schule," pp. 138–51; Bickel, "Kritik," p. 181.
287. Weindling, *Health*, pp. 119; Stölting, "Schule," p. 140; Chickering, *Men*, pp. 204–45.

thousand subscribers, the journal proved surprisingly successful in its first year, when it published articles by Naumann, Haeckel, Driesch, Hellpach, Lombroso, and even Schallmayer, but Woltmann's new friends soon did irreparable damage to its reputation. After his early death in 1907, the *Review* fell completely into the hands of radical nationalists, who promoted anti-Semitism and Aryan mysticism to a dwindling readership far from the academic circles the journal was meant to impress until it was finally banned together with the German Racist League for Protection and Defiance in 1922.[288]

A second, more successful attempt to establish racial hygiene as a science with academic credentials came from Ploetz, who founded the rival *Archive for Racial and Social Biology* with Haeckel's support in 1904.[289] While stressing the scholarly nature of his enterprise, Ploetz also realized he would need support outside the university in order to succeed, and he approached the racial anthropologists in hopes of working out a compromise, but the overtures ultimately came to nothing. The racial hygienist had more luck with the Monists, among whom environmental and hereditarian views maintained a tense co-existence in a movement united by the commitment to biology as a modern scientific means to further humanistic development, which was led by Haeckel and the energeticist Ostwald.[290] Supported by Monists, physicians, feminists, and his friends in Friedrichshagen, Ploetz founded the Society for Racial Hygiene in 1905.[291] Among its founding members were the temperance leader Gustav Bunge, the Munich medical advisor and Garden City supporter Max von Gruber, Johannes Unold and Haeckel from the Monist League, Bölsche and the Hauptmann brothers. Of the Society's 445 members in its first years, 111 were women, primarily doctors, many of whom also joined the radicals in the League for the

288. Weindling, *Health*, p. 129; Stölting, "Schule," pp. 153–58.
289. Weindling, *Health*, pp. 128–34; Stölting, "Schule," p. 140.
290. Hübinger, "Bewegung," pp. 246–59; Johannes Unold, "Monismus und Sozialpolitik," *Tat* 3, no. 1 (April 1911): 11–18. Unold looked to biology for a synthesis of individual forces and the social collective in much the same way as Bäumer: "The greater the freedom, the tighter the organization must develop, the greater the diversity the more closed the unity, if an individual or social organism wishes to increase its capacity for service."
291. Weindling, *Health*, pp. 141–54. For the founding committee, see NL Sombart 18b.

Protection of Mothers and Sexual Reform. Despite his own close ties to this group, Sombart chose not to join, however, and another member of the circle conspicuously absent from the founding meeting was Alfred Grotjahn.

While he supported Schallmayer in the Krupp prize controversy and shared his interest in "reproductive hygiene," the staunchly environmentalist Grotjahn rejected the hereditarian stance of Schallmayer and Ploetz and kept his distance from the Society. Like Ratzel (and Bäumer), Grotjahn insisted on the unity of the human race. Objecting to the term 'racial hygiene' *(Rassenhygiene)*, the medical socialist of the lectern suggested an unequivocally singular version of the word *(Rassehygiene)* before settling on 'social hygiene' as a more appropriate label for his version of the new science, which emphatically continued to support "the measures necessary to spread hygienic values among individuals and their offspring"—i.e., social reform—which Ploetz and Schallmayer had come to oppose.[292] This approach could certainly count on more support from the reform milieu, and it also proved far more successful at German universities.[293] While Grotjahn's personal ties to Social Democracy kept him from gaining an academic post—despite attempts to distance himself from the party— other physicians sharing his point of view did get appointments. Established in Vienna, the first chair of social hygiene went to Ludwig Teleky, who used it to promote social reform from the lectern after 1907, and by 1912 there were reformist professors of the new discipline in Munich and Berlin as well.[294] Finding his own movement in jeopardy, Ploetz moved to co-opt his successful friend into the Society, while Gruber did the same with Ignaz Kaup, Munich's social hygiene appointee. In the end Ploetz won out, and Grotjahn joined the Executive Committee by 1912.[295] Racial hygiene was the name that stuck, but it was the environmentalist approach that had led to its success.

The reformist impulse also brought leading members of the milieu together in the German Society for Sociology, where attempts to combine

---

292. Weindling, *Health*, p. 221.
293. Ibid., pp. 211–26.
294. The Berlin appointee Carl Flügge belonged to the Garden City Society and the Society for Social Reform; GfSR founding committee, NL Sombart 19; German Garden City Society membership list, insert, *Gartenstadt* 3 (1909).
295. Weindling, *Health*, p. 226.

biology and the social sciences in a progressive synthesis produced similar tensions, and it was here that Ploetz's Hamlet conflict was finally laid to rest. The scientific study of man emerged gradually from the interdisciplinary search for solutions to the social problem at German universities, where it remained a vaguely defined expression of the "social currents" Wilhelm Rein incorporated into his pedagogical system in Jena, until the desire for an institutional basis for this collaboration eventually led the generation of 1890 to found the sociological Society in 1909. Above all, the leaders of the new science came from national economics—Sombart, Weber, Tönnies, Herkner, Hermann Waentig, and Rudolf Goldscheid—but scholars from other social disciplines were also involved, including members of the Leipzig circle (Lamprecht, Bücher, Ostwald), as were non-academic social reformers such as Jaffé and Jastrow, the labor relations experts of the Institute for Public Welfare who helped Sombart found the Society for Social Reform, and even the revisionist socialists Bernstein and Eduard David, who joined the Berlin doctors Grotjahn, Oppenheimer, Moll, and Sommer at the founding congress.[296] In order to ensure the representation of "scientific sociology," Weber specifically urged that Ploetz be included in the Executive Committee, and it was at his request that Sombart approached the leader of German racial hygiene, who readily accepted, joining shortly after the Society was founded in 1909.[297] Ploetz had long since renounced the social commitments at the core of the new discipline, however, and his open antipathy to reform sparked a major controversy when the Society "jumped into biology with both feet" at the first German Sociologists' Congress the following year.[298]

Arguing that social reform had a "counter-selective" effect on the nation's genetic stock, Ploetz evoked a furious response from Tönnies, who had been drawn into the fray over the Krupp prize contest ten years earlier, when he had strongly defended environmental reform, and now reiterated his attack on Schallmayer's merciless social biology, ridiculing Ploetz's "sci-

---

296. Kruse, "Nationalökonomie," pp. 149–65; "Einladung zum Beitritt zur Deutschen Gesellschaft für Soziologie"; NL Sombart 18b.

297. Tönnies to Hermann Beck, October 27, 1909; NL Sombart 18b.

298. Robert Sommer, quoted in Karl-Siegbert Rehberg, "Das Bild des Judentums in der frühen deutschen Soziologie. 'Fremdheit' und 'Rationalität' als Typusmerkmale bei Werner Sombart, Max Weber und Georg Simmel," in Klingemann, ed., *Rassenmythos*, p. 107.

entific" definition of race and proclaiming social reform to be "the best eugenics."[299] Weber, who had invited the racial hygienist into the Society and was currently undertaking his own studies "On Selection and Adaptation (Career Choice and Career Destiny) of the Workforce in Enclosed Heavy Industry," noted that "personally and subjectively" he believed "the significance of the biological genotype should be highly appraised," but given the tentative state of the new science, racial hygiene had yet to produce any definitive findings useful for sociological analysis. Echoing reservations Sombart had already expressed in his "scientific" investigation of the "Jewish question," Weber went on to warn urgently against importing subjective value judgments into scholarship in the guise of objective categories, a point he drove home with examples of American scholarly prejudice against blacks.[300] The issue remained unresolved, however, and Sombart closed the congress on a conciliatory note, stressing that "the Sociological Society in no way wishes to reject the community of interests with biology."[301] For the next two years, the disagreement simmered on both sides. Apparently determined to settle the matter once and for all, Tönnies set "The Concepts of People and Nation in the Context of Race, State, and Language" as the agenda for the German Sociologists' Congress of 1912.[302] Oppenheimer led the attack on Ploetz in a speech on the "Racial Theoretical Philosophy of History," and Weber reported that he had still found no use for racial hygienic concepts in his worker-utility studies.[303] Embittered by failure to get the Jewish question included on the agenda, Sombart belittled the objections of Oppenheimer and Weber, arguing that environmental and hereditarian views were equally lacking in scientific foundations, a claim that by no means reflected his own views on the subject and opened the door for a stormy controversy over personal attitudes toward social reform that had nothing to do with science. That, at

---

299. Bickel, "Kritik," pp. 81–83, 185–95; Weindling, *Health*, pp. 121–22.

300. Sabine Frommer, "Naturalismus und Naturalismuskritik: Emil Kraepelins Arbeiterpsychologie und ihre Rezeption durch Max Weber," in Hübinger, Bruch, et al., *Kultur*, pp. 190–91, 197–204; Rehberg, "Bild," p. 108; Peukert, *Diagnose*, pp. 96–98.

301. Becker, *Geschichte*, p. 76.

302. Tönnies to German Society for Sociology Executive Committee, November 5, 1911; "Einladung zum 2. Soziologentag," NL Sombart 18b.

303. Rehberg, "Bild," pp. 108–9.

least, was the opinion of Weber, who resigned from the Society's Executive Committee in order to maintain his commitment to "value-free" scholarship.[304]

The outcome of the 1912 congress had important consequences for the future of both German sociology and social reform. Determined to stamp out the influence of Ploetz, Tönnies seized on Weber's argument for objectivity as his most effective weapon, thus severing the Society's ties to the reformist impulse that had led him and many others to sociology in the first place. When hygienists planned to found a "Social Biological Section" in 1914, the Society's chairman cloaked his objections in an affirmation of "objective" scholarship. "This is of course not meant as a judgment on the trend," Tönnies explained. "But it definitely belongs in a different context, just as social policy remains outside our social and political research projects."[305] Ruling out all discussion of social as well as racial hygiene, this "schoolmarmish pretentiousness" so enraged Grotjahn that he immediately quit the Society and used the first meeting of its new section to found an independent organization.[306] In one sense, of course, this was certainly a victory, since it rid sociology of the pernicious "scientific" attempts to master the social question linking hidden racial prejudices to the victory of Weismannism after the turn of the century, which unquestionably contributed to "the genesis of the 'final solution' from the spirit of science," as Peukert argued in his assessment of Weber's confrontation with Ploetz.[307] Yet from another perspective, it also unleashed a ruthless drive for "objective" knowledge of "biological man" that was no less subjective in orientation but had been cut loose from moorings in the humanistic values that

---

304. Weber to Beck, October 22, 1912, NL Sombart 18b. Written the day the congress ended, the letter reads: "I will no longer attend Sociologists' Congresses. It is clear that guarantees for maintaining the limits of discussion defined by the statutes are not to be had, and I would thus constantly arouse the same agitation as this time again and again." Weber resigned from the Society itself just before the hygienists founded the Social Biological Section; Weber to Beck, January 17, 1914, NL Sombart 18b.

305. Tönnies to German Society for Sociology Executive Committee, March 3, 1914, NL Sombart 18b.

306. Grotjahn to Beck, March 8, 1914; protocol of the Social Biology Section's first meeting, NL Sombart 18b; see also Bickel, "Kritik," p. 183.

307. Peukert, *Diagnose,* pp. 95–100, 108–9.

led Wilhelmine reformers to look to science for solutions and had long kept their progressive aspirations from spilling over into the "fantasies of omnipotence" Peukert discerned. It was, after all, hardly the case that "only a few like Max Weber warned" against a naively optimistic faith in science. Nor was an "uncompromising attitude against the inhumanity of a realm of racist master men" the essence of Weber's critique of Ploetz in the eyes of many contemporaries. Like Bäumer, many progressive reformers decried the refusal to acknowledge and *affirm* the subjective in the scientific study of humankind as the cowardly "half-education" of a privileged elite who could afford to remain indifferent to the personal fate of the masses and were above all responsible for the "ghastly calculation" of population policy. It was this awareness of the dark potential lurking in scientific reason that led Damaschke, Bäumer, Sombart—and Tönnies—to expressions that were indistinguishable (on the surface) from the "anti-modernism" uncovered by liberal historians in the 1960s. And it was their resolve to rescue the progressive potential of modern science and technology from this danger by binding them firmly to an avowedly subjective, humanistic agenda, to "compel these means into its service" through the "force and incandescence of the cultural ideal" of liberal humanism, that casts them beneath the "dark shadows of modernity" from the more critical perspective of recent years. With the creation of the German Society for Social Biology in 1914, the crucial link between science and humanism that sustained the search for a more livable future seemed to have been broken, along with that between sociology and social reform.

For the generation of 1890, however, these ties were strong, too strong to dissolve overnight as the result of an argument between two friends and reformers—Tönnies and Grotjahn—who had once spent their evenings together discussing the revisionist socialism of Bernstein and Heinrich Braun in Kiel. Before sociology turned its back on reform, war and revolution would have to shatter many more bonds, twisting the fabric of the anti-political reform web and distorting the vision of a new national community. In 1914, after all, Hellerau was still in its heyday, a place where Oppenheimer, Grotjahn, Ploetz, and other sociologists could lay aside their differences and engage actively in building alternative modernities. Weber was right to say that the Society for Sociology could not maintain an "objective" distance to the social question in these years. For the men and women of the milieu, science called for a commitment to *The Deed*, and no one expressed the ambivalence of its progressive message more powerfully than a leader of the sociological Society itself, Rudolf Goldscheid.

A member of the Monist League and the German Peace Society, Gold-scheid had studied national economics in Berlin and Vienna before accepting an academic post in the Austrian capital, where he established a local sociology association in 1909, the same year the German Society was founded.[308] A year after Tönnies and Ploetz locked horns at the first Sociologists' Congress, he presented his own views on the relations between science and reform in *Upward Development and Human Economics: The Foundations of Social Biology*. Refusing to describe evolution as 'descent,' Goldscheid pushed the milieu's progressive optimism well into the danger zone Peukert defined, revealing the ominous prospects ever within range of commitments to harness the power of modern science to raise the quality of life. "Just as Marx enlightened us about the economic laws of motion in modern society," he proclaimed, "the theory of ascent reveals its biological laws."[309] If humans had once been "marionettes" of the historical process, they could now become its "demigods," since "the successes of social bio-technology" were rendering superstitious fear of the laws governing life unnecessary, just as physics had enabled "our domination over inorganic matter" in the last century. "We need only seize the courage in our own ability," Goldscheid wrote. Among the comprehensive package of reforms that he promoted in order to achieve more "economy in the use of human material" was "preventive selection in severe cases of the genetically handicapped, bacterially infected, and those damaged beyond repair by alcohol or other poisons," a demand that echoed the official position taken by the League of German Women's Associations after the debates over abortion a few years earlier, as we have seen.[310]

Yet *Upward Development* also contained a 127-page assault on Weismannism, which Goldscheid denounced as an "intentionally-planned, reactionary treatment" of Darwin's ideas, and vociferous appeals for both environmental social reform and the democratization of Germany's "atavistic," authoritarian regime.[311] Like Bäumer, the sociologist insisted that rigid discipline and blind obedience were crippling the life of the nation, which needed individual initiative—"extremely mobile regulators with sufficient capacity for service"—in order to prosper in the modern world, and

---

308. "Rudolf Goldscheid," *NDB*.

309. Rudolf Goldscheid, *Höherentwicklung und Menschenökonomie: Grundlegung der Sozialbiologie* (Leipzig: W. Klinkhardt, 1911), p. xx.

310. Ibid., pp. xvii–xviii, xxvi, 447–51.

311. Ibid., pp. 225–352, quotation p. 225.

he also echoed her calls for integrating women into the public sphere.[312] Describing the women's question as the most "urgent evolutionary problem" of the day, he warned that "our present cultural system will not be fit for survival, far less capable of rising to its maximum capacity for service" unless women were hired as teachers and civil servants. This "union of motherhood and career" would build bridges from family life to the life of the nation, but Goldscheid went beyond demands for social and economic rights to call for political emancipation as well: "the family would be recognized in parliament and thus socially and organically for the first time."[313] In order to increase Germany's "organic capital," he further recommended "popular and civic education" for the "most intensive qualification of the cerebrum as central regulator," along with a host of other reforms to assist the upward-striving: workers' protection, housing reform, maternity insurance, child and juvenile care, abolition of prostitution, temperance measures, prevention of sexually transmitted diseases, and Imperial Health Departments devoted to "racial fitness" and the "preservation and augmentation of national health and the corporeal as well as psychic energy of the people." There could be "no more productive investment of financial capital," Goldscheid insisted. "It is organic surplus value that we create from the greatest technical surplus value."[314]

Lest there be any doubt about the ultimate aim of all this productive efficiency, however, Goldscheid followed his compendium of progressive reforms with a stern warning directed against those who opposed the maintenance of humanistic values in the name of objective science. "[W]e are indeed at present confronted with this sort of misuse of science. *Instead of attending only to science, we sin at the costs of science!*" the sociologist declared, after condemning visions of aristocratic breeding promoted by racial nationalists.

> We suffer the continued existence and heightening of the most unhealthy and damaging conditions for development in the secure trust that the progress of science itself will again repair all evils. And we make ourselves guilty of the same crime against humanity as we do against science. *Not with laboring under too much humanitarianism is the present to be reproached, as is falsely and wickedly asserted again and again, but with sanctioning, indeed of*

---

312. Ibid., p. 175.
313. Ibid., pp. 453–57.
314. Ibid., pp. 447–51.

seeking by all means to uphold conditions that make an excess of humanitarian measures absolutely essential if society is not to perish for want of Kultur.[315]

Goldscheid's *Human Economics,* which blended the science of Marx and Darwin to present the compelling paradigm of an integrated and efficient, yet also humane national and social community, emerged from the classrooms and social circles of the generation of 1890, just like the ideas of Damaschke, Bäumer, Sombart, and so many others in the Wilhelmine reform milieu. Familiar as it was in the anti-political space occupied by these young men and women, Goldscheid's vision seems strange to us today, but also strangely familiar—not only for the concept of "human material" later ground to dust in the well-oiled machine of National Socialist genocide, but also for the progressive evolutionism it expressed in 1911. The term that fits Goldscheid's message so well was in fact coined to describe the synthesis of economics and biology promoted by American sociologists during these same years. "Early sociologists were as much heirs of the Enlightenment as critics of it," William Fine has written in his analysis, which might easily be extended to include the German case:

They did not abandon the idea of a science of man; they believed in its positive benefits for social improvement, and the possibilities of social engineering; enhancement of democracy through public opinion and mass education; liberation of the individual from outworn institutional forms and traditional constraints; the extension of opportunity for individual achievement and mobility. Finally, they accepted the promise of modern industrialism, communications, and transportation as vehicles for social progress.[316]

In both countries, the new science evolved from a confluence of social, cultural, and intellectual currents that came together in movements for housing and land reform, women's rights, social justice, temperance, neo-Malthusianism, and "reproductive hygiene," with equally ambivalent results.[317] If enthusiasm for modern, scientific solutions led some reformers to push successfully for the first laws on sterilization and eugenicist mar-

---

315. Ibid., pp. 469–70, emphasis in the original.

316. William Fine, *Progressive Evolutionism and American Sociology, 1890–1920* (Ann Arbor, Mich.: UMI Research Press, 1979), p. 173.

317. Arthur A. Ekirch, Jr., *Progressivism in America: A Study of the Era from Theodore Roosevelt to Woodrow Wilson* (New York: New Viewpoints, 1974), pp. 40–77.

riage restrictions in the United States, leading voices demanded the preservation of ethical standards in the modern world just as passionately.[318]
Like the progressives of Kloppenberg's *Uncertain Victory,* Wilhelmine reformers also were seeking a "via media" that would lead between the excesses of positivism and idealism, liberalism and socialism, toward a common horizon where the best of both worlds might be found.[319] This was a
perilous endeavor, and the intellectuals and activists of the milieu cannot
evade responsibility if the road they found later met up with the many
others leading to the "philanthropic pathos" of Himmler's camps.[320] "In
the historical field of possibilities this too was possible," as Peukert rightly
observes; "there was also the option for racial primacy of the national body
over the individual and of the 'valuable' over the 'worthless,' " a danger of
which Wilhelmine reformers remained deeply aware. But it was not the
only outcome. Nor was it the one most of them envisioned. "Progressive
evolutionism" followed many, forking paths into the twentieth century,
some of which did not end in disaster, and many more were left untaken.
The vision of 1890 lies scattered among them all.

---

318. Donal Pickens, *Eugenics and the Progressives* (Nashville: Vanderbildt Univer-
      sity Press, 1968), pp. 75–90; Kloppenberg, *Victory,* pp. 115–44.
319. Kloppenberg, *Victory,* pp. 15–63, 395–415.
320. Peukert, *Diagnose,* pp. 111–12.

War and Revolutions

"All good history writing begins at the end," Timothy Mason aptly wrote of the treacherous business of assigning meaning to historical work.[1] "However artfully it may be disguised, however unthinkingly it may be assumed, the end of the story is there at the beginning. Where the end is judged to lie in time, what its character is, how it is defined—in taking these decisions about any piece of work, historians necessarily make their judgment about the general significance of their particular theme or period." The Wilhelmine search for alternative modernities began in the classrooms and social circles where the "younger generation" learned the social question, in the discourses of national economics and biology that informed both problem and solution, in the unforgettable moment when the reform decrees of the "Workers' Kaiser" came in February 1890. From there it led through quarrels over territory and tactics, heredity and humanism, nationalism and socialism, *Zivilisation* and *Kultur,* the matrix of issues and goals that bound Wilhelmine reformers all the more tightly to the terrain of anti-politics, where socially conscious men and women of the most diverse backgrounds managed to work together in building institutions and professional careers, the foundations of a future they hoped would be at once modern and humane. But where does the story end, and what judgments shall we make about its significance?

Let us say it ends, as this study does, in the summer of 1914. It can certainly be argued that the heyday of Hellerau marked the culmination of the milieu's historical development. While in official quarters, the re-

---

1. Timothy Mason, *Social Policy in the Third Reich: The Working Class and the "National Community"* (Providence: Berg Publishers, 1993), p. 15.

formist impulse had once more stalled in the latest of the recurrent reactions that punctuated the expansion of Wilhelmine social policy, and while the "sharper key" drove the pitch of nationalist rhetoric and tensions between left and right to new heights in the political sphere, public health and welfare institutions were employing increasing numbers of social policy experts trained by the generation of 1890, Ploetz's "Hamlet conflict" had been laid to rest with the exclusion of selectivist racial hygiene from the scientific paradigms instituted to sustain their quiet efforts, and Naumann's anti-political successes—the Werkbund and Garden Cities—stood on solid foundations. The movements led by Damaschke, Bäumer, and Sombart also seemed to have come into their own. The land reform League had been growing rapidly, attendance at its seminars had more than doubled since 1911, and with the federal capital gains tax achieved, the BDB was launching a new campaign for "homesteads" for the underclasses. Wilhelmine feminists could likewise note with encouragement the increasing employment of women in municipal institutions built to match the functions of "social motherhood" as defined by moderates and radicals alike. Winning conservative groups away from the spiritual tutelage of Stumm and Stöcker, Bäumer had finally convinced the "philistines" of the Progressive party to endorse the principle of women's suffrage, but in the summer of 1914 her attention was trained on the non-partisan, cultural politics of womanhood, on plans for a joint exhibit with the Werkbund, on the "entire web of modern life reforms" she believed were leading from "the black middle ages of industry, with their roaring, smoking, crude works . . . into its bright renaissance." Of the three case studies, only Sombart had lost faith in such solutions. But the Society for Social Reform was continuing to build on his old "Ideals of Social Policy," which seemed closer to reality than ever, and when the institution won the endorsement of Free Union leaders in its struggle against Delbrück's "reasonable social policy" in May, Sombart's former colleagues might well have echoed his own defiant affirmation of 1900—*Nevertheless!*

Of course, none of this could stop the fatal sequence of events and decisions in the corridors of power that was about to shatter the world of Wilhelmine anti-politics forever. Lack of political force had in fact defined the milieu's horizons, which were always severely limited, vulnerable, dependent on the Empire's sham constitution for both survival and success. What would become of the elaborate network of unofficial channels through which progressive reformers informed public policy without the need for political compromise if municipalities were ruled by a democratic franchise, or if the Reichstag ceased to be a theater of comic illusion? Such sweeping change was at best a remote possibility in Wilhelmine Germany, and it was only by pushing aside debates over these hypothetical issues that intellectuals, activists, and professionals were able to focus on building the framework for an alternative modernity grounded in the here and now. While progressives in Western Europe and America constructed similar networks under different conditions, the peculiarities of the German political system acted as "incubator" for the Wilhelmine reform milieu in many ways.[2] These fragile, yet protective confines were crushed by the First World War. When the Social Democrats joined with Liberals to vote for military credits, the long-standing barriers between right and left fell to reveal an altered landscape in which the "conditions of public life" held possibilities for significant change, making political engagement a "moral duty" once more. At the same time the government opened its doors to the milieu and its proposals, which sustained this "civic peace" as official policies behind the German war effort. Far behind the trenches, the terrain of anti-politics was trampled in the invasion of German social and economic life. "What is that to us today?" Bäumer asked of articles she had written just weeks before on August 13, 1914. "A voice from a sunken world. Something that no longer concerns us at all."[3]

Damaschke's "truly national" mission, the "more corporeal, more concrete" humanism of Bäumer's eugenics, Sombart's clashes with Naumann, and the resonant appeal of *Anti-Politik* all belonged to that world. There are thus good reasons for ending our story with its final days, before the deluge of war and revolutions washed out the delicate features of a landscape filled with bright prospects, dark shadows, the many alternative paths later submerged under the "spirit of 1914." What we are left with in this case is a picture of Wilhelmine political culture decidedly modern in its contours, in which moderate voices still vigorously contested the claims of radicals to the discourse of 'national community,' 'human economics,' the 'Unpolitical German,' even 'national socialism,' the meanings of which remained up for grabs. If it bears some traces of a German "special path,"

---

2. For the notion of "incubator" I am indebted to Mack Walker's analysis of the Holy Roman Empire in *German Home Towns: Community, State, and General Estate, 1648–1871* (Ithaca: Cornell University Press, 1971), pp. 11–33.

3. Bäumer, "Heimatchronik," *Hilfe* 20, no. 33 (August 13, 1914): 528.

this terrain was by no means as unfamiliar to Western eyes as has often been maintained and is perhaps no more distinctive than the routes reformers in other industrializing countries took past the same landmarks: Marxism and Darwinism, humanistic ethics, rationalization, order and efficiency, the twin Enlightenment impulses of human emancipation and scientific and technological advance. Like its counterparts elsewhere, the Wilhelmine reform milieu bordered on extremes of modern nationalism and technocratic rationalism as well as anti-modern flights of fancy, which were also a part of its world, but the broad middle ground has vanished from subsequent maps of socialized Germany along with the cutting edge of Howe's lost modernity of 1914. By ending with that summer, we preserve much of the "original ambivalence" and perhaps some of the "great potential" many found there in coming to terms with the future, adding to the rich, complex historical portrait of Imperial Germany that is gradually beginning to resurface in our continuing efforts to come to terms with the past.[4]

But there are also compelling reasons for choosing a later date. After all, both the discourse and the practices of the Wilhelmine search for alternatives survived long after the space of anti-politics had collapsed, and by the time Howe returned in 1914, the First World War had already given a new, darker urgency to his warnings about Germany's decisive advantages over the liberal democracies of the West. While many reformers of the milieu joined Rudolf Goldscheid in the peace movement, urging an immediate cessation to hostilities and a return to the status quo ante, many more seized on the "civic peace" as a realization of their pre-war visions of a reformed national community.[5] Working for the integration of socialist labor in the German Society of 1914, the Free Patriotic Union, and the National League for Freedom and Fatherland, they also joined Naumann to confer with government officials on plans to transform the wartime alliance of Central Powers into a permanent federal union built on the foundations of the new German economy.[6] Damaschke, Bäumer, and Som-

---

4. Nipperdey, *Geschichte*, vol. 1., p. 824.
5. The pacifists Gerlach, Quidde, Rade, and Helene Stöcker joined Goldscheid in the League of the New Fatherland, which sharply opposed chauvinistic or annexationist policies and was censored after 1916; Fricke, *Lexikon*, vol. 1, pp. 351–60.
6. The German Society of 1914 was a forum for government, business, and labor representatives, including Rathenau, Robert Bosch, Gustav Krupp, Alfred Hu-

bart rushed to serve the nation as well. While "Homesteads for Warriors" became the goal of the land reformer's latest campaign, receiving hearty endorsements from Hindenburg, Ludendorff, and Tirpitz, on the day of mobilization Bäumer presented the BDF's 1912 proposals for a National Women's Service to the government, which readily accepted them.[7] Social Democratic and radical feminists also pledged support for the Service, and by 1916 women had assumed leading roles in the municipal administration of the domestic war effort, as well as a place in local branches of the War Office.[8] As we have seen, Sombart welcomed the "miracle" of war, which momentarily broke the spell of his cultural pessimism, with special enthusiasm. Greeting the "national community, concentrated into unity," the economist insisted that the "heroes" of Potsdam and Weimar stood "completely in unison" against the materialistic "traders" of the "English world

genberg, Harnack, Sering, Meinecke, Jäckh, Schiffer, and Eduard David; Fricke, *Lexikon,* vol. 1, pp. 700–3. The Free Patriotic Union opposed annexationist aims and avoided close relations with government; its members included Jäckh, Gerhart Hauptmann, Harnack, and Sering; Fricke, *Lexikon,* vol. 2, pp. 663–65. The Working Committee for Central Europe included Naumann, Bosch, Herkner, Merton, Jäckh, Rösicke, and Hjalmar Schacht. Catholic members of the milieu—Behrens, Rade, Giesberts, and Hitze—pursued similar aims in the Association "Central European League of States"; Fricke, *Lexikon,* vol. 3, pp. 366–68. On Naumann's plan for a Central European union, see Friedrich Naumann, *Mitteleuropa* (Berlin: Georg Reimer, 1915).

7. Adolf Damaschke, "Der Krieg und die Bodenreform," *Bodenreform* 25, no. 16 (August 20, 1614): 482–84. The Central Committee for Warrior Homesteads was founded in March 1915 and had 814 corporate members less than four months later; "Der Hauptausschuß für Kriegerheimstätten," *Bodenreform* 26, no. 7 (April 5, 1915): 199–201: "Rundschau," *Bodenreform* 26, no. 13 (July 5, 1915). The BDB's membership also grew by leaps and bounds; see reports in *Bodenreform.* On the National Women's Service, "Versammlungen und Vereine," *Frau* 21, no. 12 (September 1914): 757; Huber, *Bäumer,* p. 86; Barbara Guttmann, *Weibliche Heimarmee: Frauen in Deutschland 1914–1918* (Weinheim: Deutscher Studien Verlag, 1989), p. 131.

8. Gertrud Bäumer, "Heimatchronik," *Hilfe* 20, no. 33 (August 13, 1914): 528; Bäumer, *Die deutsche Frau in der sozialen Kriegsfürsorge* (Gotha: Perthes, 1916); Guttmann, *Heimarmee,* pp. 23–24, 135–51; Gerhard, *Unerhört,* p. 318; correspondence between Else Lüders and Bäumer, October 14–18, 1914, HLA 13–47[2–3].

empire," which had been pieced together "like a sum of capital." While the "organic-objective" model of the state assured victory in this "*German war*," Sombart warned that the nation would have to seal itself off permanently from the decadent influence of the West to preserve its integrity after the peace: "Have no fear, dear neighbors: we won't swallow you whole. What would we do with that indigestible bit of food in our stomach?"[9]

One might easily end the story in 1915, the year Sombart and Howe saw German efficiency and solidarity as decisive advantages over the West, when Bäumer mocked British inability to comprehend "the land of state-socialist wartime regulations," and leading politicians from across the spectrum joined government, military, and labor leaders to praise Damaschke as a prophet of national community on his fiftieth birthday.[10] National chauvinism, xenophobia, militarism, an irrational emphasis on the "spirit," the utter subjugation of individuals to the state would dominate the tone of such a conclusion.[11] The ideals of ethical culture and humanism would lead not to the repudiation of Weismannism and selectivist eugenics, but instead to acclamations of a "deeply rooted reverence for service and joy in work" during the "holy war."[12] Rather than expressing an attempt to curb the excesses of laissez-faire capitalism and revolutionary socialism while preserving the promise of both progressive ideologies in a new, dynamic synthesis, critiques of Manchester liberalism and Marxism would

---

9. Sombart, *Händler*, pp. 35, 53, 76, 93, 124, 143, emphasis in the original.

10. Gertrud Bäumer, "Heimatchronik," *Hilfe* 21, no. 22 (June 3, 1915): 347. On Damaschke, see introduction to Chapter 2.

11. While Sombart's *Traders and Heroes* is a particularly extreme example, these elements can also be detected in the wartime writings of Damaschke: "Weihnachten 1914," *Bodenreform* 25, no. 24 (December 20, 1914): 677; "Zerbrochene Hoffnungen," *Bodenreform* 26, no. 12 (December 20, 1915): 350–53; "Deine Aufgabe," *Bodenreform* 28, no. 18 (September 20, 1917): 493; "Ludendorff," *Bodenreform* 29, no. 21 (November 5, 1918): 335–40. For Bäumer, see "Einkehr," *Frau* 22, no. 1 (October 20, 1914): 4–7; "Das geistige und das militärische Deutschland," *Hilfe* 51, no. 1(January 7, 1915): 7–8; "Heimatchronik," *Hilfe* 21, no. 22 and 23 (June 3 and 10, 1915): 347, 363; "Heimatchronik," *Hilfe* 21, no. 38 (September 23, 1915): 607. See also Helene Lange, "Die Umwertung aller Werte," *Frau* 22, no. 1 (October 1914): 1–4.

12. Gertrud Bäumer, "Der deutsche Geist in der Lebensanschauung," in *Schützengräben*, p. 117; Damaschke, "Deine Aufgabe," p. 493.

indicate nothing more than a reactionary, militaristic "service ideology" and the "failure of illiberalism." The passionate warnings against the dangers of fleet-building and state socialism, the powers of the bureaucracy and the "military spirit" would seem as meaningless as they had apparently become for Damaschke, Bäumer, and Sombart when they touted the civic peace as the realization of their hopes and dreams. If 1915 is a fitting end, the Wilhelmine search for alternatives has little to add to the familiar "song of the Unpolitical German and his special path."

But again, one could go further. The euphoria of 1915 quickly dissipated, and while Sombart lapsed back into despair, Damaschke and Bäumer soon repeated their past warnings against the excesses of radical nationalism.[13] Recognition that the national community of wartime contrasted sharply with the decentralized, "cleaner, quieter" version Bäumer had promoted in the "pre-August" days of peace was especially strong in the case of the BDF leader, who saw the "burden of hatred" as a tragic one and was sickened by spectacles of "hurrah patriotism" from the start.[14] After all, it was also in 1915 that she reviled the "ghastly calculation" of population policy, and her bitterness over the "inorganic" nature of compulsory restrictions, censorship, and "over-centralization" only increased as the war went on.[15] "A little democratic spirit" once again became a dynamic alternative to the stifling, "mechanistic" force of the state, as Bäumer pushed for voluntary cooperation between public and private sectors as the best means to achieve productive efficiency by stimulating personal initiative along with the incentive for profit. Condemning resistance to social reform and democratization, she denounced the Fatherland Party as a "painful renunciation of the spirit of 1914," launching a campaign for universal suffrage and the rights of women and workers to jobs and homes after the

13. Adolf Damaschke, "Ernste Zahlen," *Bodenreform* (October 5, 1916): 625–28; Damaschke, "Lloyd George und die Kriegerheimstätten," *Bodenreform* 28, no. 23 (December 5, 1917): 583–86. On Sombart's retreat, see Lenger, *Sombart*, p. 249.

14. Bäumer used the term 'voraugustlich,' implicitly comparing the revolutionary transformations of 1914 to the revolution that ended "pre-March" Germany in 1848, in "Heimatchronik," *Hilfe* 21, no. 13 (April 1, 1915): 199.

15. Gertrud Bäumer, "Heimatchronik," *Die Hilfe* 22, no. 3 (January 20, 1916): 39–40; see also Helene Lange, "Überzentralisation," *Frau* 24, no. 7 (April 1917): 403–4.

war in 1917.[16] When the revolution came in 1918, Damaschke, Bäumer, and Sombart claimed it as their own, just as they had the civic peace four years earlier.[17]

Bäumer's appeals for "organic democracy" and a new politics of womanhood (which now included a natural affinity to pacifism), the reunion of leading members of the milieu (including Bäumer and Sombart) as founders of the Democratic People's League, Damaschke's candidacy for the German Democratic Party in 1920 might offer a conclusion more in line with the broad strokes of the story before 1914.[18] While the anti-

16. See Bäumer's serial "Heimatchronik" in *Hilfe* 23, no. 38 (September 20, 1917): 583; no. 40 (October 4, 1917): 611; 22, no. 4 (January 27, 1916): 54. See also her series on "Social Questions of the Future" in *Frau*, 24, no. 1 (October 1915): 5–11; no. 2 (November 1916): 65–72; no. 3 (December 1916): 131–36; and no. 5 (February 1917): 254–62; and Bäumer, "Die Neuorientierung und die Frauen," *Hilfe* 23, no. 23 (June 7, 1917): 379–80; "Vom inneren Frieden des deutschen Volkes," *Hilfe* 22, no. 2 (July 13, 1916): 453–55; "Die Frauenfrage im künftigen Deutschland," *Hilfe* 22, no. 23 (June 8, 1916): 375–78; "Die Überwindung des Klassenkampfes," *Hilfe* 24, no. 11 (March 14, 1918): 117–19; "Aufstieg und Arbeitsorganisation," *Hilfe* 24, no. 22 (May 30, 1918): 254–55.

17. While disturbed by the dissolution of the "civic peace" into civil war, all three saw capitalism as the primary target of the revolution, which vindicated their social political standpoints; Adolf Damaschke, "An unsere Freunde," *Bodenreform* 29, no. 22(November 18, 1920): 345; Gertrud Bäumer, "Die Seele der Revolution," *Hilfe* 25, no. 15 (April 20, 1919): 179–80; "Der Geist der neuen Volksgemeinschaft," *Hilfe* 25, no. 25 (June 19, 1919); and "Der Fluch der Masse," *Hilfe* 25, no. 27 (July 3, 1919): 347; on Sombart, see Lenger, *Sombart*, p. 283.

18. Gertrud Bäumer, "Die Frau als Wähler," *Hilfe* 24, no. 47 (November 21, 1918): 560–61; "Zwischen den Zeiten," *Frau* 26, no. 3 (December 1918): 72; "Die Frauen in der deutschen Demokratie," *Frau* 26, no. 4 (January 1919): 102–6; "Die Geburt des neuen Deutschland," *Hilfe* 24, no. 46 (November 14, 1918): 76. See also Gertrud Bäumer's series on "Inner Renewal" in *Hilfe* 24, no. 46 (November 14, 1918): 543–45; and no. 48 (November 28, 1918): 575–76; and 25, no. 1 (January 2, 1918): 11–13; and another series on "Clarification on the Concept of Soviets," also in *Hilfe* 25, no. 20 (May 15, 1919): 245–46; no. 21 (May 22, 1919): 252–54; no. 23 (June 5, 1919): 282–84; and no. 24 (June 12, 1919): 294–95. Other members of the Democratic People's League included Rathenau, Bosch, Brentano, Meinecke, Giesberts, Heuss, Jäckh, Naumann,

political space of the Wilhelmine era could not be reconstructed in the Weimar Republic, the conviction that fundamental transformations of Germany's social and economic structures needed to accompany its political revolution if democracy was not to substitute "mammonarchy" for monarchy sustained the continued search for alternatives in the 1920s.[19] Once again restyled to fit new conditions, the land reform League's campaign that had begun in 1912 went on, now striving for "economic," or "housing homesteads," while Social Democratic women joined in the struggle for social status and "social motherhood" in the controversial field of Weimar welfare, and Bäumer used her new positions in the Reichstag and the Ministry of the Interior to promote "unity schools" as the foundations for a new system of national education that cut across the lines of class and confession.[20] For his part, Sombart completed the third volume of *Modern Capitalism,* in which he stressed the gradual convergence of capitalism and socialism in a new economic order, and explored the possibilities of a neo-corporatist social structure as its basis.[21] Although transformed by the upheavals since 1914, the milieu's vision of a reformed national community built on the progressive synthesis of the 1890s continued to inspire moderate efforts that competed with new and more radical extremes throughout the Weimar Republic.

War and social democratic revolution were followed by fascist revolution and another war; these too, one could argue, belong to our story. Indeed, the complex process through which the Nazis appropriated the discourse of "national socialism" is perhaps the most significant chapter in any com-

Stegerwald, Dehmel, and Oppenheimer; Fricke, *Lexikon,* vol. 1, pp. 494–95. Adolf Damaschke, "Meine Kandidatur," *Bodenreform* 31, no. 10 (May 20, 1920): 151–54.

19. Adolf Damaschke, "Zur Nationalversammlung," *Bodenreform* 29, no. 24 (December 20, 1918): 385.

20. Maureen Roycroft-Sommer, "The Quest for Normalcy in a Period of Crisis: The Single Family House Movement in the Weimar Republic" (Paper delivered at the American Historical Association Annual Conference, 1990). On the ambivalent legacy of social motherhood in Weimar, see Sachße, *Mütterlichkeit,* pp. 173–311; Hong, "Gender"; Eifert, "Terms"; Rouette, "Mothers." On unity schools, see Huber, *Bäumer,* pp. 256–58.

21. Werner Sombart, *Die Zukunft des Kapitalismus* (Berlin: Buchholz und Weißwange, 1932); "Reformer-Briefe," NL Sombart 7; "Aufruf zur Gründung einer Forschungsinstitut für Ständewesen," NL Sombart, 2h.

plete study of the German search for alternatives. "One can be seized by wrath in remembering how conscientiously and laboriously these things were once struggled for," Bäumer wrote on the National Socialism of 1928; "how easy these hysterical rabble-rousers make it for themselves on the other hand."[22] Confused, distorted, repulsive though it was, however, the Nazi synthesis of Darwinism and national community bore more than a surface resemblance to the discursive terrain Wilhelmine reformers were attempting to reclaim in the vastly altered landscape of Weimar politics. While Damaschke, Bäumer, and Sombart each maintained a critical distance from the "socialism of fools" before the Nazi seizure of power, the "spirit of 1914" remained a powerful memory, and when the Republic fell into chaos, longing for social unity led them back to the answers of state control, "spiritual revolution," and a strong "leader," just as it had in the First World War.[23] The National Socialists also did their part to encourage these affinities by directing appeals to the former members of the milieu, who appeared to offer a channel into segments of the population they had been unable to reach.[24] "Yes, indeed, we stand at your side, Adolf Damas-

---

22. Bäumer, *Grundlagen,* p. 75.

23. On Damaschke, see "Reichsbanner, Wehrwolf und die 'Front der Anständigen,'" *Bodenreform* 41, no. 39 (January 19, 1930): 17–18; Adolf Damaschke, "Mussolinis Prüfung," *Bodenreform* 43, no. 29 (July 17, 1932): 221–22. On Bäumer, see her article "Hodlers Expressionismus," *Hilfe* 24, no. 24 (June 13, 1918): 280; Huber, *Bäumer,* p. 181; Bäumer, *Grundlagen,* pp. 9–10, 14–15, 18–19, 22–23, 25. On Sombart, see Lenger, *Sombart,* pp. 293–99; Hans-Werner von Hugo to Sombart, June 20, 1932, NL Sombart 2h; Reclams-Universum "Aufruf," sent to Sombart November 14, 1932; NL Sombart 2h. Sombart's occupation with neo-corporatist ideas brought him into the proximity of fascist or quasi-fascist elements of thought; Sombart, *Zukunft des Kapitalismus;* Lenger, *Sombart,* p. 350; Nicolaus Sombart, *Jugend in Berlin 1933–1943: Ein Bericht,* 2nd revised ed. (Frankfurt: Fischer, 1991), p. 93. All three also entered into relationships of varying intensity with radical right-wing groups such as the Young German Order and the *Tat* circle; "Der Jungdeutsche Orden," *Bodenreform* 40, no. 38 (September 22, 1929): 324–26; Huber, *Bäumer,* pp. 139, 148–49, 151–58; Peter Diederichs to Sombart, March 31, 1932, NL Sombart 2h.

24. The *Völkische Beobachter* saw the land reform movement as "an opportunity here to carry the ideas of National Socialism into that segment of the bourgeoisie, which alone has struggled seriously and successfully as the result of a

chke," an article in the *New National Newspaper* proclaimed in 1931.[25] "We are a *movement* and not a party in the old sense. We don't ask: do you call yourself a socialist or a communist, are you a noble, bourgeois, or peasant; are you an academic or a factory owner? We only ask: What do you want and how do you act?" As such echoes rebounded in the final days of the Republic, the struggle over the discourse of national socialism became a muddled process of mutual appropriation lasting well beyond 1933.[26] The

real social sensitivity"; "Auftakt der Presse," *Bodenreform* 41, no. 18 (May 11, 1930): 142.

25. "Die Nationalsozialisten und das Wohnheimstättengesetz," *Bodenreform* 42, no. 14 (April 5, 1931): 106, emphasis in the original. Damaschke's response is indicative of the failure to recognize the fundamentally new character of this "movement." "How does the League of German Land Reformers stand to the NSDAP?" he asked in 1931. "As it does to every other party. What someone thinks outside of land reform . . . does not concern [the BDB]. The League is and will remain the intellectual 'round table' at which people from all camps can unite in common labor and in honest recognition of equal rights"; "Eine notwendige Klärung," *Bodenreform* 42, no. 28 (July 12, 1931): 217. These remarks, it should be noted, came during a furious exchange between Damaschke and Walther Darré, the future leader of the Nazis' *Reichsnährstand,* who sharply attacked Damaschke in the National Socialist press as a blatant Marxist. Damaschke responded by lashing out against the aristocratic and immoral breeding practices promoted in Darré's *Blood and Soil* and by emphasizing that many other high-ranking Nazi officials had endorsed the land reform movement. The BDB's major antagonist in the Weimar Republic, the Economic Party, also became involved in the conflict, and the grotesque struggle between the opponents for the Nazis' support has much to say about the way in which the first German democracy unraveled. On the hostile exchange between the BDB and the NSDAP, see "Nationalsozialistisches," *Bodenreform* 42, nos. 20 and 22 (May 17 and 31, 1931): 153–54, 169–72; "Herr Darré," *Bodenreform* 42, no. 24 (June 14, 1931): 187–89; "Ein 'innenpolitisches Phänomen' und Herr Darré," *Bodenreform* 42, no. 37 (September 13, 1931): 290.

26. "Nationalsozialisten und das Wohnheimstätten gesetz": 106. Bäumer's frantic effort to prevent the drift to the right at the end of the Weimar Republic is by far the most significant example of this process, which bears some similarity to her attempt to assert control over the conservative feminists before the First World War. The experiment with the Young German Order that led to the demise of the German People's Party was intended as a means to strengthen democratic forces by pulling radical elements into the center (Huber, *Bäumer,*

Nazis won that struggle through brute force. Trying to use the language of 'national socialism' to convince the leaders of the new Germany that they had got it wrong—especially in mistaking racial hygiene for social policy—Damaschke, Bäumer, and Sombart certainly risked reprisal, but in negotiating with a murderous regime they also engaged in disastrous complicity. By claiming that "the seven years of the *first* national social movement" had been "precursors and pathfinders for much of what bears the destiny of our nation today,"[27] by inviting young women to "stream into the new

---

p. 166), and in her struggle against the swelling support for fascism among German women Bäumer emphasized the need to accommodate the vocabulary of the Nazis (Huber, *Bäumer*, p. 171). While the former BDF leader emphasized that the women's movement had for decades been criticizing the same aspects of capitalism as the National Socialists and had been pursuing the goal of national community infused by personal rather than materialist values, she also emphasized that a Nazi victory would completely erase all of the accomplishments women had been able to achieve during the course of her lifetime. Returning to her arguments about a politics of womanhood that was indissolubly linked to peace and democracy, Bäumer opposed the Nazis with all the means in her power right up until the seizure of power. This fact is often overlooked in light of her later complicity, but it deserves to be emphasized here. See Gertrud Bäumer, "Die Stellung der weiblichen Jugend zum politischen Leben," *Frau* 37, no. 11 (August 1930): 638–45; "Psychologische Bilanz der Wahlen," *Frau* 38, no. 1 (October 1930): 7; "Die Front der Frauen," *Frau* 39, no. 10 (July 1932): 593–96; "Neuer Aufbruch—oder?," *Frau* 39, no. 12 (September 1932): 724–31; Huber, *Bäumer*, pp. 351–54. See also the BDF's election appeals that delivered strong warnings to German women about what they could expect if the Nazis gained power; "Die Frauen vor der Entscheidung!" *Frau* 37, no. 12 (September 1930): 673–74; "Aufruf zur Reichstagswahl," *Frau* 39, no. 11 (August 1932): 710; "An die Wähler und Wählerinnen," *Frau* 40, no. 1 (October 1932): 65–67.

27. Announcement of the publication of Damaschke's retitled memoirs, *Ein Kampf um Sozialismus und Nation: Vom Ringen um Boden für jeden Volksgenossen* (Dresden: Reißner, 1935), in *Bodenreform* 46, no. 22 (June 2, 1935): 121, emphasis added. Damaschke even quoted from *Mein Kampf* to show the common ground between the BDB and the Nazis (he attributed Hitler's unhappy experiences in Vienna to the housing problem), but he used such alleged parallels to warn the Nazis about the continued need to support the BDB and the consequences of failing to implement land reform. The watchdog was soon silenced. Once the Nazis officially declared that they had no use for Damas-

forms in which the German people are trying to master their fate, . . . helpfully and conscious of [their] responsibility,"[28] by endorsing "national community" that "embraces the entire people, and thus all branches of culture, not only the area of economics,"[29] they pursued the illusion that the new order could be molded to fit their visions just as they had tried to claim the civic peace of 1914, and in the end each of them merely added to the "befuddlement of frightened shipwreck victims in the present crisis."[30] While recognizing their resistance prior to 1933 and courage in criticizing it afterwards, a study that follows the careers of our three case studies into the Third Reich would necessarily stress this contribution to the second, fatal experiment in National Socialism.

1914, 1915, 1920, 1933, 1945—each carries distinctly different conclusions about the Wilhelmine reform milieu and its significance. This study closes with the faded reliefs of a moderate, "progressive evolutionism" that needs to be restored on maps of pre-war Germany, but not because it was

---

chke, *Land Reform* issued one more warning, before dropping its criticism entirely and moving on to discuss developments beyond the borders of the Third Reich; "Allerlei Hoffnungen auf die Reichsregierung," *Bodenreform* 44, no. 12 (March 26, 1933): 89–91; "Vom wirtschaftlichen Sofortprogramm der NSDAP," *Bodenreform* 44, no. 16 (April 23, 1933): 113–14; "Die alte und die neue Regierung und die Siedlungsfrage," *Bodenreform* 44, no. 17 (April 30, 1933): 125; G. Berg, "Lagarde als Bodenreformer," *Bodenreform* 44, no. 19 (May 14, 1933): 142–43; "Der Frontkämpferartikel 155," *Bodenreform* 44, no. 22–23 (June 4, 1933): 161–62; "Aus Adolf Hitlers Lehrjahren," *Bodenreform* 44, no. 43 (October 29, 1933): 297–99; "Kraft durch Freude," *Bodenreform* 44, no. 51 (December 24, 1933): 353–54; H. P., "Um ein nationalsozialistisches Strafrecht," *Bodenreform* 45, nos. 5–6 (February 4, 1934): 25–26; Damaschke, "Staatsbürgerliche Briefe," *Bodenreform* 45 (March 18, 1934); "Nationalsozialismus und Bodenreform," *Bodenreform* 45, no. 24 (July 17, 1934): 145–49.

28. Gertrud Bäumer, "Das Haus ist zerfallen," *Frau* 40, no. 9 (June 1933): 514. Bäumer not only encouraged women to join the League of German Girls but also supported "unity schools" and the obligatory year of women's service introduced by the Nazis; Huber, *Bäumer*, pp. 87, 261. Despite moral reservations, Bäumer also felt she had no choice but to support the war effort—"right or wrong my country," she wrote to Marianne Weber on December 27, 1939, NL Marianne Weber 2, page 40.

29. Sombart, *Deutscher Sozialismus*, pp. 160–61.

30. Bäumer, *Grundlagen*, p. 75.

the "end that was there at the beginning." As it was initially conceived, the research presented here had in fact been intended to fill in part of a much longer story culminating with the West German Greens and Alternatives of the 1980s. Wolf-Dieter and Connie Hasenclever's "bio-cybernetic" model of communitarian social order, Manon Maren-Grisebach's natural philosophy of motherhood, Rudolf Bahro's calls for a "new and different 1933" were foreseen as the conclusion of a study that was not about alternative *modernities* at all, but about forms of anti-modernism that followed different lines of continuity from the Garden City movement down Germany's special path and beyond the "zero hour" of 1945.[31] But the sources told a different story. If the builders of German Garden Cities bitterly criticized the industrial, capitalist modernity of their day, none of them rejected the optimistic belief in science, technology, and the potential for limitless increase in the productive capacity of the nation. The closer one looked at the diverse group of reformers, intellectuals, and activists who shaped the movement, the clearer their determination to realize that potential to the fullest measure became. Hellerau was to be a quiet place where personal fulfillment took precedence over material gain, but it was also to be a quietly efficient and profitable technical enterprise. As the contours of the milieu in which they lived and worked came into sharper relief, a strange new territory appeared on a mental landscape divided into modernist and anti-modernist camps, a bizarre middle ground that defied easy classification. How should one refer to the world in which Franz Oppenheimer strove to protect the "national body" from the hereditary ills of capitalism with the environmentalist "settlement cooperative," a world to which Ludwig Erhard's "social market economy" of the 1960s could look for inspiration as easily as the "fundos" of the Green Party twenty years later?

The discourse of Wilhelmine anti-politics made sense only on its own, strange territory, where opposites still combined to form moderate answers the extremes had yet to burst apart in 1914, and in later years it drifted with the currents of war and revolutions into a world that no longer offered

---

31. Wolf-Dieter and Connie Hasenclever, *Grüne Zeiten: Politik für eine lebenswerte Zukunft* (Munich: Kosel, 1982); Manon Maren-Grisebach, *Philosophie der Grünen* (Munich: Olzog, 1982); Rudolf Bahro, *Logik der Rettung: Wer kann die Apokalypse aufhalten? Ein Versuch über die Grundlagen ökologischer Politik* (Stuttgart: Weitbrecht, 1987), esp. p. 346.

shelter from the burdens of political responsibility. Long after the reform milieu dissolved, its language could still be heard in the arguments of opponents who otherwise shared nothing in common. This story too deserves to be told, and perhaps one day it will. But for now let us conclude in the heyday of Hellerau, when socialists and reactionaries, environmentalists and industrialists, humanists and engineers still found common ground in the search for alternative modernities.

$\bullet \quad \bullet \quad \bullet$

Select Bibliography

Archival Materials

Bäumer, Gertrud. Nachlaß (fragmentary). Bundesarchiv Koblenz.

Berlepsch, Hans. Nachlaß, files 3–6, 27. Material on the Society for Social Reform and the Institute for Public Welfare. Bundesarchiv Merseburg.

Braun, Lily. Nachlaß (fragmentary). Correspondence with Werner Sombart. Bundesarchiv Koblenz, Kleine Erwerbung 129.

Damaschke, Adolf. Nachlaß (fragmentary). Bundesarchiv Koblenz, Kleine Erwerbung 806.

Erkelenz, Anton. Nachlaß, files 103, 139. Autobiographical manuscript; correspondence with Gertrud Bäumer.

Helene Lange Archiv, Abteilungen 2/I, 5/XV–XVI, 7–9, 11–12, 14, 16/I. Bäumer's correspondence 1900–1926; BDF Executive Committee correspondence; BDF petitions on legal, moral, hygienic, employment, social and population policy, and suffrage; BDF General Assembly protocols and resolutions, 1896–1912. Landesarchiv Berlin.

Landsberger, Artur. Nachlaß (fragmentary). Correspondence with Werner Sombart. Bundesarchiv Koblenz, Kleine Erwerbung 103.

Lang, Otto. Nachlaß. Correspondence with Werner Sombart. International Institute for Social History, Amsterdam.

Naumann, Friedrich. Nachlaß, files 53, 123, 134–36, 147. NSV Executive Committee meetings, 1896–1903; correspondence with Hermann Kötzschke, Wolf Dohrn, Elisabeth Gnauck-Kühne, Minna Cauer, Charles Hallgarten, Wilhelm Rein. Bundesarchiv Potsdam.

Prussian Internal Ministry, Rep. 77, Abt. II, Sekt. 25–30, file 52; Rep. 76 V^a, Sekt. 4, Tit. X, file 82, vol. 2; Rep. 76 V^a, Sekt. 4, Tit. IV, file 47, vol. 2; Reports on the New Community and German Garden City Society 1900–1903; the Hygienic Institute in Breslau; personal records of the Breslau faculty 1888–1902, Bundesarchiv Merseburg.

Sombart, Werner. Nachlaß, files 1–2, 4–11, 13–19, 26, 28, 34–35, 37–47. Correspondence; reviews and correspondence regarding *Dennoch!, Das Proletariat, Die Juden und das Wirtschaftsleben, Händler und Helden, Der Moderne Kapitalismus* (1916), *Deutscher Sozialismus;* autobiographical; University of Berlin; seminars; Handelshochschule; Akademie der Wissenschaften; Akademie für deutsches Recht; *Archiv für Sozialwissenschaft;* German Society for Sociology; Society for Social Reform, Friedrich List Gesellschaft; Spanish lectures (1933); Academy speech (1936); *Schlesische Zeitung;* socialism; Freiburg appointment; diverse; newspaper contributions (1913–1914). Bundesarchiv Merseburg.

Verein für Sozialpolitik, Rep. 196, files 6, 8, 39, 71–79, 89, 96. Executive Committee matters; circulars; general assemblies 1905–1907, 1913–1914; consumer cooperatives committee 1912–1926; committee meetings 1903, 1909–1918; dissolution 1936. Bundesarchiv Merseburg.

Weber, Marianne. Nachlaß. Bundesarchiv Koblenz.

Weber, Max. Nachlaß, files 3–7. Correspondence to friends, colleagues, scholars, and others 1890–1918. Bundesarchiv Merseburg.

Periodicals

Archiv für soziale Gesetzgebung und Statistik, vols. 1–45 (1889–1918).

Die Bodenreform, vols. 1–52. Prior to vol. 18, no. 8 (April 20, 1907) appeared as *Deutsche Volksstimme.*

Centralblatt des Bundes deutscher Frauenvereine, vols. 9–12 (1907–1910).

Ernstes Wollen, vols. 1–5 (1901–1903).

Ethische Kultur: Wochenschrift für sozial-ethische Reformen, vols. 1–6 (1893–1899).

Die Frau: Monatsschrift für das gesamte Frauenleben unserer Zeit, vols. 1–40 (1893–1933).

Die Gartenstadt: Mitteilungen der Deutschen Gartenstadtgesellschaft, vols. 2–8 (1907–1914).

Die Hilfe: Gotteshilfe, Selbsthilfe, Staatshilfe, Bruderhilfe, vols. 1–25 (1895–1919).

Morgen: Wochenschrift für deutsche Kultur, vols. 1–2 (1907–1908).

Neue Bahnen: Organ des Allgemeinen Deutschen Frauenvereins, vols. 42–45 (1907–1910).

Die Neue Rundschau, vols. 1–14 (1890–1904). Also appeared variously under the titles *Freie Bühne für modernes Leben* and *Freie Bühne für den Entwicklungskampf der Zeit.*

Soziale Praxis: Centralblatt für Sozialpolitik, vols. 8–13 (1899–1904).

Sozialpolitisches Centralblatt, vols. 1–4 (1892–1895).

Die Tat, vols. 1–6 (1909–1914).

Published Works

Abbé, Ernst. *Sozialpolitische Schriften.* Jena: Fischer, 1906.

Accampo, Elinor, et al. *Gender and the Politics of Social Reform in France, 1870–1914.* Baltimore: Johns Hopkins University Press, 1995.

Aldenhoff, Rita. "Kapitalismusanalyse und Kulturkritik: Bürgerliche National-ökonomen entdeckten Karl Marx," in Hübinger and Mommsen, *Intellektuelle,* pp. 78–95.

———— "Das Selbsthilfemodell als liberale Antwort auf die soziale Frage im 19. Jahrhundert: Schulze-Delitsch und die Genossenschaften." In Holl, *Liberalismus,* pp. 57–69.

Allen, Ann Taylor. *Feminism and Motherhood in Germany, 1800–1914.* New Brunswick, N.J.: Rutgers University Press, 1991.

———— "The Holocaust and the Modernization of Gender: A Historiographical Essay," *Central European History* 30, no. 3 (1997): 349–64.

Altner, Günther, ed. *Der Darwinismus: Die Geschichte einer Theorie.* Darmstadt: Wissenschaftliche Buchgesellschaft, 1981.

Apel, Max, ed. *Darwin im Ringen um Weltanschauung und Lebenswert.* Berlin: Buchverlag der *Hilfe,* 1909.

Appel, Michael. *Werner Sombart: Theoretiker und Historiker des modernen Kapitalismus.* Marburg: Metropolis, 1992.

Applegate, Celia. *A Nation of Provincials: The German Idea of Heimat.* Berkeley: University of California Press, 1990.

Aschheim, Steven. *The Nietzsche Legacy in Germany, 1890–1990.* Berkeley: University of California Press, 1992.

Auerbach, Felix. *Ernst Abbé: Sein Leben, sein Wirken, seine Persönlichkeit.* Leipzig: Akademische Verlagsgesellschaft, 1918.

Bach, Marie Luise. *Gertrud Bäumer: Biographische Daten und Texte zu einem Persönlichkeitsbild.* Weinheim: Deutscher Studien Verlag, 1989.

Barkin, Kenneth. *The Controversy over German Industrialization.* Chicago: University of Chicago Press, 1970.

Bäumer, Gertrud. *Das Bildnis der Liebenden: Gestalt und Wandel der Frau.* Tübingen: Wunderlich, 1958.

———— *Die deutsche Frau in der sozialen Kriegsfürsorge.* Gotha: Perthes, 1916.

———— *Deutsche Schulpolitik.* Karlsruhe: Braun, 1928.

———— *Europäische Kulturpolitik.* Berlin: Herbig, 1926.

———— *Die Frau im deutschen Staat.* Berlin: Junker und Dünnhaupt, 1932.

———— *Die Frau im neuen Lebensraum.* Berlin: Herbig, 1931.

———— *Die Frau in der Krisis der Kultur.* Berlin: Herbig, 1926.

———— *Die Frau in Volkswirtschaft und Staatsleben der Gegenwart.* Berlin: Deutsche Verlags-Anstalt, 1914.

—— *Die Frau und das geistige Leben.* Leipzig: Amelang, 1911.

—— "Die Geschichte der englischen Frauenbewegung," in Gertrud Bäumer and Helene Lang, eds., *Handbuch der Frauenbewegung,* vol. 1. Berlin: Moeser, 1901.

—— "Die Geschichte der Frauenbewegung in Deutschland," in Gertrud Bäumer and Helene Lang, eds., *Handbuch der Frauenbewegung,* vol. 1. Berlin: Moeser, 1901.

—— *Grundlagen demokratischer Politik.* Karlsruhe: Braun, 1928.

—— *Heimatchronik während des Weltkrieges.* Berlin: Herbig, 1930.

—— "In eigener Sache." Typewritten manuscript. Hoover archives.

—— *Der Krieg und die Frau.* Berlin: Deutsche Verlags-Anstalt, 1914.

—— *Lebensweg durch eine Zeitenwende.* Tübingen: Wunderlich, 1933.

—— *Der neue Weg der deutschen Frau.* Stuttgart: Deutsche Verlags-Anstalt, 1946.

—— *Soziale Erneuerung.* Berlin: Fortschritt, 1919.

—— *Die soziale Idee in den Weltanschauungen des 19. Jahrhunderts: Grundzüge der modernen Sozialphilosophie,* 2nd ed. Heilbronn: Salzer, 1910.

—— *Weit hinter den Schützengräben: Aufsätze aus dem Weltkrieg.* Jena: Diederichs, 1916.

Becher, Paul. *Vergleich und Kritik der sozialpolitischen Auffassungen bei Lujo Brentano, Adolf Wagner, Georg von Hertling und Franz Hitze.* Munich: dissertation, 1965.

Becker, Peter. *Zur Geschichte der Rassenhygiene: Wege ins Dritte Reich.* New York: Thieme, 1988.

Beevers, Robert. *The Garden City Utopia: A Critical Biography of Ebenezer Howard.* London: Macmillan, 1988.

Behl, C.W.F., and Felix A. Voigt. *Chronik von Gerhart Hauptmanns Leben und Schaffen.* Berlin: Korn, 1957.

—— *Gerhart Hauptmanns Leben: Chronik und Bild.* Berlin: Suhrkamp, 1942.

Beier, Rosmarie, and Martin Roth, eds. *Der gläserne Mensch—Eine Sensation: Zur Kulturgeschichte eines Ausstellungsobjekts.* Stuttgart: Hatje, 1990.

Berg, Christa. *Handbuch der deutschen Bildungsgeschichte,* vol. 4: *Von der Reichsgründung bis zum Ende des Ersten Weltkriegs.* Munich: Beck, 1991.

Berger-Thimme, Dorothea. *Boden- und Wohnungsreform in Deutschland 1873–1918.* Frankfurt: Lang, 1976.

Berglar, Peter. *Walther Rathenau: Seine Zeit. Sein Werk. Seine Persönlichkeit.* Bremen: Schünemann, 1970.

Bergmann, Anna. *Die verhütete Sexualität: Die Anfänge der modernen Geburtenkontrolle.* Hamburg: Rasch und Röhring, 1992.

Bergmann, Klaus. *Agrarromantik und Großstadtfeindschaft.* Meisenheim: Hain, 1970.

Berlepsch, Hans-Jörg von. *"Neuer Kurs" im Kaiserreich? Die Arbeiterpolitik des Freiherrn von Berlepsch 1890 bis 1896.* Bonn: Neue Gesellschaft, 1987.

Bernstein, Eduard. *Evolutionary Socialism: A Criticism and Affirmation.* New York: Schocken, 1961.

Besier, Gerhard, ed. *Die Mittwochs-Gesellschaft im Kaiserreich: Protokolle aus dem geistigen Deutschland 1863–1919.* Berlin: Siedler, 1990.

Beyerchen, Alan. "On the Stimulation of Excellence in Wilhelminian Science." In Dukes and Remak, *Germany*, pp. 139–68.

Bickel, Cornelius. *Ferdinand Tönnies: Soziologie als skeptische Aufklärung zwischen Historismus und Rationalismus.* Opladen: Westdeutscher Verlag, 1991.

——— "Tönnies' Kritik des Sozialdarwinismus: Immunität durch Philosophie: Die Auseinandersetzung mit der Krupp-Preisfrage von 1900." In Klingemann, *Rassenmythos*, pp. 172–211.

Blackbourn, David. "The Politics of Demagogy in Imperial Germany." *Past and Present* (1986): 152–84.

Blackbourn, David, and Geoff Eley. *The Peculiarities of German History: Bourgeois Society and Politics in Nineteenth-Century Germany.* New York: Oxford University Press, 1984.

Bock, Gisela. "Racism and Sexism in Nazi Germany: Motherhood, Compulsory Sterilization, and the State." In Bridenthal et al., *Biology*, pp. 271–96.

Boese, Franz. *Geschichte des Vereins für Sozialpolitik 1872–1932.* Berlin: Duncker & Humblot, 1939.

Bohm, Eberhard. "Wohnsiedlung am Berliner Stadtrand im frühen 20. Jahrhundert: Das Beispiel Frohnau." *Siedlungsforschung, Archäologie-Geschichte-Geographie* 1 (1983): 117–36.

Born, Karl Erich. *Staat und Sozialpolitik seit Bismarcks Sturz: Ein Beitrag zur Geschichte der innenpolitischen Entwicklung des deutschen Reiches 1890–1914.* Wiesbaden: Steiner, 1957.

Bowler, Peter J. *The Eclipse of Darwinism: Anti-Darwinian Evolution Theories in the Decades around 1900.* Baltimore: Johns Hopkins University Press, 1983.

——— *The Non-Darwinian Revolution: Reinterpreting a Historical Myth.* Baltimore: Johns Hopkins University Press, 1988.

Boyd, Byron A. *Rudolf Virchow: The Scientist as Citizen.* New York: Garland, 1991.

Brakelmann, Günther, Martin Greschat, and Werner Jochman. *Protestantismus und Politik: Werk und Wirkung Adolf Stoeckers.* Hamburg: Christian, 1982.

Braun, Lily. *Memoiren einer Sozialistin*, 2 vols. Berlin: Hermann Klemm, n.d.

Brentano, Lujo. *Mein Leben im Kampf um die soziale Entwicklung Deutschlands.* Jena: Diederichs, 1931.

Breysig, Kurt. *Der Stufenbau und die Gesetze der Welgeschichte*, 2nd expanded ed. Stuttgart: J. G. Cotta'sche Buchhandlung Nachfolger, 1927.

Bridenthal, Renate, Atina Grossmann, and Marion Kaplan, eds., *When Biology Became Destiny: Women in Weimar and Nazi Germany.* New York: Monthly Review Press, 1984.

Bröker, Werner. *Politische Motive naturwisenschaftlicher Argumente gegen Religion und Kirche im 19. Jahrhundert.* Münster: Aschendorff, 1973.

Bruch, Rüdiger vom. "Bürgerliche Sozialreform im deutschen Kaiserreich." In Bruch et al., *Kommunismus,* pp. 61–179.

———— "Von der Sozialethik zur Sozialtechnologie? Neuorientierungen in der deutschen Sozialwissenschaft um 1900," in Hübinger, Bruch, et al., *Kultur,* pp. 260–76.

———— *Wissenschaft, Politik und öffentliche Meinung: Gelehrtenpolitik im Wilhelminischen Deutschland, 1890–1914.* Husum, Germany: Mathiesen, 1980.

Bruch, Rüdiger vom, et al. *Weder Kommunismus noch Kapitalismus: Bürgerliche Sozialreform in Deutschland vom Vormärz bis zur Ära Adenauer.* Munich: Beck, 1985.

Brümmer, Franz, ed. *Lexikon der deutschen Dichter und Prosaisten vom Beginn des 19. Jahrhunderts bis zur Gegenwart.* Leipzig: Reclam, 1913.

Buber, Martin. *Briefwechsel aus sieben Jahrzehnten,* vol. 1 (1897–1918). Heidelberg: Schneider, 1972.

Bücher, Karl. *Arbeit und Rhythmus.* Leipzig: Teubner, 1902.

———— *Industrial Evolution.* New York: Holt, 1901.

———— *Lebenserinnerungen,* 2 vols. Tübingen: Laupp, 1919.

Büchner, Ludwig. *Am Sterbelager des Jahrhunderts: Blicke eines freien Denkers aus der Zeit in die Zeit.* Giessen: Roth, 1898.

———— *Darwinismus und Sozialismus oder Der Kampf um das Dasein und die moderne Gesellschaft.* Stuttgart: Kröner, 1906.

———— *Fremdes und Eignes aus dem geistigen Leben der Gegenwart.* Leipzig: Spohr, 1890.

———— *Im Dienste der Wahrheit: Ausgewählte Aufsätze aus Natur- und Wissenschaft.* Giessen: Roth, 1900.

———— *Die Macht der Vererbung und ihr Einfluss auf den moralischen und geistigen Fortschritt der Menschheit.* Leipzig: Günther, 1882.

Buder, Stanley. *Visionaries and Planners: The Garden City Movement and the Modern Community.* New York: Oxford University Press, 1990.

Bütschli, O. *Mechanismus und Vitalismus:* Leipzig: Engelmann, 1901.

Buttmann, Günther. *Friedrich Ratzel. Leben und Werk eines deutschen Geographen.* Stuttgart: Wissenschaftliche Verlagsgesellschaft, 1977.

Cahan, David. *An Institute for an Empire: The Physikalisch-Technische Reichsanstalt, 1871–1918.* New York: Cambridge University Press, 1989.

Campbell, Joan. *The German Werkbund: The Politics of Reform in the Applied Arts.* Princeton: Princeton University Press, 1978.

———— *Joy in Work, German Work: The National Debate, 1800–1945.* Princeton: Princeton University Press, 1989.

Canning, Kathleen. *Languages of Labor and Gender: Female Factory Work in Germany, 1850–1914.* Ithaca: Cornell University Press, 1996.

Chickering, Roger. *Karl Lamprecht: A German Academic Life (1856–1915).* Atlantic Highlands, N.J.: Humanities Press International, 1993.

—— *We Men Who Feel Most German: A Cultural Study of the Pan-German League, 1886–1914.* Boston: Allen and Unwin, 1984.

Churchill, Frederick. "From Machine-Theory to Entelechy: Two Studies in Developmental Teleology." *Journal of the History of Biology* 2 (1969): 165–85.

Clark, Linda. "Bringing Feminine Qualities into the Public Sphere: The Third Republic's Appointment of Women Inspectors," in Accampo et al., *Gender,* pp. 128–56.

Coetzee, Marilyn. *The German Army League: Popular Nationalism in Wilhelmine Germany.* New York: Oxford University Press, 1990.

Coleman, William. *Biology in the Nineteenth Century: Problems of Form, Function, and Transformation.* New York: Cambridge University Press, 1977.

Conze, Werner. "Friedrich Naumann: Grundlagen und Ansatz seiner Politik in der nationalsozialen Zeit." In Walther Hubatsch, ed., *Schicksalswege deutscher Vergangenheit* (Düsseldorf: Droste-Verlag, 1950), pp. 355–86.

Crew, David. "The Ambiguities of Modernity: Welfare and the German State from Wilhelm to Hitler." In Eley, ed., *Society,* pp. 319–44.

Dahme, Heinz-Jürgen. "Der Verlust des Fortschrittsglaubens und die Verwissenschaftlichung der Soziologie: Ein Vergleich von Georg Simmel, Ferdinand Tönnies und Max Weber." In Rammstedt, ed., *Simmel,* pp. 222–74.

Dahrendorf, Ralf. *Society and Democracy in Germany.* New York: Doubleday, 1967.

Damaschke, Adolf. *Aufgaben der Gemeindepolitik,* 4th revised ed. Jena: Fischer, 1901.

—— *Aus meinem Leben.* Berlin: Hobbing, 1928.

—— *Die Bodenreform: Grundsätzliches und Geschichtliches zur Erkenntnis und Überwindung der sozialen Not,* 16th revised ed. Jena: Fischer, 1919.

—— *Geschichte der Nationalökonomie: Eine erste Einführung,* 2 vols. Jena: Fischer, 1929.

—— *Geschichte der Redekunst: Eine erste Einführung.* Jena: Fischer, 1921.

—— *Ein Kampf um Sozialismus und Nation: Vom Ringen um Boden für jeden Volksgenossen.* Dresden: Reißner, 1935.

—— *Volkstümliche Redekunst: Erfahrungen und Ratschläge.* Jena: Fischer, 1920.

—— *Was ist National-Sozial?* Berlin: Kundt, 1898.

—— *Zeitenwende.* Leipzig: Grethlein, 1925.

David, Eduard. "Darwinismus und soziale Entwicklung." In Apel, ed., *Darwin,* pp. 45–65.

Deegan, Mary Jo. *Jane Addams and the Men of the Chicago School, 1892–1918.* New Brunswick, N.J.: Transaction, 1988.

Degler, Carl. *In Search of Human Nature: The Decline and Revival of Darwinism in American Social Thought.* New York: Oxford University Press, 1991.

Diehl, Karl. *Über Sozialismus, Kommunismus und Anarchismus: Zwölf Vorlesungen.* Jena: Fischer, 1906.

Döbertin, Winfried. *Adolf von Harnack: Theologe, Pädagoge, Wissenschaftspolitiker.* New York: Lang, 1985.

Doeberl, Michael, et al., eds. *Das akademische Deutschland,* vols. 1–2. Berlin: Weller, 1930.

Dohrn, Klaus. *Von Bürgern und Weltbürgern: Eine Familiengeschichte.* Augsburg: Neske, 1983.

Dohrn, Wolf. *Die Gartenstadt Hellerau: Ein Bericht.* Jena: Diederichs, 1908.

Driesch, Hans. *Lebenserinnerungen: Aufzeichnungen eines Forschers und Denkers in entscheidender Zeit.* Basel: Reinhardt, 1951.

———— *Ordnungslehre: Ein System des nicht-metaphysichen Teiles der Philosophie: Mit besonderer Berücksichtigung der Lehre vom Werden.* Jena: Diederichs, 1912.

———— *The Science and Philosophy of the Organism,* 2 vols. London: Black, 1908.

Driesmans, Heinrich, ed. *Moritz von Egidy: Sein Leben und Wirken,* 2 vols. Dresden: Pierson, 1900.

Du Bois-Reymond, Emil. *Über die Grenzen des Naturerkennens: Die Sieben Welt-räthsel: Zwei Vorträge.* Leipzig: Veit, 1891.

———— "Über Neo-Vitalismus." In Du Bois-Reymond, *Vorträge über Philosophie und Gesellschaft* (Hamburg: Meiner, 1974), pp. 205–32.

Düding, Dieter. *Der Nationalsoziale Verein 1896–1903: Der gescheiterte Versuch einer parteipolitischen Synthese von Nationalismus, Sozialismus und Liberalismus.* Munich: Oldenbourg, 1972.

Dukes, Jack, and Joachim Remak, eds., *Another Germany: A Reconsideration of the Imperial Era.* Boulder: Westview, 1988.

Eifert, Christiane. "Coming to Terms with the State: Maternalist Politics and the Development of the Welfare State in Weimar Germany." *Central European History* 30, no. 1 (1997): 25–47.

Ekirch, Arthur A., Jr. *Progressivism in America: A Study of the Era from Theodore Roosevelt to Woodrow Wilson.* New York: New Viewpoints, 1974.

Eksteins, Modris. *Rites of Spring: The Great War and the Birth of the Modern Age.* New York: Anchor, 1989.

Eley, Geoff. "German History and the Contradictions of Modernity: The Bour-geoisie, the State, and the Mastery of Reform." In Eley, ed., *Society,* pp. 67–103.

———— "Introduction 1: Is There a History of the Kaiserreich?" In Eley, ed., *Society,* pp. 1–42.

———— *Reshaping the German Right: Radical Nationalism and Political Change after Bismarck.* New Haven: Yale University Press, 1980.

————, ed. *Society, Culture, and the State in Germany, 1870–1930.* Ann Arbor: University of Michigan Press, 1997.

Elias, Norbert. *The Civilizing Process,* vol. 1, *The History of Manners.* New York: Pantheon, 1978.

Ermann, Heinrich. *Das große Bekenntnis zur Deutschen Bodenreform.* Frankfurt an der Oder: Trowitzsch, 1928.

Evans, Richard. *Death in Hamburg: Society and Politics in the Cholera Years, 1830–1910.* New York: Oxford University Press, 1987.

———— *The Feminist Movement in Germany 1894–1933.* London: SAGE, 1976.

———— *Rethinking German History: Nineteenth-Century Germany and the Origins of the Third Reich.* Boston: Allen and Unwin, 1987.

Fine, William. *Progressive Evolutionism and American Sociology, 1890–1920.* Ann Arbor, Mich.: UMI Research Press, 1979.

Flober, Heiner. "Probleme biologischer Orientierung der Soziologie." In Klingemann, *Rassenmythos,* pp. 277–313.

Foerster, Friedrich Wilhelm. *Lebensfragen und Lebensbilder: Socialethische Betrachtungen.* Berlin: Edelheim, 1902.

Fout, John, ed. *German Women in the Nineteenth Century: A Social History.* New York: Holmes and Meier, 1984.

Freese, Heinrich. *Die Bodenreform: Ihre Vergangenheit und ihre Zukunft.* Berlin: Weichert, 1918.

Freudenberg, Ika. *Die Frau und die Kultur des öffentlichen Lebens.* Leipzig: Amelang, 1911.

Frevert, Ute. "The Civilizing Tendency of Hygiene: Working Class Women under Medical Control in Imperial Germany." In Fout, ed., *Women,* pp. 320–44.

———— *Frauen-Geschichte: Zwischen Bürgerlicher Verbesserung und Neuer Weiblichkeit.* Frankfurt: Suhrkamp, 1986.

Fricke, Dieter, et al., eds. *Lexikon zur Parteiengeschichte: Die bürgerlichen Parteien und Verbände in Deutschland (1789–1945),* 4 vols. Cologne: Pahl-Rugenstein, 1986.

Frisby, David P. "Soziologie und Moderne: Ferdinand Tönnies, Georg Simmel und Max Weber." In Rammstedt, ed., *Simmel,* pp. 196–221.

Fritzsche, Peter. "Did Weimar Fail?" *Journal of Modern History* 68, no. 3 (September 1996): 629–56.

Gasman, Daniel. *The Scientific Origins of National Socialism: Social Darwinism in Ernst Haeckel and the Monist League.* New York: Elsevier, 1971.

Gay, Peter. *The Dilemma of Democratic Socialism: Eduard Bernstein's Challenge to Marx.* New York: Columbia University Press, 1952.

Geison, Gerald L. "The Protoplasmic Theory of Life and the Vitalist-Mechanist Debate." *Isis* 60 (1969): 273–92.

George, Henry. *Progress and Poverty: An Inquiry into the Cause of Industrial De-*

pressions and of Increase of Want with Increase of Waste: The Remedy. Garden City: Doubleday, Page & Co., 1923.

Gerhard, Ute. *Unerhört: Die Geschichte der deutschen Frauenbewegung.* Hamburg: Rowohlt, 1990.

Gerlach, Hellmut von. *Erinnerungen eines Junkers.* Berlin: Verlag *Die Welt am Montag,* 1925.

────── *Von Rechts nach Links.* Hildesheim: Gerstenberg, 1978.

Gizycki, Georg von. *Grundzüge der Moral: Gekrönte Preisschrift.* Leipzig: Wilhelm Friedrich Königliche Hofbuchhandlung, 1883.

────── *A Students' Manual of Ethical Philosophy.* Trans. Stanton Coit. London: Swan Sonnenschein, 1889.

Glaser, Herman. *The Cultural Roots of National Socialism.* Austin: University of Texas Press, 1978.

Göhre, Paul. *Die evangelisch-soziale Bewegung: Ihre Geschichte und ihre Ziele.* Leipzig: Grunow, 1896.

────── *Three Months in a Workshop: A Practical Study.* Trans. A. B. Carr. New York: Scribner, 1895.

────── *Vom Socialismus zum Liberalismus: Wandlungen der Nationalsozialen,* 2nd ed. Berlin: Verlag der *sozialistischen Monatshefte,* 1902.

Goldscheid, Rudolf. *Höherentwicklung und Menschenökonomie: Grundlegung der Sozialbiologie.* Leipzig: Klinkhardt, 1911.

Gorges, Irmela. *Sozialforschung in Deutschland 1872–1914: Gesellschaftliche Einflüsse auf Themen- und Methodenwahl des Vereins für Socialpolitik,* 2nd ed. Frankfurt: Hain, 1986.

Gould, Stephen. *The Mismeasure of Man.* New York: Norton, 1981.

Grebing, Helga. *Arbeiterbewegung: Sozialer Protest und kollektive Interessenvertretung bis 1914.* Munich: Deutscher Taschenbuch Verlag, 1985

Gregory, Frederick. *Scientific Materialism in Nineteenth Century Germany.* Boston: Reidel, 1977.

Greven-Aschoff, Barbara. *Die bürgerliche Frauenbewegung in Deutschland 1894–1933.* Göttingen: Vandenhoeck & Ruprecht, 1981.

Groh, Dieter. "Marx, Engels und Darwin: Naturgesetzliche Entwicklung oder Revolution." In Altner, ed., *Darwinismus,* pp. 217–41.

Günther, Katharina. *Literarische Gruppenbildung im Berliner Naturalismus.* Bonn: Grundmann, 1972.

Gutzeit, P. *Die Bodenreform: Eine dogmengeschichtlich-kritische Studie.* Leipzig: Duncker und Humblot, 1907.

Hackett, Amy. "The German Women's Movement & Suffrage, 1890–1914: A Study of National Feminism." In J. Besuch, ed., *Modern European Social History* (Lexington, Mass.: Heath, 1972), pp. 355–86.

———— "Helene Stöcker: Left-Wing Intellectual and Sexual Reformer." In Bridenthal et al., *Biology*, pp. 109–30.

———— *The Politics of Feminism in Wilhelmine Germany*. Dissertation: Columbia University, 1976.

Haeckel, Ernst. "Deszendenztheorie und Sozialdemokratie." In Altner, ed., *Darwinismus*, 1981.

Harnack, Adolf. *Essays on the Social Gospel*. Ed. Maurice A. Canney. Trans. G. M. Craik. New York: Putnam, 1907.

———— *Thoughts on the Present Position of Protestantism*. Trans. Thomas Bailey Saunders. London: Black, 1899.

Harrington, Anne. *Reenchanted Science: Holism in German Culture from Wilhelm II to Hitler*. Princeton: Princeton University Press, 1996.

Harris, Abram L. "Sombart and German (National) Socialism." In Mark Blaug, ed., *Gustav Schmoller (1883–1917) and Werner Sombart (1863–1941)* (Brookfield: Elgar, 1992), pp. 41–71.

Hartmann, Kristiana. *Deutsche Gartenstadtbewegung: Kulturpolitik und Gesellschaftsreform*. Munich: Moos, 1976.

Haselbach, D. *Franz Oppenheimer: Soziologie, Geschichtsphilosophie und Politik des 'liberalen Sozialismus.'* Opladen: Leske, 1985.

Hauptmann, Carl. *Leben mit Freunden: Gesammelte Briefe*. Berlin: Horen-Verlag, 1928.

———— *Unsere Wirklichkeit*. Munich: Callwey, 1902.

Hauptmann, Gerhart. "Bahnwärter Thiel." In *Gerhart Hauptmann: Auswahl für die Jugend* (Berlin: Neues Leben, 1962), pp. 115–46.

———— "Fasching." In *Auswahl*, pp. 95–114.

———— *Vor Sonnenaufgang: Soziales Drama*. Frankfurt: Ullstein, 1982.

———— *Die Weber*. In *Auswahl*, pp. 147–217.

Heckart, Beverly. *From Bassermann to Bebel: The Grand Bloc's Quest for Reform in the Kaiserreich, 1900–1914*. New Haven: Yale University Press, 1974.

Heilmann, Martin. *Adolph Wagner—Ein deutscher Nationalökonom im Urteil der Zeit*. New York: Campus Verlag, 1980.

Hellige, Hans Dieter. "Rathenau und Harden in der Gesellschaft des Deutschen Kaiserreichs: Eine sozialgeschichtlich-biographische Studie zur Entstehung neokonservativer Positionen bei Unternehmern und Intellektuellen." In H. D. Hellige, ed., *Walther Rathenau, Maximilian Harden: Briefwechsel 1897–1920* (Munich: Müller, 1983), pp. 15–299.

Henderson, W. O. *Friedrich List: Economist and Visionary, 1789–1846*. Totowa, N.J.: Cass, 1983.

Herf, Jeffrey. *Reactionary Modernism: Technology, Culture, and Politics in Weimar and the Third Reich*. New York: Cambridge University Press, 1984.

Herz, Heinz. *Alleingang wider die Mächtigen: Ein Bild vom Leben und Kämpfen Moritz von Egidys.* Leipzig: Koehler & Amelang, 1970.

Heuss, Theodor. *Anton Dohrn: A Life for Science.* Trans. Liselotte Dieckmann. New York: Springer, 1991.

——— *Erinnerungen: 1905–1933.* Tübingen: Wunderlich, 1963.

——— *Friedrich Naumann: Der Mann, das Werk, die Zeit,* 2nd revised ed. Stuttgart: Wunderlich, 1959.

Heymann, Lida Gustava, and Anita Augspurg. *Erlebtes, Erschautes.* Meisenheim: Hain, 1972.

Holl, Karl, et al. *Sozialer Liberalismus.* Göttingen: Vandenhoeck & Ruprecht, 1986.

Holt, Niles R. "Ernst Haeckel's Monist Religion." *Journal of the History of Ideas* 32 (1971): 265–80.

Hong, Young-Sun. "Gender, Citizenship, and the Welfare State: Social Work and the Politics of Femininity in the Weimar Republic." *Central European History* 30, no. 1 (1997): 1–24.

——— "World War I and the German Welfare State: Gender, Religion, and the Paradoxes of Modernity," in Eley, *Society,* pp. 345–69.

Howe, Frederic C. *Socialized Germany.* New York: Scribner, 1915.

Huber, Werner. *Gertrud Bäumer: Eine politische Biographie.* Munich: dissertation, 1970.

Hübinger, Gangolf. " 'Journalist' und 'Literat': Vom Bildungsbürger zum Intellektuellen." In Hübinger and Mommsen, eds., *Intellektuelle,* pp. 95–110.

——— *Kulturprotestantismus und Politik: Zum Verhältnis von Liberalismus und Protestantismus im wilhelminischen Deutschland.* Tübingen: Mohr, 1994.

——— "Die monistische Bewegung: Sozialingenieure und Kulturprediger." In Hübinger, Bruch, et al., *Kultur,* pp. 246–59.

Hübinger, Gangolf, Rüdiger vom Bruch, and Friedrich Wilhelm Graf, eds., *Kultur und Kulturwissenschaften II: Idealismus und Positivismus.* Stuttgart: Steiner, 1997.

Hübinger, Gangolf, and Wolfgang Mommsen, eds. *Intellektuelle im Deutschen Kaiserreich.* Frankfurt: Fischer, 1993.

Hubrich, Hans-Joachim. *Hermann Muthesius: Die Schriften zu Architektur, Kunstgewerbe, Industrie in der "Neuen Bewegung."* Berlin: Mann, 1981.

Hughes, H. Stuart. *Consciousness and Society: The Reorientation of European Social Thought, 1890–1930.* New York: Knopf, 1958.

Jäckh, Ernst. *Das größere Mitteleuropa.* Weimar: Kiepenheuer, 1916.

——— *Der goldene Pflug: Lebensernte eines Weltbürgers.* Stuttgart: Deutsche Verlags-Anstalt, 1954.

Jansen, Marlies. *Max Maurenbrecher: Der weltanschaulich-politische Weg eines deutschen Nationalisten 1900–1930.* Munich: dissertation, 1964.

Jarausch, Konrad. *Students, Society, and Politics in Imperial Germany: The Rise of Academic Illiberalism.* Princeton: Princeton University Press, 1982.

————— "The Universities: An American View," in Dukes and Remak, eds., *Germany*, pp. 181–206.

Jelavich, Peter. *Berlin Cabaret.* Cambridge, Mass.: Harvard University Press, 1993.

————— *Munich and Theatrical Modernism: Politics, Playwriting, and Performance, 1890–1914.* Cambridge, Mass.: Harvard University Press, 1985.

Johnson, Jeffrey Allan. *The Kaiser's Chemists: Science and Modernization in Imperial Germany.* Chapel Hill: University of North Carolina Press, 1990.

Jung, Irma. *Lily Braun—eine Revisionistin im Spiegel ihrer Briefe 1891–1903: Untersuchung zur ideologischen Standortbestimmung einer Sozialdemokratin.* Dissertation: Hannover, 1987.

Kampffmeyer, Hans. *Die Gartenstadtbewegung.* Leipzig: Teubner, 1909.

Käsler, Dirk. "Das 'Judentum' als zentrales Entstehungs-Milieu der frühen deutschen Soziologie." In Klingemann, ed., *Rassenmythos*, pp. 50–79.

Kelly, Alfred. *The Descent of Darwin: The Popularization of Darwin in Germany, 1860–1914.* Chapel Hill: University of North Carolina Press, 1981.

Kessler, Harry Graf. *Walther Rathenau: Sein Leben und sein Werk.* Frankfurt: Fischer, 1988.

Kleinlosen, Martin, and Jürgen Milchert. *Berliner Kleingärten.* Berlin: Spitz, 1989.

Klingemann, Carsten. "Ein Kapitel aus der ungeliebten Wirkungsgeschichte der Sozialwissenschaften: Sozialutopien als sozialhygienische Ordnungsmodelle." In Klingemann, ed., *Rassenmythos*, pp. 10–48.

—————, ed. *Rassenmythos und Sozialwissenschaft in Deutschland: Ein verdrängtes Kapitel sozialwissenschaftlicher Wirkungsgeschichte* (Opladen: Westdeutscher Verlag, 1987).

Kloppenberg, James T. *Uncertain Victory: Social Democracy and Progressivism in European and American Thought, 1870–1920.* New York: Oxford University Press, 1986.

Koch, Rainer. "Liberalismus und soziale Frage im 19. Jahrhundert." In Holl et al., *Liberalismus*, pp. 17–33.

Kocka, Jürgen. "The European Pattern and the German Case." In Kocka and Mitchell, eds., *Society*, pp. 3–39.

Kocka, Jürgen and Allan Mitchell, eds. *Bourgeois Society in Nineteenth-Century Europe.* Oxford: Berg, 1993.

Köhnke, Klaus. "Wissenschaft und Politik in den Sozialwissenschaftlichen Studentevereinigungen der 1890er Jahre." In Rammstedt, ed., *Simmel*, pp. 308–41.

Kompert, Paul. *Kritische Betrachtungen über die Bodenreform.* Vienna: Manzsche k. und k. Hof-Verlags- und Universitäts-Buchhandlung, 1907.

Koonz, Claudia. "The Competition for Women's *Lebensraum*, 1928–1934." In Bridenthal et al., eds., *Biology*, pp. 199–236.

————— *Mothers in the Fatherland: Women, Family, and Nazi Politics.* New York: St. Martin's, 1987.

Koven, Seth, and Sonya Michel. "Introduction: 'Mother Worlds.' " In Koven and Michel, *Mothers*, pp. 1–42.

——— *Mothers of a New World: Maternalist Politics and the Origins of Welfare States.* New York: Routledge, 1993.

Krabbe, Wolfgang. *Gesellschaftsveränderung durch Lebensreform: Strukturmerkmale einer sozialreformerischen Bewegung im Deutschland der Industrialisierungsperiode.* Göttingen: Vandenhoeck & Ruprecht, 1974.

Kratzsch, Gerhard. *Kunstwart und Dürerbund: Ein Beitrag zur Geschichte der Gebildeten im Zeitalter des Imperialismus.* Göttingen: Vandenhoeck & Ruprecht, 1969.

Krause, Werner. *Werner Sombarts Weg vom Kathedersozialismus zum Faschismus.* Berlin: Rütten und Loening, 1962.

Kroll, Jürgen. *Zur Entstehung und Institutionalisierung einer naturwissenschaftlichen und sozialpolitischen Bewegung: Die Entwicklung der Eugenik/Rassenhygiene bis zum Jahre 1933.* Tübingen: dissertation, 1983.

Krüger, Dieter. "Max Weber and the 'Younger' Generation in the Verein für Sozialpolitik." In Mommsen, ed., *Contemporaries*, pp. 71–87.

Kruse, Volker. "Von der historischen Nationalökonomie zur historischen Soziologie: Ein Paradigmenwechsel in den deutschen Sozialwissenschaften um 1900." *Zeitschrift für Soziologie* 19, no. 3 (June 1990): 149–65.

Kunz, Andreas. "The State as Employer in Germany, 1880–1918: From Paternalism to Public Policy." In Lee and Rosenhaft, eds., *State*, pp. 37–63.

Lamprecht, Karl. *Die kulturhistorische Methode.* Berlin: Gaertners Verlagsbuchhandlung Hermann Heyfelder, 1900.

——— *Moderne Geschichtswissenschaft: Fünf Vorträge.* Berlin: Weidmannsche, 1909.

Lange, Helene. *Lebenserinnerungen.* Berlin: Herbig, 1921.

Lee, W. R., and Eve Rosenhaft, eds. *State, Social Policy and Social Change in Germany, 1880–1994.* New York: Berg, 1997.

Lenger, Friedrich. "Die Abkehr der Gebildeten von der Politik: Werner Sombart und der 'Morgen.' " In Hübinger and Mommsen, eds., *Intellektuelle*, pp. 62–77.

——— *Werner Sombart 1863–1941: Eine Biographie.* Munich: Beck, 1994.

Lenoir, Timothy. *Instituting Science: The Cultural Production of Scientific Disciplines.* Stanford: Stanford University Press, 1997.

——— *The Strategy of Life: Teleology and Mechanics in Nineteenth Century German Biology.* Chicago: University of Chicago Press, 1982.

Lepsius, M. Rainer. "Parteisystem und Sozialstruktur: zum Problem der Demokratisierung der deutschen Gesellschaft." In Gerhard A. Ritter, ed., *Deutsche Parteien vor 1918* (Cologne: Kiepenheuer & Witsch, 1973), pp. 81–99.

Lewis, John D. *The Genossenschaft-Theory of Otto von Gierke: A Study in Political Thought.* Madison: University of Wisconsin Press, 1935.

Lichtblau, Klaus, " 'Alles Vergängliche ist nur ein Gleichnis': Zur Eigenart des Ästhetischen im kultursoziologischen Diskurs der Jahrhundertwende." In Hübinger, Bruch, et al., eds., *Kultur,* pp. 86–121.

Lidtke, Vernon. *The Alternative Culture: Socialist Labor in Imperial Germany.* New York: Oxford University Press, 1985.

—— *The Outlawed Party: Social Democracy in Germany, 1878–1890.* Princeton: Princeton University Press, 1966.

Lindenlaub, Dieter. *Richtungskämpfe im Verein für Sozialpolitik,* 2 vols. Wiesbaden: Steiner, 1967.

List, Friedrich. *Das nationale System der politischen Oekonomie.* Berlin: Cotta'sche Buchhandlung Nachfolger, 1925.

Lüders, Else. *Minna Cauer: Leben und Werk.* Gotha: Klotz, 1925.

Lüders, Marie-Elisabeth. *Fürchte Dich nicht: Persönliches und Politisches aus mehr als 80 Jahren.* Köln: Westdeutscher Verlag, 1963.

Lunn, Eugene. *Prophet of Community: The Romantic Socialism of Gustav Landauer.* Berkeley: University of California Press, 1973.

Machatzke, Martin, ed. *Gerhart Hauptmann: Tagebücher 1897 bis 1905.* Berlin: Propyläen, 1987.

Mason, Timothy W. *Social Policy in the Third Reich: The Working Class and the "National Community."* Trans. John Broadwin. Providence: Berg, 1993.

Meyer, Alfred G. *The Feminism and Socialism of Lily Braun.* Bloomington: Indiana University Press, 1985.

Milles, Dietrich. "Industrial Hygiene: A State Obligation? Industrial Pathology as a Problem in German Social Policy." In Lee and Rosenhaft, eds., *State,* pp. 164–202.

Mitchell, Allan. "Bourgeois Liberalism and Public Health: A Franco-German Comparison." In Kocka and Mitchell, eds., *Society,* pp. 346–64.

Mitzman, Arthur. *The Iron Cage: An Historical Interpretation of Max Weber.* New York: Knopf, 1970.

—— "Personal Conflict and Ideological Opinions in Sombart and Weber." In Mommsen, ed., *Contemporaries.*

—— *Sociology and Estrangement: Three Sociologists of Imperial Germany.* New York: Knopf, 1973.

Mommsen, Wolfgang J. *The Age of Bureaucracy: Perspectives on the Political Sociology of Max Weber.* Oxford: Blackwell, 1974.

—— *Der autoritäre Nationalstaat: Verfassung, Gesellschaft und Kultur im deutschen Kaiserreich.* Frankfurt: Fischer, 1990.

—— *Bürgerliche Kultur und künstlerische Avantgarde: Kultur und Politik im deutschen Kaiserreich 1870 bis 1918*. Berlin: Propyläen, 1994.

────── *Bürgerstolz und Weltmachtstreben: Deutschland unter Wilhelm II, 1890 bis 1918*. Berlin: Propyläen, 1995.

────── *Max Weber and German Politics, 1890–1920*. Trans. Michael Steinberg. Chicago: University of Chicago Press, 1984.

────── "Max Weber: Ein politischer Intellektuelle im deutschen Kaiserreich." In Hübinger and Mommsen, eds., *Intellektuelle*, pp. 33–61.

──────, ed. *Max Weber and His Contemporaries*. London: Allen & Unwin, 1987.

Mosse, George. *The Crisis of German Ideology: Intellectual Origins of the Third Reich*. New York: Schocken, 1964.

Müssiggang, Albert. *Die soziale Frage in der historischen Schule der deutschen Nationalökonomie*. Tübingen: Mohr, 1968.

Muthesius, Hermann. *Der Deutsche nach dem Kriege*. Munich: Bruckmann, 1915.

────── *Die Zukunft der deutschen Form*. Berlin: Deutsche Verlags-Anstalt, 1915.

Na'aman, Shlomo. *Lassalle*. Hannover: Verlag für Literatur und Zeitgeschehen, 1970.

Naumann, Friedrich. *Mitteleuropa*. Berlin: Reimer, 1915.

────── *Neudeutsche Wirtschaftspolitik*, 3rd revised ed. Berlin: Fortschritt, 1911.

────── "Religion und Darwinismus." In Apel, ed., *Darwin*, pp. 99–123.

Nichols, J. Alden. *Germany after Bismarck: The Caprivi Era, 1890–1894*. Cambridge, Mass.: Harvard University Press, 1958.

Nipperdey, Thomas. *Deutsche Geschichte 1866–1918*, 2 vols. Munich: Beck, 1992.

────── *Nachdenken über die deutsche Geschichte: Essays*. Munich: Beck, 1986.

Oppenheimer, Franz. *Erlebtes, Erstrebtes, Erreichtes: Lebenserinnerungen*. Düsseldorf: Melzer, 1964.

────── *Großgrundeigentum und soziale Frage: Versuch einer neuen Grundlegung der Gesellschaftswissenschaft*. Berlin: Deutsche Verlags-Anstalt, 1898.

────── *Die Siedlungsgenossenschaft: Versuch einer positiven Überwindung des Kommunismus durch Lösung des Genossenschaftsproblems und der Argrarfrage*. Leipzig: Duncker & Humblot, 1896.

Pagel, Julius. *Biographisches Lexikon hervorragender Ärtzte des 19. Jahrhunderts*. Berlin: Urban & Schwarzenberg, 1901.

Pascal, Roy. *From Naturalism to Expressionism: German Literature and Society, 1880–1918*. New York: Basic, 1973.

Pataky, Sophie, ed. *Lexikon deutscher Frauen der Feder*. Berlin: Pataky, 1898.

Pauck, Wilhelm. *Harnack and Troeltsch: Two Historical Theologians*. New York: Oxford University Press, 1968.

Paulsen, Friedrich. *Das deutsche Bildungswesen in seiner geschichtlichen Entwicklung*. Leipzig: Teubner, 1909.

────── *The German University and University Study*. New York: Scribner, 1906.

Peukert, Detlev. *Max Webers Diagnose der Moderne.* Göttingen: Vandenhoeck & Ruprecht, 1989.

Phillips, D. C. "Organicism in the Late Nineteenth and Early Twentieth Centuries." *Journal of the History of Ideas* 31 (1970): 413–32.

Pickens, Donald K. *Eugenics and the Progressives.* Nashville: Vanderbilt University Press, 1968.

Pierson, Stanley. *Marxist Intellectuals and the Working-Class Mentality in Germany, 1887–1912.* Cambridge, Mass.: Harvard University Press, 1993.

Ploetz, Alfred. "Der Konflikt zwischen Individualhygiene und Rassentheorie." In Altner, ed., *Darwinismus,* pp. 122–33.

Pogge von Strandmann, Hartmut. *Walther Rathenau: Industrialist, Banker, Intellectual, and Politician: Notes and Diaries, 1907–1922.* Oxford: Clarendon, 1985.

Proctor, Robert. *Racial Hygiene: Medicine under the Nazis.* Cambridge, Mass.: Harvard University Press, 1988.

Pulzer, Peter. *The Rise of Political Anti-Semitism in Germany and Austria.* New York: Wiley, 1964.

Quataert, Jean. "Women's Work and the Early Welfare State in Germany: Legislators, Bureaucrats, and Clients before the First World War." In Koven and Michel, *Mothers,* pp. 159–87.

Rabinbach, Anson. *The Human Motor: Energy, Fatigue, and the Origins of Modernity.* Berkeley: University of California Press, 1992.

Rammstedt, Otthein, ed. *Simmel und die frühen Soziologen: Nähe und Distanz zu Durckheim, Tönnies und Max Weber.* Frankfurt: Suhrkamp, 1988.

Rathenau, Walther. *In Days to Come.* London: Allen & Unwin, 1921.

——— *The New Society.* New York: Harcourt, Brace & Howe, 1921.

——— *Zur Kritik der Zeit.* Berlin: Fischer, 1912.

Ratz, Ursula. *Sozialreform und Arbeiterschaft: Die "Gesellschaft für Soziale Reform" und die sozialdemokratische Arbeiterbewegung von der Jahrhundertwende bis zum Ausbruch des Ersten Weltkrieges.* Berlin: Colloquium, 1980.

Ratzel, Friedrich. *Anthropogeographie,* 2 vols. Stuttgart: Engelhorn, 1899.

——— *Politische Geographie oder die Geographie der Staaten, des Verkehres und des Krieges.* Munich: Oldenbourg, 1903.

Reagin, Nancy. *A German Women's Movement: Class and Gender in Hanover, 1880–1933.* Chapel Hill: University of North Carolina Press, 1995.

Rehberg, Karl-Siegbert. "Das Bild des Judentums in der frühen deutschen Soziologie. 'Fremdheit' und 'Rationalität' als Typusmerkmale bei Werner Sombart, Max Weber und Georg Simmel." In Klingemann, ed., *Rassenmythos,* pp. 80–127.

Rein, Wilhelm. *Outlines of Pedagogics.* Syracuse, New York: Bardeen, 1893.

——— *Pädagogik in systematischer Darstellung,* vol. 1: *Grundlegung.* Langensalza, Germany: Beyer, 1911.

Rein, Wilhelm, A. Pickel, and E. Scheller. *Theorie und Praxis des Volksschulunterrichts nach Herbartischen Grundsätzen,* vol. 1. Leipzig: Bredt, 1898.

Ringer, Fritz. *The Decline of the German Mandarins: The German Academic Community, 1890–1933.* Cambridge, Mass.: Harvard University Press, 1969.

Rissom, Renate. *Fritz Lenz und die Rassenhygiene.* Husum, Germany: Mathiesen, 1983.

Ritter, Gerhard A. "Bersteins Revisionismus und die Flügelbildung in der Sozialdemokratischen Partei." In Ritter, ed., *Die deutschen Parteien vor 1918* (Cologne: Kiepenheuer & Witsch, 1973), pp. 642–57.

Rollins, William. *A Greener Vision of Home: Cultural Politics and Environmental Reform in the German Heimatschutz Movement, 1904–1918.* Ann Arbor: University of Michigan Press, 1997.

Rosenhaft, Eve, and W. R. Lee. "State and Society in Modern Germany—*Beamtenstaat, Klassenstaat, Sozialstaat.*" In Lee and Rosenhaft, eds., *State,* pp. 1–36.

Roth, Guenther. *The Social Democrats in Imperial Germany: A Study in Working-Class Isolation and National Integration.* Totowa, N.J.: Bedminster, 1963.

Rouette, Susanne. "Mothers and Citizens: Gender and Social Policy in Germany after the First World War." *Central European History* 30, no. 1 (1997): 48–67.

Ruff, Peter W. *Emil du Bois–Reymond.* Leipzig: Teubner, 1981.

Sachße, Christoph. *Mütterlichkeit als Beruf: Sozialarbeit, Sozialreform und Frauenbewegung 1871–1929.* Frankfurt: Suhrkamp, 1986.

Scaff, Lawrence A. *Fleeing the Iron Cage: Culture, Politics, and Modernity in the Thought of Max Weber.* Berkeley: University of California Press, 1989.

Schäffle, Albert. *The Quintessence of Socialism.* New York: Scribner, 1894.

Schmoller, Gustav. *Charakterbilder.* Munich: Duncker & Humblot, 1913.

——— *Grundriß der Allgemeinen Volkswirtschaftslehre,* 2 vols. Leipzig: Duncker & Humblot, 1901, 1904.

——— *Die soziale Frage: Klassenbildung, Arbeiterfrage, Klassenkampf.* Munich: Duncker & Humblot, 1918.

——— *Über einige Grundfragen der Sozialpolitik und der Volkswirtschaftslehre.* Leipzig: Duncker & Humblot, 1904.

——— *Zur Social- und Gewerbepolitik der Gegenwart: Reden und Aufsätze.* Leipzig: Duncker & Humblot, 1890.

Schmoller, Gustav, Max Sering, and Adolf Wagner, eds. *Handels- und Machtpolitik: Reden und Aufsätze im Auftrage der "Freien Vereinigung für Flottenvorträge,"* vol. 1. Stuttgart: J. G. Cotta'sche Buchhandlung Nachfolger, 1900.

Schorske, Carl. *Fin-de-Siècle Vienna: Politics and Culture.* New York: Vintage, 1981.

Sheehan, James J. *The Career of Lujo Brentano: A Study of Liberalism and Social Reform in Imperial Germany.* Chicago: University of Chicago Press, 1966.

——— *German Liberalism in the Nineteenth Century.* Chicago: University of Chicago Press, 1978.

Smith, Helmut. *German Nationalism and Religious Conflict: Culture, Ideology, Politics, 1870–1914*. Princeton: Princeton University Press, 1995.

Smith, Woodruff D. *Politics and the Sciences of Culture in Germany, 1840–1920*. New York: Oxford University Press, 1991.

Sombart, Nicolaus. *Jugend in Berlin 1933–1943: Ein Bericht*. Frankfurt: Fischer, 1991.

Sombart, Werner. *Allgemeine Nationalökonomie*. Berlin: Duncker & Humblot, 1960.

———— *Der Bourgeois. Zur Geistesgeschichte des modernen Wirtschaftsmenschen*. Hamburg: Rowohlt, 1987.

———— *Dennoch! Theorie und Geschichte der gewerkschaftlichen Arbeiterbewegung*. Jena: Fischer, 1900.

———— *Die deutsche Volkswirtschaft im neunzehnten Jahrhundert und im Anfang des 20. Jahrhunderts*, 4th ed. Berlin: Brandi, 1921.

———— *Deutscher Sozialismus:* Berlin: Buchholz und Weißwange, 1934.

———— *Die drei Nationalökonomien: Geschichte und System der Lehre von der Wirtschaft*, 2nd ed. Berlin: Duncker & Humblot, 1967.

———— *Gewerbewesen*, 2 vols. Leipzig: Göschen, 1904.

———— *Die gewerbliche Arbeiterfrage*, 2nd revised ed. Berlin: Göschen, 1912.

———— *Händler und Helden*. Munich: Duncker & Humblot, 1915.

———— *Die Juden und das Wirtschaftsleben*. Leipzig: Duncker & Humblot, 1911.

———— *Krieg und Kapitalismus*. Leipzig: Duncker & Humblot, 1913.

———— *Kunstgewerbe und Kultur*. Berlin: Marquard, 1908.

———— *Liebe, Luxus und Kapitalismus: Über die Entstehung der modernen Welt aus dem Geist der Verschwendung*, 2nd ed. Berlin: Wagenbach, 1983.

———— *Der moderne Kapitalismus*, 2 vols. Leipzig: Duncker & Humblot, 1902. Second revised ed., Munich: Duncker & Humblot, 1916.

———— *Der moderne Kapitalismus*, vol. 3. Munich: Duncker & Humblot, 1927.

———— *Noo-Soziologie*. Berlin: Duncker & Humblot, 1956.

———— *Das Proletariat*. Frankfurt: Rütten & Loening, 1906.

———— *Der proletarische Sozialismus ("Marxismus")*, 2 vols. Jena: Fischer, 1924.

———— *Sozialismus und Soziale Bewegung im 19. Jahrhundert*, 1st ed. Frankfurt: Europa, 1966.

———— *Über Pacht- und Lohnverhältnisse in der römischen Campagna*. Berlin: dissertation, 1888.

———— *Vom Menschen: Versuch einer geisteswissenchaftlichen Anthropologie*, 2nd ed. Berlin: Duncker & Humblot, 1956.

———— *Warum gibt es in den Vereinigten Staaten keinen Sozialismus?* Darmstadt: Wissenschaftliche Buchgesellschaft, 1969.

———— *Warum interessiert sich jedermann für Fragen der Volkswirtschaft und Sozialpolitik*. Leipzig: Dietrich, 1904.

———— *Die Zukunft der Juden.* Leipzig: Duncker & Humblot, 1912.

———— *Die Zukunft des Kapitalismus.* Berlin: Buchholz und Weißwange, 1932.

Spael, Wilhelm. *Friedrich Naumanns Verhältnis zu Max Weber.* Sankt Augustin: Liberal-Verlag, 1985.

Sperber, Jonathan. "*Bürger, Bürgertum, Bürgerlichkeit, Bürgerliche Gesellschaft:* Studies of the German (Upper) Middle Class and Its Sociocultural World." *Journal of Modern History* 69, no. 2 (June 1997): 271–97.

Stachura, Peter D. *The German Youth Movement, 1900–1945.* New York: St. Martin's, 1981.

Steinmetz, George. "The Myth of the Autonomous State: Industrialists, Junkers, and Social Policy in Imperial Germany." In Eley, ed., *Society,* pp. 257–318.

———— *Regulating the Social: The Welfare State and Local Politics in Imperial Germany.* Princeton: Princeton University Press, 1993.

Stern, Fritz. *The Failure of Illiberalism: Essays on the Political Culture of Germany.* New York: Knopf, 1972.

———— *The Politics of Cultural Despair: A Study of the Rise of the Germanic Ideology.* Berkeley: University of California Press, 1974.

Stölting, Erhard. "Die anthroposoziologische Schule: Gestalt und Zusammenhänge eines wissenschaftlichen Institutionalisierungsversuchs." In Klingemann, ed., *Rassenmythos,* pp. 130–71.

Strauß, Lulu von, ed. *Eugen Diederichs: Leben und Werk.* Jena: Diederichs, 1936.

Temkin, Oswei. "The Idea of Descent in Post-Romantic German Biology, 1848–1858." In Bentley Glass et al., *Forerunners of Darwin: 1745–1859* (Baltimore: Johns Hopkins University Press, 1959), pp. 323–53.

Tennstedt, Florian. *Sozialgeschichte der Sozialpolitik in Deutschland.* Göttingen: Vandenhoeck & Ruprecht, 1981.

Terra, Otto de. *Soziale Verkehrspolitik.* Berlin: Heymann, 1895.

Theiner, Peter. "Friedrich Naumann und der soziale Liberalismus im Kaiserreich." In Holl et al., eds., *Liberalismus,* pp. 72–83.

———— *Sozialer Liberalismus und deutsche Weltpolitik: Friedrich Naumann im Wilhelminischen Deutschland (1860–1919).* Baden-Baden: Nomos, 1983.

Tönnies, Ferdinand. *Gemeinschaft und Gesellschaft: Abhandlung des Communismus und des Socialismus als Empirischer Culturformen.* Leipzig: Fues, 1887.

Tönnies, Ferdinand, and Friedrich Paulsen. *Briefwechsel: 1876–1908.* Kiel: Hirt, 1961.

Turk, Eleanor. "Thwarting the Imperial Will: A Perspective on the Labor Regulation Bill and the Press of Wilhelminian Germany." In Dukes and Remak, eds., *Germany,* pp. 115–38.

Viehöfer, Erich. *Der Verleger als Organisator: Eugen Diederichs und die bürgerlichen Reformbewegungen der Jahrhundertwende.* Frankfurt: Buchhändler-Vereinigung, 1988.

Volkov, Shulamit. *The Rise of Popular Anti-Modernism: The Urban Master Artisans, 1873–1896.* Princeton: Princeton University Press, 1978.

Wagner, Adolf. *Die akademische Nationalökonomie und der Socialismus.* Berlin: Becker, 1895.

——— *Briefe, Dokumente, Augenzeugenberichte 1851–1917.* Ed. Heinrich Rubner. Berlin: Duncker & Humblot, 1978.

——— *Lehr und Handbuch der politischen Oekonomie,* 4 vols. Leipzig: Winter, 1892.

———*Theoretische Sozialökonomik, oder Allgemeine und theoretische Volkswitschaftslehre: Grundriß tunlichst in prinzipieller Behandlung,* 2 vols. Leipzig: Winter, 1909.

Walther, Franz, Viola Denecke, and Cornelia Regin. *Sozialistische Gesundheits- und Lebensreformverbände.* Bonn: Dietz Nachfolger, 1991.

Weber, Marianne. *Max Weber: Ein Lebensbild.* Tübingen: Mohr, 1926.

Weber, Max. *The Protestant Ethic and the Spirit of Capitalism.* New York: Scribner, 1958.

Wehler, Hans-Ulrich. *Deutsche Gesellschaftsgeschichte,* vol. 3: *Von der "Deutschen Doppelrevolution" bis zum Beginn des Ersten Weltkriegs.* Munich: Beck, 1995.

——— *The German Empire, 1871–1918.* Dover, N.H.: Berg, 1985.

——— "A Guide to Future Research on the Kaiserreich? *Society, Culture, and the State in Germany, 1870–1930,* edited by Geoff Eley." *Central European History* 29, no. 4 (1996): 541–72.

Weindling, Paul. *Darwinism and Social Darwinism in Imperial Germany: The Contribution of the Cell Biologist Oscar Hertwig (1849–1922).* New York: Fischer, 1991.

——— "Eugenics and the Welfare State During the Weimar Republic," in Lee and Rosenhaft, eds., *State,* pp. 134–63.

——— *Health, Race and German Politics between National Unification and Nazism, 1870–1945.* New York: Cambridge University Press, 1989.

Weingart, Peter, et al. *Rasse, Blut und Gene: Geschichte der Eugenik und Rassenhygiene in Deutschland.* Frankfurt: Suhrkamp, 1988.

Weller, B. Uwe. *Maximilian Harden und die "Zukunft."* Bremen: Schünemann, 1970.

Wenck, Martin. *Geschichte der Nationalsozialen 1895–1903.* Berlin: *Hilfe* Verlag, 1905.

——— *Geschichte und Ziele der deutschen Sozialpolitik.* Leipzig: Wigand, 1908.

Wenzl, Aloys, et al. *Hans Driesch: Persönlichkeit und Bedeutung für Biologie und Philosophie von Heute.* Basel: Reinhardt, 1951.

Wheeler, L. Richmond. *Vitalism: Its History and Validity.* London: Witherby, 1939.

Wiebe, Robert H. *The Search for Order, 1877–1920.* New York: Hill and Wang, 1967.

Wiese, Leopold von. *Posadowsky als Sozialpolitiker: Ein Beitrag zur Geschichte der Sozialpolitik des Deutschen Reiches.* Cologne: Christlicher Gewerkschaftsverlag, 1909.

Winkel, Harald. *Die deutsche Nationalökonomie im 19. Jahrhundert.* Darmstadt: Wissenschaftliche Buchgesellschaft, 1977.

Wittich, Dieter, ed. *Vogt, Moleschott, Büchner: Schriften zum kleinbür gerlichen Materialismus in Deutschland.* Berlin: Akademie-Verlag, 1971.

Wobbe, Theresa. *Gleichheit und Differenz: Politische Strategien von Frauenrechtlerinnen um die Jahrhundertwende.* New York: Campus, 1989.

Wohl, Robert. *The Generation of 1914.* Cambridge, Mass.: Harvard University Press, 1979.

Wrede, Richard, ed. *Das geistige Berlin: Eine Encyklopädie des geistigen Lebens Berlins,* 3 vols. Berlin: Wrede, 1897–1898.

Zahn-Harnack, Agnes von. *Die Frauenbewegung: Geschichte, Probleme, Ziele.* Berlin: Deutsche Buch-Gemeinschaft, 1928.

Ziegenfuß, Werner. "Werner Sombart: Geist, Gesellschaft und Wirtschaft." *Schmollers Jahrbuch* 69 (1949).

Zmarzlik, Hans-Günther. "Social Darwinism in Germany, Seen as a Historical Problem." In Hajo Holborn, ed., *Republic to Reich: The Making of the Nazi Revolution* (New York: Pantheon, 1972), pp. 435–74.

Index